THE STORY OF CRICKET

Robin Marlar

Marshall Cavendish London & New York

INTRODUCTION

There are games and there are great games. Cricket is a great game. Baptism can be baffling for the laws of cricket may seem perversely complicated, and its language obtuse, but the early enthusiast is likely to become addicted – drawn by those very subtleties and the game's infinite variety, its potential for surprise and its moments of brilliant unpredictability amid apparent calm. That cricket has an inbred philosophy and is a sort of civilised oasis in an often uncivilised world is well understood, but recently the game has proved its ability to adapt to the rougher commercial demands of the present and future. Professional cricket has become a lively reality, Test matches, since the great cricket revival of recent years, go from strength to strength and perhaps most importantly of all, the cheerful matches in city parks and village greens, where fathers and sons, old schoolfriends and neighbours meet every dry weekend of the summer, seem set to last forever.

All this and much more is evoked in Robin Marlar's splendid history. The origins of the game and its earliest exponents, the growth of the county game and its export all over the world are recounted. The greatest players of past and present are recalled, together with their records, and the development of cricket in recent years is examined. With a skillful combination of massive research and personal knowledge and recollection Robin Marlar has assembled a marvellous exploration of this great game.

The Story of Cricket includes extensive, comprehensive and up-to-date statistics for cricket and cricketers all over the world, and is illustrated in colour and black and white throughout.

Edited by **Susan Hill**
Designed by **Rob Burt**
Picture Research **Mark Dartford**
Tables and statistics compiled by **C.J. Bartlett**
Published by Marshall Cavendish Books Limited
58 Old Compton Street
London W1V 5PA

Printed in Singapore

ISBN 0 85685 707 6

Right: W.G. Grace
Preceding page: Geoff Boycott drives off Jeff Thomson at the Oval in 1977, England v Australia
Page one: Mr Hope of Amsterdam, by Sablet
Endpapers: The first England touring XI en route for North America in 1859

CONTENTS

THE MISTS OF TIME

Games like cricket are not conceived and born like the mortals who play them. Nor if they give enjoyment are they allowed to perish; They are more likely to be adapted to suit the changing times. Having no traceable beginning, so they will have no sudden end.

Preceding page: the Hambledon Club at Halfpenny Down, 1777. Right: leaning on her bat, a fashionable lady awaits the bowler

Indeed, when authority, whether Church or State or both, has tried to repress cricket, the game has reacted as would a plant with a well-developed root system. Instead of dying, cricket has become stronger. Games are like jokes. Thoughtful comedians tell us that their gags are all variations on familiar themes, all of them well-used. Many games belong to the 'to and fro' category; football, for example—a game invented in England, where people have always been gregarious, and subsequently exported all over the world as both a participation and a spectator activity. Hockey, although different in that the players use an implement, is comparable, and so, for that matter, are the racquet games, all of them to-and-fro games, even those in which a wall is used to keep the ball in play.

Then there are the games in which the players hit or throw away from a mark, usually towards another. Into this category come golf, croquet and quoits. Finally, there is the group which combines the to-and-fro element of the first class with the despatch of an object, the key characteristic of the second class. In this respect cricket shows common features with baseball. Both have their roots in a game like stool-ball, still frequently played in that area of Surrey, Sussex and Hampshire widely accepted as the cradle of cricket thanks to the effect of some of the game's earliest literature, which has proved most effective propaganda for the men of Hambledon. As Christopher Brookes has pointed out in his history, cricket's roots are to be found in the folk-games played in the villages of medieval England, and stool-ball is the only one to survive relatively unchanged.

These days it is fashionable to pooh-pooh the idea that it was simple human instinct that provided the impetus for the invention of these folk-games. Yet if it is instinctive for us to move, the acts of throwing or kicking are close to basic, and that of hitting a missile with a club not much further removed. Certainly the instinctive enjoyment of these physical actions is what united the earliest groups of cricketers. With no hard evidence available it is really a matter of speculation as to how cricket evolved from these early instinctive pleasures. Certainly the ready availability of useful timber was an important factor.

In medieval times only the King's business was important enough to be recorded—filed and guarded in an undisturbed state for centuries. We read that John of Leek, Chaplain to King Edward I's son, had to pay out 100 shillings, a lot of money in those days, for 'creag et alios ludos' in the Palace of Westminster on 10 March 1299, perhaps in the indoor school, the cloisters, as it was rather early in the season. Was 'creag' in fact cricket, as historians have trained us to believe? It is pleasant to think so.

Etymologically, the origins of some of cricket's trappings disappear into Anglo-Saxon times, well before Edward II, a poor king who probably did not have the steadiness of temperament required of a Test captain. Cricket, wicket, bat, crease, stump and bail are all words of great antiquity. My personal favourite is bail, or beil, the moveable cross-bar on top of the stakes or stumps.

By 1598, nearly 300 years later, official documents were being written in English. The then Coroner of Guildford, one John Derrick, refers to a piece of ground in the town recently turned into a timber yard as a place where he had played cricket in the 1550s, when he was a scholar of the Free School at Guildford.

It is almost certain that local variations of the game were legion until the middle of the next century, the seventeenth, the age of the great cultural leap forward as witnessed, for instance, in the art of portrait-painting. How could it be otherwise when new ideas took as long as people to move from one country to another? Rowland Bowen suggests that cricket spread but slowly, and that it was not widely played in Cornwall or Cumbria, or indeed in

Left: a slightly later print depicts a member of the Oxfordshire Cricket Club in front of his wicket and pavilion

Herefordshire or Monmouthshire, until the nineteenth century. By that time it was already a familiar pastime in faraway places like North America and India. Indeed, Bowen has unearthed a seventeenth-century jet-setter, Samuel Filmer, who took part in the first recorded match at Coxheath in Kent in 1646, the year in which the Scots handed Charles I over to Parliament. Filmer next emerges in Virginia before returning to England at the time of the Restoration. This match was the first time a game of cricket was used as a vehicle for betting; this may help to explain why in Cromwell's time a game at Cranbrook in Kent was described by the prosecution as unlawful.

Oliver Cromwell, according to Royalist propaganda, had earned himself the 'name of royster' by establishing a reputation for enjoying football, cricket, cudgelling and wrestling as a young man. Later, poor fellow, he acquired a reputation as a killjoy, leading men into death and destruction. By 1656 he was burning cricket bats and balls in Dublin. Two years earlier the churchwardens of Eltham in Kent—near where W. G. Grace is buried—had fined seven parishioners two shillings each for playing cricket on Sunday, the Lord's Day. The Puritans were in charge. During Cromwell's rule the remaining rich and would-be courtiers scattered to the country and only returned to London with the accession of Charles II, royal protagonist of leisure and freedom—not least the freedom to gamble.

All over Europe there was war in the seventeenth century. In terms of the general duration of hostilities the British Isles suffered a comparatively short disruption. In terms of its effects on the entire population, the Civil War was nevertheless comprehensive. A great mingling took place as the old order, and with it the remnants of the feudal world of the folk-game, were thrown down in the conflict and its repercussions.

As the classes mixed, as the land prospered, and as the early factories and craft workers yielded time and resources for leisure activities, cricket benefited. It was in these middle years of the seventeenth century that the game developed the basis for its claim of being England's national game.

In Charles II's time cricket—no longer creag but now indisputably cricket—was in receipt of royal patronage and therefore by extension that of the newly revived court. Officially that sexy and stylish monarch Charles II died childless, but in fact the then Earl of Sussex was his son-in-law, and from the year 1677 there survives a ledger in which the Treasurer noted that his Lordship had taken £3 from petty cash to go to the cricket match at Dicker Common. Dicker lies north of the Sussex Downs, and the nearest sporting attraction in recent years has been the Eastbourne Speedway at nearby Arlington Stadium. In these days it was the last village on the road from Lewes Market to Hailsham Market; where they made the best pottery in East Sussex.

By March 1700 (again that early start!) they were playing the best of five games on Clapham Common 'for £10 a head each game and £20 the odd one'. In 1707 a well-advertised eleven-a-side match took place in Lamb's Conduit Fields in London, and two years later county cricket was born when Surrey took on the Kentish men.

Young men playing the game as the seventeenth century became the eighteenth lived well into the newspaper era. William Bedle, who died in 1768, was at one time the most expert cricketer in England. Yet beyond the dates of his birth and death only his reputation remains. Matches were taking place in London, Kent, Surrey, Sussex and Gloucestershire before 1750. The Henfield Cricket Club, whose players now sport a white Sussex hen on a green cap, can show proof of games played in the village as long ago as 1727. Teams took county titles because by now the great patrons of the game were gathering together

Right: a young cricketer, engraved from a picture attributed to Gainsborough.
Far Right: cricket on the village green

the best cricketers from both town and village. It was an expensive business to promote at the rate of a guinea to each player for home matches and a guinea and a half for travelling. Yet thousands, sometimes as many as 20,000, came to watch and pay their sixpences, all we were to be charged some two hundred years later.

After the Articles of Agreement between the Duke of Richmond and a Mr. Brodrick in 1727, the first written Laws of Cricket to survive date from 1744 and refer to the game as played on the Artillery Ground in London. We can take this date as signifying cricket's emergence from its archaeological chrysalis into the sunshine of regular recorded fact. The origins of some of cricket's curiosities have been explained by dedicated historians of the game, and some of the paths they have opened up are worth following here. Although the basic activities of cricket, throwing and hitting, are instinctive to us, there is nothing instinctive about the formation of a cricket eleven. Why not a ten or a twelve? Ten is the number on which the Romans based the metric system, while the Anglo-Saxons handed down a haphazard numerical system in which the number twelve features strongly. Furthermore, while 'bat' and 'ball' are words which need no further explanation, from where does the word 'cricket' derive? And why do we insist on baffling Americans and occasionally even ourselves by using the word 'wicket' to describe both the pitch and the stumps?

Rowland Bowen, who published his history in 1970, draws our attention to the first conclusive reference to cricket in the *Archives de France*. In 1478 the game was being played near St Omer in the Pas de Calais, the last part of France to be surrendered up by the Kings of England. Queen Mary, you will remember, went to her grave with Calais inscribed on her heart. And it was in this area that there was a numbering system based on *eleven* inches, or *lignes*, to a foot. As to the word 'cricket', there are those who claim it derives from the bat and those who believe it describes the mark which the cricketer defends. Harry Altham, whose first *History of Cricket* appeared in 1926, cites the old English translation of the Twenty-third Psalm ('Thy rod and staff comfort me', where *cric* was the original word for staff) as proof that cricket is derived from the bat. The outer shape of the early bats bears some similarity to that of the old shepherd's crook. On the other hand the Flemish word *krickstoel*, meaning a low stool like those used in churches for kneeling to prayer, tends to support the argument that cricket, like stool-ball, takes its name from the mark. 'Stool' is an old Sussex word for the stump of a tree, an ideal mark to aim at or defend, bearing in mind that originally bowling was under-arm.

Most of us who have tried to explain cricket to the uninitiated know how confusing they find the similarity between the words 'cricket' and 'wicket'. Wicket gates are traditionally associated with shepherds and the penning of their sheep. In the North Country, and indeed in North America, 'wicket', or sometimes 'wickets', was the name of the game itself. As for the bail, originally, as we have seen, spelt beil, this was the slip-rail the shepherd moved to unlock the wicket gate.

Cricket dimensions will always defy the metric system, that Roman legacy to Europe. Small wonder that some of us Englishmen resist the uniformity of measurement required in the Common Market, based appropriately on the Treaty of Rome! What hope have we when the length of our cricket pitches is the same as the width of the Saxon acre-strip, which was the basis of the great system of field-farming which survived until the eighteenth century.

Representation of the Noble GAME of CRICKET as played in the celebrated Cricket Field near White Conduit House. 1787.

Not before this period did his Lordship's busy officials go about enclosing strips to form the great estates which glorified acreage at the expense of the old rods, poles and perches. While the bailiffs were enclosing, his Lordship was often either playing in, staging or betting on the big cricket matches.

As for the stumps and the crease in front of them, these measurements derive from the textile trade of small-town England, the Hong Kong of the Middle Ages. The cloth-yard was forty-five inches, the length of an arrow for a long-bow. The wicket was half an arrow's length in height and an eighth of it in breadth.

Under the wicket was the popping hole into which the ball had to be dropped for a run-out. Subsequently a run-out was judged on the popping crease—a ditch an inch deep and an inch wide was cut at the end of every pitch right up until the time of W. G. Grace in the 1860s, when the chalk-mark took its place.

As for the bat, its width was not regulated until thirty years after the first Laws, and only then because a man from Reigate called 'Shock' White shook his opponents by taking guard with a bat wider than the stumps. What villainy—but what invention! Later on, bats and balls were both subject to the gauge.

When cricket became a double-wicket game (and it is difficult to be certain when and how this came about) balls were bowled alternately from either end, four balls to the over. Harry Altham has advanced the theory that it was at this stage in the game's development that two umpires became essential—each would carry a bat and a run would only be completed when the batsman touched the umpire's bat with his own. This was a great help to the scorer who could rely on a crash of bats as well as sight of the game, and also explains why old prints show the umpires much closer to the wickets than they stand today.

HAMBLEDON

The trend towards the aristocratic acceptance of cricket that had begun with the Restoration in 1660 and been sustained by national notables throughout the remaining years of the Stuart dynasty continued with the arrival of the Hanoverians.

Preceding page: the cripples of Hughenden play a Buckinghamshire county side on their village green

Right: young boys from Harrow School play cricket in 1765. The public schools have long been training grounds for county and national sides

The first George may not have been able to speak English, but many of the leading figures in the land had played cricket as children and so the old folk-game remained fashionable.

The devotion of George I's grandson, Frederick, who was born in 1707, represented cricket's biggest emotional capture since Edward II. In Frederick's case, there was to be no change of heart as had occured in Oliver Cromwell. Not that everyone has regarded Frederick, Prince of Wales, as a 'good thing', to use the language of *1066 and All That*. The *Encyclopedia Britannica*, admittedly an American publication, describes the cricketing Prince of Wales as the 'absurd' father of George III, the King who lost the American Colonies. Perhaps if this Prince of Wales had lived his full span instead of dying at the age of 44, the game and the British connection might have taken deeper root in the Colonies and survived, thus saving the United States from having to suffer baseball as their national game.

It was a cricket ball in fact which determined our history hereabouts, for it was such a blow that lead to the death of the Prince of Wales in 1751. But not everyone was happy with the game. Some unknown author, writing in the *British Champion* of 1743, thought it ridiculous and unseemly that lords and gentlemen, clergymen and lawyers should associate themselves with butchers and cobblers in such diversions. An opinion which was perhaps a foretaste of the Gentlemen and Players match some sixty years later.

The beerage as well as the peerage were becoming involved in patronage, even at a relatively humble level. For example, 'Lumpy' Stevens, the most famous bowler of his generation, was engaged by an innkeeper with the appropriate name of Porter in Chertsey, nearly twenty miles away from his home in Shamley Green.

Purses needed to be deep for the great occasions. In 1735 the Prince of Wales and the Earl of Middlesex, son of the Duke of Dorset, played a match at Moulsey Hurst for £1,000 a side. The Prince's side comprised eight from the London Club and three from Middlesex, and the Kentish men played for the Earl. Kent won by three wickets. A fortnight later, the return match was played on Bromley Common. The aristocracy certainly got their priorities right: 'I'll attend the Board of Admiralty when at leisure from cricket,' the Earl of Sandwich told his colleagues. It was another son of the Duke of Dorset, Lord John Sackville, who made the critical catch in the famous game on the Artillery Ground in 1744 between Kent and All-England. We know all about this great match because it is the subject of James Love's long poem:

Hail Cricket! Glorious, manly, British Game!
First of all Sports: the first alike in fame!

Alas, we don't write cricket reports like this any more. Love was obviously an eye-witness of the game. Kent led England by 13 runs after the first innings (53 to 40), but at their second attempt the 'Rest' had done much better, and Newland, with the best score of the match (18) already standing to his name, was going strong once more with 15 to his credit:

The champion strikes. When scarce arriving fair,
The glancing ball mounts upward in the air.
The batsman sees it, and with mournful eyes
Fixed on the ascending pellet as it flies,
Thus suppliant claims the favour of the skies.
O, mighty Jove, and all ye powers above,
Let my regarded prayer your pity move;
Grant me but this: whatever youth shall dare
Snatch at the prize descending through the air,
Lay him extended on the grassy plain,
And make his bold adventurous effort vain!
He said: the powers attending his request,
Granted one part, to winds consigned the rest.
And now illustrious Sackville where he stood,
The approaching ball with cautious pleasure viewed,
At once he sees the chief's impending doom,
And pants for mighty honours yet to come.
Swift as the falcon darting on its prey,
He springs elastic on the verdant way;
Sure of success, flies upward with a bound,
Derides the slow approach, and spurns the ground.
Prone slips the youth, yet glories in his fall,
With arm extended shows the captive ball.

James Love's real name was Dance, and his father was the architect who designed the Mansion House, still only ten minutes' walk from the ground where this match was played. Kent won, by the way, largely because Sackville caught Richard Newland at that crucial stage in the second innings.

The Prince of Wales watched this match and so did his brother the Duke of Cumberland, the son sent by King George II to sort out the Scots after the rebellion of 1745 in favour of Bonnie Prince Charlie. If 'Butcher' Cumberland was keen on cricket no wonder most Scots took to golf!

In the 1750s, cricket suffered a recession, perhaps because more important matters needed attention, like the Seven Years' War, a conflict about issues more serious than its predecessor Jenkins's Ear—the winning of an Empire and the capture of export markets for the game of cricket. Nevertheless the game re-established its appeal to all classes. What was now needed was a similar leap forward in technique. This improvement was to come from the men of

Hambledon, who gave cricket its air of romance, a gift more precious even than that of the great patrons who had provided it with the upper crust of social standing.

Dance's poem showed that cricket could inspire feats of imagination and create its own literature. Now the Hambledon men became heroes because they could match their skills against the best from anywhere in the land. John Small's boast that he would play at cricket with anyone in England was far from bombastic. As the game grew in popularity in the Midlands and the northern and western shires, so the fame of the Hambledon men spread. Perhaps we have developed a slightly idealized view of the Hambledonians because of the stories John Nyren told about his father Richard Nyren to Charles Cowden Clarke, whose works *The Young Cricketer's Tutor* and *Cricketers of my Time* are a veritable goldmine for those who want to study cricket in the years leading up to and immediately after the French Revolution.

John Nyren, cricket's earliest regular chronicler, was five years old and the Hambledon Club about nineteen when the first recorded century partnership took place in 1769 on Broadhalfpenny Down, that upturned saucer of a field across the road from the Bat and Ball Inn, kept by Richard Nyren. This century partnership was made by Tom Sueter and George Leer, wicketkeeper and long stop, tenor and counter-tenor in the Hambledon church choir, and on this occasion opening batsmen for Hampshire against Surrey. Not that all the records were falling to Hambledon men: at Wrotham, another famous ground, John Minshull, batting first wicket for the Duke of Dorset, hit the first recorded century, 107 out of a second-innings total of 236. Minshull had his reward: the Duke appointed him his gardener a few weeks later for wages of eight shillings a week.

There was no greater patron than this Duke. His cricket cost him over £1,000 a year in the early 1780s. He respected the players and won their respect. He gave John Small a new fiddle, whereupon Small, proud enough not to be upstaged, sent the Duke two bats and two balls in return. Eventually the Duke of Dorset went to Paris as Ambassador, and early in 1789 he asked the Foreign Secretary, the Duke of Leeds, for a gesture of goodwill towards the French monarchy, then having what one of our latest patrician Prime Ministers, Harold Macmillan, might have described as some little local difficulties over dividing Marie Antoinette's cake. 'Send a cricket team' was the request, but the Duke of Dorset, now fleeing from the guillotine, met the cricketers at Dover and wisely called off the visit. Life insurance had not been invented. This was the first but not the last tour to be called off for political reasons.

'Lumpy' Stevens was the first out-and-out

HOME BLOCK.
London. Baily, Brothers, Cornhill.
Printed by C. Graf.

Left: a stylised and delicately coloured Victorian print dated 1845 shows how the bat has already become quite modern, as has cricketing clothing

cricketer whose portrait has survived. It hangs at Knole House, near Sevenoaks, and shows the face of a hard man. Stevens was a great bowler of shooters and always wanted to choose not only the end from which he would bowl but also where the wicket should be pitched on fields which were usually anything but level. What he wanted was a downward slope, because 'Honest Lumpy did allow, he ne'er could pitch but o'er a brow'.

In 1775 Stevens played as the 'given' man for Kent in a five-a-side match against Hambledon on the Artillery Ground near Finsbury Circus in London, where the Honourable Artillery Company still play the game. Several times he beat the bat of John Small and the ball fizzed through the double wicket and under the bail. When Small, the last man, had walked to the wicket Hambledon had needed 14 runs, and with that sort of luck they were bound to get them. Betting must have been heavy and the laments of the losers long, for soon afterwards a third stump was added to the existing wicket.

We shall never know whether John Small was playing with a bat curved at the bottom like a hockey stick or with a straight bat with shoulders such as we use now. From Petersfield, born in 1737, seventy-five years in the choir, John Small was one of the greatest technocrats of the game.

Here lives John Small,
Makes bat and ball,
Pitch a wicket, play at cricket
With any man in England

read the sign outside his door, and it was during his playing career that the straight bat became more than just the game's chief implement. Against the length bowling of the likes of 'Lumpy' Stevens, John Small stepped towards the ball to play the off-drive and the draw, a stroke so difficult to control and therefore dangerous that none now play it, at least deliberately, for it meant purposely playing the ball between bat and leg down to long stop's left hand. Now it is regarded as a lucky stroke, described by Etonians as the 'Harrow drive' and by north-of-the-Thames men as the 'Surrey cut'.

By the time the Hambledon men like John Small were establishing their reputation in the 1770s, cricket had already suffered its first recession. The 1760s were as barren as the 1960s and the game was said to be losing its fashionable support to golf. Also, inflation was hitting cricket equipment as hard as it is now. The price of bats went up from half a crown ($12\frac{1}{2}$p) for eleven—yes, eleven!—to four shillings (20p) each between 1766 and 1773! Balls were more expensive than bats in those days, William Pett of Sevenoaks charging 3s. 6d ($17\frac{1}{2}$p) for a couple in 1766.

On the field the men of Hambledon wore shirts with full sleeves, knee-breeches, stockings and buckled shoes. These were dangerous, and Silver Billy Beldham told how John Wells, another Hambledonian, tore off his fingernail on a buckle as he tried to pick up the ball. Top-hats were not then part of the uniform. In the Hambledon team of the 1780s and 1790s, men like Beldham, who lived until 1862 (when he was the grand old age of ninety-six), wore purpose-built cricket shoes.

The portrait of 'Lumpy' Stevens shows him wearing a stock, waistcoat and jacket. Off the field the players wore sky-blue coats with black velvet collars and the letters CC, standing for Cricketing Club, engraved on their buttons.

Richard Nyren was the key figure of this period, the go-between linking the patrons and the players, the keeper of the Bat and Ball Inn, secretary of the Hambledon Club for nigh on forty years, the King Arthur of this Round Table. He learned his cricket from his uncle Richard Newland, one of three brothers from Slindon in Sussex, the first such trio to be recorded playing in organized cricket and as such the forerunners of the Graces of Gloucestershire.

Nyren was a left-arm bowler of slow lobs, always to a length, although it was as a talent spotter and coach that he was to play such a prominent part in both the Hambledon teams, old and new. The art of bowling was becoming more sophisticated. The first bowlers had simply heaved the ball along the ground, hence the passion for shooters, whether on the first, second or any old bounce. But the length bowlers, who tossed the ball under-arm on to the spot, were capable of giving the ball some bias after it had pitched; usually, in the case of a right-hander, from leg to off. With the renowned Brett and Richard Nyren, right- and left-arm men respectively, Hambledon's bowlers could set some problems. Then along came the little downland farmer with a name appropriate for a shepherd—Lamborn—who was to under-arm bowling what the first leg-break bowlers were to over-arm. By flipping the ball over his wrist he could make it move from off to leg, and when his Hambledon team played All-England the men of Surrey and Kent 'tumbled out as if they had been picked off by a rifle corps!'

It was said of the 'Little Farmer' (as Lamborn was known) that 'his comprehension did not equal the speed of lightning', and Richard Nyren spent hours trying to persuade him to pitch his off-breaks outside the off-stump instead of straight as was his wont when practising with his sheep hurdles. The lesson was hard to learn, and Lamborn once missed the Duke of Dorset's leg-stump by such a hair's breadth that he let out the earliest recorded bowler's cry of anguish: 'Ah, it was tedious near you, Sir.'

Another notable member of the team was the long-fielder, Peter Stewart, whom they called Buck—a shoemaker and carpenter, and the funny man of the party. Once when the Hambledon caravan overturned, the optimistic Buck insisted on staying in it, hoping for supernatural intervention, and claiming that 'One good turn deserved another'.

Then, as now, great teams petered out, and after some poor results in 1770 the Hambledonians all but fell apart. However, they came back to fame during the next ten years by playing fifty-one matches against teams labelled 'All-England' and the like, and winning a staggering twenty-nine of them. Some village! Some players! Years later John Nyren set down the names: David Harris, John Wells, Richard Purchase, William Beldham, John Small junior, Harry and Tom Walker, Robert Robinson, Noah Mann, Thomas Scott and Thomas Taylor. 'No eleven in England,' he wrote, 'could have had any chance with these men, and I think they may have beaten any two and twenty.'

Of those mentioned, David Harris was a great bowler, quick enough to draw blood from a batsman's hands though not from rustic Tom Walker's, whose skin was 'like the rind of an old oak, and as sapless!' John Nyren tells us he was an ungainly fellow who 'toiled like a tar on horseback'.

John Wells came from Farnham, where he was a baker: a useful cricketer, and whether bowling, fielding or batting 'a servant of all work'. Noah Mann kept an inn at North Chapel near Petworth in Sussex, so he had a twenty-mile ride to play or even practise cricket. On arrival he was apt to demonstrate his party piece, picking up handkerchiefs at full gallop. Swarthy as a gypsy, he was a left-handed hitter and bowler and a fine sprinter in the field: he covered Leer at long stop and sometimes would let a ball through deliberately so that he could attempt to run out the batsman. He was once credited with a hit for ten on Windmill Down—the Hambledon men had moved their field here because Broadhalfpenny was too bleak.

Noah Mann came to a sad end: one autumn night after going shooting and celebrating his successful bag, he insisted on being left to sleep in his chair by the fire. In the night he fell on to the embers and died of his burns within twenty-four hours. His son was named after Sir Horatio Mann, the boy's godfather, one of the great patrons from Kent: Richard Nyren had been the go-between in this happy relationship between landowner and publican. On another more controversial occasion, Nyren had words with Sir Horatio, who successfully enticed away a young

Below: the close fielders poised, the batsman prepares to receive an underarm delivery, and villagers loll on the banks. A print by Pyne, 1805

Hambledonian, James Aylward, to be his bailiff at Bishopsbourne in Kent. Aylward held the record score for many years, hitting 167 out of a total of 403 for Hambledon (alias Hampshire) against England in 1777; he went in at five o'clock on a Wednesday and batted until three o'clock on Friday. No wonder Horatio Mann wanted him for Kent!

William Beldham, 'Silver Billy', was a man of Farnham like John Wells. He was younger than the others and thus still a Hambledonian when the club began to fade in the early 1790s. He perfected the cut, taking the ball 'twixt wind and water', as James Burke was apt to take the House of Commons in the same period. Beldham played his last match for the Players at the ground we know today as Lord's as late as 1821. He was fifty-five and made 23 not out.

These, then, were the players. The atmosphere they engendered was of the Hampshire earth itself—rich and natural. John Nyren remembered it well: 'How strongly are all those scents of fifty years gone by painted in my memory! and the smell of that ale comes upon me freshly as the new May flowers.' The fifth toast at these Hambledon dinners was always to Madge, but despite considerable research no-one has succeeded in discovering the identity of this damsel. No wonder, for, according to Rowland Bowen, Madge was an eighteenth-century word for the female reproductive organ. Cricket dinners have not changed overmuch!

However brilliant the Hambledonians' cricket however romantic it became thanks to John Nyren's ability to broadcast the tradition with filial affection, there was little possibility that Hambledon would survive. London was the centre of attraction, and elsewhere there were patrons as resolved as Horatio Mann to field a team fit to take on the best, no matter how unscrupulously they had to recruit. In 1791 Richard Nyren left Hambledon. In 1796 the last minutes of the club he had fostered were taken. Eventually even the ground was returned to the plough, though the Bat and Ball retained its hold on the memory of cricketers everywhere. In 1925 a commemoration match was played on Broadhalfpenny Down, a field now looked after by Winchester College. To Harry Altham, a man whose scholarship and teaching were always at cricket's service, and a former president of MCC, belongs the credit for saving the field from the plough and for the game. Now from time to time the Lord's Taveners play there, their teams always full of notables and fun. So, if the ghosts of the great cricketers of Hambledon wish to appear, they know whose fixture list to consult, for there are great occasions still on the hallowed down, and perhaps the ghosts of cricketers past watch and applaud—or criticise—the games and players they observe.

A MATCH AT
CRICKET

WILLIAM CLARKE & THE PROFESSIONALS

William Clarke, born in Nottingham soon after the lamps had dimmed for good on Hambledon, was trained as a bricklayer, his father's trade. He was an under-arm bowler, preferring that style to round-arm bowling, although that was legal throughout his time.

Preceding page: William Clarke and his professionals engaged in a match against Leicester around 1829

Left: William Clarke trained as a bricklayer but became one of cricket's early architects. He selected the first All England eleven in 1846

He was a solemn-looking fellow and bowled from under a tall hat, his arm whipping backwards and forwards at the maximum height allowed. His appearance must have become even more formidable after 1830, the year of revolutions in Europe when Charles X of France lost a throne and William Clarke, keeper of the Bell Inn at Nottingham, lost an eye.

In 1837 he married as his second wife the widow Chapman, who kept the Trent Bridge Inn. Within a year he had not only seduced the cricketing clientele away from the Bell Inn, where they always supped, but he had also obtained a field behind the public house which became the Trent Bridge ground. At first the new ground was not entirely successful, despite the fact that there was a charge to enter. Nevertheless Clarke stayed there until 1847, by which time he had discovered another, more profitable way of earning his living. The previous year, he had selected his first all-England XI, the first of the travelling teams of professional cricketers, now regarded as the most significant games-playing development in England's sporting history, one that was to last for twenty-four years.

Why did Clarke do it? For profit. This wandering cricket show was, in today's terms, a 'service' business providing a substantial income for a small and controllable capital outlay. Were there other motives? Certainly the lot of the cricketer who wanted to play all summer long for match money was hard in Nottinghamshire. In the middle of the nineteenth century the Dukeries were great sporting estates. They still were in the 1920s, as D. H. Lawrence reminds us, but the Dukes who lived in the great houses, like Portland, were not known as patrons of county cricket in Nottinghamshire.

In 1842, for example, only one match was played, and this paltry fixture-list had grown merely to an inadequate five by 1845. Such places in the county eleven as were available were often snapped up by amateurs of minimal skill. Clarke himself was known in cricket circles as 'Old Clarke'; hardly surprisingly since he was forty-six before he played for England. His first selection for the Players in one of the great matches at Lord's came at the age of forty-eight. From then on he averaged 340 wickets a season, and although he broke an arm at the age of fifty-two he played for three more years, taking a wicket with his very last ball. However good must he have been in his prime? But being born in Nottinghamshire was to be born to blush unseen.

Whether he began his version of a cricketing circus with any wider intent than profit with enjoyment we cannot be sure. But there is evidence that he knew what would happen. A conversation with another of the game's entrepreneurs, James Dark, the manager of Lord's, has been handed down. 'It's a going to be, Sir, from one end of the land to the other, you may depend on that,' said Clarke, 'and what is more it will make good for cricket for you as well as for me. Mark my words, you'll sell cartloads of your balls where you used to sell dozens.' There can be no doubt that the travelling teams took cricket to new towns and villages, places it would only have reached more slowly without the travellers. The interest in their matches only began to fade when conflicts about fixtures and money began to receive public airing. But there were other factors coming to the fore which prompted the independence of Clarke, Wisden and the like. Quite apart from the evidence the professionals could all see of the MCC's preference for promoting one or other form of amateur cricket, there were technical issues of great moment over which the professionals were arguing with the amateurs, especially the diehards among the latter. Over-arm bowling was obviously a better method of launching the ball than delivering with a round arm, because a bowler could keep the ball straighter. And, by and large, the task of bowling had landed squarely on the strong legs and shoulders of the game's artisans, the professionals, while the gentlemen took up the more elegant pastime of batting.

But one factor in particular was essential to the success of the new venture—railways. Without the mobility they provided the programme Old Clarke devised would have been impossible. He set himself to play between twenty and twenty-five matches every season and 'could have had three times as many if we could have found the dates'. Suddenly the possibility of cricket six days a week for five months of the year had opened up. No longer was it crucial that a man good at cricket learn a trade or find a patron, as had been the case with the players of the Hambledon era. As an added incentive, certainly in the Midlands area, where most of the men were textile workers, the industrial revolution had made working conditions far less agreeable than five months in the cricket fields of England. As for the erstwhile patrons, they were getting fewer: nor were they so necessary, for as the game spread through the schools and travelling clubs, so did the number of players skilled enough to cope with the game at its highest level increase. William Clarke, then, was hailed, at least at the beginning of this era, as a great benefactor. The players were paid £5 a match (sometimes £6 if the journey involved was long), but they were obliged to pay for travel and board out of their own pockets—and sometimes there was little enough left.

As time passed Clarke became more parsimonious,

Below: Fuller Pilch, a demon batsman of his day, was born in 1803 at Horningcroft, Norfolk

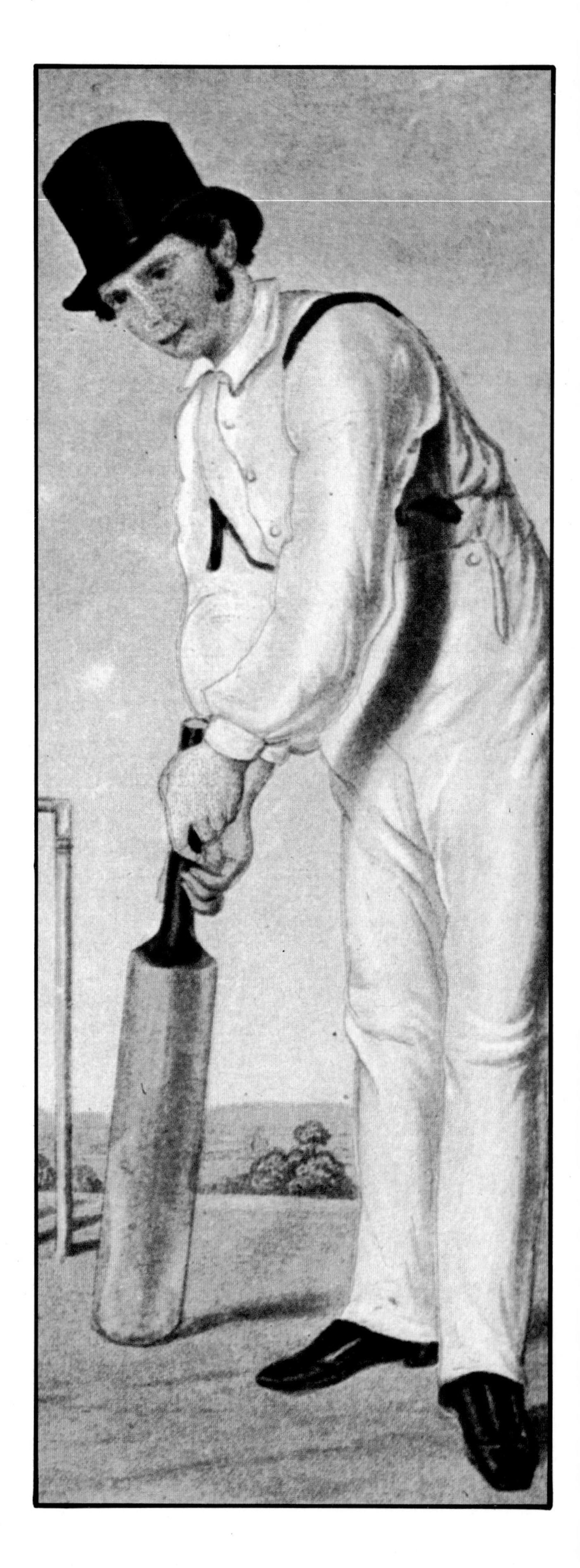

and eventually two of his players led the southern men into exile, where they reformed under the title the United England XI in 1852. Despite the anger of John Wisden and James Dean, who hoped for a complete break with their former colleagues, the United England XI maintained their connection with the All-England XI and for ten years the matches between the two teams were the finest in the land. This state of affairs even survived Clarke's death, when George Parr, another of the Trent Bridge greats, took over the management of the All-England XI.

Some of the journeys undertaken by these travelling teams were testing. Not all could be made by train. One such, from Wisbech to Sleaford, a distance of some forty miles, was completed only because Martingale, one of the players, shinned up a signpost in the middle of the night, somewhere in the depths of the Fenland, after the coachdriver had lost his way. Some of the grounds were rough, too. On one occasion Fuller Pilch had to scythe the field before a start could be made, and even then one of the players put up a covey of partridges. Nor were all the hazards to be faced of the natural variety. At Hull, the ground was prepared by inmates of the local lunatic asylum. There has always been a strong connection between cricket and mental asylums (a connection on which I do not intend to comment further!), but usually only the staff get near the action. On this occasion one lunatic took an iron bar out of the roller and hit Job Greenwood, one of the players, over the head with it.

Eventually a decline in the playing ability of the professionals, the strength of the amateur tradition sustained at Lord's, and the rise of the county clubs (which hoped to provide for the growing county towns what MCC at Lord's and Surrey at The Oval were offering the London cricketing public) all combined to throttle the great professional elevens. The arguments against them were best summed up by the Rev. James Pycroft writing in *Cricketana* in 1865. John Arlott quoted this long passage in his history of cricket published in 1953, but now that we have Kerry Packer in our midst its sentiments are even more ironically relevant.

From *Cricketana*:

> The getting-up of an All-England match in a country place is very much in this wise:
>
> The secretary of All Muggleton is an elderly gentleman—no player, but an eating or smoking member, yet ambitious to distinguish himself, and perhaps to have his photograph taken as the Father of the Muggleton Club. Whereupon, as the cheapest kind of immortality, about October he begins to talk, and goes on talking all the winter

Below: William Lillywhite, of the famous Sussex family. Largely responsible for the introduction of round-arm bowling

of his determination to 'book the All England Eleven' for the coming season. He soon has a subscription list with his own name at the head, and does not doubt (till he tries) that George Parr will take 'the gate'—though all the parish can creep through the hedge—instead of payment for his Eleven. But soon a polite letter comes, hinting that Muggletonian enthusiasm is not so certain as to make anything less than £70 or £80 a sufficient consideration.

Then comes the question of how to raise the wind. Whereupon the gentleman goes about with his subscription-list in hand, trying to persuade every tradesman, and, above all, every innkeeper within five miles round that the All-England match will be the making of the town and trade of Muggleton and its vicinity, and they must be public-spirited and subscribe. As to asking any players to subscribe it seems very hard to take a man's money and not to put him into the Twenty-two; yet everybody wants to be in the Twenty-two, and everybody who is left out is so sure to be offended—especially if he happens not to be in Muggleton society, for then he feels doubly snubbed,—vowing the Muggleton Club is likely to come to a speedy dissolution 'all through our secretary's match'. However, money is picked up by driblets, and a ten-pound note is volunteered by the victualler, who thus knowingly secures a monopoly of all the diluted spirits, weak beer, and shabby dinners, which are remembered by grumbling spectators for weeks after . . .

As to these All-England matches, you do not play against All-England or its best Eleven by any means. At present there are two All-Englands—two bests! which is rather strange, certainly. Not only so, but neither of the two can be called best in any sense. We will speak now of Parr's Eleven, 'the All-England'; for Wisden's Eleven, 'the United All-England', having six Surrey men, play comparatively few matches, for fear of spoiling the Surrey county matches. They only play when Surrey has no fixture. . .

When a travelling circus goes round the country, you are rather staggered, as you pay your money, in looking up and seeing the face, all red and white chalk, of Mr. Meryman the clown taking the cash without a smile on his countenance, unless one is painted there, and not all like the Fool, but in the most sensible and business manner possible.

In the same way the All-England Eleven—'the gate' being part of the bargain—you pay your sixpences to a creature in flannels, pads, and spiked shoes, ready at a moment's notice to start to have his innings, which innings, no doubt, he

Below: Thomas Box guards his wicket. The professionals were paid the princely sum of £5 per match—£6 sometimes if they had to travel far

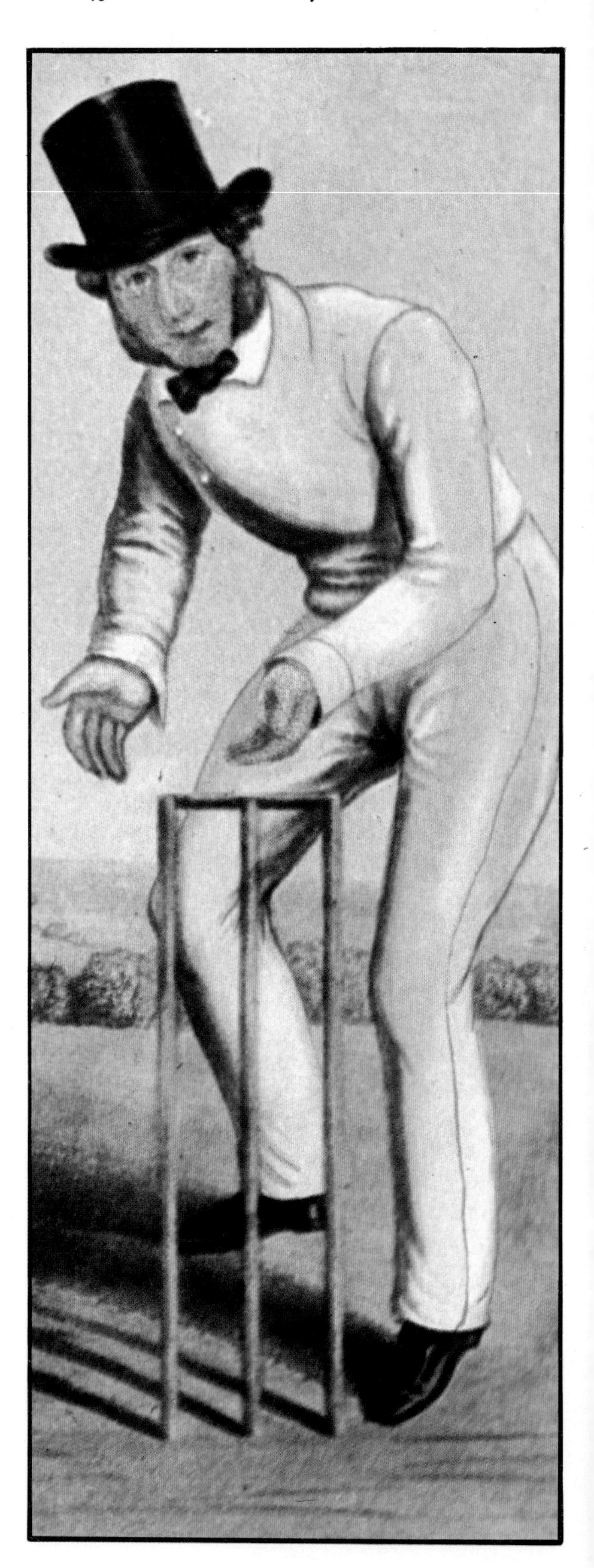

hopes will be a creditable one to himself; but as to the issue of the match he does not care a button, not he. No; he does not play for the score—he only plays for the till. And cricket is one of those games that must be played with a will to be played well. This is especially true of old and experienced players. Boys play their best for the fun and the novelty; but there can be no novelty to a professional cricketer; and the difference between concentrated energy and the mere mechanical performance makes all the difference between the finest bowling and that which is just good enough to make the batsman play his best against it. This intensified energy, this concentration of all the powers of bowlers, wicketkeepers, and fieldsmen to one point, makes a difference of half the score.

So the truth comes to this: even if you had All-England men, you cannot have All-England play when your side is not worth beating, and when not the runs but the sixpences are all they care for . . .

But the chief reason of all that men in the All-England Eleven rarely play like themselves is this: they are fagged and jaded—stale and overdone from the beginning of the season to the end.

Imagine two matches a week, and most of their rest taken in railway trains. We remember they came to play at Bath, just landed from Ireland, half of them sea-sick. The first day they were not fit to play a decent school; still our friends flattered themselves the score they made was against All-England men! about as true as if they had been drunk. Why, as to play, we are reminded of the travelling circus over again. 'I might be fond of music,' said the French horn, 'but I am not the man to blow all day to please anyone.' Sometimes the said All-England bowlers have hardly a leg to stand on—such as cricketers' legs ought to be. We could name men we have seen quite groggy—with sore feet and swollen legs—blessing Providence for the chance of going to bed (for that's what they do) when the rain came down in torrents.

The contrast between the faces of the All-England Eleven—when paid not by 'the gate' but by the job—and the faces of the rest of the field on a rainy day, is amusing to any lover of the ridiculous. Being very civil fellows, they feel bound to seem a little disappointed, as naturally as they can, when they pass some promising young players looking much bluer than the sky is likely to be. Perhaps they may also say a sympathetic word to the caterer, whose cold lamb and cucumbers is already in a state of watery solution; but if anyone could hear their private and confidential communications, he would hear something like this: 'A good

Below: James Cobbett of Surrey. His fellow players did not wear a uniform as such, but established the rudiments of cricket clothing

chance for your bad legs, John. Another such a day as this, and I shouldn't wonder if some of Jackson's bowling would come back again.' Now this is all we get for our money—this is the delusion we practise on ourselves when we book our clubs and grounds for one of the vacant days of the All-England Eleven. We have that Eleven, it is true, but all the powder and the spirit is out of them; and one would think that no man who had ever made one of twenty-two with two bowlers given, all fresh and lively, against eleven stiff and steady ones, could ever want to do the same thing over again.

'But if we do like to amuse ourselves,' someone will say, 'what does it matter to anyone?'

Why, it matters a great deal. It is nothing to draw the best players away from fine county matches, which are better worth seeing by far? Very commonly the members of the Surrey Club—than whom no club has ever done more to encourage county cricket—have had a difficulty in their fixtures, because All-England matches are encouraged on the same days.

We trust all true lovers of cricket will take this into consideration before they have anything to do with these 'All-England' games. For, which is better—that for three summer months the finest matches possible shall be arranged by the Marylebone and the Surrey clubs chiefly in London, but with return matches in other counties, or that these arrangements should be spoilt for so poor an apology for a match as we have already described?

It does appear at present that there is a feeling of opposition on the part of the All-England Eleven, or certain of them, to the promoters of country matches. Surely nothing can be more suicidal. Who brought forward these very men to their present positions? Who find the sinews of war? Who provide the money for matches and the labour fund? We admit that there may be one or two men so situated that they may see little personal danger in opposing their former friends and patrons; though even they may commit the fatal mistake of kicking away the ladder before they have done with it. But let us ask—Do cricketers act wisely in supporting them? Should the rest of the All-England Eleven agree to play on days when they are wanted for our leading clubs?

We trust that this will be amicably arranged; otherwise, we should say that the Marylebone and the Surrey clubs should make it a rule that men who belong to an Eleven so regardless of their fixtures should never be employed either at Lord's or at The Oval.

(Rev. James Pycroft, *Cricketana*, 1865)

MARYLEBONE CRICKET CLUB

Given the increasing popularity of cricket, the Marylebone Cricket Club was to become an essential feature of the social life and topography of London.

Preceding page: Gentlemen v Players at Lord's, by Dickinsons, 1845

Right: Thomas Lord, cricket's greatest early entrepreneur, who gave his name to the most famous cricket ground in the world

Great houses and terraces were being built by the likes of John Nash close to clubland and in the area between Hyde Park and Regent's Park. If Thomas Lord had not acted as MCC's midwife as the eighteenth century drew to a close, someone else would have established a club or a cricket team in London to rival the men of Hambledon. Indeed, it is surprising that one had not already been established.

Thomas Lord had the right name for promotion to the upper classes. But he was a worker. He had to be, for his father—once a wealthy Yorkshire landowner—had lost his estates through his support for the Jacobites during the 1745 uprising. It is hard to appreciate what a divide such events created throughout the length and breadth of England—equivalent, perhaps, to the way in which wartime France was split between Gaullists and supporters of the Vichy régime. Young Thomas Lord was obliged to sell anything and everything to make a living. In one of his ventures he sold wine to the King and, even more important as it turned out, to the Earl of Winchilsea, one of the new generation of cricket patrons. The Earl belonged to the White Conduit Club, which played in Islington, a ground not nearly exclusive enough for the Earl's taste. Encouraged by the enthusiasm of Winchilsea and his friends, Thomas Lord leased a piece of land, now Dorset Square, from the Portman family. The first game at Lord's, in 1787, was between Middlesex and Essex, then minor counties, but a few weeks later the White Conduit Club, with six men, met All-England and lost.

Lord himself liked his cricket and was able to hold his own as a bowler. He could not, however, hold back the rapid development of London, and within twenty years he was obliged to move his ground to Lisson Grove, then owned by the Eyre family. Later, in the winter of 1809-10, Lord transported the actual turf from the old ground, its value as a pitch providing remarkable evidence of the technical developments being made in the game. When Parliament bisected his field with the Regent's Canal in 1813, Lord moved the turf yet again, to the present ground. It was probably just as well that this further move had been forced upon him, as the second ground did not prove popular. The MCC played there only three times. By this time the MCC were recognized as the premier club in the land. Their laws were the scratching post for the whole country and then, as now, they were frequently revised.

A study of the laws reveals many surprises. The earliest, dating from 1721, delineated only two issues: that a match should be of two innings, and that the batsman should have some right to charge down an opponent trying to catch him. Clearly there were other laws, and when the matches were important enough instructions to players and umpires were recorded. By 1755 a group was meeting at the Star and Garter in Pall Mall (also the home of the Jockey Club), and here the great men of cricket produced revisions to the laws of the game, culminating in 1744 in the *New Articles of the Game of Cricket.* Sir William Draper was chairman of the group and the Duke of Dorset, Sir Horatio Mann and the Rev. Charles Pawlett, a Hambledonian, were members. As a result, the weight of the ball was fixed between five-and-a-half and five-and-three-quarter ounces, the bat's width, *pace* 'Shock' White, at four-and-a-quarter inches, the height of the three stumps at twenty-two inches, and the width of the bails at six inches. The creases and the pitch measured as they do today.

By virtue of this set of revised laws, the away team was given choice of innings and where to pitch the wicket. Batsmen could be dismissed much as they can be today, including leg-before-wicket, lbw, 'if the batsman had a design to stop the ball and actually prevented the ball from hitting his wicket'. By this time no batsmen, 'whether under pretence of running a notch or otherwise', could impede a would-be catcher.

By 1788 the Star and Garter group, later renamed the White Conduit Club, had moved to Lord's first ground and become the Marylebone Cricket Club. Henceforward changes in the laws issued by the MCC remained unchallenged. Even today the International Cricket Conference grants to MCC the right of final custodianship of the Laws of Cricket.

Because of its pre-eminence, there have been attempts to disfavour this ancient club, the Marylebone Cricket Club, the MCC, the private club with the public function. This is nothing new. In 1864, W. G. Grace noted that an attempt by certain newspapers had been made to question the authority of the MCC and to have it replaced by a parliament of the counties. The Doctor was happy to see such a notion fail. Historians, too, while legitimately challenging the facts as presented by previous generations of chroniclers, have shown a tendency to minimize the particular flavours of the Club's history. Lord, as we have seen, gave MCC much of its early character. His training was as a wine merchant, and the aristocracy were likely to be better customers than the *hoi polloi* who played in Islington's public fields. The successive moves within the Borough of Marylebone were designed to protect the relative exclusivity the Club enjoyed, and to encourage and control the expansion of MCC as a private club.

Right: unlike other sports which merely have rules, cricket has laws

Even in the 1860s, the structure of cricket was much less formalized than it is today, when a computer is needed to arrange fixtures. Whereas the principal games in the early days at Lord's were between teams labelled MCC or named after one or other of the counties, the advent of other fixtures began to establish in the game the principle of exclusivity which was eventually to extend even as far as county cricket. Many of these games, which grew into traditional fixtures, were arranged between schools, by pupils past and present. Sometimes they were banned because they led to trouble between the boys of these schools. Dr. Heath, the flogging headmaster of Eton, tried to prevent Eton playing Westminster, for instance. Eton and Harrow first played in 1805, and again in 1818, but their games did not become an annual fixture until 1822. It was in this event that Charles Wordsworth and Herbert Jenner, the men who were to arrange the first fixture between Oxford and Cambridge five years later, first met on the cricket field. By 1836, the University match too had become an annual fixture. Another of the traditional Lord's fixtures, the game between Gentlemen and Players, represented the ultimate exclusivity in class teams. Later it came to epitomise the distinction between unpaid (later known as amateur) players and the professionals, a distinction which was to last, albeit often cynically blurred, right up until 1962.

In the early days of the event, however, the Gentlemen were obliged to engage Players to even out the sides in order that the match might make a better vehicle for betting. Betting was the passion of MCC members, and so in order to provide the right conditions for an even wager the vagaries of selection to which Gentlemen and Players were subjected included allowing the Gentlemen sixteen players, or inviting the Players, with no option, to defend wickets twice the normal size. As betting had become such an important appendage of the game, trouble was bound to follow. By the end of the eighteenth century the 'legs', the bookmakers' assistants, used to buy up players in the Green Man and Still, a pub frequented by cricketers in Oxford Street. William Lambert (the professional employed by Squire Osbaldeston, one of the great sporting figures of the early 1800s who resigned in pique from MCC after a celebrated duel with Lord George Bentinck) was eventually barred from Lord's in 1817 after he was alleged to have sold the match between England and Nottingham played on the ground. Lambert resumed his trade as a miller, and eventually gravitated into the Fuller's Earth business making and selling material now used for filtering swimming pools.

William Ward's benefaction in purchasing the Lord's lease saved the ground from the builders and for the future of cricket. The pavillion, alas, could not be saved for, in that same year, 1825, it went up in flames; these also consumed all the earliest precious records of the game.

In 1835 the lease was passed on to J. H. Dark, a man in the Thomas Lord tradition, a proprietor for whom profit was the principal motive. Dark staged displays of all sorts—Red Indians, canaries, pigeons—but there was no groundsman to tend the field. However, cricket was his business and he was fond of it and it must have been frustrating for him that the MCC, to whom he let his ground for cricket, could not or would not buy the freehold from the heir of the estate when it came up for sale in 1860 at a price of £7,000. Six years later the club did buy it, for £18,000.

For all its long history, there have been only eleven

secretaries of MCC. Initially it was an honorary appointment. Benjamin Aislabie, to whom Tom bowled slow lobs in *Tom Brown's Schooldays*, was the first to hold office, from 1822 until his death in 1842, by which time he weighed about twenty-six stone. Still playing, he was allowed a runner.

His successor was Roger Kynaston, who served until 1858, throughout the period when the first professional circuses were in full swing. Reputed to be fussy, he had difficulty with his staff, for these were the days of change—revolution was in the air and the cities, with their factories and a new generation of wealthy men, were expanding.

After Kynaston came Alfred Baillie who remained for a five-year-spell, until illness forced him to resign in 1863, whereupon Robert Alan Fitzgerald was nominated as his successor at the young age of twenty-nine. On 1 January 1868, five years after taking up the appointment, Fitzgerald became the first paid MCC secretary. He organized the first MCC tour overseas—to Paris in 1867, when he was thirty-three and young enough to enjoy it, and to the United States and Canada five years later. He was a batsman good enough to hit the ball over the old tennis court in St John's Road on one occasion, but the lasting legacy of his term of office are the present red and yellow colours of the club, changed from the original sky-blue, although no-one knows why the change was made. After Fitzgerald came Henry Perkins, 'Perkino' as he was called, whose term lasted for the next twenty-one years. He was a barrister, small in stature but with a huge beard, who walked about Lord's dressed in a grey suit with a tail-coat. His successor, Francis Lacey, was also a barrister, a man whose manner during his period of office (1898-1926) was said to be cold and official, tending towards an over-rigid interpretation of rules and regulations; nevertheless it was during Lacey's term of office that the affairs of MCC and, indeed, of cricket the world over, were put into some sort of order. He was careful, even restrictive, about such mundane matters as club finances and facilities, especially refreshment facilities, and during his period in office the first sub-committees were formed. The Mound Stand was built a year after he took the job, and many were his other accomplishments particularly as far as the laws and regulations of the game at the highest level were concerned. It was to Lord's that the leading cricketers of the day automatically turned for guidance. Thus a County Cricket Council was formed in 1887 to deal with county classifications and qualifications, and in 1898 the counties asked MCC to form a Board of Control for Test matches. Three years later it was Lacey who suggested to the counties that an advisory committee should be set up to act as a forum for considering changes in the laws. By the time of the Australian season of 1903-04, MCC in England had accepted a request from the Melbourne Cricket Club (the MCC in Australia) through its secretary, Major Wardill, that future tours should always be organized from Lord's. In 1909, the Imperial Cricket Conference was established, All-England delegates being nominated by the MCC.

Lacey's successor was Billy Findlay, who had been the second assistant secretary after captaining Eton and Oxford. He spent ten years in office, from 1926 to 1936, a period which included the notorious bodyline tour and its repercussions. Findlay himself, a courteous and charming man, probably did not relish all the scrapping that took place at that time between England and Australia.

His successor was Colonel R. S. Rait Kerr, a shy

Right: a small, faded velvet bag and a tiny urn containing cricket's mythical Ashes
Below: a landmark at Lord's. Old Father Tyme on the roof of the pavilion, symbolises one of the most crucial factors in any game—friend to the defensive side, enemy of the attacking

and efficient soldier whose daughter Diana, with encouragement from her father, created almost single-handedly the Lord's library. Colonel Rait Kerr possessed an encyclopedic knowledge of the laws and increasingly complicated regulations of cricket, and in many instances was approached as a last resort for settling disputes.

Ronnie Aird, his assistant and eventual successor, was a man of great charm who succeeded to the post in 1952 and held it for ten years. It seems that MCC's decline as the guiding force in cricket either began or accelerated during his term of office. Whether or not this was due in part to his stewardship is a judgement best left to those better placed to be objective.

By the time his successor, 'Billy' Griffith, took office, the game was in a state approaching ruin, in England principally but also elsewhere. Griffith was a former secretary and captain of Sussex and a Test cricketer who made his first century in his very first Test match. He then became a cricket-writer on the *Sunday Times* before finding his proper niche at Lord's. The boom following the 1939-45 war had come to an end and a social revolution had taken place, and yet the attitude of the game's councils seemed too complacent and outmoded for cricket to be able to adapt and survive.

During these difficult years, in which matters were not improved by the onset of several formidable and insoluble cricketing conundrums such as the South African situation, Billy Griffith was one of the few men swimming, strongly albeit somewhat slowly, in the right direction. Out of the agony of the 1960s came new ideas which in turn led to the comparative prosperity of the 1970s, to such an extent, in fact, that cricket and cricketers became a much more attractive proposition for exploitation by commercial pirates.

When Griffith bowed out of office he handed his MCC responsibilities and those of secretary of the ICC over to Jack Bailey, another administrator with a cricketing background. Those of his duties which related to the Test and County Cricket Board, the more significant body in so far as cricket in England was concerned, were passed to another of his assistant secretaries, Donald Carr, one-time captain of Derbyshire. To suggest that relations between these two bodies (the North and South Towers in the Lord's pavilion) have been easy during the last decade would be as nonsensical as suggesting that there have been no problems between Soviet Russia and China. Suffice to say that whereas the office of secretary of MCC is now significant chiefly in its historically important role of maintaining a club which still has custodianship of the greatest traditions in cricket (especially as keeper of the laws of the game), it is the office of secretary of the ICC which has become the key appointment of the late 1970s. Thus far, when tested by the likes of Kerry Packer, the Australian broadcasting entrepreneur, the ICC's administration has been quite simply disastrous. By all accounts, Sir Francis Lacey and, from personal observation, Colonel Rait Kerr, won respect because they were always correct in their judgments.

If the office of secretary has received most attention it is because that of president, the position in the public eye, has, except in war-time, been held only on an annual tenancy. Many of the figures who have held the office have been substantial influences on the development of cricket, but the office itself has usually been only incidental to that influence. Nevertheless, by studying the roles of MCC presidents certain trends in the club's history can be traced. A love of cricket, in the majority of cases, and a facility for playing the game have been the

principal qualifications for holding an office aptly described by the fifth Earl of Cardigan (then Viscount Chelsea), president in 1783, as the woolsack of cricket. Of the first nine men known to have been president, only two were titled and both of them, Lord Frederick Beauclerk and the Honourable George Ponsonby, were outstanding players, as were most of the others who held office in a decade increasingly characterized by the Duke of Wellington's civilian influence.

In the hundred years following 1834, there were only nine presidents of MCC who had no hereditary title, and one of these was a knight. From 1934 to 1964 the position changed only statistically. Beside Stanley Christopherson, who was president from 1939 until 1945, only four other commoners have held the office. By ancient tradition (and an admirable one in a private club) the president of MCC nominates his successor, and normally the secret of this man's identity is maintained until the anniversary dinner at which the appointment is announced. The time will come, no doubt, when a lady will receive the nod, but it may be a few years yet if precedent is any guide.

Above: the girls of Wycombe Abbey School, who played for the county of Buckinghamshire, present grave faces for the camera. Main picture: the ladies of Surrey meet the ladies of Hampshire in a delightfully vulgar cartoon, 1811. Below: in recent years women's cricket has gained popularity but still struggles for complete acceptance

WOMEN'S OWN

THE EVOLUTION OF THE COUNTY CHAMPIONSHIP

From 1946, the first year of the resumption of cricket after the War, until 1963, when one-day cup competitions were introduced, the County Championship, still a three day affair, remained the only form of competition between the counties.

Left: from 'Georgie's Money Box' a typical Victorian children's illustration depicting schoolboys chairing the match-winning batsman off the field

Preceding page: Ray Illingworth, Captain of Leicestershire, raises the Benson and Hedges Cup after his side beat Middlesex in the 1975 final

Cricket played between elevens labelled as counties (rather than as towns, villages or clubs) began in the middle 1700s, but the next century was more than a third gone before the first county cricket club, Sussex, was formally created, and it had only five years to run before the structure of a county championship was established in a form universally recognizable and recognized. It was not until 1895 that MCC was given, and willingly took upon itself, the task of officially declaring the champion county. Long before that it had been obvious to all but the blindly partisan which county had earned the title of champion in most seasons. But the method of scoring tended to be rudimentary, especially in view of the fact that counties all arranged their own fixture-lists. Whereas a county like Surrey, already famous and well established at The Oval, might play as many as sixteen matches, a poor eleven like Derbyshire could arrange only six or seven matches. Derbyshire were in fact the only county ever to drop out of the Championship, albeit briefly.

Not until the publication of the 1911 edition of *Wisden's Cricketers' Almanack* was a list of champion counties published, dating back to 1873. There were special reasons for choosing the year 1873, as we shall see. However, first let us trace how the nine founder members of the Championship—Derbyshire, Gloucestershire, Kent, Lancashire, Middlesex, Nottinghamshire, Surrey, Sussex and Yorkshire—developed in the formative decades of the middle of the nineteenth century. This was a period of rapid development in the country as a whole. Towns grew, funded by the profits generated by mine and mill, and the land prospered despite a population growth that terrified the economist Malthus, who had been the first to prophesy the island ant-heap we now know and sometimes love. Canals and then, rapidly, railways and better roads linked the whole together. In the midst of this expansion cricket tended to represent the good life, a feature of the game's appeal that has survived until today. Cricketers found both patrons and audiences without much difficulty in this age of penny income tax. These were the conditions in which William Clarke set up his professional troupe. When this venture failed, sufficient vested interests remained to promote the county game in all parts of the land, whether predominantly aristocratic, industrial or plain bourgeois.

We must begin with the oldest club, Sussex. Not only are they the senior county club, but following their formation, and indeed perhaps causing it, they fielded a team which could beat even Kent, then the acknowledged masters, nine times in eleven seasons. In 1847, with the greatest of Kent cricketers,

Right: a 1921 portrait of Dartmouth Cricket Team

Alfred Mynn, in the Sussex side, they defeated All-England. Lillywhite and Wisden were Sussex 'names', family names, later given to the great chronicles of the game that began to be published towards the end of the century, the *Annual* and the *Almanack*. So were Broadbridge, (he and Lillywhite formed the first pair of round-arm bowlers); Thomas Box, a wicket-keeper for no fewer than twenty-four summers; and the Eton and Cambridge batsman C. G. Taylor, a real all-rounder, an acting member of the 'old stagers' during Canterbury week, and enough of a tailor by inclination and by trade to walk down King's Parade in Cambridge wearing a pair of trousers of his own making.

The next county to be formed was Surrey—in 1845. From the very first, their home was at The Oval, where the opening match was played as the Montpelier Cricket Club against Clapton Cricket Club in that same year. It was from the Montpelier Club that Surrey sprouted, with William Ward, the saviour of Lord's, taking the role of both midwife and gardener, as it were. In June 1846 they beat Kent by ten wickets in the first county match on the ground. In the late 1850s Surrey were a real force, as they were to be again exactly a hundred years later. Captain F. P. Miller, William Caffyn, the cricketer who was to do so much to foster the game in Australia, Julius Caesar (not a *nom de plume*), and H. H. Stephenson, the wicketkeeper who captained the first England team in Australia, were all pillars of the side.

Surrey's great bank-holiday rivals were Nottinghamshire, the next county to be founded in 1859. Nottinghamshire players really made their mark even before the redoubtable William Clarke, for the notorious Sam Redgate was a faster round-arm bowler even than Alfred Mynn. Redgate's most famous over (four balls at that time) was bowled for England at Town Malling in Kent in 1839. The first shaved Fuller Pilch's wicket, the second bowled him out, the third knocked down Alfred Mynn's stumps, and the fourth bowled another Kent player, Shearman. It is said that the bowler downed a glass of brandy after each success. Whether this is legend or fact, drink was to be the death of poor Sam Redgate.

Clarke himself played in the side, of course, and there were no fewer than three Parrs in the original eleven, including George Parr, after whom the famous tree at Trent Bridge was named, and who subsequently went on to captain the All-England professional eleven that Clarke founded.

John Jackson was Redgate's successor as Nottinghamshire's fast bowler, but in the forty years from 1861 to 1901 this poor fellow slumped from the peak of his career as the greatest bowler in the world to a miserable death in the infirmary of a Liverpool workhouse, where even the Cricketers' Fund Friendly Society could not save him. A fifteen-stone six-footer, he was once asked if he had ever taken all ten wickets. 'No,' he replied regretfully, and then his face lit up. 'But I clean bowled nine once, and lamed John Wisden so's he couldn't bat. That'd be near enough, wouldn't it?'

Charlie Brown was the wicketkeeper in this fine team. A dyer by trade, he was apt to become so enthusiastic when talking about cricket at work that he would splash his own colour into everybody else's tub. Remarkable players tumbled out of Nottinghamshire, generation upon generation: Richard Daft, who married a Parr daughter, and built a reputation for dealing contemptuously with the most difficult balls, even shooters; his contemporary Alfred Shaw who, in a thirty-one-year career, bowled more than half his overs as maidens, so effective was his off-theory; Oscroft, who became captain of the county; and Arthur Shrewsbury who, according to W. G. Grace, was the best batsman in all the world, the first to use his pads as a second line of defence.

Gloucestershire began to play matches in 1868, and by 1870 the senior Mr. Grace, W. G.'s enthusiastic father, had enlisted support from friends and a county club was established. Naturally they were known all over the country as the county of the Graces.

For a while it seemed as if Cambridgeshire, too, would develop into a county club able to hold its own with the very best. Buttress and Tarrant, as dangerous a pair of bowlers as ever walked out on to a cricket pitch, the one a leg-breaker and the other a fast round-arm specialist, played regularly for this county. Buttress's appeal must have been interesting: a lamplighter by trade, he was also a ventriloquist, with a predilection for scaring nervous Victorian ladies in railway carriages by throwing his voice to represent a cat meowing under their seats. No batsman, he was once found under a tree when his time to walk to the wicket came. 'If I miss 'em I'm out, if I hit 'em I'm out, so what is the use—let's start the next innings,' he said. But instead of Cambridgeshire it was Derbyshire, founded in 1873, who took a place in the founding nine. William Mycroft's bowling was their great asset at this time, but despite this they were never a strong side.

Kent stood as unrivalled champions for many years in both the 1700s and the 1800s. The reason why a club was not founded until 1873 lies not in the poverty of that country's history, but in its very richness.

We have already seen teams under the Kent

banner in action during Hambledon times and even before. In the early part of the nineteenth century, the West Kent Club was a miniature MCC, with its own professionals. The Town Malling Club, founded by Tom Selby, a businessman who turned land-owner, brought Fuller Pilch from Norfolk to manage a local pub. He in turn engaged Martingell, a Surrey man, at a salary of £60 a year, for Town Malling. Even such a man as Pilch regarded 'Gentlemen as gentlemen and players as much in the same position as his head keeper may be.'

Canterbury Week, with its cricket and concert parties, began in 1842 and settled at the St Lawrence Ground five years later. In these days Kent had only one amateur, Alfred Mynn. Mynn, incidentally, missed the entire season in 1837 after taking the bowling of Redgate on his front leg for hour after hour playing in the historic North *v* South match at Leicester in 1836. Doctors thought he would lose the leg. Blood had run down and stained his stockings—pads were not yet in use. He was taken home to Kent strapped to the roof of a stagecoach, a journey which all but killed him.

Alfred Mynn was a splendid all-rounder, one of the round-arm men, one of the first in a long line of England all-rounders that would later comprise the incomparable Dr. W. G. Grace and Walter Hammond, and whose current representative may well be Ian Botham.

In 1858 the Kent County Club was formed, and the Baker family, with Fuller Pilch as a retainer, merged their own club, the Beverley Club, with the new body so hoping to revive the fortunes of the county now that Mynn, often the only amateur in this great eleven, and Pilch had retired. On the original committee sat both Alfred Mynn and Edward Wenman, a professional. Although he later resigned, his presence on the committee reflects the long Kentish tradition of former professionals assisting in administration. In recent times Les Ames, now the controller of the Hoppers, a Kent Cricketing Club with almost Masonic characteristics, has epitomised this tradition as secretary-manager of the country club at Canterbury. We ought to note in passing that Kent and Sussex, two counties which have been at loggerheads with the other counties in recent times, were also the leading counties in the dispute over the establishment of a parliament of cricket in 1864.

The date of the first published list of champions coincides with a series of meetings held among the counties between December 1872 and June 1873, most of which took place at the Surrey County Club's behest. Their purpose was to lay down qualification rules to determine eligibility. We have already seen how, at one stage, Alfred Mynn of Kent took the field under Sussex colours. The eligibility rules eventually agreed in The Oval pavilion

Left: A. E. 'Stoddy' Stoddart played for Middlesex, MCC and for England, opening many stands with W. G. Grace. In one afternoon he hit 485. He also won 10 Rugby caps for England

Below: Richard Daft played for Nottingham, for the Gentlemen and the Players, and the All England XI. He is said to have played an innings of 140 in club cricket in his 60th year

on 9 June 1873 stood for many years. They were:

1. No cricketer, whether amateur or professional, should play for more than one county during the same season.
2. Every cricketer born in one county and residing in another shall be free to choose at the commencement of each season for which of those counties he will play, and shall, during that season, play for the one county only.
3. A cricketer should be qualified to play for any county in which he is residing and has resided for the previous two years; or a cricketer may elect to play for the county in which his family home is, so long as it remains open to him as an occasional residence.
4. Should any question arise as to the residential qualification, the same should be left to the decision of the committee of the Marylebone Cricket Club.

When these rules were submitted to MCC for approval the latter wanted a clause inserted allowing amateurs to play for a county in which their parents had property. When this was rejected by the counties MCC attempted to stage their own championship by inviting sixteen counties to challenge for a silver cup. In the end, only Sussex and Kent offered such a challenge. They played an unhappy match on an extremely poor wicket and the scheme was abandoned.

What was not settled in 1873 was the method of deciding the Championship. This remained a knotty issue for twenty years and indeed has been the subject of debate and amendment ever since. Essentially, the method adopted was that the county with fewest matches lost should win the title. Except for one or two seasons, this method has produced results similar to more sophisticated point-scoring schemes. Gloucestershire and Nottinghamshire, for instance, are judged to have shared first place in 1873, and Gloucestershire to have been outright winners in 1874. Thereafter, the principal rivalry was between Nottinghamshire and Surrey.

Nottinghamshire's great bowlers were Shaw and Morley. It was Morley who, in one memorable match against Surrey in 1880, bowled 19.2 overs at the opposition, who were bowled out for 16 on a treacherous wicket on which he, Morley, conceded only 9 runs for 7 wickets. That gives some idea of the intensity of rivalry of matches a century ago.

The potential for argument and the need for arbitration were particularly notable in 1886, for in that year the *Lillywhite Annual* indicated joint champions—Nottinghamshire and Surrey. Nottinghamshire were unbeaten with seven wins and seven draws; Surrey won five more matches, twelve out of sixteen, but lost three times and were therefore adjudged second in the title race. The rivalry between these counties was as intense as that between Yorkshire and Lancashire in the 1920s and 1930s.

The first significant change in the Championship scoring system was the introduction of the points method: one point for a win, half a point for a draw. But with such a haphazard list of fixtures, and no real agreement as to which counties were first-class, the system was far from perfect. It was perhaps fortunate that Surrey's clear pre-eminence in the period of George Lohmann, Tom Richardson, Bill Lockwood and Bobby Abel was widely accepted by the cricketing public in the early 1890s; otherwise the arguments might have wrecked the Championship as they had eventually wrecked the touring sides thirty years before.

Despite the arguments, it was clear that Nottinghamshire and Surrey were the outstanding teams in the first twenty-two seasons of formal county cricket. Nottinghamshire were champions six times, four of them in succession, and also joint champions four times, whereas Surrey, who also won six times, shared the title only once. Gloucestershire, the team of all the Graces, judged outright winners in 1874, also won in 1876 and 1877. Yorkshire, who have now won the title twenty-nine times, had to wait until 1893 to take it for the first time.

Derbyshire lost all their matches in 1887 and withdrew from the Championship, but Somerset made the number up to nine again in 1891 and three years later Derbyshire returned with Essex, Leicestershire and Warwickshire. Hampshire became an acknowledged first-class county in October of the same year. By this time yet another point system was in operation. This had been agreed in 1889 by the county secretaries, and provided that losses should be deducted from wins and no points given at all for a draw.

As the Championship entered the modern era it was fourteen counties strong. It had an agreed system for deciding the eligibility of players and a completely new scoring system: one point for a win, a point deducted for a loss and a proportion of points for games completed settled the order of merit. Above all, the County Championship now had an arbitrator. From 1894, MCC were to decide which games were first-class, and ten years later, in 1904, they set up the Advisory County Cricket Committee which was to last as the County Championship's ruling body until the formation of the Cricket Council in 1969.

Although MCC had donned the mantle of Solomon, the County Championship was still by no means an easy package to disentangle or on which to make judgments. With fourteen counties involved, the number of matches played had all but doubled from 71 to 131, but of this total Essex, for example, had some difficulty in acquiring even a minimum fixture-list of eight matches. Furthermore, draws were becoming common. This was the golden age of batting, heralded by a marked improvement in the wickets. The bowlers had to work harder for less success and so the percentage of draws crept up to a figure of over forty per cent.

In 1910, the long-established point system (one point for a win and one point deducted for a defeat, calculated as a percentage of matches played) was amended to wins as a percentage of the whole. This system lasted for one year only, for in 1911 the first-class counties adopted the idea, already implemented by the minor counties, of giving some points to a county which had a lead on the first innings. This of course was an essential feature of any two-day competition. Later, in 1911, upon Somerset's instigation, a scheme was adopted whereby five points were awarded for a win, three for a first-innings lead, and only one for a draw, a county's final score being the number of points gained expressed as a percentage of the maximum possible, with no-decision matches (those affected by rain) ignored altogether. Eventually this system was found to be statistically unsound. A county with a high rating, that is to say over three points a match, could find its total unfairly reduced because of a first-innings lead, and so a team challenging hard, for example Nottinghamshire in 1929, would deliberately throw a match into the no-decision category.

It was Tom Richardson, who walked from his home in Mitcham to The Oval and back every day—a twelve mile stretch—whose bowling won the first modern championship for Surrey. He took no fewer than 237 wickets with his great strength and pace; by August this great cricketer, described by Charles Fry as an Italian-looking bandit, must have travelled a fair distance in Surrey's service! Like many another great cricketer, unable to cope with life without the game which he loved, it is believed that Richardson eventually committed suicide.

Yorkshire ran a close race with Surrey for the

Championship in the next year, and then Surrey subsequently faded away to fourth place. In the twenty years up to 1914, when cricket was suspended with the onset of the Great War, Yorkshire won the title eight times and were never below number eight in the table. In that period of total supremacy, they won 286 of their 545 matches, and only 68 were lost.

Yorkshire held the title for the first three years of the twentieth century—seasons in which they won 57 of their 99 matches. Somerset, spurred on by Sammy Woods, beat Yorkshire in Yorkshire in 1901 and 1902, these defeats making news up and down the country, as well as providing evidence that Somerset were then, as indeed they always have been, capable of surprising the cricketing world. The scores in the match at Leeds in 1901 still hold pride of place in the Taunton pavillion. Somerset were all out for 87 in the first innings and 238 adrift after Yorkshire batted. But then Lionel Palairet and Len Braund, two of the legion of greats who played for the smaller counties, put up 222 for the first Somerset wicket in the second innings, out of a total which eventually climbed to 630; whereupon Yorkshire, weary and worn, were bowled out for a mere 113.

Middlesex took the title in 1903 with a thin fixture-list compared with that of Yorkshire, the scoring system being such that a few wins and a high proportion of draws were virtually unbeatable. Incentive to win was thus reduced, and when Yorkshire managed outright success in fifty per cent of their games during this season only to be rated no higher than third, the north/south argument was again revived.

Lancashire took their second title without argument in 1904 with Yorkshire runners-up. The places were reversed in 1905, the year in which Northamptonshire entered the Championship for the first time.

In 1906, Kent won their first title. Their roll-call was as impressive as any side's, particularly as it included the names of the two great left-handers, Woolley and Blythe. Colin Blythe, or Charlie as he was known, a talented violinist, was killed at Ypres in 1917.

Nottinghamshire, Yorkshire, Kent for two seasons running, Warwickshire, Yorkshire, Kent again, and finally, in 1914, Surrey—these were the Champions in the years before the shells and bullets of the Western Front took out a whole generation of cricketers, some with reputations, others with promise of them. Cricket would never be the same again.

Although the Championship now took up half the English cricketing summer, most county programmes allowed sufficient blank days for country-house cricket to be played by many of the leading batsmen and bowlers, especially the amateurs—this, sadly, was a form of cricket that was never wholly re-established after the War.

Cricket began again in 1919 with two-day fixtures only. It was a dry summer, and because the Championship was decided on the old formula of percentage wins to matches played, drawn games became an epidemic and then a plague—56 out of a total of 124. Yorkshire had a new captain, D. C. F. Burton, but their players retained their old mastery, with Rhodes taking his usual 100 wickets, and the opening pair of Holmes and Sutcliffe heading the batting averages for the first time.

In the following year, first-innings points came back into the reckoning and matches were restored to three days. Thereafter, scoring methods were changed too frequently to chronicle in detail. Each change presented the captains with new challenges and new opportunities, although not all were in the best interests of the game. For example, it was decided in 1927 that all games in which it had been possible to hold less than six hour's play without a pair of innings completed be rated no-result games, and thus qualify each side for four points. This gave the captain having the worst of it every incentive to stay in the pavilion.

The season of 1920 was Plum Warner's last as captain of Middlesex, and although Yorkshire, Surrey and Kent all seemed to have a chance of winning, Middlesex took the title with Lancashire as runners-up. They won again in 1921 under Frank Mann, father of George Mann, the present chairman of the Test and County Cricket Board. The great batsmen at Lord's at this time were Patsy Hendren and Jack Hearne, who in the course of this season hit thirteen centuries between them. Six of Patsy's seven were hit at Lord's, and five of 'Young Jack's', as he was known, were scored away from home. This produced as much contemporary chatter as did the home and away bowling figures of Laker and Lock when Surrey were winning so often in the 1950s. Great players get results anywhere, but runs and wickets against Yorkshire and Australia, the hardest nuts in the game, have always earned special respect from cricketers all over the world.

From 1922 to 1925, Yorkshire won consistently. Wilfred Rhodes was one of five batsmen to score 1,000 runs in 1922 for the White Rose, and four bowlers, none of them what we would now call fast took 100 wickets. George Macaulay began life as a bowler of genuinely fast pace, but later developed into one of the earliest seam bowlers, and a very successful one. In 1923, Maurice Leyland played his first full season in the Yorkshire team, strengthening the side even more. He also made 1,000 runs.

Middlesex ran a close race with Yorkshire in 1924.

Left: the cigarette lends Charles Parker a rakish air. A legendary Gloucestershire wicket-keeper and a protege of W. G. Grace

War was declared between the two counties when Middlesex refused to play any more fixtures against Yorkshire because of the incessant noise made by the Sheffield crowd. The atmosphere of special hostility between these counties lingered. It was a Yorkshireman who attempted to denigrate Denis Compton by labelling him 'the Brylcreem Boy', and at Sheffield in the 1950s, John Warr (subsequently paid a great honour by the Australians, who nominated him one of their representatives to the International Cricket Conference) was asked none too politely, after taking some stick whilst bowling, if he and his colleagues 'had come up there just to get tha' penknives sharpened'.

Not only did Yorkshire lose at Lord's that season, they also lost at Leeds in the Roses match, when Dick Tyldesley and Cecil Parkin, in one of the most famous of these closely fought encounters, bowled them out in an hour for 33 when Yorkshire needed a mere 57 to win. In 1925, Yorkshire, now captained by A. W. Lupton, were unbeaten in their thirty two games, and during the course of this season. Holmes, made 2,000 runs, whilst Roy Kilner, an all-rounder whose left-arm bowling was rated superior to Rhodes' at this time, received a bumper benefit of £4,000.

After Yorkshire's run it was Lancashire's turn: for three years they took the Championship. Ted McDonald, the great Australian fast bowler, obtained 163 wickets in 1926 and Ernest Tyldesley, cousin to Dick and as thin and upright as Dick was round, batted with rare style and consistency.

In the next year Nottinghamshire looked a certainty for the Championship. All they had to do at the end of August was to beat the Rag, Tag and Bobtail Glamorgan team in their last match. Yet they lost by an innings. Glamorgan had entered the Championship in 1921, the last county to do so, and they owed much in those early days to Maurice Turnbull, who had begun to play for the county as a seventeen-year-old and who thereafter became not only a pillar of Cambridge cricket but also chief administrator of Glamorgan. He was secretary until he went off to fight in the Second World War—he was killed in Normandy in 1944. Jack Mercer, still scoring for Northamptonshire in 1978 at the age of 83, a Sussex man by birth and during the first part of his career, took 6 for 31 for Glamorgan in this match with his off-spinners.

In May 1928, Charlie Hallows of Lancashire hit 1,000 runs. Hammond had done it in 1927, and W. G. back in 1895. With this supreme individual prizewinner in their ranks, Lancashire went through the season without defeat. Watson, Hallows' partner, was in his best form ever, and five batsmen in the team averaged over 50, while McDonald took even more wickets than usual—178. Nottinghamshire by now had their fast bowlers, Larwood and Voce, in harness, and captained by Arthur Carr, a redoubtable cricketer, they won the title in 1929. Their batting was thinner than that of their principal rivals, but with George Gunn and the young Charlie Harris following in the older players' deliciously eccentric footsteps, Nottinghamshire could never be dull.

Does anyone doubt that the Australians stood in awe of Larwood? We were still hearing stories of his pace as youngsters in the 1950s. But despite his mammoth contribution Nottinghamshire were removed from the top by Lancashire in 1930, Eddie Paynter's first full season. Then Yorkshire, out of the limelight for five years, took the title for another three. At one stage in 1931 they were no higher than eighth place, but they won five games in a row, three of them on their southern tour, all of them by an innings, and once they arrived at the top they could not be shifted. By now Hedley Verity and Bill Bowes had joined their bowling attack and had become the chief wicket-takers, and Herbert Sutcliffe was capable of averaging 97 as he did in that season. In the next year he and Percy Holmes put on 555 for

C. B. Fry
comes out to bat
in the 1914 Gentlemen v Players match

the first wicket on a beautiful pitch at Leyton. It took just five minutes under seven-and-a-half hours to score this pile of runs, the largest ever accumulated by an opening pair until the record was beaten by Waheed Mirza and Mansoor Akhtar for Karachi Whites *v* Quetta in 1976-77.

In 1933, A. B. Sellers took over from F. E. Greenwood as captain and began to strengthen his reputation as a formidable skipper. The following season, Leonard Hutton, then eighteen, scored his first century for Yorkshire at Worcester. But it was Lancashire who took the title that year—the season that Cyril Washbrook began to make a mark for them.

In 1935 Yorkshire won again and the following year Derbyshire, captained by A. W. Richardson, took the title in what remains to this day a statistically improbable achievement. Only three of their

Jack Hobbs

batsmen—Worthington, Townsend and Smith—averaged over 30, and none was rated among the best in the land. But this was the year in which Bill Copson, he of the red hair and long arms, was at his fastest and most devilish. He took 140 wickets, while the leg-breaks of Tommy Mitchell, the greatest billiard-ball spinner, also claimed over 100. The next season Yorkshire were first again, and there they stayed for three years. This must have seemed a long time to all the other counties, especially Middlesex, who had been runners-up every season from 1936 to 1939—a most disheartening experience, particularly as they could boast Jim Sims bowling his leg spinners and the young Edrich and the brothers Compton coming to full maturity. Be that as it may, Yorkshire's run of seven titles in the 1930s remained the most monopolistic hold on the Championship in its long history thus far.

THE COUNTY CHAMPIONSHIP 1946-1978

From 1946, the first year of the resumption of cricket after the War, until 1963, when one-day cup competitions were introduced, the County Championship, still a three day affair, remained the only form of competition between the counties.

And every year since 1963, at the presentation ceremonies, the county captain lucky enough to have led his team to victory in the Championship has been asked the same question: 'It's still the best competition, isn't it?' And always the same answer comes back: 'Yes.'

Many times there have been attempts to alter the structure of the Championship. Many committees have sat and much midnight oil has been consumed. Suggestions made have included abandoning the Championship altogether because of falling attendances, turning it into a smaller, four-day competition in which the counties play each other only once during a season, or, at the other extreme, increasing the number of County Championship matches. This latter alternative was actually instigated at one point, and for several years the Championship was a competition in which each county played each of its rivals twice over a three-day period—a true championship, in fact. Currently, each county must play twenty-two matches.

Just as the number of matches has altered over the years, so too has the method of scoring points continued to change. Indeed, at one stage the changes were so frequent as to be quite baffling to the spectators, but eventually the legislators recognized that continuous meddling with the Championship was bringing the competition into disrepute. Against this background of constant change the present system, which incorporates the system of scoring bonus points initiated in 1968, must be judged a considerable success. For a win twelve points are awarded, for a tie five points, and for a draw (equal scores) the side batting in the fourth innings scores five points. Additionally, each county is awarded bonus points during the first innings of the match, which is limited to 100 overs. These points are awarded for scoring each successive 50 runs once a total of 150 has been reached, and as the shutters come down at 300 this means that there are four points available to the batting side. There are also four points available to the bowling side, who must take a minimum of three wickets before they can begin to register their bonus points. Of course, there have been attempts to manipulate the rules by declaring before the full complement of wickets has been taken and by conceding runs as part of a trade-off for a declaration, but on the whole the system has worked well.

The introduction of a limited-over first innings caused many older cricketers to shake their heads. They felt that this was an unwarranted interference with the captain's right to plan a match, just as the system of limiting the leg-side field, introduced in 1957, was regarded by many as a catastrophic step backwards, initiating as it unquestionably did the decline in the significance of spin bowling in all forms of cricket. The limitation has varied over the years, standing in 1966 at sixty-five overs and at other times eighty-five overs. Under this restriction it proved more worthwhile for captains to pack their side with economical seam-bowlers rather than include spinners in their attack, a factor which prompted a dramatic change in the composition of county teams. Whereas in the 1950s the normal pattern of a bowling attack was three spinners and two quicker bowlers, now it is almost always customary for teams to have three, if not four, seam bowlers, and often counties go into the field with but a single spin bowler. Whether this is progress or not only the crowds can tell. Certainly attendances have continued to diminish, spectators patently preferring the alternative of one-day cricket.

But despite what was to happen later, the summer of 1946 began a cricketing boom which lasted for fully five years. It represented the end of hostilities and a need on the part of everyone to return to old habits—such as watching the best cricketers in the country at play. Yorkshire won the title in 1946 with Brian Sellers still their captain. One of their outstanding bowlers that season was Arthur Booth, who had earlier been discarded because of the pre-eminence of Hedley Verity, now dead. Remarkably, Booth came back to head the national bowling averages and won his Yorkshire cap at the ripe old age of forty-three.

In 1947, Middlesex, who had run Yorkshire close in 1946, took the title. It was a gorgeous summer, and Edrich and Compton played in masterly fashion through the season until by September hardly a day's cricket passed without a record being broken. Compton averaged 96 in that season, Edrich 77, and there were three others in the team whose average was over 40: Robertson, Thompson and Brown. Both Compton and Edrich broke the record aggregates for a summer in England, and Compton, with eighteen centuries to his credit broke the record of sixteen which Jack Hobbs had set when he was forty-

Below: shady trees, a perfect day, church spires, deckchairs and an unhurried game. County cricket at Worcestershire

two. The spinners, Jack Young, with slow left-handers, and Jim Sims, the leg-spinner, took most of the wickets, and Walter Robins, in his last season as Middlesex's captain, was as full of zest and trickery as he had been when he first began to play for his county.

1948 saw Glamorgan at the head of the table, a remarkable achievement for the junior county, traditionally one of the weakest. Glamorgan bred some but not enough of its own players, and had always been obliged to recruit from elsewhere in the country. However, under the captaincy of Wilfred Wooller, who had been a distinguished centre three-quarter for Wales, Glamorgan established a reputation for fearless fielding and driven on by this tall, angular man scored enough runs and took enough wickets to beat their rivals. Perhaps the most pleasing feature of their win was that Johnnie Clay, who had played in the side which first entered the Championship in 1921, was a member of the team which beat Hampshire at Bournemouth towards the end of August, a crucial match that clinched the Championship. He was then fifty-one and he took nine wickets in this game, following figures of 10 for 66 in the preceding game. Willie Jones, the Gloucester stand-off half and the greatest dropper of goals in post-war rugby, headed the batting averages. Emrys Davies, a veteran of the 1930s, and Gilbert Parkhouse, a young player who was later to win caps for England, fronted the batting strength. Len Muncer, an off-spinner from London, took 139 wickets, but success did not smooth his Cockney tongue which could be heard around the Lord's ground, where he was one of the chief coaches, until his retirement in 1978.

In 1949, Middlesex and Yorkshire shared the title, and the following year Surrey, under Michael Barton, divided the honours similarly with Lancashire. The latter side were bringing on some magnificent new cricketers in this period, particularly bowlers—spinners like Tattersall, Hilton and Berry, and the young Brian Statham.

In 1951 Warwickshire took the title for the first time in forty years. Their splendid side, under captain Tom Dollery, lost only two matches during the season, partly because few of their team were required for Test matches. Runs came thick and fast from men like Dollery, Gardner, Hitchcock, Spooner (the wicketkeeper) and Townsend; and Eric Hollies and Tom Pritchard from New Zealand (as fast a bowler as any in England) spearheaded the bowling attack.

The following season it was Surrey who were to return to the limelight, now under the captaincy of Stuart Surridge, a member of the family famous for its bats and balls. Surridge achieved an unprecedented record: in his five years as captain he led Surrey to five consecutive Championship victories.

Right: Kent team-mates congratulate Godfrey Evans on a brilliant catch in his first county match after an eight-year absence
Below: the summer's greatest prize for any county cricket side —the simple but beautifully crafted championship trophy

He was a whirling dervish of a batsman and a useful away-swing bowler with the new ball, but his principal contribution to Surrey's achievements was the remarkable spirit he inspired in his team, particularly in the field (he was the forerunner of the suicidally close short-legs). Fired by his example Surrey developed into a superb all-round side, not only because their fielding was so excellent (particularly with Tony Lock, the best backward short-leg in the history of the game, in the team) but also because their batsmen and bowlers were so uniformly competent. Three of their bowlers (Lock, Alec Bedser and Jim Laker) were automatic selections for England, all of them the outstanding practitioners of their respective styles. Bedser's combination of in-swing and cut from leg could be unplayable, and almost always entailed an early breakthrough for his county. Later he came to be supported by the fierce, whippy pace of Peter Loader. Lock was challenged as a left-arm bowler throughout this period by Yorkshire's Johnny Wardle, but there was no comparison between the two on wet wickets where Lock's action, subsequently much criticized and not least by himself, made him able to generate such pace and lift as to be virtually unplayable.

As for the County's batting strength, once the young May had become a Surrey player there was no shortage of class. Others who served the county so well in this period were players such as Bernard Constable, so difficult to dislodge even after wickets had begun to fall, David Fletcher, who promised so much but subsequently faded, reliable Tom Clark, and finally the exciting newcomers who were to go on and play many times for England: Ken Barrington and Mickey Stewart.

After Surridge's retirement Peter May took the county to two more Championships. In May's first year, 1957, the distance between Surrey and Northamptonshire, the runners-up, was huge, and they had completed their Championship by 16 August, a very early date. Yorkshire won in 1959, a remarkable feat with their young, re-built side. But Yorkshire also had a post-war generation of outstanding merit, headed by Freddie Trueman, perhaps at the end of the day the most notorious fast bowler of all time. Irrespective of the records that he set, Trueman's contribution to a cricket side on the field was immense. He had not only pace but movement and stamina, and he was able to provide a continuous element of surprise. Add to that his fielding ability, which was second only to Lock's, and his whirlwind batting performances, and here was a figure around whom others of less character could be successfully grouped. Among the young Yorkshire tigers of this era were Close and Illingworth, now both at the peak of their capabilities and both future captains of England, and the new generation of batsmen led by Stott, Taylor and Padgett, none of whom quite developed as Yorkshiremen hoped. The captain was Ronnie Burnett, who successfully weathered his inheritance of a troubled team in which Johnny Wardle although a great comedian off the field, was not the easiest of dressing-room comrades. Yorkshire had lost the services of Bob Appleyard, whose career was cut short by tuberculosis just as he had established himself both in county and on tour for England as a wicket-taker of unusual skill and penetration.

In 1960, Vic Wilson, a farmer from Malton, one of Yorkshire's veteran players, was appointed captain, and Yorkshire again won the Championship. Jimmy Binks their wicketkeeper, who could claim eventually over 400 consecutive matches for his county, took 100 victims behind the stumps in this season. Although Yorkshire had been the principal challengers to Surrey during the latter's seven-year reign as champions, their team at the beginning of the 1960s was not quite good enough to emulate Surrey's feat, and in 1961 a new name was engraved on the Championship board—that of Hampshire. Both Yorkshire and Middlesex challenged strongly, but Hampshire held top position throughout August. Colin Ingleby-Mackenzie was their captain, and a more glamorous figure has never been seen in county cricket. After Hampshire had won the title, the Ingleby-Mackenzie legend grew. He claimed his team had trained on wine, women and song, and not too much of the latter; the only rule he insisted upon was that his players should be in bed by breakfast-time. The Hampshire team on the whole were a hard-bitten lot who had had to struggle for success in cricket, but they regarded their young captain with amusement, tolerance and, in the end, almost reverence, not least because he won so many matches that year through declarations. Horton, Gray and Leo Harrison, the wicketkeeper, were steady players at the top and in the middle of the order, and among their bowlers Hampshire boasted the incomparable Derek Shackleton, whose length and movement were a phenomenon of cricket at this time. The best cricket sides require above-ordinary pace in their attack, and this was provided by the rollicking figure of 'Butch White'. Unable to establish himself in Warwickshire cricket, White came to Hampshire and eventually became as natural a Hampshireman in looks and behaviour as any in the team. So, in his cricket at least, was Roy Marshall, the most exciting batsman in the side. The first overseas player of any distinction to join the county cricket circuit after the war, Marshall joined Hampshire in 1951 and played with the greatest distinction for the county for twenty-one years. He was a rarity in his age, an opening batsman who put bat to ball from the first delivery of the innings. Between the Wars there had been many such cricketers—Charlie Barnett of Gloucestershire comes readily to mind. Roy Marshall was in the same mould, and he gave real pleasure to cricket-lovers all over the country and most especially in Hampshire. Had it not been for him the club might have suffered considerably because it was not one of the strongest counties financially.

Vic Wilson led Yorkshire back to the Championship in 1962, his last year in the first-class game. This was an exciting season because everything hinged upon the last match, Yorkshire's game against Glamorgan. Worcestershire were ten points ahead in the table when Yorkshire put Glamorgan in to bat on a drying wicket and established a position of considerable strength on the first day. The second day was a complete wash-out, and on the third the Yorkshire spinners managed to bowl the Welshmen out cheaply yet again, whereupon Yorkshire romped home in a low-scoring match by seven wickets.

Yorkshire won again in 1963 (their centenary year), a season in which Brian Close captained them for the first time. Close was a player of outstanding natural ability and must look back over his career regretting that he did not make more runs and take more wickets than he did. It was not until he was over thirty that he began to demonstrate for the

Right: Sussex and Gloucester in May 1973. The season only just underway, the county championship is well in its stride

world to see the courage and the acute cricketing brain that were to make him such a respected figure in the country at large. The team he led was a strong one, with Trueman to bowl and Philip Sharpe to catch so many batsmen at slip. Above all it was the first full season of the young Geoffrey Boycott, who made three 100s in this summer, including a quite superb innings at Sheffield in one of the last Roses matches played on this great ground.

1964 was the year of Worcestershire's centenary, and a few months before the actual birthday Don Kenyon led the county to their first ever Championship. Kenyon himself was a son of the county with a Brummagem accent which was almost impenetrable at times. For nigh on twenty years he was the man who had to be got out in the Worcestershire eleven, a fine opening batsmen who, once established, could tear bowlers to shreds on the superb Worcestershire ground. He was joined now by Tom Graveney who had left Gloucestershire in 1961 and enjoyed one of his best seasons in this Championship year, and also by Ron Headley, son of the great George Headley, the West Indian batsman whose son's Birmingham accent rivalled that of the captain. But it was the bowlers who had a year to remember in 1964, Jack Flavell, a Black Country lad, and Len Coldwell, a Devonian, both taking over 100 wickets.

The Worcestershire centenary was actually celebrated in 1965, and appropriately the side won the Championship again. They had been well down the table in ninth position towards the end of July, but thereafter they won ten of their final eleven matches and came through to finish with one of the strongest runs in memory. Their cricket was much strengthened by the appearance for the first time of the South African Basil d'Oliveira, who had joined them the previous year. In his opening season he hit five centuries in the Championship.

From 1966 to 1968, Yorkshire won three Championships in a row. The first was a tight affair with everything depending on the last matches, in which they beat Kent, but Worcestershire, challenging again, went down against Sussex. This summer the Yorkshire bowlers were strengthened by the appearance of Tony Nicholson, an in-swinger of high skill, and he, Trueman and Don Wilson all took over 100 wickets, while Boycott headed the batting averages. In 1967 Yorkshire needed to beat Gloucestershire to decide the Championship; they managed it in two days. A constant threat throughout the history of the Championship has been the Yorkshiremen's ability to take the title from the pack when there are very few opportunities for scoring championship points left. So many times, when confronted with a last-ditch affair, they have come out on top. Close led his county to victory for the third time in 1968, again helped by the superb batting of Boycott, with the Yorkshire spin bowlers having an especially good season.

Glamorgan had been developing another good side during the 1960s, and in 1969 their efforts finally bore fruit when they won the Championship. They fielded a number of players who had joined the county from elsewhere. Ossie Wheatley, a fine

away-swing opening bowler, who had captained them for several years, was still playing, and they now could call on the services of Majid Khan from Pakistan and Cambridge, and Brian Davis from Trinidad, as well as their Bristol-born but South African-raised all-rounder, Peter Walker. Walker had been capped for England because of his all-round skill and was accounted one of the finest short-leg fielders in the country. The team was led by Tony Lewis, who like so many of his Welsh-born predecessors was not only an outstanding cricketer but also a fine rugby player until injury ended his career.

In the following year, their centenary year, Kent won the Championship. The summer was a tribute to the quality of the Championship as a competition, because on 1 July Kent had been at the bottom of the table. Five of their players—Cowdrey, Denness, Luckhurst, Knott and Underwood—were called

Right: Mike Denness, who had an unhappy spell as captain of England until 1976. He led Kent to success in the Gillette Cup in 1974

upon by England. It was the first triumph of a team which has seldom been out of contention in the 1970s.

In 1971, Surrey took the title, although the issue was not decided until 13 September. Mickey Stewart, in his last season as captain of a county for which he had given so much service, led the team to triumph. John Edrich, Graham Roope, Pat Pocock, Geoff Arnold and Bob Willis (before his move to Warwickshire) were all in that Championship-winning side.

In the following season, 1972, Warwickshire, the team often unkindly called the United Nations, won the title. They had eleven Test players in the county, including no fewer than four from the West Indies—Kanhai, Kallicharran, Murray and Gibbs. Objectively examined, this was an absurd position. No-one begrudged Warwickshire their Championship, but the presence in the champion county of so many players not able to play for England was plainly not in the best interests of English cricket. Bob Willis, although he was not allowed to play for Warwickshire until 1 July after leaving Surrey, nonetheless featured in the run-in to the title for the second season in succession.

The winners in 1973 were Hampshire, who had the good fortune not to lose any players to the Test side. Like Warwickshire in 1972 and Glamorgan in 1969, Hampshire came through the season unbeaten, and also took every advantage of the relatively new bonus-points system, taking 84 for batting and 81 for bowling. This gave them an overall lead over Surrey of 31 points in the final table.

Hampshire were always able to get off to a splendid start because of the batting of Barry Richards and Gordon Greenidge, an opening partnership that, when future histories come to be written, will have to be acknowledged as one of the finest in all English cricket.

Hampshire challenged strongly in 1974. They were at the top of the table at the end of May and stayed there for three months, but Worcestershire had narrowed the gap to two points by the middle of August and with some help from the weather were able to creep into the lead and take the Championship by the very narrow margin of two points.

This was the first season in which the first-innings 100-over limit was applied. If the team batting first failed to use up their 100 overs, the remainder would be given to the side batting second. This, combined with the bonus-points system, seems to have satisfied the players with its fairness, and there have been no changes since.

1975 saw another late result. Not until 15 September were Leicestershire declared the winners, for the first time in their history. This was a great achievement for Raymond Illingworth, perhaps all the more sweet because his former county Yorkshire were runners-up. In fact the only real challengers for the title were Lancashire, who finished fourth, with Hampshire lying third and Kent fifth. The Leicestershire side had been shrewdly strengthened by their secretary-manager, Mike Turner, who was prepared to engage players of talent no matter where they came from; the Leicestershire batting averages were headed by Brian Davison from Rhodesia, and also in the team were players like Illingworth, Balderstone and Birkenshaw, all from Yorkshire, McVicker from Lincolnshire via Warwickshire, Ken Higgs from Lancashire, and Graham McKenzie from Western Australia.

Under Mike Brearley, a young Middlesex side deserved the Championship in 1976. Not only did they win more matches than their three nearest rivals, but they also toppled the dominant West Indian tourists. Graham Barlow, a left-hander, headed the batting averages with Brearley himself second, and four of the bowlers, Titmus, Selvey, Alan Jones and Phil Edmonds all took over 60 wickets, a big haul in the modern Championship.

In the following year, Middlesex shared the title with Kent, the first time since 1950 that there had been joint leadership. The fact that Middlesex played one more match than Kent and two more than Gloucestershire, who suffered with the weather, caused tongues to wag. Middlesex avoided the three worst days in the summer because their county fixture with Essex was re-arranged so that they could complete their Gillette Cup semi-final. Given a points scoring system whereby a team had merely to play to be certain of at least some points, this caused considerable controversy. The finale was exciting. Gloucestershire were ahead by four points as they began their final match, but Kent beat them without much difficulty. This left Middlesex needing to beat Lancashire at Blackpool to make sure of the title, with Kent virtually certain to beat Warwickshire at Edgbaston. Emburey and Edmonds, the Middlesex spinners, took 17 wickets, and their young batsman Mike Gatting scored 110 in the match which was more than Lancashire's entire first-innings total.

In 1978, Kent, joint champions in 1977, took the title almost unchallenged. They were able to do this because they had a number of fine players registered with World Series Cricket who were nevertheless eligible to play for them all through the summer. Derek Underwood enjoyed a particularly fine season. However, the presence of so many Packer players in the Kent team meant that this White Horse Championship win was less rapturously received than others had been.

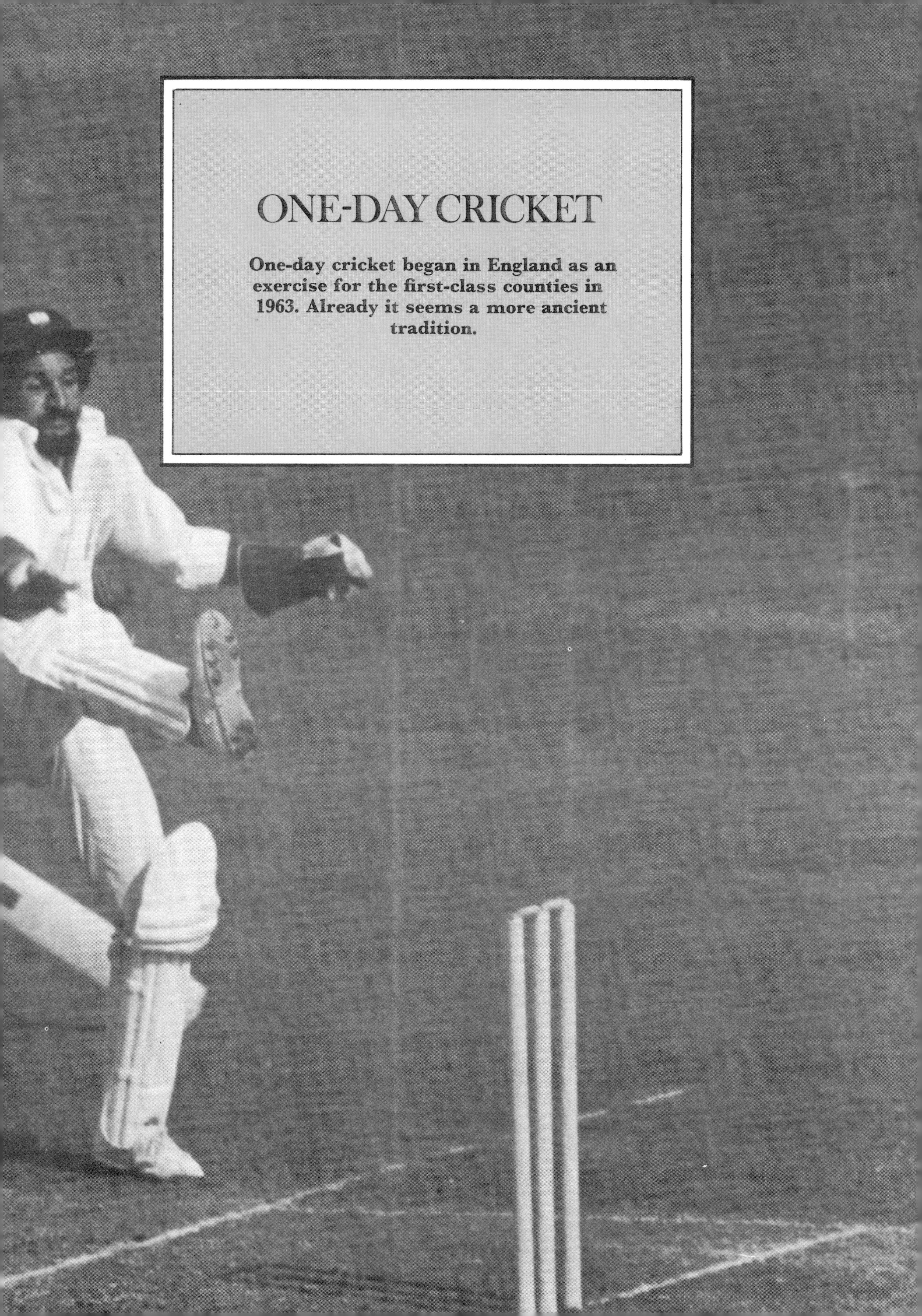

ONE-DAY CRICKET

One-day cricket began in England as an exercise for the first-class counties in 1963. Already it seems a more ancient tradition.

Preceding page: the Prudential World Cup, first held in 1975 was a massive success, with West Indies beating Australia in the final

The effect was comparable to that of a blood transfusion on an ailing patient, for make no mistake, cricket was dying as a national pastime in the 1960s. The decline had begun in the previous decade, following the first rush of enthusiasm for cricket after the end of the Second World War. By the late 1950s gates were declining and the appeal of the County Championship, the bulwark of first-class cricket in England, had dissipated, certainly as far as the general public were concerned, if not in the players' eyes.

It was a bad time for the game, and somehow this was reflected in a lack of zest in contemporary Test matches. Far too many Tests against Australia in the 1960s were ending in draws. Furthermore, there was a lack of new talent entering the game, which had never been the case before, and what few players of class there were (May and Dexter, for instance) seemed to be deserting cricket just as soon as they became household names.

Colin Cowdrey was one of the few members of his generation who stayed constant through good and bad times and survived to usher in a new, different and better era. For this was what was implied by the first one-day knock-out cup competition held in 1963. Already a trial one-day competition involving the four Midland counties—Leicestershire, Derbyshire, Nottinghamshire and Northamptonshire—had taken place in May 1962. It was an unqualified success, and plans for a full scale tournament in the following year went ahead. The main problem was the question of weather. What would happen should rain affect play, thus delaying the outcome and causing disproportionate expense to those counties whose matches were interrupted or extended by bad weather? Originally, the sponsorship of Gillette, which in its first year totalled £6,500, was designed in order to provide some insurance for the counties against the increased expenditure that might be necessary in the event of rain. However, the enormous popularity of the competition in its first year and the sell-out for the final at Lord's on the first Saturday in September ensured that the competition would be a financial success. Indeed, so enthusiastic was the crowd at that first Gillette Cup final that the atmosphere was more electric even than expected at a Test match against Australia. Subsequently, therefore, sponsorship was gradually increased. Now it is normal for sponsors to come forward with sums well in excess of £100,000, although inflation has rendered figures such as this rather meaningless. The purpose of sponsorship, whether it be in England or any other country of the world, is now far removed from the concept of insurance against wet weather, the original notion of the Gillette Company, its Managing Director, Mr. Henry Garnett, and its PR expert, Gordon Ross, an experienced journalist and promoter. Often, when competitions become successful enough to be regarded as institutions, the founding fathers are forgotten as the story unfolds, for not every innovator can be as memorable as Christopher Columbus. Not so these two; they not only helped to launch the Gillette Cup, as it quickly became known, but also gave cricket sponsorship its style of non-interference. This was a precious gift and one which could easily have been abused. Perhaps the fact that cricket had more than its share of scandals as long ago as the 1820s, when players were accused, and justly accused, of throwing matches when large sums of money were involved, has enabled the game to remain free of such charges in this modern era. In the 1960s charges were made, and made to stick, against certain soccer players of selling games for money. Even though the funds flowing into cricket have increased to the point where the game earns over £1,000,000 from sponsorship, there have been no such suggestions made against cricketers, nor have there been many complaints by members of the cricketing public about the use of advertising boards or promotional materials by the companies involved. Certainly there have been rows about the positioning of such boards and the use of advertising by the media, but these arguments have been restricted to the various professionals involved and have seldom come to the notice of those who watch the games with evident enjoyment and in steadily increasing numbers. Even a sustained campaign against tobacco sponsorship by the anti-smoking lobby has had little effect. Cricket has long enjoyed the best of relations with the tobacco companies, who have been loyal supporters of the game when it has needed funds most desperately. Indeed, two of the four domestic competitions in England are sponsored by tobacco companies, the John Player League covering the Sunday afternoon games, and Benson & Hedges taking sponsorship of the first of the full-scale knock-out competitions to be played in the season. The first tobacco company to become involved with cricket was Rothmans, who fielded a team called the Rothmans Cavaliers, playing mostly for the benefit of players at the end of their careers. Such were the relationships established at that time that Sunday cricket became a feature of the first-class scene with relative ease.

As far as the merit of the cricket played is concerned, the players themselves are in no doubt that the 60-over game is best for a one-day competition. The 40-over variety of the Sunday League, with its restrictions and its various compulsions on bowlers and batsmen, tends to debase the game to a certain

Below: Victorious West Indian Captain, Clive Lloyd, who made a flashing 101 in the final, holding the Prudential Trophy

extent, and yet there is no doubt that the excitement, the hilarity even, of these matches has re-established cricket's previously fast-diminishing popularity. Many are the children who have been brought up on 20-over evening cricket up and down the country, and their appreciation of cup cricket has been thankfully extended to the first-class game at a time when the greatest possible attendance has been needed, not only from the financial point of view, but also because of the opportunity afforded of influencing the younger generation.

At first there was much scepticism as to the value of the new competitions, but one individual who was intrigued by the format and did his utmost to understand it was Ted Dexter. He subsequently led Sussex, who had hitherto won nothing, to success in the first two Gillette Cups. Even now Sussex remains a team which performs better in one-day cricket than in the more traditional form of the game.

There have been some memorable individual performances in one-day cricket. Outstanding in my memory is the innings played by Boycott when Yorkshire won the Gillette Cup in its third year. His 146 against Surrey that day remains among the most brilliant innings I have ever seen. It was played on a pitch which neither the captains nor the umpires thought was fit for play, which in itself is a reminder of how cup cricket and large attendences have forced players to get on with the game when voices of caution have said that it would be better to remain in the pavilion. It was only on the insistence of the then MCC secretary, Billy Griffith, that the above-mentioned match was started with only an hour's delay.

The success of sponsorship for those companies prepared to devote a part of their advertising budget to this end has been so self-evident that now sponsors have come forward for the County Championship, for Test matches, and for one-day internationals. Cricket in England now has two insurance companies, the Cornhill and the Prudential, a food and drink company, Schweppes, two tobacco companies, Imperial and Gallagher, and a manufacturer of what are best described as sundries, Gillette, as its valued sponsors. Of course it has to be part of the policy of the game's administration to ensure that there is always sufficient potential goodwill from sponsors waiting in the wings in the event of any of those currently involved deciding to drop out. The idea that sponsorship is fixed for all time is a most dangerous one to entertain in the case of an institution like cricket, or indeed any other sport.

Not surprisingly, as each new development has been announced there has been anxiety lest the intrusion of yet more commercial interests should start to affect the game adversely. In fact, only when the media itself has taken a hand in sponsorship has the game been threatened, as witnessed by the intervention of Kerry Packer's Channel Nine in Australia. This of course was a development to be expected, but once a television station, with all its particular requirements, enters the sponsorship area, then it is clear that the needs of the game are likely to be sacrificed for what seems to be a good gimmick for television. An example has been the installation

Left: Max Walker of Victoria and Australia. Walker, one of a group of exciting Australian bowlers to emerge in the late seventies

of microphones around players and wickets which the BBC attempted to follow, then wisely abandoned. If the game is to hold any enjoyment for the players, as it must, and if they are to communicate that enjoyment to the crowds, then the players must have some element of privacy.

The example set by sponsored cricket in England has now been followed in other countries where inevitably difficulties have appeared. These are usually due to geographical factors, and the difficulty of arranging one-day matches when huge distances have to be travelled—often they tend to be tacked on to longer matches. Differences of national temperament have also dictated that certain countries should accept the one-day version of the game with greater enthusiasm than others. For example, the West Indians have always relished it, whereas it has been considered rather inferior sport in Australia until recently. The Australians shared their lack of enthusiasm with Yorkshire, but eventually cricket's hardest men have come to appreciate that the one-day game, if sufficiently extended, can be as demanding as three- or five-day matches. Now the Gillette Cup final in Australia is an established tradition. If at some time in the future sponsorship is needed in India or Pakistan it will surely be as successful there. The West Indians are the poorest of all the cricketing fraternities, and they would be lost without their Shell Shield competition between the island teams, and their Benson & Hedges Cup for the knock-out matches.

The most significant point of all is that the one-day format has provided the opportunity for the creation of a World Cup which alone can bring together all the cricketing countries of the world, now numbered at twenty-four. Within the one-day format teams can compete without the total loss of dignity that must have been a danger in the old days when the odds would be stacked heavily in favour of one team or another. The first World Cup in 1975 was a resounding success, with the two outstanding teams, Australia and West Indies, contesting the final and the West Indies winning for the second time against Australia in that series with a superb exhibition of cricket skills. The second World Cup, in May and June 1979, was an even bigger and better organized affair. Fifteen Associate Member countries Argentina, Bangladesh, Bermuda, Canada, Denmark, East Africa, Fiji, Gibraltar, Holland, Israel, Malaysia, Papua New Guinea, Singapore, Sri Lanka and the U.S.A. took part in the preliminary rounds to decide which two should join the six full members—Australia, England, India, New Zealand, Pakistan and the West Indies.

THE INTERNATIONAL GAME

In this section, which traces the ebb and flow of cricketing success in the countries of the International Cricket Conference, the first and last chapters, dealing respectively with Associate Members and the West Indies, are the longest.

Preceding page: This late Victorian print shows a game in Corfu

No apology is offered for this. As holders, at the time of writing, of the first World Cup the West Indies are demonstrably the best players. Their story, which follows the development of the game from a colonial pastime to the point where it has become, like calypso music, an expression of independence and special flair, is fascinating in itself.

What makes it more so is the uncertainty of the future of West Indian cricket. At present, due to the sudden influx of money, it seems to have degenerated irretrievably into a spectacle which is unhealthy in its rejection of many of the values for which cricket is alleged to stand.

The future of cricket may well lie in the hands of the Associate Members, who continue to represent internationally the recreational element in cricket. It is unlikely that the game in these countries will achieve a professional structure as long as the Test countries seek to keep their best players gainfully employed.

Cricket in the United States and other parts of the world.

Stool-ball was established in New England soon after the safe arrival of the Mayflower. In the next century it was possible for a man to play cricket on both sides of the Atlantic Ocean, and evidence exists that this happened. The game was played not only in Virginia but also in New Amsterdam, later to become New York. By the middle of the eighteenth century cricket was being played all the way from Boston down to the recently founded Carolinas and Georgia, where evidence of it dates from 1737. Four years later, when the settlement of Savannah was only eight years old, the game was played there on Christmas Day.

When the laws of cricket were re-written in 1744 the older game continued in America, but a steady influx of immigrants from England ensured that there was no permanent divergence in the way in which the game was played. However, there is evidence that in the nineteenth century some Americans were still playing with the old-fashioned low wicket.

The game was similarly established in Ontario, Canada, and in 1840, when Fred Lillywhite became the first round-arm bowler to take 100 wickets in England, the first international match was played between the Toronto Cricket Club and St George's Cricket Club in New York. A few years later this encounter developed into a series of matches between representative teams of Canada and the United States, a series which only lasted for two years because in 1846 the teams fell out when the Canadians, while batting, tried to charge down the fielders who attempted to make a catch. This was clearly a reversion to the old-fashioned law of obstruction which permitted such deliberate collisions.

The 1859 tour by George Parr's team gave rise to the first book on the game of cricket by Fred Lillywhite, who acted as scorer; this has become a rare collector's piece. The tour took place in the North Eastern States in October and November, and finished in a snow-storm! In the 1860s clubs were established in American universities such as Harvard and Princeton, and also on the West Coast, especially British Columbia. A second English tour, led by Edgar Willsher, was arranged in 1868, and although this team beat a United States side with some ease it was held to a draw by a Canadian team. W. G. Grace himself was on the third tour to North America in 1872. In 1874 the Halifax Cup was established during a tournament between the British Army and Philadelphia and this subsequently became an annual competition in the Philadelphia area between 1880 and 1926. By this time there were a dozen teams in the United States as good as any English side.

In 1878 the first United States Cricket Association was formed, and also in that year an Australian team visited America for the first time. The Association still exists although it was reformed in 1961. In 1880 a Canadian team came to the United Kingdom, but the tour was not a success and had to be abandoned halfway through the planned itinerary. It was now normal for teams to stop off in the United States on their way to Australia, and the Americans were proving themselves quite capable of holding their own in eleven-a-side matches, as they showed when they defeated the Gentlemen of Ireland.

In the 1880s individual American cricketers were taking over 100 wickets and scoring 1,000 runs in a season, and similar feats were being achieved in Canada. It was in this period that the Americans adopted a six-ball over and developed their own leg-before-wicket law, giving due emphasis to the real purpose of the law, namely to prevent batsmen indulging in deliberate obstruction. However, within the decade they had reverted to standard English law in order to avoid dissimilarity of practice between the two countries. The Americans also adopted the practice of captains being able to declare at any time during a match, well before this became common practice in England.

In 1891 Lord Hawke took the ninth English team to visit the United States. By now there were exchanges between America, Canada and the island

THE FIRST OVERSEAS TOUR

At the end of the 1859 season, twelve professional cricketers undertook the first-ever overseas cricket tour to Canada and the United States. It was organized in North America by the Montreal Cricket Club, another MCC, and in England by W. P. Pickering, Edmund Wilder, President of the Cricketers' Fund, Fred Lillywhite, the scorer and first touring cricket correspondent, and by two players, George Parr and John Wisden, leaders of the two touring elevens of the day. It had taken three years to organize, but with a guarantee of £50 a head to sustain them the twelve finally set off on 7 September. Of the twelve, Parr, Grundy and Jackson were from Nottinghamshire, Wisden and John Lillywhite came from Sussex, and of the remaining seven, three were Cambridgeshire men (Hayward, Carpenter and 'Ducky' Diver) and the last four were from Surrey—H. H. Stephenson, Julius Caesar, Lockyer and Caffyn. The passage took fifteen days and the party arrived off the Heights of Abraham close to Montreal almost exactly a hundred years after General Wolfe, who first captured the place for the British monarchy. George Parr's lobs were too much for the Canadians in the first match and the tourists took 16 for 25 in the first game in the United States. Both matches were well attended, 25,000 people turning up for the game in New York. The team also played in Philadelphia on 10 October with the aid of two wagon-loads of sawdust. Philadelphia fielded twenty-two and were coached by an old Kent player, Halward. After the first scheduled match at Hamilton an extra match was arranged at Rochester, but this was ended by a heavy fall of snow. The team won all their matches and were back in Liverpool on 11 November, richer by £90 a head once all the expenses had been deducted.

of Bermuda, and these have lasted until the present day. Towards the end of the 1890s an institution such as Harvard College was strong enough to tour England, competing against public schools. This practice continued until 1925.

Tour by English cricketers were by now an annual affair. 'Plum' Warner took a team in 1897 and 1898, and in 1899 Ranji skippered a team which beat Philadelphia in both the matches they played. One of Ranji's opponents was the legendary Bart King. He was a man of lesser means than many of the rich Americans playing in the Philadelphia area, and although these people disliked the idea of professionalism entering their game, King was discretely subsidized. In 1905 he made 315 in a Beaumont *v* Germantown match, and his score of 344 not out the following year remains a record. In 1908 King, while on tour in England, took 87 wickets for an average cost of 11 runs, a figure not bettered for fifty years in English first-class cricket. Pictures of King show what a fine high action he had. Not surprisingly, he was a master of movement in the air. In the following year he took all ten wickets for 33 against the Gentlemen of Ireland, every one of them clean-bowled.

In 1921 the last tour by a Philadelphia team, the Philadelphia Pilgrims, came to the United Kingdom, and by 1928 the Philadelphians had played their last game, a drawn match with Bermuda. With 375 matches recorded in the area in the year before the First World War, how was it that cricket in and around Philadelphia declined so drastically within such a short period? The answer is to be found in two factors: firstly, the preference of American club members for the game of tennis, which was easier to stage, and secondly, the exclusive attitude of Philadelphian clubs to each other and to the community at large. These clubs were essentially for the rich; there was no attempt to encourage cricket at all levels of society. And unfortunately the game had long ceased to be a practical proposition in other cities, where property development was widespread enough to account for any large open space near a city centre. Also, despite all the exchange visits that took place between England and the United States, no significant assistance in the form of coaching or organization were made available to the United States Cricket Association by MCC or anyone else in England, even though by the end of this period England were travelling under the colours of the MCC, as they were to Australia. Whatever the reasons, the sad fact remains that when Arthur Mailey took his Australian team on that long tour of the United States and Canada, during which Don Bradman played so many innings and scored such a stack of runs, they did not even visit Philadelphia. Nowadays the influx of West Indians ensures some enthusiasm for cricket in the United States, although at the game promoted by Tony Grieg in the Yankee Stadium in New York in September 1978 not enough spectator interest was aroused to suggest that it could be revived on any large scale.

Because cricket was more widely established in Canada, and especially in the schools, it continued at a relatively steady level throughout this period, and MCC teams continued to visit throughout the 1930s and again from the 1950s up to the present day. There is now a Canadian Shield competition between the provinces, organized on an annual basis. In 1954 the Canadians, under the captaincy of H. B. Robinson, a noted off-spin bowler who went up to Oxford in the late 1940s, completed their only first-class tour in England during which they met and lost to Pakistan at Lord's in a three-day match. Had the result been different the Canadians might well have established first-class status on a permanent basis. Nevertheless, interest in cricket remains steady, particularly in the English-speaking areas of Toronto and British Columbia. The United States, Canada and Bermuda remain Associate Members of the International Cricket Conference.

The other country in the American continent where the game has long been established is the Argentine. This interest dates from 1806 when a British expedition to the River Plate was imprisoned. Those incarcerated began to play cricket, as British prisoners have done ever since, arousing the curiosity of their captors. In the nineteenth century the development of the meat industry and the railways, with a resulting influx of Britons and large expatriate colonies, ensured the game's survival. The Buenos Aires Club was founded in 1831 and similar clubs were established in Mexico City and Rio de Janeiro. By the time of the First World War an Argentinian Cricketers' Association had been established. In 1924 Argentina came to the United Kingdom for the first time and two years later Plum Warner took an MCC team there. By 1932 Clem Gibson, a Cambridge blue, had brought a South American team to the United Kingdom which was recognized as first-class. Since the Second World War teams have gone from England to Argentina under the captaincy of England cricketers Hubert Doggart and Alan Smith and it is now a regular feature of the MCC touring programme, although South American cricketers can no longer lay serious claim to first-class status.

East and West Africa are both members of the International Cricket Conference. The first recorded mention of cricket in the Gold Coast, now Ghana, is in 1888. Two years later it was being played in Zanzibar, on the other side of the continent. The first important cricket match in Kenya was played in 1899, and a club formed at Entebbe, in Uganda, in 1901. Three years later the first inter-colonial match in West Africa took place between Lagos and the Gold Coast. In 1914 a Kenyan team visited Uganda. When the former German East Africa was taken by British forces in 1916, cricket was also played in Tanganyika.

The game also has a long history in Egypt, although it was played only by expatriates. The tradition of annual matches at the Gezira Club with teams visiting Cairo from England was maintained even between the 1914-18 and the 1939-45 wars. Many outstanding cricketers, Australian, Indian and English, played in these matches during the Second World War for the entertainment of the troops. In one of the services matches Dudley Nourse hit nine sixes in nine balls. Cricket in Egypt ceased at the time of the Suez invasion!

By 1929 teams were coming to England from East Africa as the three touring teams, the Kenyan Kongonis, the Tanganyika Twigas and the Uganda Kobs were established. The first inter-territory match in East Africa took place in 1951 between Kenya and Tanganyika; Kenya played Uganda the following year. In the 1950s teams from Pakistan and India played in East Africa; the Kenyan Asians visited South Africa and also received in Nairobi a non-white South African team which was good enough to beat the combined East African side. In the early 1960s England captains F. R. Brown and M. J. K. Smith led MCC tours to East Africa, and in 1966 Bert Oldfield, the Australian wicketkeeper, took a team of Australian schoolboys. East Africa now included Zambia as part of the African Conference. The first MCC tour of West Africa visited the four countries, Gambia, Sierra Leone, Ghana and Nigeria, in the 1975-76 Christmas holiday period.

Britons have often played cricket in the strangest circumstances. There is an engraving at Lord's of sailors playing on the ice of the Arctic Circle; matches have taken place on the Goodwin Sands at low tide; and the first mention of cricket played abroad, which dates as far back as 1676, comes from Aleppo, referred to as a merchant town in *Macbeth*. Horace Walpole watched the game being played at Neuilly, now a most fashionable suburb of Paris, in the second half of the eighteenth century. It has been played just as long in the Netherlands. The Dutch have on record mention of an Amsterdam merchant, with the very English name of Hope, playing cricket in Rome in 1793. Towards the end of that century instruction books were printed in both the German and Danish languages.

Although teams nowadays go from England to play in Germany and France, the three principal

European countries where cricket has survived and grown as a national sport are Denmark, Holland and Gibraltar, all of them Associate Members of the International Cricket Conference. The first clubs in these countries were formed in the 1850s and 60s, and the two oldest surviving clubs, Deventer in Eastern Holland and in Copenhagen, recently celebrated their centenaries. So well established was the game in Holland that the Dutch Cricket Association was formed in 1883; it is the oldest of all national cricketing organizations and in 1958 was awarded the title of 'royal' by Queen Juliana. Both Danes and Dutchmen have regularly played at Lord's, and a procession of touring sides have visited Holland. On one celebrated occasion the Dutch beat the Australians in a one-day match. The game, organized on a league basis and played on matting wickets, continues to flourish in both countries.

There are other parts of Europe where cricket is played not only by expatriate Britons. The game took root in Corfu in the days before Greece became independent of Turkish rule in the early part of the nineteenth century. Tours from England take place regularly, and many leading players have taken part in the matches, which are held in the municipal car park on the island. In Portugal the first recorded game was played by sailors in Lisbon in 1736, but by 1861 a regular fixture had been established between Oporto and Lisbon. Wine-trade cricket occasions have become famous. The Portuguese also exported the game to what is now Mozambique.

In Asia are to be found a number of Associate Members of the ICC. Bangladesh, the last member to be admitted, is the one country with an international cricket stadium, at Dacca. In the first few years of independence from Pakistan the Bengalis were not much encouraged by their leaders to play cricket, but in recent years leagues have been rapidly formed and the national team is now fully organized—so much so that over the Christmas holiday period of 1976-77 an MCC team under the captaincy of Ted Clark, formerly of Middlesex, visited the country, a tour repeated two years later. Fewer Bengalis have shone at cricket than players from other parts of the subcontinent but enthusiasm for the game is huge, as can be deduced by the regular crowds of 40,000 people who watch in the stadium at Dacca.

Sri Lanka is probably the strongest of the Asian Associate Members, and certainly the country where cricket has been longest established. The Colombo Cricket Club was founded in 1832 and the Ceylon Cricket Assoiation dates from 1922. When Associate Membership status was initiated in 1965, Ceylon, together with Fiji and the United States, was the first country to benefit. The first MCC tour of Ceylon took place in 1926-27. Ceylon then visited India in 1932. Since then matches with English teams *en route* to Australia, Australian teams *en route* to England, or between the three countries of the Indian subcontinent, have been regular and increasing. A number of Singhalese (or Srilankans) have played cricket in this country, often as members of Oxford or Cambridge teams. The most famous of them was Gamini Goonesena, who captained Cambridge and subsequently played for Nottinghamshire where he was rated one of the best leg-spin bowlers in the world at that time. Recently there has been some suggestion that Sri Lanka should become a full member of the International Cricket Conference, but it is hard to believe that a country without a first-class domestic competition could become a fully fledged Test country.

Cricket was played in Singapore as long ago as 1837. The island ground, close by the magnificent harbour, is one of the most beautiful in the entire world, and certainly the nearest to a major city centre. 'Test' matches between Singapore and Malaysia began almost one hundred years ago, and there has been a long tradition of matches between cricketers from that part of South-east Asia and Hong Kong and Shanghai. Sir Julien Cahn took an English team there in 1936-37, and the MCC first visited this part of the world officially on the way to New Zealand in 1960-61. Since then, because it is an attractive area and a pleasant one in which to play cricket, Singapore and Malaysia have been host to teams from Australia, Ceylon, India, New Zealand and Pakistan.

Like Singapore and Malaysia, Hong Kong has attracted cricketers from all parts of the world. From 1840 right up until the 1970s, the Hong Kong Cricket Club's ground was in the middle of the city centre which, considering the scarcity of space, is a remarkable testimony to the game's popularity and significance for the inhabitants.

Cricket was established in Fiji even before Britain became involved in the government of the islands. In the 1890s a team comprising seven Britons and six Fijian chiefs toured New Zealand and won several of their matches. The aim of Fijian cricketers is to hit the ball as hard as they can and to bowl as fast as possible, which gives their game a delightfully abandoned air!

Finally it should be noted that a game approximating cricket, but spelt krikit, is occasionally played in Jugoslavia, exported to that country, perhaps, by an English gentleman, as Lawrence Durrell did in Corfu.

HONOLULU

THE TEST ARENA

The seven major cricketing nations of the world compete in Test matches in gentle rotation all the year round

Clockwise from upper left: the New Zealand side of 1973, Andy Roberts of West Indies bowls a bouncer to Graham Yallop of Australia, England's Chris Old, Gavaskar of India, flanked by Pakistani fielders, Bari, Sarfraz and Miandad, and Arthur Nourse of South Africa.

AUSTRALIA

Cricket began in Australia in the 1800s while Europe was wrestling with the consequences of the French Revolution. The desire for adventure, conquest and wealth (which we now call imperialism) was beginning to find rampant expression; the Australian adventure had only just begun.

The early games of cricket were played in churchyards, just as they had been in England, or on sheep or cattle tracks. In 1826 the first clubs were formed in Sydney—the Military and the Australian. Gradually the game gravitated to a new cow-paddock in Sydney's outskirts, where the first inter-colonial match was to be played in 1857.

The Melbourne Cricket Club, Australia's MCC, began playing in 1838, and like Lord's its ground had to be moved, first from an allotment in William Street to a site on what is now part of the Spencer Street railway station, then to a wheat-field between the river Yarra and Emerald Hill, and finally to the Richmond Paddock on which the first ever match between Victoria and New South Wales was played in the 1856-57 season. Now the world's largest cricket stadium stands there.

The first game played in Adelaide was staged by a local publican about the same time that William Clarke was learning how to manage both the pub and the cricket ground at Trent Bridge. As was usual elsewhere, the South Australian pitches were full of holes and in the first match against New South Wales in 1862 the twenty-two Queensland batsmen collected no fewer than eighteen ducks. The score-book shows that one of the three New South Wales bowlers took 17 wickets for 26 runs in the match, and that Queensland's top scorer in the first innings won promotion in the batting order for the seond innings, but only from number twenty to number nineteen.

The first tour from England had come and gone before club cricket was organized on a proper footing in the chief Australian cities. This occurred in the 1870s, the decade of the early English County Championships. By this time the Australian and Albert clubs of Sydney, as well as the Melbourne Cricket Club, were helping to bring the game into new districts as these were opened up by pioneering farmers. The Albert Club produced David Gregory, Australia's first captain, the country's first century-maker, Charles Bannerman, and the most famous of all Australian fast bowlers, F. R. Spofforth, 'the Demon'—a fair trio. This club's progress was given an enormous boost by the coaching of Charles Lawrence, who had been left behind when the first English touring team sailed away for the old country, thus setting a trend for county professionals to spend agreeable winters involved in training young cricketers in the southern hemisphere.

This first touring team left Liverpool on 15 October 1861 and arrived in Melbourne on Christmas Eve after a nine-week voyage. The tour was sponsored by Messrs Spiers and Pond, a Melbourne catering firm. As soon as they arrived, the team were taken on a coach drawn by six greys to their first Australian meal in the Café de Paris in Bourke Street, Melbourne. Many players in England had turned up their noses at this tour, despite a fee of £150, but certain Surrey players persuaded others to take part under the captaincy of H. H. Stephenson, who had been on that first-ever tour to North America in 1859. Within eight days they were in action in Richmond paddock before a crowd of no fewer than 15,000. It was the first day of 1862.

Each player wore a different sash and hat-ribbon to corresponding to a colour on the score-card. The Englishmen made 305 and won by an innings and 96 runs. Of their twelve matches, they won six, drew four and lost twice—to a side from Castlemain, and in Sydney to the side selected from Victoria and New South Wales. Spiers and Pond, be it noted, cleared £11,000 for their brave new venture. Successful, private, commercially sponsored cricket tours evidently have a long history in Australian cricket.

George Parr took the second team in 1863-64, among them E. M. Grace, W. G.'s elder brother. Again the team was universally successful against adverse odds, although a New South Wales side came to within a single wicket of victory. William Caffyn of Surrey stayed behind this time, and worked both as a cricket coach and as a barber in the two leading Australian cities, Melbourne and Sydney.

Between the first and second tours from England over-arm bowling was introduced in Australia. The subsequent success of Australian cricketers against England stemmed largely from their ability to make the best use of the new method of bowling. Another cause of improvement was a spectacular change in the nature of Australian wickets because of the concentration of grounds in the large cities, especially Melbourne and Sydney.

In the 1870s the game spread. The South Australian Cricket Association was formed, based on the Adelaide Oval, and apart from one season this has subsequently been the only ground used for first-class cricket in the city. In Queensland an

Left: William Lloyd Murdoch (right) poses with W. G. Grace. Right: Australia's best all-rounder before World War One, Montague Alfred Noble

Association was founded in 1876. It was in this season that the fourth English team, captained by Lillywhite, made the long trip out and played the first of two Test matches in Melbourne. Australia won the first and lost the second.

The first Test century was scored by Charles Bannerman, who made 165 for Australia. In 1878 the first select Australian team came to England under David Gregory, though no Test matches were played; this team also visited New Zealand, Canada and the United States. Spofforth took a hat-trick at Lord's against the MCC who were beaten by the Australians in a single day by nine wickets. In the winter of 1878-79 Spofforth took another hat-trick, the first in a Test match, in the England first innings, during the only match played at Melbourne when Lord Harris was captain of the side. Once again Australia won the important match.

Money had become an important factor in the organization of these tours. As an example of what was possible, W.G. (a medical student at the time) demanded, and actually received, the sum of £1,500 for the 1883-84 tour, not including his expenses—the value of this fee in today's terms would be almost incalculable. But apart from money there were other disruptive factors on the touring scene in the 1870s. Gregory and his Australian team complained about the umpires in England, and also protested vigorously when W.G. insisted that Midwinter (who had been born in, and was under contract to, Gloucestershire) should play for his county rather than for the Australians at Lord's. The worst scene of all took place when Gregory had a dispute with Lord Harris over the English side's umpire and refused to play, whereupon a mob invaded the pitch and threatened the English players who had to be protected by mounted police. As a result of all this the Australians came to England in 1880 without a settled fixture-list. Luckily, Murdoch, their captain, who subsequently played for Sussex, managed to patch up the quarrel with Lord Harris.

During this tour the first Test match ever was played in England. Australia were beaten. W.G., opening the batting with his brother E. M. Grace, made 152. His score was topped by one run when Murdoch batted throughout his team's short innings to score 153 not out. Spofforth did not play in this match but his deeds elsewhere at this time were

Left: Jack Blackham in characteristic pose—close to the stumps. Right: Warren Bardsley, one of Australia's greatest left-handers

astonishing. He took all 20 wickets for 48 runs, every single batsman bowled, in a match at Bendigo, the town in which the first double century had been scored in Australia by W. E. Midwinter twelve seasons before.

In the 1881-82 season, Midwinter played for England as a member of Alfred Shaw's team which played four Tests against Australia. Two of these were lost and two drawn. This was a prelude to the third Australian tour of England, again under Murdoch, when victory was once again Australia's. They beat England by 7 runs at The Oval in the match which gave rise to the obituary notice in *The Sporting Times* and the beginning of the tradition of the Ashes. Spofforth took 14 wickets for 90 runs in this match. In the following season, Ivo Bligh's team drew all three representative matches.

In 1884 the Australians came to England again under Murdoch, stopping off in Ceylon on the way. This time they did lose a match, drawing the other two of three Tests. Spofforth, however, had lost none of his power, and on this tour took no fewer than 205 first class wickets at an average of 12.50.

During the following winter the first five-Test series was played in Australia. England won three of the rubber matches to two under the captaincy of Arthur Shrewsbury, all matches being played to a finish. This was the first series in which a Test match was played at Adelaide. The Australians were in some disarray this year, having fielded no fewer than four captains for the series, each State virtually choosing its own side.

In 1886-87 Arthur Shrewsbury's team again won both Test matches, and encouraged by this trend two English teams visited Australia in the next season: Shrewsbury's, captained by Charles Aubrey Smith, and a team led by G. F. Vernon. The two teams actually joined forces under W. W. Read of Surrey to play one Test; Australia were beaten, bowled out for 42 and 82, but the two-tour winter in Australia meant that neither of the teams made money. The experiment was never repeated.

By the end of the 1880s the practice of regular Test matches had been established as a popular summer attraction. The Australians came again in 1888 and 1890, and despite their splendid bowling, with Taylor taking 283 wickets in first-class matches in the 1888 tour, a strong England team nonetheless won more of the Test matches, two to one.

During the 1890s Australian teams not only came regularly to England but also often went on to play in Philadelphia on the way back to Australia. Here they were handsomely beaten by an innings in both 1893 and 1896. In 1894-95, England under A. E. Stoddart—'my dear victorious Stod' as W.G. called him; one of few men to play both cricket and rugby for England—won three and lost two Test matches.

The following year the Australians toured England for the first time on an official basis. The MCC (Marylebone as opposed to Melbourne Cricket Club) made all the tour arrangements and the Australian Cricket Council selected a side in advance; previously it had been done on an *ad hoc* basis. Not that the result was any better from Australia's viewpoint; once again England won the series by two to one. However, when Stoddart took the next tourists to Australia in 1897-98 he was thoroughly beaten in the series by four to one, even though he had such luminaries as Ranjitsinhji and Archie MacLaren in his side. In 1899 the Australians won the only finished match in the first rubber of five Tests played in England. They won again in the 1901-02 series, when Archie MacLaren's team was beaten in Australia four to one. In 1902 the Australians, at this time under Darling's captaincy, won the series by two to one. This was the summer in which Victor Trumper made 2,570 runs in an English season, and a wet one at that. On the way home Darling's team played in South Africa, the first Australians to do so. They were a busy team for they also entertained another English side during their season, this time under Plum Warner. However, no Tests were played in that year, which was a dress rehearsal for the following winter when the first MCC team went to Australia under Plum Warner's captaincy. This was the occasion on which the Ashes, which had started as a joke and continued as a private contest between the English and Australian sides of 1882, were elevated by Plum Warner, a scholarly cricketer with a deep understanding of the game's history and its relationship with the public, into a trophy for regular competition between England and Australia. The fictions of history are notorious, and this one was particularly helpful in promoting cricket matches between the two countries. Eventually, however, the tradition of the Ashes and their Urn (which incidentally never leaves its cupboard at Lord's) was to have unfortunate consequences—namely, a series of boring Tests. Once the issue of the Ashes has been settled a number of captains have been prepared to settle for stalemate, even after victory in the opening Test, to the detriment of the series as an entertainment.

Plum Warner's strong team was successful in the rubber by three matches to two. In 1905, the Australians, still captained by Darling, were beaten in England, but they won again most convincingly under Monty Noble, one of the great Australian all-rounders, in their 1907-08 season. Their 1909 team, under Noble, found the England selectors in less than startling form, which helped them to win by two to one with two matches drawn, in the last of which Warren Bardsley, a supreme left-hander, became the first batsman to score two centuries in a Test match.

In the 1910-11 season Australia entertained the South Africans for the first time and won the series comfortably by four matches to one. In the following winter the third MCC team, originally captained by Plum Warner and later by J.W.H.T. (Johnny Won't Hit Today) Douglas when Warner fell ill, won four out of their five Tests. This was a prelude to the triangular series of 1912, the year in which the Australians were much weakened because of the first major dispute between the Board and their players over the question of fees. King George V became the first monarch to view a Test match when Australia were playing at Lord's.

All cricket was suspended during the 1914-18 War, but the Australian Imperial Forces embarked on a long tour of England in 1919 and visited South Africa on the way home. Such was the enthusiasm for the restoration of cricket that the MCC had to send a makeshift team to Australia in 1920-21 under Johnny Douglas; they lost all five Tests.

Australia were exceptionally strong under the powerful figure of Warwick Armstrong, who was able to field the first pair of fast bowlers in McDonald and Gregory, the best since the days of Spofforth. In England under Armstrong, the Australians won all three of the matches finished in the five-Test series. Charlie McCartney, known affectionately by Australian crowds as 'the Governor-General', was the outstanding batsman. Against Nottinghamshire he made no fewer than 345 runs in a single day.

The following winter the Australians went to South Africa. There was then a break until 1924-25, when Arthur Gilligan took the MCC to Australia, yet again to be soundly beaten, for his team lost the rubber comprehensively by four Tests to one. The leg-spin bowling of Arthur Mailey, and in the fifth test of Clarrie Grimmett, was the key factor. In this series the first wireless commentary on Test matches took place.

In 1926 a four-year cycle was established for the England-Australia series. Under Collins, the Australians drew four of their Test matches in England but lost the fifth and with it the series. In the following winter season Victoria made 1,107 runs against New South Wales at Melbourne, New South Wales succumbing by an innings and 656 runs, a result of historic proportions.

In 1928-29 the MCC visited Australia under Percy Chapman. This time, for once, the Australians were relatively weak, and they went down by four Tests to one. This was the first season in which a Test match was played at Brisbane and was notable for the first appearance in a Test match of the young Don Bradman, the batsman who was to dominate cricket between the two countries for twenty years. When he came to England for the first time in 1930 under Bill Woodfall as captain, Bradman scored 1,000 runs by the end of May, the first Australian to do so. He also

Below: Jack Fingleton
Below: The Chappell brothers, Greg and Ian
Far right: Jeff Thomson

hit 309 runs in a single day during a Test match at Leeds. In 1930-31 he amassed a pile of runs against the West Indian side, although Herman Griffith bowled him out in the last Test match for a duck. Bradman never played in the West Indies nor in South Africa, but the South Africans were the next side to feel the weight of his run-making. He scored 299 against them at Adelaide, an Australian Test record in Australia at that point. In 1932 he joined the lengthy tour of Canada and the United States organized by Arthur Mailey, and such were his exertions in a procession of one-day matches that he was never quite so hungry for runs thereafter. Certainly he was relatively exhausted in 1932-33 by the time the MCC arrived under D. R. Jardine, the hard-headed Oxonian, for what became known as the bodyline tour with Larwood, Voce and Bowes comprising the first formidable battery of English fast bowlers to engage in a Test match. Bradman was top of the Australian averages, but England nonetheless won a bruising series which left deep and lasting scars, by four matches to one.

In 1934, when he came again to England, with Woodfull still as captain, Bradman set up a second-wicket partnership of 451 with Ponsford at The Oval. Revenging their defeat by Douglas Jardine's team, the Australians won the series by two matches to one, with two matches drawn. In 1936-37 Gubby Allen took the MCC side to Australia—a famous occasion for the Australians, for having lost the first two matches they went on to win the remaining three to take the series. The following year the Australians again came to England. Bradman repeated his feat of scoring 1,000 runs before the end of May, but this was a season which was notable for the highest Test score ever, Len Hutton's 364, hit at The Oval. This was the match in which the Australians were confronted by an England total of 903 for seven, the highest ever in a Test. The English bowlers were spared having to face Bradman, who sprained an ankle and took no part as a batsman.

In 1946-47, Walter Hammond, a professional before the War and an amateur after it, led the MCC tour to Australia. His team were badly beaten by Bradman's Australians, losing the three matches in which there was a result. For the first time, England came up against the bowling combination of Miller and Lindwall, who could count on Bill Johnston, one of the most successful bowlers in Australian cricket history, to support them. The Australians came to England in 1948, having beaten the Indian side under Lala Amarnath in their 1947-48 season. This was Bradman's last tour, the twentieth by the Australians, and one of the most successful. Australia went through the tour unbeaten, won four Tests and

Right: in 1977 England won the Ashes
Australian Rodney Marsh.
seen here at Old Trafford facing Underwood

drew the fifth. In 1949 Bradman was knighted and retired from the game, to be succeeded by Lindsay Hassett, who led Australia against the 1950-51 MCC team. After a long losing sequence England eventually managed to win a Test at Melbourne, although they had already lost the series. The tide had turned, however, and when the Australians came to England in 1953 Len Hutton led the home side to victory in the only Test finished that summer, the final one at The Oval. Hutton, the first professional captain of England since Arthur Shrewsbury led the next MCC side to visit Australia in 1954-55. He was again successful and retained the Ashes by winning the series three to one, with one draw. England once again had a full complement of fast bowlers—Statham, Tyson and Loader—with a fine cricketing side in support who thoroughly deserved their victory.

After this series, in the spring of 1955, Australia went to the West Indies for the first time ever. The Australians were notoriously reluctant to tour in the half-century leading up to the 1960s—the fact that they had thus far played only one official Test in New Zealand, in the 1945-46 season, bears this out graphically enough. Ian Johnson led Australia to victory in the West Indies, but when he brought the side to England in 1956 he was beaten two to one, with two matches drawn. Australia did not recover the Ashes until they had thrashed the South Africans in 1957-58 under Ian Craig. The following season, with Richie Benaud installed as captain, they beat the England team captained by Peter May by four matches, with one drawn—this was perhaps the most astonishing result in the history of Tests between the two countries, because the English side was one of the strongest ever fielded.

In 1960-61 the West Indies visited Australia for the third time under Frank Worrell. The first game of this rubber ended in a tie, the only instance of this in the history of Test cricket. Some 90,000 people attended the second day of the fifth Test at Melbourne, which gives some measure of the popularity of the cricket played by the West Indies and Australia in this series. The following year, Richie Benaud's talented team beat England two to one in England and Australia continued to hold the Ashes for another year because Ted Dexter's MCC team played an even series in 1962-63, when only two of the five matches were finished, with one victory.

For some time a dispute had been smouldering between the two countries on the question of throwing. England was fielding some notorious 'chuckers', not all of them fast bowlers. One was Tony Lock, who subsequently reformed his action completely and, like Larwood and Tyson, eventually settled in Australia, in Perth. The Australians, meanwhile, had developed a number of fast bowlers whose actions were highly questionable, most notably Meckiff and Rorke. Not only was their delivery far from conventional but they also often let fly from a range of less than twenty yards because of their extended drag. In the end the decisive influence in settling the question was that of Sir Donald Bradman.

Richie Benaud was succeeded as Australian captain by Bobby Simpson, who led the Australians to victory in England in 1964, making a personal score of 311 in the Manchester Test. The 1965-66 tour of Australia by MCC under Mike Smith was drawn yet again—one match to each side, with three matches undecided—so Simpson retained the Ashes. In the following winter the Australians lost in South Africa.

After a gap of twenty years the Indians visited Australia for the second time in the 1967-68 season, and once more the Australians won easily, victorious in all four Test matches. In 1968 the Australians followed up this success by coming to England, with a weak side which was nonetheless able to draw the series: one match each, with three matches left unfinished. This rubber represented a low point in the history of Test matches between the two longest-standing contestants: the quality of the cricket was poor and the public stayed away. In 1970-71 England went to Australia with a strong fast-bowling attack led by John Snow. Bill Lawry's Australian side could not hold them, although many moderate State bowlers were called to the colours, including a tearaway from Western Australia called Dennis Lillee.

For over a decade, Graham McKenzie (known as Garth) had spearheaded the Australian attack. He had helped Australia to beat the West Indies in Australia in the 1968-69 season, and now he was to play a major role in India in the season following the 1968 visit to England. At this time Australia were engaged in the toughest programme imaginable—fifteen tests in fewer months—and Bill Lawry found his team soundly beaten in South Africa. But Australia began to revive under the stimulus of Ian Chappell and his brother Greg, both batsmen of skill and determination, and a squared series in England in 1972 featured a remarkable victory at Lord's when Bob Massie, a swing bowler, came good in his first Test to the extent of 16 wickets. Massie faded, but Chappell won his first series in the West Indies in 1972-73, took three victories in three matches from the Pakistanis and three in six from New Zealand in the following season, and in 1974-75 watched his two fast bowlers, Lillee and Thomson, scatter England to all four corners of Australia in the

second of the six-Test series. Jeff Thomson, with his long-arm action, was to grow into a classical yet original Test bowler of considerable status. Beaten in the 1975 World Cup Final, Australia retained the Ashes in the following short Test series.

Ian Chappell relinquished the captaincy to his brother Greg for the next rubber, a hurriedly arranged visit to Australia by West Indies, called in as replacements for South Africa. Again the Australian fast bowlers carried the day, even against the best West Indian players. The next season, however, the Pakistanis, under Mushtaq Mohammad, held the Australians to a draw. This was followed by an Australian victory in the Centenary Test against England, a social and cricketing *tour de force* in which two entertaining players, Rodney Marsh, the Australian wicketkeeper, and Derek Randall, the Nottinghamshire batsman, made attractive centuries.

This was the last Test before the schism. Undoubtedly the modest fees paid to the players and the lack of forceful negotiation of TV contracts by the Australian Board created resentment among Australian cricketers. But whatever the reasons for wholesale defection to Packer's 'Circus', the young team that Bobby Simpson, called back as captain at the age of forty-two, led to ultimate and exciting victory against India and then took to the West Indies early in 1978 conducted itself proudly on and off the field. They were no match for the West Indian fast bowlers but succeeded against the team that remained after the Packer players had been excluded. Rebuilding an entire Test side is a complex business which takes many years, and the 1978-79 series against England served to show how merciless the Test spotlight can be when the players involved are not of sufficient calibre.

ENGLAND

We have seen how George Parr's team became the first cricketers to venture abroad when they voyaged by sail and steam to Canada and the United States in the autumn of 1859.

The experience was a daunting one for many of the players because of the difficulties of travelling by land and sea; the bumpy Atlantic did not seem to yield to the heavy roller! Nonetheless, several members of that team went to Australia in 1861-62 under the captaincy of H. H. Stephenson. It was during this tour that the expression 'Test match' was first used, although none of the matches played were played on level terms. Whereas individual benefactors had put up the money for the tour to Canada and the United States, the first trip to Australia was sponsored by a company of Melbourne caterers. It was such a success that the second team in 1863-64, also under George Parr, extended its visit to include New Zealand, returning home to find that over-arm bowling, already widespread in both Australia and England, had been made legal on 10 June 1864.

The only England teams bearing that name were the professional touring teams, the All-England Eleven and the United Eleven, and their derivatives. For many years these two sides had played a benefit match for the Cricketers' Fund Friendly Society, but in 1867 the matches between North and South and between the two All-England elevens, the two great fixtures of the season, were abandoned because of the acrimony between the two groups. Their secretary-managers, Parr from the North and Wisden from the South, were given short shift by Fred Lillywhite in his account of the first tour to Canada and the United States in which both took part.

Batting in England became easier after the first use of the heavy roller at Lord's in 1870. In 1871 W. G. Grace had his finest season; and the whole business of run-making was helped in the following year by the first experiment at Lord's in covering the wicket.

In 1876-77 the first Test match between England and Australia was played. Australia won. In the summer of 1878 they came to England to defeat a strong MCC England by nine wickets in a single day under Dave Gregory's leadership, and thereafter attention was focused less on the County Championship or such matches as the Gentlemen and Players fixture than on these games between the best of England and the best of Australia. The first Test match in England in 1880 became something of a contest between W.G. and Willie Murdoch; W.G. made 152, and Murdoch decided he would have to get more and did so, scoring 153 not out. Two years later Australia won their first Test match in England by sevens runs at The Oval; a spectator was to die from the excitement of it all. The tour of 1882-83 caused some confusion about the Ashes. Ivo Bligh's team discovered when they got to Australia that matches had been arranged not only with Murdoch's 1882 team but also with a team representing the best of Australian cricket at that time. Originally, only those matches played against the 1882 side were designated Ashes matches. When the Australians next came to England they found the present Lord's Pavilion being built—this was completed by 1889.

England won all three matches in the 1886 series, two of them by an innings, with Arthur Shrewsbury making 164 in the second match and W.G. 170 in the final one. This was the start of a good run by England who won both the matches played in Sydney in the following winter and were victorious again in the 1887-88 season when Lohmann and Peel bowled Australia out for 42. England also won the next rubber in 1888 by two matches to one with W. G. Grace captaining England in the final two Tests of the series.

The first England visit to South Africa followed, and then the Australians returned in 1890 when the home side, again with W.G. captaining, won both at Lord's and The Oval. W.G. then took England to Australia in 1891-92, and lost the first two matches. C. T. B. Turner was largely responsible for this defeat, for he took an enormous number of wickets and, incidentally, bowled six-ball overs, although only five-ball overs were permissible according to the Laws.

England's next visit to South Africa was curious, because in the England side at Capetown were Murdoch, now playing for Sussex, and J. J. Ferris, both of whom had played for Australia, while Frank Hearne, who had played for England in the previous rubber, now scored most runs in both innings for South Africa. This was not the first case of players changing countries, however, for Midwinter, an Australian, had also played for England against Australia.

England won the 1893 Test series, beating Australia at The Oval by an innings in the only match which was finished. Johnny Briggs of Lancashire, a fine left-handed wicket-taker, took 10 wickets in the match. The 1894-95 series opened with a tight match

Left: Herbert Strudwick, known as 'Struddy' was England keeper in 28 Tests and Surrey's for 25 years

which England won by 10 runs after heavy rain on the fifth night of the match. On the following morning, Bobby Peel took 6 wickets for 67. This was to be an exciting series in which Albert Trott, who was to become a professional with Middlesex, distinguished himself for Australia. England won the fifth and deciding match by six wickets.

The following winter England returned to South Africa, with Lord Hawke as captain, and won relatively easily. The Australians returned to England in 1896, when Richardson and Lohmann got England off to a good start by bowling them out for 53 at Lord's. England lost at Manchester but won at The Oval, where six of the England players asked for £20 for the match instead of £10, and two of them, Gunn and Lohmann, were left out of the side because of this. Neither man went to Australia in the following winter when England were badly beaten by four matches to one, Darling and Hill making many runs, and Trumble, Noble and Jones taking most of the wickets.

England went to South Africa in the last close season of the nineteenth century, and Australia returned in 1899 when W.G. made his last Test appearance at Nottingham in the first match. England took the field thereafter under Archie MacLaren. Both Clem Hill and Victor Trumper made 100s at Lord's, where the Australians won by 10 wickets. This was the only match of the five-match series which ended in a result. Archie MacLaren took the 1901-02 team to Australia, the Australians winning the series by four matches to one. In 1902 England fielded a golden team against Australia—all eleven had made 100s in first-class cricket. Wilfred Rhodes bowled Australia out in the first match in Birmingham, with help from George Hirst, Australia escaping with a draw because of bad weather. They came back into the series by winning the only Test every played at Sheffield, where Clem Hill made a match-winning 100, and then won at Manchester by three runs when Fred Tate, at number eleven, was bowled out for 4 after dropping a vital catch. He left the ground vowing that he would one day make the Australians suffer; a vow that was eventually to be fulfilled by his son, Maurice Tate. However, Australia won the most exciting series thus far by two matches to one. Plum Warner revived the legend of the Ashes in the next series in Australia, also an exciting one, his side beating the team led by Noble by the narrow margin of three matches to two.

In 1905 Stanley Jackson captained England against Darling's Australians and won the series. Not only did he make two centuries, he also fulfilled the first and still the most important role of the captain by winning all five tosses.

South Africa won their first match against England in the following season—their ninth attempt. Indeed, they won four matches of this rubber, the selectors choosing a team which remained the same throughout all five Tests, an experiment which has never been repeated. When they came to England for the 1907 series, South Africa were beaten even though they had a clever band of googly bowlers, but England lost the next rubber against Australia on Jack Hobb's first overseas tour. They selected their team for the 1909 series in an astonishing fashion, going into two of the matches without a single fast bowler. Not surprisingly, the series was lost, and deservedly so. England also went down three-two to South Africa in that winter of 1909-10. The domestic programme received attention in the two years following, but touring was revived in 1911-12 when England won a great victory in Australia. Plum Warner was again nominated captain, but Johnny Douglas took over when Warner became ill. Hobbs, Rhodes and Barnes won the series for England, with support from the rest of a strong team. In the last season before the First World War, England won easily in South Africa under Johnny Douglas, but after the hostilities readjustment did not come easily and Australia, with Armstrong as captain, not only won a clean sweep of games in their own summer of 1920-21, but also came to England in 1921 and won the first three Tests of that five-match series. England beat South Africa in 1922-23 and again, and this time substantially, in 1924. Australia were a tougher proposition, however. In 1924-25 England went

Left: Peter May and Colin Cowdrey come in after their massive stand against West Indies at Edgbaston in 1957. Right: Tom Graveney applauds his skipper, Colin Cowdrey, who in the Edgbaston Test against Australia in 1968 had just completed a century in his hundredth Test

down again with Arthur Gilligan as captain to a side led by Herbie Collins in which Arthur Mailey took the most wickets. In the 1926 series everything depended on the result of the fifth Test, the first four having been drawn. Fifty years later so many draws suggest a boring series, but Tests in England were not played to a finish as they were in Australia. Over 100,000 people watched the last match at The Oval. England won it by 289 runs. From 22 behind on the first innings they were brought back into a commanding position by the vital opening partnership between Hobbs and Sutcliffe, who put on 172 runs. Both men scored 100s in an innings total of 436, and subsequently Larwood and Rhodes took 7 Australian wickets in the second innings which tumbled to 125 all out. After that the Australians were, for a change, easy to beat. It was a very changed England side that afterwards went to South Africa for a five-match rubber.

In the 1928 season the West Indies came for the first time, and subsequently England sent a team to Australia under Percy Chapman. This was the most successful side before the Second World War and faced a weak Australian opposition, so weak that they were obliged to try out a young batsman called Bradman, although he was left out of the team for the second match. In 1929 England beat South Africa, winning the only two matches which were finished, and after featuring teams in both New Zealand and West Indies during the winter, they returned in 1930 to face Woodfull's Australians, bent on revenge for their defeat in 1928-29. This was a splendid series. England won the first match by 93 runs, but Australia took the second at Lord's by 7 wickets, Woodfull making 155, Ponsford 81, Kippax 83 and Bradman a huge 254 out of a total of 729 for 6 declared. Percy Chapman made twice as many runs as anybody else in England's second innings, 121 out of 375, but the Australians equalled this total for the loss of only 3 wickets. The next two matches, in one of which Bradman made a triple century at Leeds, were drawn because of the weather, and the teams came to The Oval still locked. Australia won by an innings and 39 runs, even though Herbert Sutcliffe made 161 for England out of a first-innings total of 405. The Australian batting order seemed incapable of failure: Ponsford made 110, Bradman 232, and their total of 695 was enough to secure an innings victory.

South Africa beat England that winter, winning the only match finished, and then it was the turn of New Zealand and India to come to England during the following summers before England again went to Australia in the winter of 1932-33, with Plum Warner as manager and Douglas Jardine as captain. This was a formidable combination of charm and will and developed tactics which were to unhinge the Australian batting, so triumphant in 1930. Reading through the roll of batsmen the names and achievements of this series are unforgettable. For example, Sutcliffe, Hammond and the older Pataudi all scored 100s for England in the first match, while Stan McCabe made 187 for Australia. Bradman had to be content with only one century in the series but he still made many scores of 50. England, level after two Tests, came to the fifth and last with the Ashes already theirs and finished with a 4-1 victory. They had to beat Australia's largest series total of 435 and managed to do so by 19 runs, with Walter Hammond making 101 and Larwood hitting no fewer than 98 as night watchman at number four.

The West Indies came again in 1933 and England went to India in the winter. And then the Australians returned under Woodfull. This time there was no doubt as to the outcome for Australia won both the first and the fifth match with Ponsford and Bradman scoring double 100s out of a total of 701, while Grimmett took 8 wickets in the match.

South Africa won their first rubber in England in 1935. India came in 1936, and Bradman then succeeded in leading Australia to a three-two victory, after losing the first two Test matches, in 1936-37, with O'Reilly taking 25 wickets in the series.

England beat New Zealand without pressure in 1937 and Australia visited again in 1938, still under Bradman, playing a high-scoring four-match series which was drawn at one match each. Australia won at Leeds, O'Reilly taking 10 wickets, and lost at The Oval, where he took 3 for 178 and Fleetwood-Smith 1 for 298 as England, inspired by Len Hutton's 364, accumulated the record score in Test cricket of 903 for 7.

England went to South Africa after this, winning the only finished match, the third Test at Durban. The fifth Test was also staged at Durban and lasted for ten days, breaking any number of records as the longest and slowest Test ever played. In the end England had to leave the field with the game unfinished in order to catch the boat home; they were 42 runs short of victory with five wickets in hand. In 1939, the last summer before the Second World War, England won the only Test finished against West Indies, the first, by eight wickets, despite George Headley making 100 in both innings. The West Indies once again demonstrated that they were somewhat inhibited when playing in England; it was not until later that they were able to let loose their real talent.

After the War, England settled into a routine which involved her cricketers being engaged winter and summer, almost without a break. In 1946 the Indians came to England under the older Pataudi and in a pleasant summer re-launched the first-class game. Later, under the captaincy of Walter Hammond, with Bradman leading Australia, England had a disastrous series against an Australian team as strong in both batting and bowling as any in the field. In 1947 England inflicted terrible punishment on a talented South African side, with Denis Compton and Bill Edrich scoring runs almost at will in the summer in which they broke every single aggregate record in first-class cricket. In the following winter a somewhat weakened side set off for the West Indies under Gubby Allen, who had captained in Australia more than a decade before, and because of injury and lack of ability found itself struggling against the rising tide of West Indian cricket. It was not good preparation for the Australian visit of 1948, with Bradman again leading a side armed with every talent. Once again England were white-washed. Brilliant though England's players seemed, they were never a complete enough team to hold Australia; there were no fast bowlers, for instance. Yardley was now captain, but the party which set off for South Africa was led by George Mann who had a most successful series there to re-emphasize that England were second only to the Australians in cricketing strength. The 1949 summer saw the last of the three-day Tests when Walter Hadlee's New Zealanders demonstrated that this format was an inadequate frame for achieving results: the series was frankly a bore.

In 1950 Ramadhin and Valentine spun England to defeat as the selectors experimented with a new generation. Whatever the results of these experiments, they were not successful enough to hold the Australians in the 1950-51 season, when Freddie Brown quickly found his team in a losing position in the second post-war rubber in Australia. However, at Melbourne in the fifth and final Test England scored what Jim Swanton always referred to as the 'elusive victory', and it was after that success that the tide of English cricket turned. It continued this winning run for more than half a decade until Peter May's astonishing reverses in Australia in 1958-59. The South Africans were beaten again in 1951, a second-grade team had a relatively successful tour of India under difficult conditions in 1951-52, and when the Indians came here they were destroyed by the fast bowling of Fred Trueman.

In 1953 the Australians came again, and Len Hutton, the first professional captain of England since Arthur Shrewsbury, succeeded in inflicting a defeat on them which was celebrated in wild scenes at The Oval. A year later, after a tough but drawn series in the West Indies, England were forced to lower their colours against the newly arrived Pakistan team at The Oval, although the rubber was drawn. More important, in that winter England succeeded in holding the Ashes in Australia. According to many judges, Frank Tyson, now the Victorian cricket coach, bowled faster than any man has done either before or since.

In 1955 Jack Cheetham's side, a brilliant fielding combination, found the post-war generation of

English cricketers at their best under the captaincy of Peter May, an inspired batsman and one of the longest-serving of England captains. The series was a close one with every match finished, England winning three matches to two. The following year England had a two-one victory against Ian Johnson's Australians, who in complete contrast with England were a talented side who played poorly under a less inspired captain. May's next task was to take England to South Africa, and this time the South Africans held on for a drawn rubber, two matches each with one undecided. In 1957 the West Indians were in England again under the captaincy of John Goddard, and England had what was to be their last crushing victory against the West Indies, succeeding in all three of the games that were finished. Goddard's team performed far below their potential. In 1958, with May still England's captain,

Left: Ian Botham, one of a very bright new bunch of England all-rounders

the New Zealanders lost four of their five matches, but that winter May's team came unstuck against the captaincy of Richie Benaud in the famous series marred by the throwing controversy. This defeat against all the form was a great personal disappointment for Peter May. England won easily against India in 1959, and the 1959-60 tour of the West Indies found them victorious in the only match finished. May himself was plagued by illness, and retired prematurely from first-class cricket and from the captaincy of England.

In 1960, the South Africans under Jackie McGlew lost the last five-Test series ever played by them in England by three matches. In the summer of 1961 Richie Benaud was able to beat the England side now led by Ted Dexter by two to one, his own leg-spin bowling at Old Trafford clinching the series. In 1962 Pakistan came for the second time and England won the four Tests completed. The following year Frank Worrell's West Indians fulfilled their great potential with a three-one victory, and in 1964 the Australians under Bobby Simpson were successful in the only match with a result. This period can perhaps rightly be regarded as a low point in the cricket played between these two countries. The Ashes and the need to retain them had become an all-important factor, and no longer were Australian matches considered an end in themselves. The powerful desire not to lose the Ashes prompted captains on both sides with the first game of a series under their belt to adopt an over-cautious posture. Whereas previously over half the Tests had been finished, this proportion now dropped below one in four.

Ted Dexter's visit to Australia in 1962-63 was a very dreary affair, and again relatively poor cricket was played by both sides on the 1965-66 tour when Mike Smith was captain. Meanwhile, earlier in the year the first split English summer had taken place, with South Africa and New Zealand each playing three Tests. England were beaten by South Africa in the only match finished in the first of these mini-series, although they successfully defeated John Reid's New Zealanders in all three matches. At this point England had sunk to fourth position in world ratings behind Australia, S. Africa and the W. Indies.

In 1967 the summer was again divided, this time between India and Pakistan, and England were able to beat both countries, taking five out of the six Tests played. The following year, Australia, who were very properly not scheduled to share a series, drew under the captaincy of Bill Lawry, again only two matches being completed out of five. The result of this series meant that of the twenty-five England-Australia Tests played up to the end of the 1968 tour no fewer than fifteen had been drawn, which clearly demonstrated why during the 1960s Test cricket suffered a drop in public popularity.

In 1970 the South Africans were due to play a full five-match series, but the after-effects of the d'Oliveira affair and the increasingly powerful voice of the anti-apartheid campaign caused the visit to be cancelled. Instead, a series against the Rest of the World was staged which, while an interesting exhibition, failed to capture the imagination either of the spectators or of the statisticians.

Ray Illingworth, England's successful captain against the West Indies in 1969, now built a formidable side around the batting of Boycott and John Edrich, both of them to become makers of a century of centuries, and the fast bowling of John Snow. Australia, as weak as they had ever been, were swept aside in 1970-71, and although the Indian spinners snatched a victory in 1971, a split summer in which Pakistan, the first to arrive, failed, Australia were held in 1972 so that Illingworth retained the Ashes.

However, the side was creaking again and was not successful on tour in India under Tony Lewis in 1972-73. Snow did not possess the wicket-taking capabilities of a Trueman in England, and the West Indies took England apart at Lord's so easily that Illingworth was removed from the captaincy. Under Mike Denness the team was able to draw in the West Indies, thanks to Boycott's batting and Greig's off-spin bowling in the final Test. Denness had an easy summer in 1974 against India and Pakistan respectively, but his team had a disastrous tour of Australia in the following close season, so much so that Denness had to drop himself because his own batting fell to pieces against Lillee and Thomson. Not even the arrival of Colin Cowdrey could save a sinking ship. Tony Greig took over from Denness in the World Cup summer, but England were beaten by Australia in the crucial one-day match and subsequently lost the only Test of four finished in the following short rubber.

In the following year Clive Lloyd's West Indies team brushed England aside yet again, but Grieg systematically rebuilt the team's morale in India and keenly contested the Centenary Test although his was the weaker of the two sides.

Then came the great divide. Mike Brearley took on Greig's team, now good enough to defeat an Australian side debilitated by Packer defectors and without Dennis Lillee to partner Jeff Thomson. England batted, bowled and caught well and followed their success up with four more short and successful series with Pakistan and New Zealand before setting out for Australia, Packer's home ground, to meet the Test team Australia was trying to rebuild under the TV man's shadow.

INDIA

Cricket, like so many other British products, was taken to India by sailors of the East India Company as early as 1721, and just as the game drew stronger in England during the eighteenth century so did it in India.

With increasingly large British armies stationed in the country during the wars against the princes and moguls, the game spread, and there are records of it being played in Bombay and in Southern India, in Seringapatam near Mysore, after the successful siege of that old Moslem city.

At the outset it was very much an expatriate game, the first known century in the country being scored, in 1804, by R. Van Sitart for the Old Etonians against the Rest of Calcutta. It was another thirty-five years before the first Indian community, the Parsees, began to play the game in Bombay. In the 1860s the Hindus followed the Parsees into action in the same city, and the first recorded match took place between Madras and Calcutta. Instructional books from England were translated into Hindi and into Urdu, and in that same decade round-arm bowling superseded under-arm bowling among the Parsees. Some of the army games were particularly exciting: for example, a fixture recorded at Lucknow, scene of a bitter siege during the Mutiny when the Royal Irish Lancers and the Fusiliers played a tied match. By the 1870s, two soldiers, (Private Sheiring and Quartermaster Sergeant Miller) had recorded the first double century and the first bag of ten wickets in a single innings respectively. The Parsees were now proposing to visit England and Australia, but they did not succeed in so doing at this time; cricket had also become established in Indian universities.

In the 1880s the Moslem's became the third community to establish a cricket club, and a tournament developed in Bombay between the various gymkhanas. The Parsees finally set sail for England in 1886; they came again in 1888 and in the following winter season an English team visited India. It was a Parsee team that recorded the first major victory over an English team, beating Lord Hawke's touring side in 1892-93.

During the following English summer, in his last year in residence, Ranjitsinhji became the first of a long succession of Indian cricket blues at Cambridge. Not only did he establish a distinctive Indian approach to cricket in English eyes, he also revolutionized the art of batting. His keenness of eye and strength of wrist together with a fine judgment enabled him to perfect the leg-glance with which he scored so many of his runs. Ranji was a delightful patrician who invested a very considerable amount of his family's then ample fortune in his own and other people's cricket. As an undergraduate it was his practice to engage half a dozen professionals to bowl at him; there is one celebrated story of how such a team returned to bowl at him somewhat the worse for wear after a session in the nearby Prince Regent pub, still a happy haunt for cricketers. Ranji proceeded to give them all fielding practice, including a series of steepling catches as high as the nearby Catholic church spire which were altogether too much for the less sober brethren. The Jubilee Book of Cricket, which he wrote in collaboration with his great friend and colleague Charles Burgess Fry, is one of the classics of cricket literature. Ranji still holds the record (fourteen) for the number of double centuries scored by an Indian. V. M. Merchant, the greatest Parsee cricketer, comes next with eleven.

The first All-India tour to England was mooted for the season of 1904 but fell through for financial reasons, although all the fixtures had been arranged. Eventually it came in 1911 under the second of the three Maharajahs of Patiala to be passionately involved in cricket. (For years it seemed necessary that the Indian cricketers should be captained by a prince, which may not always have been in the best interests of their cricket.) In 1922 a team of South African Indians visited India and played cricket in Calcutta. Gandhi was to spend many formative years in South Africa, but over the years exchanges such as this grew less and less possible.

India were admitted to the Imperial Cricket Conference in 1926 and in the following season the first official visit by the MCC took place under the captaincy of Arthur Gilligan. In April 1927 an Indian Board of Control was established, setting a precedent for the state associations that were later to be formed. During 1932 the second Indian tour came to England with the Maharajah of Porbander as nominal captain, but this team played but a single Test in which C. K. Nayudu led the team.

MCC's second visit took place in 1933-34; they played a three-match rubber and Douglas Jardine's team won both matches that were finished. It was in this period that the Cricket Club of India was founded in New Delhi as the Indian version of the MCC. It later moved to Bombay and established itself in magnificent premises in what came to be known as the Brabourne Stadium, after the Governor of the same name. The ground was opened in 1937

Below: England won the series in India in 1977, but there were moments of triumph for India

with Lord Tennyson's team of English county cricketers playing there. However, the Cricket Club of India's assumed pre-eminence in Indian cricket aroused considerable jealousy, particularly as the CCI seemed to be an exclusive preserve for the remaining practitioners of Parsee cricket. Gradually the Bombay Cricket Association came to resent the significance of the CCI to such an extent that in the early 1970s a new stadium, the Wankhede, was built within three-quarters of a mile of the old Test centre. At once it became the official Test match ground, a vast bowl of concrete and steel, lacking much of the character of the CCI ground, although duplicating most of Brabourne's facilities.

In the 1934-35 season the Ranji Trophy, the provincial tournament on which first-class cricket in India is based, was established. In the second year of this tournament the Maharajah of Patiala sponsored an unofficial tour by a team of Australians, led by Jack Ryder. Then the third Indian tour of England took place under the captaincy of the Maharaj-Kumar of Vizianagram, and again two of the three Tests were lost.

Cricket continued uninterrupted in India throughout the Second World War, and a number of leading English Test players came to the country, notably Denis Compton and Joe Hardstaff. When the game was resumed elsewhere in 1946 it was an Indian side, this time led by the older Nawab of Pataudi, that occupied first place in the English programme. The

tour was not a successful one in terms of Test match quality, but it did establish one quite delightful record between two bowlers, Sarwate, the leg-spinner, and Banerjee, one of the fast bowlers. In the match against Surrey at The Oval they scored centuries batting at ten and eleven respectively and by so doing added 249 for the last wicket. This figure remains the highest for the tenth wicket in both English and Indian cricket.

Thus far India had produced three cricketers of undoubted genius: Ranji, his nephew Duleep (who was incidentally the first victim of South African racial policies in cricket), and Merchant, a most prolific run-maker. A number of other Indians have achieved eminence by their run-making or bowling capabilities; for example, the two Nayudus, Mankad and Amarnath, two cricketers who produced sons also destined to play for India, and Vijay Hazare, one of the quietest Test cricketers in the history of the game and as near to a round-arm bowler as has been seen in the twentieth century. Hazare was such a gentle soul that he hardly deserved to be captain when Indian cricket sank to its lowest point. At Leeds in 1952 the Indians faced a scoreboard which read four wickets for no runs, their batsmen scattered by the pace of the young Fred Trueman, who had found Indian resolve notably lacking.

For the next twenty years, despite frequent visits by overseas teams, Indian cricket followers had to be content with only a few morsels of success. They had beaten the MCC team which toured in the winter of 1951-52 under Nigel Howard, but that had been a far from full-strength team. India also scored victories against Pakistan before the period when matches between these two countries degenerated into a procession of draws. The 1959 tour to England was also a failure, all five Tests being lost during the first series of five-day matches played against

Left: In the third Test at Madras in 1977 Lever was caught by Kirmani off the devastatingly effective bowling of Bedi

England. The following winter, Benaud's Australian side dropped a Test match in India, but India subsequently lost all five in the West Indies. They salvaged some pride by drawing all five Tests against Mike Smith's MCC team and won another match against the Australians, but it was not until the New Zealand tour of 1967-68 that India won its first series away from their own wickets. It was at this time that the frustration of the Indian crowds at the lack of success began to make itself felt in unpleasant forms. One of the matches involving New Zealand on their next tour to India was abandoned because of a riot which started following a disagreement between the two captains on the drying of the pitch.

In the early 1970s, however, the Indian team under A. L. Wadekar, who succeeded the younger Pataudi as captain, scored victories against the West Indies and England away from home, and then won the series against England on Indian wickets in 1972-73. Wadekar seemed to be the first captain of either Pakistan or India to instil in his team an understanding of the need for first-class fielding as support for the bowlers. For all his brilliance with the bat and his occasional successes, Pataudi, although himself a superb fielder away from the wicket, had not been able to achieve such a fine standard for close fielding as Wadekar set. The catching near the wicket gave great support to the outstanding spin bowlers, Bedi, Chandra, Prasanna and Venkat, who represent India's latest significant contribution to world cricket. On their own wickets and on wickets in the West Indies and Australia, these players have proved themselves time and again the finest spin bowlers of their generation. Furthermore they have continued to emphasize to the public the importance of spin bowling when other countries seem to be besotted with speed or seam bowling of a uniform steadiness and dullness.

Two young batsmen, Gavaskar and Viswanath, appeared in this period to further strengthen the team with their capacity for regular century-making. The Indian side was thus able to compete strongly in the apparently hostile one-day framework of the first World Cup in 1975.

Thereafter their fortunes have been more mixed, and the England team which toured India in 1976-77 under Tony Greig was able to take their first three Tests with a display of positive cricket helped by the indifferent performance of the Indians under their new captain, Bishen Singh Bedi. India's problem since Partition has been that of finding adequate, or indeed any, fast bowlers. At the moment there are few signs of any developing, and those that do come forward often have suspect actions. Obviously it is hard to sustain pace under the mid-day sun, where only Englishmen and mad dogs venture if the song is to be believed, and the problem is aggravated because India seems unable to produce large men who can even attempt to bowl fast. Partition removed the tallest players to Pakistan, and the smaller men whom they have tried to develop as fast bowlers seem to have been unable to sustain the pace required for an adequate Test attack, even with helpful wickets.

One of the saddest events in Indian cricket was the accident to the younger Nawab of Pataudi. His left eye was seriously injured in a car crash in 1961 on the Brighton front when he was playing for Sussex, whose team he graced for a number of years. There may have been other sixteen-year-olds in first-class cricket, but few have had the same ability. Whereas his father had played for Worcestershire, the young Nawab decided to join Sussex because he had been coached by Sussex players George Cox and Hubert Doggart at school at Winchester. It so happened that his first match for his county was against Worcestershire, whose fast bowler Jack Flavell let fly one of the nastiest bouncers ever bowled to greet a teenager. That he should have come back to play with only one sound eye against the world's fastest bowlers is a remarkable tribute to his courage. England lost the services of Colin Milburn whose eye damage, in 1969, similarly sustained in a car crash, was more serious than Pataudi's.

Pataudi is one of a number of Indian cricketers who in effect have been schooled outside the country. The drive within India at the moment is to develop more and better players capable of making their mark in Test cricket; the following for the game is vast (some 200,000,000 people listen to Test matches on the radio) and the Indian people will not be satisfied until their cricketers are capable of holding their own with the rest of the world. To that end much of the revenue of Indian cricket, previously principally devoted to expanding their now massive stadia, is being channelled into a full-scale coaching scheme in all the various provinces. Up until now national coaching has been virtually non-existent, due mainly to the old Indian social system whereby the princes engaged cricketers and saw to it that they were properly coached. Now that the princes are no longer able to afford their once normal patrician style of living, the central sporting bodies are having to do more to maintain the flow of talent into the game. In a country as large as India this is a mammoth task. Fortunately, as in England, many of the old Test cricketers are devoting themselves to coaching young talent, and the exchanges at schools level between England, India, the West Indies and Australia are working to every country's advantage.

NEW ZEALAND

The year of the great Reform Bill, 1832, is the year in which there is first mention of cricket in the islands of the southern ocean, not only in Hobart but in New Zealand, where Charles Darwin, the great explorer, wrote about Maoris playing the game at Christmas-time.

As the two islands of New Zealand began to attract more and more settlers so the game spread, although it is easy to forget how small the population of New Zealand remains to this day: some 3,500,000, roughly comparable to the Republic of Ireland.

The Domain, still used for Test matches in Auckland, first became a cricket ground in 1853, and by the end of that decade Wellington and Auckland were playing against each other. There is early evidence that they were prepared to experiment: while the first match between them consisted of six-ball overs in the second year they used five balls. New Zealanders have always been prepared to change this particular rule, bowling alternatively six or eight balls; eight is the current number. The length of time that elapsed between the commencement of cricket in these islands and a visit from England was relatively short, for in the 1863-64 season George Parr brought a team after touring Australia for the second time. This team experienced a number of unscheduled events, not the least of them a narrow escape from a raging flood when their coach became stuck in the mud of a river-bed during a thunderstorm.

In 1868 the Basin Reserve in Wellington, still the capital city's Test match ground, was first used for cricket. About this time J. W. A. Marchant not only scored the country's first century but also took nine wickets in a match, these feats being achieved for two different teams, in two different islands furthermore, thus demonstrating how mobile the population was even at that time.

In 1876-77 Lillywhite's team also went on from Australia to New Zealand, a pattern of visits that was maintained until recently. Two years after that visit the first New Zealand side travelled overseas when Canterbury went to Victoria and Tasmania. It was in the 1877-78 season that the Australian team first played in New Zealand, a second tour following in the 1880-81 season with the team eventually coming on to the United Kingdom. The following year Shaw's English team became the first to play at Lancaster Park in Christchurch.

In 1883-84 Tasmania sent a team to New Zealand. The tours had become almost an annual event, an Australian visit in 1886-87 being followed by an English side led by the famous Hollywood actor, Charles Aubrey Smith, known as 'Round the Corner' Smith because of his angled approach to the wicket when bowling. In 1894 the New Zealand Cricket Council was established, and in that season a Fijian side under J. S. Udal, the famous judge, toured in New Zealand, winning four out of six matches.

Although an Australian side in New Zealand in 1896-97 was still playing against odds, the New Zealanders were forced to admit two years later that they were unable to cope with the high and rising standard of cricket in Australia. When they toured as a representative side in 1898-99 they lost both their first class matches, and in the following season Melbourne Cricket Club were able to beat a representative New Zealand eleven on their own. After P. F. Warner had taken his side to New Zealand in 1902-3 and the Australians had visited again in 1904-5, the sixth English team, the first sent by the MCC, visited New Zealand in 1906-7. In the same year the Plunket Shield Competition (now the Shell Cup) was started among the major associations, Canterbury winning it in the opening season. The Shield was originally contested by Auckland, Wellington, Otago and Canterbury, although in recent years two more associations have been added—Northern Districts, which comprise the teams around Auckland, and Central Districts, which covers all those outside Wellington. Organizationally New Zealand cricket has remained relatively stable and free from controversy compared to other national associations.

Another unsuccessful visit to Australia was made in 1909-10, but in 1913-14 a New Zealand team beat Queensland, their first victory in first-class cricket in Australia. That same season, J. N. Crawford, the Surrey amateur, made 354 against a fifteen from South Canterbury, playing for Sim's unofficial Australian side which included Victor Trumper; the latter hit 293 runs against Canterbury to establish a New Zealand first-class cricket record. After the First World War official Australian and MCC teams both visited New Zealand, and they were followed by New South Wales and Victoria. When New Zealand visited Australia for the third time, they failed to win a single match, but since then, although New Zealand were admitted to the then Imperial Cricket Conference in 1926, the number of tours by Australian sides to New Zealand has been lamentably few. Although New Zealand first sent their team to England in 1927 the first Test matches were not

Right: John Reid, New Zealand's most successful captain was also an outstanding all-rounder. He led his country to their first ever Test win, against West Indies in 1956

played until Harold Gilligan took a team to New Zealand in the 1929-30 season.

In 1931 the New Zealanders returned to England, this time to play Test matches. They lost only one of the three matches, drawing the other two. The captain on this occasion was Tom Lowry, who had also been in charge four years earlier; he had made a reputation for himself as a batsman at Cambridge. Among other talented New Zealanders on the tour were C. C. Dacre, Roger Blunt and Bill Merritt. The 1931-32 season saw the South Africans begin their series of Test matches against New Zealand, and the following winter Douglas Jardine drew both his matches there, and in 1935-36 a tour of Australia MCC tour almost exclusively engaged in New Zealand and sent forth under Errol Holmes, the captain of Surrey, and all four representative matches were drawn as indeed was the single match between the two sides in the following year, when MCC's Australian tour of 1936-37 was extended to cover one unofficial test match. The following summer New Zealand returned to England, achieving exactly the same result as on their previous visit: one Test lost and two drawn. In the season immediately after the Second World War, Bill Brown took an Australian team to New Zealand and won the only Test match played, and in 1949 the fourth New Zealand tour came to England. This time Walter Hadlee, now Chairman of the Cricket Council, was captain. He set out to demonstrate that his side was capable of drawing all that season's Test matches, which were scheduled as three-day events in order to minimize disruption of the English County Championships. This New Zealand duly did.

Subsequently three-day Tests were discontinued, being demonstrably absurd. The oustanding player in the team was Martin Donnelly, and both he and Bert Sutcliffe, another great left-hander, made 2,000 runs during the course of the season, the first New Zealanders ever to do so.

In the 1950s tours became a regular feature of New Zealand cricket, West Indies visiting again after their tour to Australia, followed by South Africa. A New Zealand side went to South Africa for a full tour for the first time in 1953-54. John Reid, subsequently New Zealand's longest-serving captain, led the team, but they proved less formidable opponents for the South Africans than the All-Blacks were for the Springboks at rugby. New Zealand won their first-ever Test victory against Dennis Atkinson's West Indies team in the 1955-56 season, but Reid and his side could do nothing in England in 1958 when New Zealand lost four and drew the fifth of their five five-day Test matches. Seven years later, on the next New Zealand tour of England, John Reid was still captain; this time the team embarked on a real world tour, visiting India, Pakistan, Holland, Bermuda and the United States as well as England, where they featured in one of the earliest split summers. This method of dividing the English season is particularly suited to New Zealand because almost all their cricketers are amateurs, and in view of the ever-increasing demands on their time they have found it difficult to make themselves available for full, professional programmes like those followed by the best English, Australian and West Indian cricketers.

Five-day tests were played in New Zealand for the first time in the 1967-68 season, when India visited under the Nawab of Pataudi. New Zealand

won one of the four matches, India the other three. They snatched a game from the West Indies, under Gary Sobers, in the following season, and managed to square this three-match series one-all with a final draw. In 1969 New Zealand won a Test series for the first time in Pakistan, where they took the only completed match of a three-match series under the captaincy of Graham Dowling.

Since the retirement of John Reid, New Zealand have produced two players who have made an impact on cricket all over the world: Glenn Turner, who came to England to play for Worcestershire and, as a member of the touring New Zealand side of 1973, became, the first player for many years to score 1,000 runs by the end of May and Bevan Congdon, who has remained an amateur, one of the last able to play virtually full-time cricket without turning professional. Two other New Zealanders also deserve a mention, namely Dayle and Richard Hadlee, the sons of Walter, whose bowling skills in a period when Test teams can hardly hope to contend seriously on a world scale without quick bowlers. have helped to keep New Zealand in contention, if not quite on a par, with the other major cricketing nations.

One agreeable feature of New Zealand cricket as it is now played is its spirit of attack. Gone are the days when New Zealand teams, desperate to establish their country's reputation and sensing how little they were respected when compared to the apparently all-conquering All-Blacks, sought only to draw matches all over the world. At present both bowlers and batsmen are prepared to have a go with bat or ball whenever they can. There was an air of rustic charm about the New Zealanders' cricket in England in the summer of 1978 not apparent in other national sides. Could it be that the players are happier too?

Below: Australia have played in New Zealand relatively infrequently. Australia won the 1976-77 tour, but New Zealand batted well

PAKISTAN

India was partitioned in 1947, an event that was to have direct effects in the Punjab, the area which produced the greatest number of cricketers. Even now there is much evidence to support the idea that Gandhi and Lord Mountbatten, the last Briton in Delhi, were right to oppose partition right up to the very end.

Some idea of the irony of it all as far as cricket is concerned can be deduced from the fact that in 1974, at an Asian Cricket Conference, the two leaders of the Pakistan and Indian delegrations had not seen each other since they had both been playing members of the same cricket club in Lahore. Both had changed their names, and Abdul Hafeez, now known to the world as A. H. Kardar of Pakistan, did not even recognize R. P. Mehra as the man with whom he had played in pre-Partition days.

Originally, Pakistan consisted of five provinces: Punjab and Sind, covering Lahore and Karachi (the two most populous), the Northwest Frontier and Baluchistan in the west and, in the east, East Bengal, centred on Dacca. With the exception of Peshawar in the Northwest Frontier province, all Pakistan cricketers have been based either in Lahore or Karachi, or in the cities that have developed as cricket centres in the two provinces of Punjab and Sind. At first Pakistan had to feel its way in Test terms; the first team to visit was the West Indies, who played one unofficial match at Lahore under John Goddard in 1948-49. But in that same season Pakistan visited Ceylon and won both unofficial Test matches and in 1949 Pakistan also beat Ceylon at home. That same winter they played a Commonwealth side in one unofficial Test and lost it, and in the 1951-52 season Nigel Howard took the MCC team which was touring India to Pakistan and won one of the two unofficial Tests. It was in that summer that Pakistan were admitted to the ICC, and at the same time the first Pakistan Eaglets team came to the United Kingdom. This was the first of eight vital tours which developed a solid core of Pakistan cricketing talent. Alfred Gover, once a Surrey and England bowler but now running a cricket school in Wandsworth, London, was the man who promoted and helped these early generations of cricketers from a new country.

In 1952-53 Pakistan, now internationally recognized, went to India, winning one and losing two of the five Test matches. In the next season a domestic competition, the Quaid-e-Azam trophy, was started, subsequently to become the basis of the Pakistani first-class game. Again under A. H. Kardar, Pakistan returned to England in the summer of

Left: winning the toss rarely meant much advantage to either side when India and Pakistan met in the 1960s

1954 to play four Test matches, a successful tour culminating in victory over England in the last match at The Oval. There were a number of outstanding cricketers in this party of whom four should be singled out: Kadar, the captain, who had played for India before the war and on the tour of 1946, and who had subsequently played in England for Oxford and Warwickshire—a man of pioneering character; Fazal Mahmood, his vice-captain, a talented fast-medium bowler fit to be ranked with the likes of Bedser and Tate, whose bowling at The Oval won Pakistan the match; Hanif Mohammad, a batsman already established as the senior member of the most remarkable cricketing family in history and a player who exhibited from the outset that ability to stay at the crease which was eventually to bring him the world's record batting total—499 for Karachi against Bahawalpur in the 1958-59 season; and finally, in Imtiaz Ahmed, Pakistan had a wicketkeeper-batsman fit to rank with any in the world.

Nonetheless, when in the subsequent winter Pakistan entertained India to a five-Test series with Vinoo Mankad as Indian captain all five matches were drawn. Overall, this left India leading by two matches to one with seven of the first ten games played between the two countries abandoned as draws. Subsequently relations between India and Pakistan deteriorated to the point of outright warfare on a number of occasions. Following a further all drawn series in the 1960-61 season, there was a gap of nearly twenty years before Tests were resumed in the 1978-79 season.

Above: India and Pakistan fight it out during a Madras Test

Pakistan were by now anxious to receive tours in their country every winter in order to develop the game; MCC agreed to send an 'A' team under Donald Carr, now the Secretary of the TCCB, which lost two of the four Test matches and thus the series. It was during this tour that the famous water-squirting incident occurred: one of the umpires was attacked with water-pistols by members of the MCC team during a party, a joke intended in good part perhaps, but which nevertheless caused considerable offence. This was the first of many ugly incidents which have marred the enjoyment of cricket in Pakistan, incidents which continue to the present day. Sometimes the language barrier lies behind the problem. A Pakistan journalist once asked Donald Carr what A. H. Kardar's nickname had been when they played for Oxford together. 'I think we sometimes used to call him the Mystic of the Orient,' replied Carr. When the piece appeared Carr was somewhat perturbed to read that 'at Oxford, according to Donald Carr, Abdul Hafeez Kardar was known as the Oriental mistake'.

The Pakistan government were anxious that their cricketers should tour wherever they were invited, and in 1956 they went to East Africa, later receiving the Australians under Ian Johnson. In 1958 they travelled to the West Indies, also visiting Bermuda, Canada and the United States. That winter the West Indies visited Pakistan with Gerry Alexander as captain, and suffered defeat in a three-match series. In 1959-60, before the visit by Australia, matting wickets were banned in first-class matches in Pakistan. Some idea of the excellence of the now standard rolled-mud wickets can be deduced by the fact that in the following year, when MCC were visiting Pakistan, no fewer than four batsmen, Hanif Mohammad, Imtiaz Ahmed, Alimuddin and Mushtaq Mohammad, all made 1,000 runs in the short Pakistan season.

In the 1960s, overseas tours continued to be a regular feature of the Pakistan season, with teams from England playing their part to the full in developing cricket in the country. It was at the end of that decade, when Colin Cowdrey was captaining MCC in Pakistan, that a tour had to be cancelled because of political riots on the Karachi ground. The following year New Zealand had an appalling season because of continuing riots which prevented matches being finished.

During the 1970s, before the intervention of Packer, the Pakistan team gradually developed into one of the four strongest in the world, although the

Below: Zaheer Abbas made 235 not out in the 2nd Test at Lahore, against Pakistan in 1978. Abbas has also played for Gloucestershire

administration of their game has been plagued by some strange decisions, especially regarding the captaincy. Intikhab Alam, one of the most popular of the many Pakistanis playing in county cricket in England, twice found himself deposed as captain, despite having led Pakistan on an unbeaten tour of the British Isles, the only side apart from Bradman's Australians to achieve this feat. Intikhab was not even selected for the 1975 World Cup squad.

The full Pakistan team's finest performance came in Australia in the 1976-77 season, shortly after beating New Zealand at home. Thanks to the bowling of Imran Khan, who helped them to win the third match in Sydney, they shared a three-match series, before going off to the West Indies to meet an all-conquering side who nevertheless only managed to beat them by two matches to one.

The Pakistan Board of Control, although continuously attacked by critics within the country, decided to react to the recruitment of its leading

Below: During the same match Chandrasekhar was bowled by Imran Khan

players by the Packer group by banning them from two series against England in 1978. After a crushing defeat that decision was subsequently rescinded, probably on political grounds. The notorious instability of Pakistan opinion, so readily seen in the streets, so often seems to spill over on to the cricket ground. One particularly undesirable feature of Pakistan cricket which seems to have taken root, especially in Bangladesh, is a fear of losing in front of their own crowds. This has resulted in the preparation of wickets which are too dull to produce good cricket and must explain why average attendances in Pakistan are much smaller than those in India, where decisive results are normally possible. Unless there is some improvement during the 1980s potential visiting teams will look at conditions in Pakistan both on and off the field and wonder whether this is any longer a worthwhile trip to make. That they should be put in such a position by the authorities is tragic, because everywhere in Pakistan there is great enthusiasm for the game and, more significant still, such a wealth of talent and such skill in coaching cricketers to Test standards that a succession of first-rate national teams seems a certainty.

In Pakistan the tradition of the Great Moghul is still alive—the top man in the country is all-powerful whether he is a military man or a civilian. Certainly he is powerful enough to determine the membership of the Pakistan Board of Control. Wholesale changes there led to a recall of the Packer players for the 1978 series with India—stronger on paper, Pakistan were decisively victorious in both matches. Even so, during a one-day match the Indian captain Bedi took his players off the field in the final stages when the Pakistan umpires refused either to halt a persistent barrage of bouncers or at least call them as wides—yet another indication of the problems which simmer not below but very much on the surface.

SOUTH AFRICA

Cricket was played in the Cape a few years ahead of any recorded mention of the game in Australia – in 1808, a match was played between officers of the Artillery Mess and the Colony in Capetown.

Thereafter progress was relatively slow until the 1840s, when the game began to spread quickly, both Port Elizabeth and Maritzburg establishing teams. At first the game seems to have been organized according to social groupings, as was the case in India, although at this stage there was no segregation according to colour. Thus, in 1854, a match took place between the Hottentots and the Afrikaaners in the Cape which the Hottentots won. In 1860 the first match took place between Maritzburg and Durban in Natal and the following year cricket seems to have become established in the Transvaal. Two years later a fixture was established in Capetown between players from the Mother Country and Colonial-born cricketers, and for many years this was the most important fixture in that province.

There is evidence from Queenstown, in what is now Border Province, that by 1865 cricket had been played in which Kaffirs or Bantus had taken part. In the 1875-76 season a champion-bat competition was established in the Cape Colony which subsequently developed into the Currie Cup Competition, named after the man who presented the trophy, Sir Donald Currie, the shipowner and philanthropist. The first winners of the Currie Cup in the 1889-90 season were Transvaal. By then South Africa had already received a visit from an English team, captained by Charles Aubrey Smith, of Sussex and England; Bobby Abel of Surrey made 120 in the second representative match—the first first-class century to be hit in South Africa.

In April 1890 the South African Cricket Association, which was to become the governing body for White cricket in South Africa, was formed. In the first season of its jurisdiction a match between Transvaal and Griqualand West achieved considerable notoriety; it lasted for seven days during which time 1,402 runs were scored for the loss of 40 wickets. It is worth mentioning in passing here the practice of declaration, which has had a profound effect on the game. Purists still believe that declarations are foreign to the spirit of cricket, certainly in the first innings, and that if the option of declaration were abolished then games would be finished within the alloted time. Clearly there is much evidence from South Africa for and against this argument, for it was in Durban in 1938-39 that the historic timeless Test was played and eventually left unfinished after ten days as the England team left to catch the boat back.

In 1891 the first match was played in Rhodesia—a fixture between the Police and the Civilians in what was then called Fort Salisbury. In that same season a second tour by an English team visited South Africa under W. W. Read of Surrey. On that occasion Read's team met eighteen Malays; this remains the only occasion on which an England team has competed against non-Whites in South Africa, although non-White teams have left South Africa to play in, for example, East Africa.

In 1894 a South African team came to England for the first time, although the tour was not acknowledged as first-class. Even in these days there was a certain amount of controversy about the composition of the party, because Hendricks, their fast bowler, described as Coloured, had been omitted as a result of pressure on the selectors. In 1895-96, not only did a team from England under Lord Hawke visit South Africa, but a remarkable match took place in which eleven members of the Hofmeyr family played together at Stellenbosch. The Edrich family is not the only one to have given several generations of players to cricket—in the 1950s Murray Hofmeyr was a distinguished batsman for Oxford University and a fly-half of distinction for both Oxford and England in rugby football.

In 1897 the Barnato Trophy was presented for competition between Coloured teams, and the South African Coloured Cricket Board was established. Lord Hawke took the fourth England team to South Africa in 1898-89, and on this occasion they also visited Rhodesia. In 1900 a match was planned at Lord's between a South African team and the West Indies, but the fixture never took place because of the South African War. During the war a curious fixture took place in Colombo, Ceylon, between Boer prisoners-of-war and a mixed-race Ceylonese cricket club. As late as 1973 Hassan Howa, then leader of the Coloured cricketers in the Cape, took the view that it was easier for him to relate to those of Dutch descent than to those of English!

Australia first visited South Africa in 1902-03 under Darling, after their tour of England, and in 1904 a South African team came to England and would have played India at Lord's had India's tour not been cancelled. Neither South Africa nor India, of course, were recognized as Test match countries at that time. When MCC, captained by Plum Warner,

Below: Lee Irvine scored his maiden Test century on his 26th birthday during the fourth Test in Port Elizabeth against Australia in 1970

visited South Africa in 1905-06, they did play five Tests—South Africa won four and lost only one of them. At this time South African googly bowlers were beginning to make themselves a power in cricket. In recognition of the skill of these bowlers and their impact on batting, on South Africa's fourth tour of England three official Test matches were designated of which South Africa lost one and drew two. By sowing doubt in batsman's minds as to which direction the ball would take after bouncing, the googly bowlers effectively destroyed the charging drive so often seem in old photographs of the game. In 1909-10, MCC's second touring side under Shrimp Leveson-Gower was also beaten, this time by three matches to two. Vogler and Faulkner, two of the googly bowlers, took 65 wickets on the mat. In 1910-11 South Africa visited Australia where they won their first Test, the only one out of five. In the 1912 season in England there was a triangular tournament, the only one, involving South Africa, Australia and England. South Africa lost all three matches to England and two of the three they played against Australia. Pegler, another googly bowler, took 189 wickets on that tour.

In the season before the 1914-18 war, Johnny Douglas took MCC's third team to South Africa. It was by far the strongest so far and they won four out of five Tests. Sydney Barnes took 17 wickets in one of the matches, and overall on the tour 104 wickets, the first time any bowler had exceeded 100. Australia once again travelled from England to South Africa after their 1921 tour and won a three-match series played in November which was the first officially recognized between the two countries. In 1922-23 Frank Mann whose son George was to lead an MCC side in the 1940s, took the fourth tour to South Africa and won the five-match rubber two to one. The South Africans next came to England under Herbie Taylor and had the misfortune to be bowled out for 30 by Arthur Gilligan and Maurice Tate, who finished the job in 75 balls in one of the early Test matches at Edgbaston. By the 1926-27 season turf wickets instead of matting had become mandatory for all Currie Cup matches in South Africa. Domestic cricket was by now completely segregated, and in 1928 the first of the Bantu cricket unions was established.

In 1930-31 Percy Chapman took the sixth MCC team to South Africa, and this time the South Africans won the only match finished in the five-match series. After visiting Australia in 1931-32, South Africa's next engagement away from home was in England in 1935. This time they won their first Test victory in England, and by drawing the other four matches took a series for the first time. In 1947 the South Africans returned to England under Alan Melville; they brought with them two of the finest of their batsmen in Bruce Mitchell, who made 2,000 runs in the season, the only South African ever to do so, and Dudley Nourse. Unfortunately they encountered an England side that included Compton and Edrich in their prime, and which destroyed them in the only three matches finished, the other two being drawn. The following year, when George Mann took the eighth MCC team

Below: Graeme Pollock hits a four to the boundary off Gleeson. Brian Taber keeps wicket for Australia in Port Elizabeth in 1970

out, England again won the rubber by two matches to nil, with three drawn, the first by virtue of a leg-bye scored off Cliff Gladwin's hip. It was Gladwin who made famous the tail-enders' battle cry: 'Cometh the hour, cometh the man.'

In 1951 South Africa, under Dudley Nourse, were again beaten in England. When New Zealand first visited South Africa in 1953-54 under Geoff Rabone, South Africa had more success, winning four Tests with the fifth drawn. In 1955 Jack Cheetham brought the South Africans to England for the first time, and for once all five matches in the series were finished, South Africa going down narrowly by three matches to two. It was Cheetham who established the South African's reputation for brilliant fielding. In 1960 Jackie McGlew brought the last full South African tour to England. The tourists lost three of the five Tests while the other two were drawn. Politically the omens were not propitious, and when South Africa left the Imperial Cricket Conference on becoming a Republic the threat that her cricketers would become outcasts was plain to see, most of all for English cricketers who had been there with MCC or as coaches to the white South African schools, whence came a stream of superb young players.

In 1963-64 the South Africans were developing into a magnificent cricket side under Trevor Goddard's captaincy, and for the second time they drew a series in Australia with Barlow and the Pollock brothers leading the team to records. But in the following season M. J. K. Smith's MCC team won the only Test match finished in South Africa; however, in the next English summer, under Peter van der Merwe's captaincy, South Africa won a three-match series in a divided England summer by taking the one match finished. Once again this team showed what a wealth of talent there was in South African cricket by trouncing the Australians for the first time when Bobby Simpson took his side there in the 1966-67 season. Denis Lindsay, who would have overtaken John Waite's figures as a Test wicket-keeper-batsman had his career run its full course, scored a record 606 runs in the series.

The year 1968 was the fateful one for the future of South African Test cricket against England. It was ominous that Colin Bland, a Rhodesian cricketer, was refused entry because his country had declared its independence. Throughout the previous summer there had been a strong probability that Basil d'Oliveira, a coloured South African, would be a key member of the England team to tour the land of his birth. However, the England selectors, who were at their collective worst, dropped him after the first Test against Australia and ignored him until the final Test. In this match d'Oliveira scored the century and took the crucial wicket that enabled England to scramble a draw in a series that should have been won easily. The night after that victory the party to tour South Africa was named—without d'Oliveira. It looked to all the world as if South African pressure, actual or imagined, had prompted the decision to drop him as had been the case with Duleepsinhji more than thirty years before. Subsequently Tom Cartwright withdrew from the party through injury and d'Oliveira was nominated as his replacement. The South African government announced that the party would not be welcome with d'Oliveira as a member and the tour was cancelled. Had the England selectors chosen d'Oliveira in the first instance on merit, as they unquestionably should have done, then there is no knowing what might have happened. On the evening of the announcement, before going on BBC radio to give my views, I rang up Billy Griffith, then Secretary of M.C.C. and a great personal friend, and told him with the utmost

sadness that I was going to criticize unmercifully the selectors for what had happened—I can recall telling him then that it was the end of South Africa as a cricketing nation. Ten years later there is no reason to change that assessment and with hindsight I put the blame fairly and squarely on the England selectors who cravenly allowed themselves to be diverted from the proper course of action by a whole series of suggestions from politicians and diplomats instead of treating the affair first and foremost as a cricketing matter. If they had done this, and if South Africa had then declined to admit an English team with d'Oliveira as a member, there would have been no possible doubt as to where the blame lay, and without question much subsequent agony would have been avoided.

The Australians continued to maintain relations with South Africa for a few years, and a team under Bill Lawry visited in the 1969-70 season after a long and exhausting tour of India, where they were trounced four Tests to nil, the first time Australia had ever lost so heavily on tour. That season Barry Richards and Mike Procter represented a marvellous influx of young talent in a very strong side. Tragically, no further Test matches involving South Africa have ever been played so that these players could establish their true places in the hall of fame.

A tour of England planned for 1970 was abandoned nine days before it was scheduled to leave because of a political campaign mounted by Peter Hain then of the Young Liberals. James Callaghan, then Home Secretary, advised MCC to call off the tour because he could not guarantee the maintenance of law and order. It was the only decision possible in the circumstances, and resulted in the England series against the Rest of the World about which statisticians have been arguing ever since—were they or were they not Test matches?

A number of South African cricketers, notably Dr Ali Bacher, the last Test captain, have done their courageous best to bring about a reform in the system under which cricket is played in South Africa in order to conform with the International Cricket Conference's ruling that no further Test matches can be contemplated until there is multi-racial cricket at club level in South Africa. Along the broken way a number of other people have been prepared to act in a valiant fashion, notably Derek Robins, who took a number of sides containing black players like John Shepherd of the West Indies and Younis Ahmed, Surrey's Pakistani batsman, to South Africa. Having watched some of these contests it is obvious that the South Africans feel that much progress has been made towards integrating cricket in their country. Nonetheless, there has been little of the social contact which is such a normal part of cricket in other parts of the world, and it is this deep-seated malaise which has to be cured before the situation will be righted. Now that so many politicians have become involved in the issue, particularly in the Indian sub-continent and the West Indies, there seems to be no hope that South Africa can ever again be admitted to the International Cricket Conference, no matter how the country conducts itself in the future.

The pendulum has swung across to a position of absurdity equal to that which prevailed when cricket was organized on a strictly racial basis. The people who suffer are the South African cricketers themselves, because they are deprived of Test cricket. Of all the players in the world they at least have every justification for seeking to join a cricket organization such as World Series Cricket. Only in this way can they evaluate their own abilities against the best cricket players in the rest of the world.

WEST INDIES

England, Spain, Britain and France had fought through the Caribbean string of pearls since the days of good Queen Bess, and it was not until the final exile of Napoleon that territorial ownership was finally settled.

Barbados is one of the few islands in the West Indies which has known only English as its language. Cricket was being played at St Anne's Club on the island during the Napoleonic wars, and the planters and garrison schools, such as Codrington College, named after the great admiral of the South American independence campaign, or St George's in Kingston in Jamaica, already included cricket in their curriculum. A club existed in Trinidad before Alfred Mynn and Felix contested the last of their great single-wicket matches. In the 1850s the founding of the Vere Club in Kingston and the Georgetown Club in Guyana spread cricket even further through the old British dependencies.

In the next decade competition between the territories began. In 1865, Guyana played on the Garrison Savannah in Bridgetown and on the parade-ground in Georgetown—what the wickets were like, history does not reveal. Four years later Trinidad played in Guyana. In 1880, the Kingston Club first took possession of Sabina Park, and four years later the Bourda ground in Georgetown was first occupied.

Soon West Indian cricketers were ready to take ship, and in 1886 they played thirteen matches in Canada and the United States. In the following year the United States team returned the visit and beat the West Indies in the one representative match. In 1891 Trinidad and Guyana teams gathered in Barbados where they played a triangular tournament on the Wanderer's ground; this was won by the home side. Two years later a cup was presented for these matches and a tradition established that all games should be played to a finish, which usually entailed five days or more.

In 1895 the first team from England toured under the captaincy of R. Slade-Lucas, who shared in the first opening partnership of 100 in those parts, and also saw one of his bowlers, H. R. Bromley Davenport, complete the first first-class hat-trick in Guyana.

1897 was a vintage year for West Indian cricket. Not only did they receive a visit from Lord Hawke, but also from a second team under A. Priestley. It was in that year too that H. B. G. Austin entered the record books by featuring in a partnership of 263 for the second wicket for Barbados against Trinidad —a huge score in those days.

Sir Pelham Warner played in one match for the first West Indian side to come to England in 1900 under the captaincy of his cousin R. S. A. Warner, sharing in the first double-century partnership for the West Indies, against Leicestershire. Two years later the West Indies won two of the three matches played against R. A. Bennett's eleven, and in 1906 H. B. G. Austin brought to England the first team from the Caribbean considered worthy of first-class status. MCC's teams visited the islands in 1911 and again in 1913 under A. W. F. Somerset, and on both occasions the party was successful, winning two of the three big matches.

Already, exciting things were happening in West Indian cricket. A tie was played in Jamaica featuring P. H. Tarilton, who with Austin and G. M. Challenor were the outstanding batsman in Barbados, in which both tenth-wicket pairs added 100 to the score, surely still a unique statistical curiosity. Tarilton was to become, in 1920, the first West Indian to score a double century in a first-class match. Three years later Austin brought the third West Indies team to England and Challenor (known as Lord Runscome in his own island) made a very stylish 1,000 runs during the course of the tour. Of the twenty-six games played the visitors won twelve. The side contained the first famous West Indian fast-bowling partnership; the two Georges, Francis and John, and the young Learie Constantine, whose father had already established his family's name in cricket, C. R. Browne, nicknamed Snuffy, took 91 wickets. I saw him play myself in the 1950s and can visualize him still: dark skin, kind countenance, interested eyes, and hair of the purest white.

The next MCC contingent, the strongest so far, came under the captaincy of F. S. G. Calthorpe, the honourable Freddie, captain of Warwickshire. Among the young members was Leonard Crawley, a superb striker of both golf and cricket ball, a man who, as a very senior golf correspondent, tried to teach me about life in Fleet Street. There were professionals in this party too,—Percy Holmes, for instance; but although there had been professionals in the West Indies (one of whom, F. Heinz, had taken all ten wickets in a Trinidad club match) they were not allowed to play in what were then called colony matches. The strength of Freddie Calthorpe's team, and the beating it received, can now be seen as the prelude to recognition for the West Indies in international cricket.

In June 1927, the West Indies Board of Control was formed with H. B. G. Austin as the first president.

Above: Lance Gibbs, the most devastating fast bowler of his era, broke Fred Trueman's Test wicket record. Inset: Wicket keeper John Hendriks catches Doug Walters, at 242, in 1959

The following summer, the first official West Indian Test tour was scheduled. It would have been a fitting reward for the father of West Indian cricket if he had captained the side. At first Challenor accepted, but now aged thirty-nine he subsequently thought better of it, and so Carl Nunes from Jamaica led the team. fiftieth anniversary celebration of Test cricket, was found to be suffering at the ripe old age of eighty-five from, of all things, Athlete's Foot) was also in the side. Much depended on seniority in those days. Griffith would have been a more fearsome proposition five years earlier in 1923, but being junior to the two Georges he had to wait until he was thirty-one before he made his first trip abroad. Griffith was one of the very few on that team to keep his reputation intact, because it was not a success—all three Tests were lost by an innings, and only five of the thirty matches won. Herman Griffith still refers to his captain in those days as Mr Austin, and talks of him as a disciplinarian with no doubts as to how the game should be played. 'Did you bowl bouncers?' I asked the old man recently, to which the reply was, 'If I bowled short on purpose, Mr Austin would have taken me off. When a batsman was set, I used to have a man down there'—pointing to deep extra cover at the Kensington Oval—'to save boundaries. Not that I minded; what's the sense in saying to yourself, "This man can play, therefore I must knock him down"?—that's not cricket.' The pity of it all was that the West Indies felt that they had let themselves down, but perhaps the explanation for their failure is to be found in the improved ability of the England side rather than in the poor collective and individual performances of the West Indians (Constantine averaged only 15, and took a mere 5 wickets). In 1923, the post-war generation of England cricketers had not yet flowered, but by 1928 it was in full bloom. Griffith took the wickets of Tyldesley, Hammond, Leyland, Hendren and Chapman in an hour at The Oval, but while only 44 were scored to give his team their one chance, England were still strong enough to make 438; this gave them a lead of 200, and in the third and final innings of the match the West Indies were all out for

129.

The next MCC team to play the West Indies, again under Freddie Calthorpe, was not much stronger than the 1926 vintage. There had been a tour of Australia and New Zealand in the same year, and many of the top players took a winter's rest after retaining the Ashes under Percy Chapman. As a result the team included Wilfred Rhodes (52), George Gunn (50) and Patsy Hendren (40). Two of the younger players were Bill Voce and Les Ames, at 20 and 24 respectively. The organization of the tour from the West Indian point of view was as haphazard as the selection of their players, some of whom could not get time off from work, Constantine among them. As a result no fewer than twenty-eight men were called upon for the Test matches. But even stranger was the fact that each centre picked its own captain and its own eleven; the Board of Control's authority stretched nowhere at all, it seemed. A pity, because the autonomy of the four centres, so obvious in this first home series, has remained a tradition which has not been entirely helpful to West Indian cricket. The series was drawn once again. The last match was to have been the decider and should have been played to a finish in Jamaica, where the pitch had been made to last. England made no fewer than 849, of which Andrew Sandham hit 325 and Les Ames 149. Instead of enforcing the follow-on, England batted again, whereupon George Headley scored a double century, hoping to bat until the rains came. On the ninth day it poured with rain and it continued to do so for two more days, whereupon the England team were given permission to leave their business unfinished and took ship for home. Thus was the precedent set for England's departure from Durban in early 1939. There has never been a timeless Test since.

One good result of the West Indies' skilful if unsuccessful exhibition in 1928 was an invitation to visit Australia in the 1930-31 season. C. G. McCartney, the famous Australian batsman of the early 1920s, saw them in action in England on a good day and encouraged the visit. Expecting fast wickets, the West Indians selected all their fast bowlers. Instead, the Australians took them to pieces on slow wickets on which Clarrie Grimmett, one of the oldest and baldest beginners in Test cricket, took 33 wickets with wrist-spin. The West Indian fast bowlers were magnificent, especially when, for the final Test, Monty Noble, the real administrator of Australian cricket, alive to taunts that the Australians had doctored the pitches, ensured that the West Indians were able to play on a fast wicket for the first time. The Australians had no quick bowler in their own side and the West Indians won the match, their fast bowlers taking 12 wickets. Only Alan Fairfax made 50, although he did so in both innings. Constantine was the baby of the three fast bowlers at 28, the age at which most fast bowlers are reckoned to be over the hill. George Francis was 33 and Herman Griffith, who bowled Bradman for a duck in the last innings of the tour with 'one I held back a bit', was then 37. Test cricket never saw these men at their best; Griffith, for example, claims he was at his quickest a whole decade before he bowled Bradman. But it is not age or technique that constitute the greatest difference between the old-timers and the modern timber. Griffith stands at 5ft 7ins, George Francis and George John were men of medium height, and so were Manny Martindale and Learie Constantine. Sir Learie, as he later was, would have been obliged to raise his eyes to gaze up at Joel Garner, a full foot taller than himself. The effect of height on speed and length is as yet an inexact science, but common sense indicates how devastating will be the change in the angle of bounce of the short ball when delivered by a giant as opposed to somebody below average height.

Nor were Herman Griffith's days with the West Indies on tour yet over. He was 39 when he came to England in 1933. Manny Martindale was also selected for this team at the age of 23, but Constantine was now 30 and playing as a professional in the Lancashire league, and the Board could not secure his release for all matches. Freddie Martin, the counterbalance to Connie's bounce, trod on a ball in the Middlesex match at Lord's, twisted his ankle and missed all the Tests. The two Tests that were finished were lost by an innings and the third was drawn. This last was an interesting match, the only time bodyline was ever seen in England. Both sides used it, but whereas Nobby Clark, the Northamptonshire left-hander, was a less able practitioner than the combination of Larwood and Voce had been in Australia, Constantine and Martindale knocked the England batsmen about considerably. Hammond was hit on the chin, and when he returned from hospital was caught in the leg trap. The one player quite unmoved by it all was Douglas Jardine, a man possessed of a remarkable and unusual cricket brain. As for the West Indies, the 1934 edition of Wisden stated: 'Not suited temperamentally for matches of such an important nature.' These words were to backfire before the next issue appeared, however, for by then the West Indians had won their first series against England, a two-one victory in a four-match programme in 1934-35. For this series they had the benefit of a settled team under Jackie Grant, who was later to do missionary work in Rhodesia for nigh on forty years. The West Indies won despite losing the first match in Barbados, a Test classic played on a wet wicket. There were two declarations, and yet three of the four innings totalled less than 100 runs. In these days of heavy covering such games can never be staged, to cricket's great loss in my judgment. Only George Headley was able to cope with these devilish pitches, and in the first innings he was run out batting with number nine, having made 44 out of 102. By the close England were 81 for 5. Play began after tea on the second day and two more wickets fell without a run being scored, so Wyatt declared. That night West Indies reversed their batting order and were 4 for 3, although they recovered to make 33 by the close. Rain again delayed the start the next day; this time the West Indies lost 3 wickets for 18 and declared, setting England a target of 73 for victory. Ken Farnes and big Jim Smith, the fast bowlers, were sent in to open, but they and four others were back in the pavilion for 48. Patsy Hendren, a month short of 46, made a precious 20, and Wally Hammond finished the match with a six off Martindale.

For some reason Wyatt reversed his batting order in the second innings of the second match, in very different circumstances on the mat in Trinidad, when England were chasing 325. England batted badly throughout this game, but particularly in this upside-down innings in which they made only 107. They lost the match easily, and when they reached Jamaica they lost again, this time by an innings. George Headley, in front of his own crowd, made 270. The Australians had forced him to change his batting style by bowling at his legs, and whereas previously he had been a great off-side player he had now established himself as one of the finest on-side players in the game. He was almost impossible to bowl at in this match, and the West Indies hit 535 in all.

West Indies were not engaged again until 1939, when they came to England; Headley made a century in both innings of the first Test at Lord's, although England still won by eight wickets in three days. Len Hutton made 196 and the young Denis Compton, blooded against Australia the year before, hit 120 in 2 hours and 20 minutes at the age of 21. The other two matches were drawn, and the tour ended on the very verge of the Second World War. Some matches in fact were cancelled; Sussex lost their fixture, although a cable went out from Brighton declaring: 'Essential to play match tomorrow, keep the flag flying.' Had the West Indians waited to play they might have been torpedoed on the *Athenia* on the night of 2/3 September, before war had even been declared. As it was, they returned home via Montreal.

By the winter of 1947-48, when England next visited the Caribbean, the West Indian team was immensely strong; they had continued to play island matches during the War, and by now the three 'Ws', Walcott, Weekes and Worrell, perhaps the most famous trio of batsmen in all cricketing history, were in full swing. The West Indians were eager for more success. Jeff Stollmeyer and Gerry Gomez had survived the long wait after 1939, and Cyril Christiani had sadly died of malaria, but Robert, his brother from Guyana, was also in the team, and so were Alan Rae and J. K. Holt from Jamaica, both sons of famous cricketing fathers. Faced with such talent, but not comprehending it, England chose this moment to take a party without Hutton, Washbrook, Edrich and Compton, the first four in the normal batting order; they also left behind Alec Bedser and Doug Wright, the one unquestionably the best bowler in England, and the other alleged to be the most difficult to play on fast wickets. 'Gubby' Allen, then aged 45, led the side, which should have been managed by the staff of St Mary's and St Thomas's hospitals, so long was the list of injured. Eventually Len Hutton arrived as a replacement, a vital move as it turned out. By no means the least amazing feat by the West Indians was that of 'Foffie' Williams, who hit his first six balls in Test cricket for 6, 6, 4, 4, 4 and 4. The Trinidad match also contained some bizarre events. Billy Griffith, one of the few fit men left, was chosen to open the innings for no better reason than that he was the first man through the dressing-room doorway after net practice—on such decisions is history made! Griffith had never batted first before in a first-class match and never played in a Test, but he nevertheless hit his maiden century. Andy Ganteaume, later to become manager of the West Indies team in 1973-74, also hit a century in what turned out to be his one and only Test innings, a personal tragedy, but so strong was the competition for places in the West Indian side that there was simply no appropriate place for him. Despite all this, England were not beaten until the third Test, although they lost again in the fourth at Kingston where Everton Weekes was booed when he came on instead of J. K. Holt, the local favourite—that is until he made 141 with 15 fours, when he was cheered all the way back to the pavilion.

West Indian cricket now ventured into India, the first team to visit that country after independence. In those days it was a rough trip, involving long journeys and without the ease and gracious living offered by the Indian princes. Frank Worrell did not go along although the Indians had specifically asked for him to come. By now he was a professional and was hardly to be tempted by £3 15s. a week to

Right: West Indian fielders crouched and poised in attack. Gary Sobers, perhaps cricket's greatest ever all-rounder, is in the centre

cover his out-of-pocket expenses, although this was a big advance on the thirty shillings a week Herman Griffith and others received for their first overseas trip twenty years before. Everton Weekes had a run of four Test centuries on this tour, but not until the fourth Test at Madras was there a result, when the Indians collapsed. In the final game the Indians needed 6 to win off the last ball, but the last ball was never bowled because the umpire pulled up the stumps and called time. He had miscounted.

As the brains of West Indian cricket began to plan for the historic 1950 tour of England with the quiet determination and dedication so typical of the last generation of white West Indian leadership, John Goddard and Jeff Stollmeyer, captain and vice-captain, were faced with some ageing and none too reliable fast bowlers among the candidates. The ones they selected were Hines Johnson, then in his fortieth year, Prior Jones, aged 33, and Lance Pierre, the guitar player, aged 29. Of the spinners, Wilfred Ferguson was the best leg-spinner available, a likeable man whose physical features were not his greatest asset—to such an extent that his team-mates joked that they would fetch Fergy to frighten any children who misbehaved. Rightly the two West Indian strategists figured that wrist-spinning was not the answer to the conditions they would encounter, so they chose two untried finger-spinners. As the calypso later put it: 'Those two little pals of mine, Ramadhin and Valentine.' Comparisons in cricket are pointless but it seems to me to be safe to affirm that never in the history of Test cricket has a pair of spin bowlers so dominated a series. Usually spin bowlers are relatively old in their prime, the opposite of the fast men, but Ram and Val both celebrated their twentieth birthdays within three days of the start of that tour. Snow stopped play in the opening match at Eastbourne. In the first Test at Old Trafford, England's lucky ground, England were 88 for 5. Valentine had taken all the wickets. Trevor Bailey, batting with Godfrey Evans, a player less at home against speed than spin, now saved England. Bailey batted through for 82 not out whilst Evans hit his first century in first-class cricket at a crucially important moment. Valentine's 8 for 104 in the innings were the best ever figures for a bowler in his first Test. By their own high standards the West Indian batting failed twice, and England scored almost as many runs the second time around. West Indies thought little of the pitch, which had helped the spinners from the start. Nevertheless, they came to Lord's determined to square the series, and they did so in what has become known as the Calypso Test, their first win in England.

England were troubled with injuries, among them Compton and Bailey, and they picked the wrong team—all three spinners wanted to bowl from the Nursery End. Alan Rae scored a century in the first innings and Clyde Walcott did so in the second. Ramadhin, in his finest hour, took 11 wickets in the match and Valentine 7. At Trent Bridge, it was Worrell and Weekes who destroyed the England bowlers; Worrell made 261 and Weekes scored a century. England's batting failed and West Indies took a firm lead in the series, with only The Oval Test to come. Hutton made 204 of England's 447 runs in that match, 202 of them being scored in the first innings on a rain-affected wicket. It was an innings which greatly impressed the young Cowdrey, watching his first Test. All out for 103 at the second attempt, England went down by an innings. This time the spin twins took 14 wickets, and John Goddard, no great cricketer but as tough as a coconut shell, took 5 of the remaining 6. Compton was run out as non-striker at the bowler's end.

This was the series which catapaulted the West Indians above the South Africans and England in world cricket ratings making them second only to Australia. It also changed the whole character of West Indian cricket. From now on the West Indies players were constantly striving for the crock of gold which they saw men like Hutton collecting. (This was Hutton's benefit year and he raised £10,000. Bradman, too, had received that sort of money for his testimonial in Australia.) Furthermore, it became important to keep the West Indian cricketers playing winter and summer. From 1928-50 they had played only nine Test series, seven involving England, one in Australia, and one in India. But since the epic victory of 1950 they have played no fewer than thirty-four series in twenty-eight years, although some of the tours have been appendages (New Zealand on an Australian trip, Pakistan at the end of a visit to India) and some have been three-Test tours. The fact remains that there have been few winters where there has not been either a tour to or by the West Indies. Furthermore, because cricket in the West Indies is not rich enough to sustain top cricketers, the country has emerged as a major cricket exporter, with the rest of the world happy to buy because of the excellence of the product.

Before they had finished with England in 1950, the Australians invited the West Indies again. Wise heads advised caution. Tony Cozier's father, Jimmy Cozier, now the grand old man of Caribbean journalism, tried to persuade the West Indian Board to play host to the Australians before they visited that country. In the event, Australia won 4-1 at home as they had done twenty-one years before. The West Indians had no fast bowling to counter

Lindwall and Miller, then at their peak, and their batting fell to pieces. Valentine took more wickets than anyone (24) but the Australians, notably Miller and Lindwall, so chased Ramadhin and got on top of the little man that he was never again able to dominate a series. The West Indies played only one first-class match before the first Test, a crazy piece of programming, and they were two Tests down when they came to Adelaide, where the wicket was wet. Frank Worrell and John Goddard bowled Australia out for 82 but that glorious left-handed bowler Bill Johnston, as graceful in his way as Frank Worrell himself, took 6 wickets, leaving the West Indians with only a tiny lead. Australia batted their tail-enders first and Doug Ring, the big Victorian leg-spinner, made the top score of 67. The West Indies began attacking their winning target of 233 on Christmas Eve and duly reached it on Christmas Day, with Gomez and Christiani at the crease. What a Christmas present that was—a first victory in Australia! But a thrilling match was lost at Melbourne, where Ring and Johnston, batting last, made the 38 runs needed to win while the West Indians got into more and more of a muddle until, according to Gerry Gomez, they were running around like chickens without their heads. One of the problems was where to place the field on the huge Melbourne ground in which Ring kept lobbing the ball over the fielders' heads.

The West Indians lost the fifth match too, but went on to win at Christchurch in New Zealand by five wickets on their first visit there, which was some consolation, particularly as they also drew the second Test.

Now it was India's turn to visit the Caribbean. They too were pioneers, because only English teams had made the trip previously, not counting tours by teams from America at the turn of the century. Just as the West Indians had arrived in England to be greeted and lauded by the local West Indian community, so the Indians found huge support in both Trinidad and Guyana, where many of their own people were working as contract labourers in the sugar estates. Of the five matches played, only the Test in Barbados was finished, and that the West Indians won. One Indian who made a great impression and on whom a lasting impact was made by the tour was the leg-spinner Subhash Gupte, still regarded by many as the greatest of all time, who took 27 wickets and married a West Indian girl. Valentine topped this total by taking 28 wickets, but the Indians, so badly beaten in England in 1952, were prepared to settle for drawn matches all the way through the series. Ramadhin took 5 for 26 in the crucial innings at the Kensington Oval, but by the end of the tour he had been dropped from the side.

The next visitors were England, who were intent on avenging their defeat of 1950. For the first time Hutton captained as strong a side as the selectors could muster. To the West Indian way of thinking, this team behaved poorly both on and off the field. They frequently challenged the umpires' decisions, and Len Hutton ignored the Jamaican Prime Minister, Mr Bustamente, as that gentleman foolishly sought to congratulate the batsman as he was coming back up the pavilion steps after scoring an exhausting but match-winning double century in the last Test. Undoubtedly the tour party had set off in fine spirits, thinking that they were off for a prolonged party in the sunshine. Possibly Len Hutton had an inkling of what was in store, but he had never been the most communicative of people. But by the time England found themselves two matches down, the team, young by English standards at least, had lost all their illusions. Ever since, the West Indies tour has been recognized for what it is—tough, hard cricket.

England won the match at Georgetown, but not before Hutton had made his famous decision to stay on the field despite a shower of bottles which rained down after the local wicketkeeper, Clifford McWatt, known to the English as McCatt because he had nine lives, was given run out to end a stand, heavily backed as an eventual century stand by the punters, on a score of 99.

At Port of Spain, the three 'W's' had their finest match together as West Indies made 681—Weekes 206, Worrell 167 and Walcott 124. This was the last match on the mat at Queen's Park, and it was drawn as so many others had been on this surface. Since then Trinidad Tests have been the most likely of all to be finished, mostly on turning wickets.

Next to arrive in the islands were the Australians, in 1955; they enjoyed a much easier passage than England. Again the combination of Miller and Lindwall was lethal and the Australians, still an impressively powerful team, were once again on top of the West Indians with the bat as well as the ball. They won the first Test when Miller and Harvey hit 100s, drew the second largely because Walcott hit his second and third 100's in four visits to the crease, and won in Georgetown to go two ahead with two to play. The Bridgetown Test was drawn. Dennis Atkinson taking 5 wickets in an innings and making a double century, an astonishing double. Keith Miller took 6 for 107 in the fifth match in Kingston, and then scored 100 to equal the performance of four others—Harvey, who made 204, Archer, McDonald and Benaud.

Walcott hit a century in each innings for West Indies but found himself nonetheless a member of a team which lost by an innings, an extraordinary result if ever there was one. Ten years were to pass before the West Indies were eventually able to topple Australia.

The West Indies next played a four-match rubber in New Zealand, the first since England took a side of less than full strength there in 1929-30; they won the first three matches and lost the fourth. After this pleasant but untesting interlude, the West Indies' next engagement was in England. By the summer of 1957, England's first post-war cricketing generation were in their prime, while the West Indies found themselves sadly lacking. Goddard was captain instead of Atkinson, who had led in New Zealand. What sealed the West Indies' fate was the failure of Ramadhin and Valentine to finish England off when they took a first-innings lead of 288 at Edgbaston in the first Test. England had lost 3 wickets for 113 early on the fourth morning and were, to all intents and purposes, sunk, but May and Cowdrey, the fourth-wicket pair, batted until after lunch the following day, the last, and made no fewer than 411. Goddard claims that the stand survived 100 appeals. Ramadhin bowled 98 overs in the innings, the most ever recorded in Test cricket. West Indies lost 7 wickets for 72 in the final innings, and after this reversal, the party lost heart. At Lord's the match was lost by an innings, and although fine batting by Worrell and Smith saved the game at Trent Bridge, thereafter the tour followed a downwards progression, as has so often been the case when the West Indies have been worsted in a series.

There followed the first visit by Pakistan to the West Indies which was notable for two of the highest Test innings ever played. At Bridgetown Hanif Mohammad batted 16 hours and 10 minutes for 337 in the first match of the series, the only one left drawn, and then Sobers beat Hutton's 1938 record of 364 by reaching a massive 365 not out in the third match at Sabina Park. The astonishing feature of this innings was that it was his first Test century, scored against a Pakistan team which could field only two fit bowlers. Three down and much afflicted by injury, the Pakistanis won the final Test by an innings and one run, whereupon they returned home to prepare for a visit by the West Indies in the 1958-59 season. This long trip started in India, without the three 'W's, and it finished without Gilchrist, one of the fastest West Indian bowlers of all time and also one of the more unruly. His use of the beamer, a ball universally outlawed by cricketers themselves, led to his being sent home by Gerry Alexander the captain, who as wicketkeeper was in a good position to judge whether or not such deliveries were bowled with murder in the man's eyes. West Indies won the second, third and fourth Tests against India; the other two were left drawn. In Pakistan it was a different story. The matches were low-scoring, and although Wes Hall made a big impact on Test cricket for the first time, West Indies lost matches at Karachi and Dacca before they won at Lahore, where Rohan Kanhai hit his second double century of the tour.

In the following season, England visited the isles once again. The memory of 1957 was still acutely painful, but England had been beaten just as badly in Australia as ever the West Indies had been, and with new players out of bud and into flower hopes were high in the Caribbean, though tinged with tragedy—Collie Smith had been killed in a car crash while travelling with other West Indian cricketers from Manchester to London.

Left: Gary Sobers in one of his last Test appearances in England at Edgbaston in 1973

In the first match at Bridgetown the century-makers for England were Ken Barrington and Ted Dexter, and for the West Indies Gary Sobers and Frank Worrell. Anyone doubting the variety, the all-consuming grandeur and the grace and power of cricket, would surely have been converted if they had watched the five days of this match. In the second Test at Port of Spain, West Indies were bowled out for 112 and 244 and lost by a large margin. As Trueman and Statham reached the end of their deadly fast-bowling mission, bottles rained on to the field and play was abandoned for seventy-five minutes. There was no excuse for such behaviour (there never is) and Eric Williams, the island's Prime Minister, sent cables of apology to all concerned. The next two matches were drawn, and England also drew the last match. May had returned home leaving Cowdrey as captain for the last two Tests.

Before their next engagement in Australia the West Indies underwent a change in leadership, and Frank Worrell became captain. Now 36, Worrell had lived in England for many years, and having overcome a drink problem had grown into a man of considerable stature. He was also very much a man of his time—the first black man to captain the West Indies on tour, an appointment he won through ability alone and which won him in return the undying respect of his colleagues. The first match, the greatest Test match of all time, took place at Brisbane. Australia led after the first innings and West Indies had to bat well to survive against Davidson at the second attempt. In the end the target Australia were set was 233, at under a minute a run. Hall took four of the first five wickets and Worrell himself the fifth for only 57 runs, but Mackay and Davidson pulled Australia through to 92 for 6, whereupon Davidson and Miller, going for their shots, put together a century partnership before Davidson was run out by a direct hit from Solomon. 6 runs were needed off the last eight-ball over with 3 wickets in hand. First ball, leg bye. Second, Benaud caught off a bouncer, bowled it is said against the captain's orders. Nothing. A bye—four balls gone. Grout skied the fifth and Hall dropped it. Another run. Meckiff hit the sixth to leg for runs: one, two, and then on the third Hunte's throw to the top of the stumps found Grout diving in vain for home. Ball number seven—Lindsay Kline made contact and ran as pre-arranged, but Solomon came in from square leg and threw down the stumps at the keeper's end with Meckiff run out. A tie, a unique Test match result.

Australia won the second match by seven wickets. At Sydney, in the third game, the West Indies batted first on a spinner's pitch, whereupon Valentine and

Right: Port-of-Spain, Trinidad, has one of the most breathtaking settings of any ground in the world

Lance Gibbs, who was selected in preference to Ramadhin, took 8 wickets each, the Australians failing to reach 250 in either innings. Rohan Kanhai made a century in each knock at Adelaide, and Worrell and Alexander made half-centuries in both innings. Gibbs took a hat-trick (Mackay, Grout and Misson to finish the first innings), but Mackay and Kline held out for a draw at the end, batting over an hour together. There was a lot of controversy about the final stages of this match. Frank Worrell believed that West Indies were cheated of victory, not so much by bad umpiring, but by the attitude of the players. Alexander was deliberately impeded when going for a catch, and Mackay clearly caught by Sobers off Worrell's bowling. In usual circumstances, no batsman will stay for a catch made before his very eyes. Even so, with the new ball, the West Indies had an opportunity to finish the game. They failed, and the effect on the team's morale was such that even Worrell could not lift his players to their natural attacking game once more. So the final Test, the decider, was laboured through in a totally different atmosphere. Bobby Simpson got on top of Hall in the first innings; Australia always had the winning of the match, and came home by two wickets. The West Indies left Melbourne to a ticker-tape farewell, an unprecedented tribute to a visiting cricket team, and the Australian board presented a Frank Worrell trophy to be competed for henceforth.

After the dramas of this tour, the West Indies began to prepare for a visit by India, again under Worrell's captaincy. To say that the team was welded into a unit by this great man is an understatement: there were no splinter groups, no back-biting jealousy, but rather a harmonious whole dedicated to victory. All five matches against India were won—the first time in the history of West Indian cricket. In Barbados, Nari Contractor, the Indian captain, was almost killed by a bouncer from Charlie Griffith and never played again, and Pataudi, at 21 had to take over the side. The fast bowlers, Hall, Chester Watson, Griffith and Lester King, were too powerful for the Indians.

Despite a bad knee, Worrell had one more ambition to fulfil—victory in England. It was the year of the Wisden centenary, and to celebrate a trophy was provided by the publishers. Worrell and his men carried it off by three victories to one. This was a perfect side—Conrad Hunte had developed into a fine opener, and behind him came Kanhai, Basil Butcher, and Sobers at his peak, with Worrell batting as a grand old man should at number six. Hall and Griffith were a formidable pair, Sobers was three bowlers in one, Gibbs was to become the highest wicket-taker in the world, and Deryck Murray, at 20, started a career which was to outlast all the others. The West Indies took the lead at Old Trafford; Gibbs took 11 wickets on the ground on which Laker had taken 19 in 1956. The match at Lord's was an epic draw which neither side deserved to lose, and England won at Edgbaston, where the West Indies succumbed to Trueman, who took 12 wickets in the match, bowling the West Indies out for 91 in the second innings. Charlie Griffith came into his own at Headingley and The Oval, taking 6 wickets in an innings on both grounds, and with Colin Cowdrey out of action with a left arm broken at Lord's by Hall, England's batting could not manage 300. It was in this year that the shared-tour idea was born. Quite apart from being good for West Indian cricket, the tour had proved good for cricket business as a whole, the gates swollen by thousands of West Indians. When, therefore, the West Indian Cricket Board put forward the idea of the split summer it was welcomed as an initiative that would prevent such long gaps between the arrival of touring sides in England, and would help to sustain the interest of the public throughout the season.

In historical terms, there were still two more rivers for West Indies to cross—two more rubbers to be won against Australia, both home and away. The home leg proved to be the easier one. The team Worrell handed to Sobers was better than the one Benaud passed on to Simpson. The latter was especially weak in bowling, whereas Sobers had considerable talent at his disposal: Hall and Griffith were in their prime, and so was Gibbs. West Indies went two up in three matches; the third match at Port of Spain, a high-scoring affair in which only three innings were completed, was drawn, and the fourth at Bridgetown saw 1,640 runs scored. Lawry, Simpson (the first openers ever to achieve this feat together) and Nurse all scored double centuries. In the final match, also at Port of Spain, Australia won by ten wickets in three days. The series was marred by a charge of throwing laid against Charlie Griffith.

The West Indians returned to England in 1966 and again won the series, this time under Sobers, by three matches to one. This had been no new Everest to climb, but the journey to the top once again greatly excited the crowds. The match at Old Trafford was won by an innings, the Lord's game left drawn, with further victories at Trent Bridge and Headingley before England won by an innings at The Oval. This tour saw Sobers in his prime. He hit three centuries and a 90 and averaged 103.14, as well as taking 20 wickets. To cap it all, he won the toss before all five matches. What more could a

captain do?

West Indies next undertook a short tour of India during December 1966 and January 1967. Sobers made runs in almost every innings and took wickets too, and the West Indies won two of the three matches with plenty to spare, although the side was beginning to lose the strength of purpose it had derived originally from Frank Worrell. The latter was now Sir Frank Worrell, and by good fortune happened to be in Calcutta, able to calm the atmosphere when the crowd rioted over the issue of thousands of forged tickets.

The next series, at home against England, was lost—only one match of the five was finished in Trinidad, and that only after a declaration by Sobers. To lose a Test on a declaration was an unheard-of event, and Sobers (even Sobers!) was put in the dock by public opinion, his effigy hung in Independence Square. Perhaps Sobers thought he could win by bowling England out in under three hours. Perhaps he was infuriated by England's slow scoring-rate in the match. However, his team was by no means deflated after their loss and came to within a wicket of victory in the last Test where the English number eleven, Jeff Jones, safely fended off the final over from Gibbs.

The West Indian team that Worrell built finally disintegrated in Australia in 1968-69. Sobers by now had taken his fill of cricket—he failed to give a lead, just as Hammond had failed with an England team of senior players twenty-two years before. The average age of Sobers' side was twenty-nine, high for a West Indian party. The fast bowlers were all but finished, and the deterioration showed worst of all in a plague of dropped catches. If this series proved anything, it was that brilliant individual performances, like pebbles in the sand, can never hold back the rising tide; something solid, a team performance, alone can do that. The time had come, said the Barbados advocate, for someone to shake the tree and let the old fruit drop. Even during the following three-Test tour of New Zealand the team did not succeed, for after winning at Auckland they lost at Wellington and drew at Christchurch. And the next prospect was yet another tour of England. Fortunately for the West Indies, now in a transitional stage, their 1969 tour was the first split tour and they were first to arrive. Sobers again led the side, but by now his knees were beginning to suffer.

Only one century was scored for the West Indies in this series, by the hitherto unknown Charlie Davis. The bowling was weak, with Gibbs the vice-captain as jaded as Sobers, having been forced into the role of stock bowler in Australia. The West Indians lost at Manchester, the Lord's Test was drawn, and at Headingley they lost by 30 runs in a tight finish. Two players from the smaller islands, Findlay, a wicket-keeper from St Vincent, and Shillingford, a fast bowler from Dominica, were included in the team, and this represented a rapid first dividend from the inclusion of members of the combined-island Shell Shield side. The Shield had begun as the first sponsored tournament in the West Indies in the 1965-66 season, when Barbados inevitably and appropriately became the first winners. Thereafter it was contested every season when there was not a full touring team visiting the West Indies, and the prize was soon being shared among the islands. This commercial sponsorship was essential if the by now independent territories were ever to meet at all, such was and is the expense of travelling, accommodation and the like. Barbados, traditionally the strongest cricketing island, was one of the weakest on terms of finance available. The West Indies Board's kitty as a whole had never been full; one reason for this was that a massive ground-improvement programme was underway, most obviously in Port of Spain, where the crowds were largest and where two Tests per tour had now become the rule.

The early 1970s were a poor period for the West Indies—fifteen home Tests produced not a single victory. The first visitors were India, who not only won their first Test match against the West Indies anywhere in the world, under Wadekar's captaincy, but also took the rubber. No fewer than twenty players were used by the West Indies for this tour, although the complement included not a single known bowler. As for the Indians, they were cresting the waves. Gavaskar broke all records, scoring centuries in both the third and fourth Tests, and finishing with a single and a double century to his credit. West Indies followed on in the first innings of the first match, not knowing that the follow-on had been reduced to 150 because rain had made the match a four-day affair; nevertheless, they held on for a draw. The second Test was at Port of Spain, sometimes a spinner's wicket, and India won there by seven wickets, even though Jack Noreiga, the local off-spinner replacing the out-of-form Gibbs, became the first West Indian ever to take 9 wickets in a Test innings. The last three matches were all drawn.

After India came New Zealand, and their five-match series was also shared in that not a single match was finished. This was to be Sober's last series as captain—he had led West Indies into 39 Tests. The new batsmen, Rowe and Kallicharran, appeared in the team for the first time, but their runs were more than countered by the performance of Glenn Turner, who hit four double centuries on the tour as Patsy Hendren had done back in 1930.

Australia won the 1973 series by two matches to nil under Ian Chappell's captaincy, winning at Port of Spain and Georgetown. The West Indies were by now in a muddle. Kanhai was the obvious successor to Sobers, but there was much support in Trinidad for Murray, the wicketkeeper. This situation was not helped by the fact that Clive Lloyd, eventually to become Kanhai's successor as captain, was not included on the Board's list of players to be returned to the country for the series at Board expense—eventually he was flown back from a contract with a club in Australia at the personal intervention of Mr Forbes Burnham, the Guyanan prime minister. Worst of all, Sobers, who had finally undergone the cartilage operation he had been resisting, asked not to be considered for the first Test. When he was ignored for the second he announced that he was fully fit, and was asked by the Board and its selectors to prove it in a two-day match. This of course effected a heated verbal exchange, and the result was that Sobers did not play at all in the series. That he was needed was obvious, and Ian Chappell said as much at the end of the trip. The first two matches were drawn because the bowling was poor. The younger Jamaican fast bowler, Uton Dowe, was excluded from the game by his own crowd. 'Dowe shalt not bowl', was the crowd's commandment. The Australians were beginning to adopt the tactic of talking batsmen out, or sledging, short for sledge-hammering, as it was subsequently called. Kallicharran was the first regular victim of this psychological warfare. In Guyana, Lloyd hit 178, but even so the West Indies collapsed in the second innings and were all out for 109, thus losing for the second time by 10 wickets.

Virtually the same team came to England in 1973, but with very different results. This time they played their three Tests in the second half of the summer, much more suitable for a dry-wicket side, and they won the first game at The Oval and the third at Lord's, in-between drawing at Edgbaston. No fewer than eleven members of the team were established county players who knew England and her players better than they knew conditions in the Caribbean. Sobers was back for his fifth tour, and he and Kanhai both made their last centuries at Lord's. Sobers' innings was interupted by a stomach complaint, but he showed no lack of application as he picked up six catches close to the wicket to establish yet another cricketing record for West Indies. Six months later, England returned to the West Indies where each side won a Test at Queen's Park, the West Indians the first and England, once again slow to start, the fifth. Inbetween there were two matches dominated by the West Indies and another, in Guyana, by rain. Kanhai the captain was shaken. He thought, and West Indians agreed, that the series should have been sewn up before the final Test, but in reality the bowling was not quite good enough. Gibbs was at the end of his career, Andy Roberts only just starting his, while the other members of the battery that was to develop later in the decade were still playing among the schoolboys. The first Test included the controversial incident when, at the end of a day's play, Tony Greig threw down the wicket of Kallicharran when the latter was on his way to the pavilion assuming that play was over. The episode was more unfortunate than criminal, and while Kalli should not have left his crease when he did it was right that he should be restored to it at the start of play the next day.

The West Indian tour of India in 1974-75 was one of the best series ever played. Under their new captain, Lloyd, the reconstructed West Indian team were full of promise, with their new batsmen, Gordon Greenidge and Viv Richards, having a notable debut. They won the first two Tests, lost the next two to the Indian spinners, and then won the final Test, the first played at the Wankhede Stadium in Bombay. From there the team went to Palistan, where two drawn matches tested the bowlers, among them Roberts, who took 9 wickets in the heat at Lahore.

Early in 1975 the West Indians took the World Cup, beating Australia twice at The Oval in the preliminary rounds and again at Lord's in the final to establish themselves as the kings of one-day cricket. For the next Australian season they were invited to substitute for South Africa as tourists; the West Indian Board were happy to give the team the opportunity of playing as much cricket as possible. The tour turned out to be a grave disappointment as the West Indians went down by five matches to one, an even worse result than in the 1968-69 series. Australia won at Brisbane but Lloyd's team were successful on the fast wicket at Perth where Roy Fredericks played the innings of his life, hooking Lillee and Thomson as neither had ever been hooked before or since: he scored 169 in three and a half hours, a remarkable rate in modern cricket. Complacency after this innings victory, a fatal mistake against any Australian side, undermined the team's next performance. During the fourth Test Boyce dropped a catch in the slips which Lloyd blamed for the loss of the series in a newspaper article. The practice of players writing articles during the course of matches in which they are involved has long represented an unacceptable face of professionalism in cricket, and its potential for harm was clearly revealed in this series. All the West Indians were able to salvage was the form of Vivian

Below: Viv Richards hooks a bouncer from Jeff Thomson during the 2nd Test in Perth, 1975. Clive Lloyd looks on

Richards and Lance Gibbs' record haul of Test wickets. After nineteen years and seventy-eight matches, he overtook Fred Trueman's total of 307.

Back in the West Indies the team took their frustration out against the Indians in one of the most unpleasant series in history. Little by little cricket has developed into a game which it is possible to win through fast bowlers bowling short of a length and at the slowest rate of overs per hour possible, without the umpires taking any action. The West Indies umpires are notoriously reluctant to act against their own side in front of highly excitable crowds, and although during the course of this series three Indian batsmen were unable to bat after being struck by Holding and Holder, still no action was taken. Bedi, India's captain, called it war. The West Indians took the series by two matches to one with one game drawn.

Four fast bowlers came to England in 1976 and they took 84 out of the 92 wickets which fell as West Indies retained the Wisden Trophy by three matches to nil—the first West Indian side to achieve a clean sweep in England. The team batted brilliantly in this summer of prolonged sunshine; Richards made a record number of runs for the West Indians—829, including two double centuries. At the start of the tour the England captain, Greig, had said that he was determined to make the West Indians grovel, and this was not forgotten as Greig himself was bowled out time and time again by fast yorkers.

Having bombarded Edrich and Close, whose combined ages added up to eighty-four-years, as they won their first victory in the third match at Old Trafford, the West Indians then introduced newcomer Wayne Daniel at Headingley, with considerable success. Another fast bowler, Holding, took 14 wickets at The Oval, hitting the stumps or getting a leg-before decision against twelve of his victims.

The West Indians next entertained the Pakistanis, and won a five-match series by two to one with two matches drawn. These two sides had played an

exciting match in the World Cup, and this time, although Holding and Daniel were injured, Croft took 9 wickets in the victory in Trinidad. However, in the second match on the ground, the fourth in the series, Mushtaq had a splendid all-round match and Pakistan won. This left the Jamaican Test, the last, as the decider; on this occasion Gordon Greenidge played a match-winning innings and Pakistan lost by 140 runs.

In the following West Indian season, the Australians arrived again, for what was to prove the most tragic Test series in history. The West Indian Board, faced with the Packer threat, took the decision to proceed normally and to delay making decisions about their Packer players until the last possible moment. While the Australians picked no-one involved in World Series Cricket, the West Indians had a full side and proceeded to bounce the young inexperienced Australians out of the first two Test matches, the only rejoinder coming from Thomson, who virtually bowled himself into the ground at Bridgetown.

When it became obvious that the West Indian Packer players would not be available for their forthcoming tour of India the West Indies fielded a new side under Kallicharran and this time Bobby Simpson's Australians came back into the series by winning at Georgetown. There were demonstrations against the West Indies Board before the second Test at Queen's Park and attendance was much reduced. Finally there was a riot at Sabina Park when it looked as if the Australians would win the final Test, and the umpires refused to stand. The series ended in chaos, a wretched augury for the future with many more problems and much misery visible on the West Indian cricketing horizon. It even seems possible that the various countries may eventually go their various ways, leaving the Test grounds open for the staging of exhibition matches. Will there be a cricketing version of the Harlem Globetrotters? It is a blood-curdling prospect.

Below: Colin Croft, one of a very bright new crop of West Indian fast bowlers, in action at Port-of-Spain in 1978

GREAT GROUNDS

All of us who like to watch or play cricket have our favourite grounds, whether they are used by a school, a village, a League club or a county.

Preceding page: Lord's cricket ground an oasis of calm amid the residential and office blocks of north London,

In themselves cricket grounds can determine the sort of cricketer who treads them: how would Oxford and Cambridge cricket have retained first-class status if the Parks and Fenner's were not two of the happiest grounds in the country, with Fenner's boasting an additional attraction in one of the best wickets in England?

West Country cricket has a life of its own, especially in Somerset. Taunton—historic, wooden, still smelling of years gone by—is different from the seaside pocket-handkerchief of Weston, and different again from Bath whose eighteenth-century atmosphere accommodates the cricket field so snugly. Travelling north, the Queen's Park ground at Chesterfield is as attractive as any, and so too in its symmetry of stone and steel is Bradford Park Avenue. Scarborough boasts a fine history and is now featuring as a one-day ground; St Lawrence, Canterbury has its famous tree to give it a special distinction; Hove has its sea-fret as a last-ditch border; Grace Road, Leicester is to be rebuilt under its now thriving management; and there are those who believe that Worcester, so long the first stop for touring sides, is the most beautiful of all.

But whatever our preferences, due mainly to our familiarity with the various great grounds, the Test match arenas have a magic all of their own. Increasingly these are the great centres of the game, and they represent cricket's investment in the future—an investment to be treasured, because as the death of Bramall Lane in Sheffield has shown there are vandals about quite capable of tearing down a cricket ground full of tradition and erecting in its place a white elephant of hideous aspect.

England

Lord's

Jack Fingleton, master Australian observer of the game's spirit and skills, both as player and writer, has conducted a long love-affair with Lord's, the fairest of all cricket grounds: 'No other, as I have seen them, can compare with Lord's in its colour and peaceful majesty.' To Fingleton Lord's is, quite simply, the Mecca of cricket, 'for there has never been an outstanding player from any country who has not played at Lord's.' To score a century there is every batsman's ambition, and if the bowlers, cricket's humbler echelon, can never hope to make such a claim, a little quiet singing in the capacious baths can sound sweet even to the tone-deaf after a haul of five wickets, even if the baths do take an age to empty and fill.

The freehold of the main ground was first sold by the Eyre family for £7,000 in 1860. The buyer was not the club, which failed to bid, but one Isaac Moses, who later sold the ground to MCC, William Nicholson, an old Harrovian, putting up £18,000. Twenty-one years later the 3½ acres of Henderson's Nursery were bought for £18,500; no longer were tulips and pineapples reputed to be the best in the country to be grown there. Four years later the present site (from Wellington Road to Grove End Road) was completed by the purchase of the clergy's Female Orphan School.

The Pavilion is the glory of Lord's. The foundation-stone was laid in 1889, a year after MCC finally defeated the Great Central Railway's bid to drive their line through the ground instead of under the practice area at the Nursery End. The two towers, suitably grand bases for the great flags of the game, are like hands holding up the three watching tiers of the Pavilion. But the special glories of the structure are not out in the open but behind the huge picture windows: the Long Room, the Writing Room, the Committee Room and, above, the players' dressing-rooms, each with its own precious balcony. The dressing-rooms are, quite simply, the most comfortable in the land. The sofas are huge and as rich in the smell of well-used leather as the smoking-rooms of any club in Pall Mall. In each room there is, or used to be, a bed for massage or for sleeping. The ancient wooden dressing-tables, with their mirrors mounted in the centre, have reflected the looks of many a hero who, having excelled on London's most famous field, was setting out to lay the night-time town by its heels.

The Committee Room below the home dressing-room on the south side has always been the holy of holies, with its binoculars mounted upon a tripod. It was there in 1905 that the young 'Plum' Warner (described to me by Nigel Haig as being a man of two parts—Prim Pelham and Frisky Francis, though few of us young ones had met the latter) once suggested to the then President, C. E. Green, himself a rebel in his youth but since grown into a purple reactionary, that there should be a wider screen at Lord's. 'Good Heavens,' said the senior man of cricket, 'I never knew you were such a radical, Warner.'

If we move out from the Committee Room and across the corridor into the Long Room, and onwards in time to 1939, we are reminded of the famous story of the two members who had sat all afternoon without speaking, even though cricket had ended early on this September day. One of the MCC staff came into the Long Room, covered up the bust of W. G. Grace and removed it. Suddenly, one of the two members spoke. 'My God, that can only mean one thing—war!' It did, and those of us who had to take similar action in 1944 can still look wryly at the picture of the Services XI flat on their stomachs as a German V1, a doodlebug, ran out of fuel overhead.

Then there are the other rooms: the Writing Room, the members' sanctuary, the bars, open all day, where many a liver has been ruined, and the offices not long ago declared unfit for use under the Factories, Shops and Offices Act, so great was the fire risk from the old wiring.

Behind the Pavilion the green hut by the garden still houses the Middlesex County Cricket Club, which has called Lord's home since 1877 but is still obliged to adopt the role of second-class citizen. Next to that is the tennis court, another peaceful spot, the nearest equivalent to a church in the whole world of sport, where the quiet is broken only by the ritual call of the score. Behind the tennis courts are the squash courts; above them, the priceless library. Alongside this the museum stands on the site of the 'new' racquets court, whose destruction some still mourn. Racquets is arguably the best court game in the world, and for years a court stood where the Mound Stand is now to be found, in the south-east corner of the ground.

The Mound Stand, and the free seats where London's muted answer to the barracking of the Sydney Hill is staged, represent far better value for money than the Grandstand, a handsome building but an economic disaster. Built in the 1930s along with 'Q' stand between the Pavilion and the south clock-tower by Sir Herbert Baker, the cost per seat was huge, especially in view of the fact that cricket is quite invisible from so many of them. But in recent years the boxes in the Grandstand have come into their own. In providing such facilities for members to wine and dine their guests, the game of cricket, so often accused of being behind the times, has proved itself once again a leader. Subsequently, Ascot, Wembley and progressive football clubs like Manchester United and Aston Villa have followed suit.

Because Father Time has become so famous, an observer might be forgiven for thinking that all that mattered about the Grandstand was the weather vane—old Father Time with his scythe and hour-glass, the very symbol of Lord's. In 1940 he became an unwitting victim of London's defence against Hitler's Luftwaffe: the cable of a barrage balloon unseated the old gentleman and he slid down into the balcony seats. Fifteen years later a left-handed farmer from Malton in Yorkshire would perform the same trick; presented with a full toss from a young off-spinner who should have known better, Vic Wilson hit the ball high over the short leg-side boundary, higher still over the balcony, until it hit the ironwork under Father Time himself. The biggest straight hit at the Pavilion was Albert Trott's clearance of it—the poor fellow ruined his batting by using heavier and heavier bats in an attempt to repeat the feat. Schumann tied rocks to his third finger in a similarly counter-productive pursuit of aesthetic satisfaction.

The Warner Stand was finished in 1958, and this was followed by the redevelopment of the Tavern in the 1960s. To old-timers this is still a tragedy, but the original building dated in part from Thomas Lord's era and had served its time.

Cricket has all but monopolized Lord's, but the old ground has known other events: in modern times, the running of pony races, the launching of a balloon, and hockey matches. Today it stands exclusively serene, the outfield mown in light and dark stripes, the recently laid drain-pipes showing dark or light through the surface, so indicating the extent of the summer's rainfall.

Lord's has known misfortune and criticism. George Summers, a Nottinghamshire player, died a few days after being hit on the head by a ball in 1870. Then there is the famous ridge, now levelled except for those with cynical minds: if a ball pitched on the bowler's side, then fingers were rapped or broken; if it pitched on the batsman's side, it turned into a shooter of which 'Lumpy' Stevens would have been proud. Once, in the days when the mower used to go round and round—they preferred sheep to motor mowers in the early days—someone dared protest to Sir Pelham Warner about the outfield after a ball had bounced over his head and rattled on to the Mound Stand fence. The reaction was the same as it would have been if a rude noise had been made in church; nevertheless the outfield did improve. Even as late as the summer of 1978 Lord's could throw up a bad wicket, but taken all in all, to rephrase Shakespeare you cannot see its like anywhere else in the wide world. Truly the Grace gates, a tribute to the best-known of all cricketers, lead into the game's most graceful home.

The Oval

Many great Test matches have been played at The Oval. They include the first played in England in 1880, and the Ashes victory of Australia two years later. Few realize today that the then Surrey Secretary, C. W. Alcock, arranged that first Test at

Right: a dropped catch during a match between England and Australia at Trent Bridge, where homely buildings back on to the ground

short notice, persuading Sussex to give up their fixture with W. L. Murdoch's first Australian side. He was a shrewd impresario—40,000 people attended the match and The Oval's reputation was made.

Like parts of Lord's, The Oval was a market garden until 1844, and even after the Montpelier Cricket Club had brought turf from Tooting Common for the cricket field, the area was still used for poultry shows and sundry other attractions. Ten years later the Duchy of Cornwall was ready to sell the land for building, but more royalty, this time in the Germanic shape of Albert, the Prince Consort, came to the rescue. Since then cricket has been relatively safe in Kennington—thankfully, an ambitious scheme to redevelop the ground in the late 1960s failed for lack of finance. Other sports, notably soccer, whose early cup-finals were staged there, but also rugby and even roller-skating, have been staged at the ground.

Surrey began to build there in the 1850s, and in 1890 the extension was added; right from the beginning this housed the amateurs of both sides, who alone enjoyed the luxury of a bath. Now, happily, the dressing-rooms are no longer segregated; in earlier days the captain would have to ring down to the rest of his team to ensure that his progress to the wicket was not a lonely one. Once again the need to provide rooms for entertainment and the earning of revenue has dictated some re-shaping, but the Long Room is still the main feature of a pavilion not unlike that of Lord's in its design and construction. The atmosphere, however, is different. The Oval has been described as a 'workaday' ground: surrounded by its gas-holders, flats, Archbishop Tenison's old school, and an endless procession of buses, The Oval of today is far removed from the Londoners' ground when Kennington Church was once as notable a feature as St John's Wood church is at Lord's.

The Oval's attraction lies not in its appearance or its facilities, splendidly though these have been modernized, but in its matches. Indeed, were the ground situated in New York, pressure for car-parking space would have forced Surrey to seek a new home further from the inner-city area. The New York Giants and Brooklyn Dodgers migrated to California in order to accommodate the motor-car. Cricket has and will continue to resist change. But it has to be recognized that the motor-car, as a means of transport, a makeshift grandstand, and an occasional pub and diner for family and friends, adds enjoyment to cricket and has to be accommodated. By making plentiful provision for car-parking Kent, for example, have added to their financial and cricketing success. By contrast, Surrey, unable to do so, have had a hard time. Years ago it seemed that The Oval was doomed as a Test centre; the threat is still there.

But whatever the future there have been great games: the Tests of 1880 and 1882, of 1902, when Gilbert Jessop hit 104 in 75 minutes and England's last-wicket pair, George Hirst and Wilfred Rhodes, made the 15 runs needed to win. ('Come on, Wilfred, we'll get 'em in singles.') It is said that John Berry Hobbs, batsman supreme and practical joker dangerous, did not figure in a truly significant Test on his own ground, where his name adorns the beautiful gates. But Len Hutton, in direct line of succession, did, because it was his 364 which kept England rattling along as the team climbed to 903 for 7—the highest Test score which in turn led to the biggest Test victory, by an innings and 579 runs. In this result, too, there was precedent at The Oval, because as far back as 1888 Surrey had given Sussex (poor old Sussex), the worst beating in county cricket—an innings and 485 runs. Fifteen years later, when it seemed that England had almost forgotten how to beat Australia, there was the sight of Len Hutton, a player scarred by defeat and one to whom victory meant so much, holding aloft the Ashes urn on the Pavilion balcony. Never can champagne have tasted sweeter.

Trent Bridge

Trent Bridge was the creation of William Clarke, the Kerry Packer of the nineteenth century. In 1837 Clarke was already established as an innkeeper in Nottingham when he married the widow Chapman, who kept the Trent Bridge Inn. He enclosed the field, brought an England eleven captained by Fuller Pilch to the ground five years later, and lived to see his cricket field established as his county's headquarters. Nowadays Trent Bridge suffers, like The Oval, from a lack of car-parking facilities, at least during Test matches.

There were always good wickets at Trent Bridge in the early days, and that was one reason why in Arthur Shrewsbury's time Nottinghamshire were so strong. A true, reliable bounce enabled the players to hit to leg, and precisely because he struck it so often one of the ground's elm trees was known as George Parr's tree; it still is, although these days all that remains of it is in the Pavilion (a veritable treasure trove for the historian) and in Parr's grave, for a piece of the tree was buried with him.

Like most other pavilions Trent Bridge has its Long Room, and away to one side of it are the

dressing-rooms, one above the other: the home side always uppermost! Stands veer away to the left where the new Trent Bridge Inn is to be found, and to the right, beyond the Committee Rooms and Ladies' Pavilion, green terracing takes the eye round to the giant scoreboard, the only one in the country to rival the biggest in Australia. This was installed in the 1950s, when the controls were a five-day wonder. The other new building is at the back of the Pavilion, where there are new offices and squash courts which ensure that the ground is used in the winter. Trent Bridge is a handsome field, a country meadow masquerading as a city ground, just as it was in William Clarke's day.

Old Trafford

Old Trafford is most correctly the home of the Manchester and Lancashire CC. As in St John's Wood in London, so at Old Trafford in Manchester: the ground had to be moved a mile in 1856, to a pavilion with an excellent wine-cellar, because the civic authorities wanted its first site for an exhibition of art treasures. Since 1884, Test matches have been played on the ground, which is as suitable for modern Tests as any in the country. But only Lancastrians are more choosy in their entertainment than Londoners; being less inclined to part with cash for advanced bookings, Old Trafford, which should be an automatic Test ground, finds itself missing a match every so often because of the rota system involving Trent Bridge and Edgbaston.

The Pavilion at Old Trafford is, I feel sure, the largest of all the Test pavilions in terms of what the estate agents would call net-lettable. It is easy to get lost in its spacious rooms, some with a purpose seemingly long-forgotten, and so it has become an ideal venue for dinners and other functions. Acres of parking space ensure its continued success.

Like other Test grounds Old Trafford has its Long Room—square on to the wicket, with terracing spreading out on either side. It was here that the crowd burst into 'Auld Lang Syne' when Jack Hobbs played for the last time in George Duck-

Right: the crowd invades the pitch at Sydney Cricket Ground after a flood-lit one day World Series match between Australia and West Indies

worth's benefit match. This is also Neville Cardus's ground, where he acted as midwife to dozens of cricketing characters. But of all the heads that appear out of the crowd to offer a discerning membership their great deeds, the one who stands out most is Jim Laker. Never again is a bowler likely to take all 10 wickets in a Test match innings as Laker did against Australia in 1956; still less bag a total haul of 19 wickets in the match for a mere 90 runs. There are two odd features of this achievement, surely one of the greatest in all cricket: first, that Tony Lock, a fine spin bowler, took only one wicket in the match, and second, that it was only when Laker, apparently as phlegmatic a character as ever played the game, got to Lichfield on the way home that he realized just what he had done, and then only because he heard others talking about his bowling in reverential terms.

Headingley

Of the six Test grounds, Headingley comes nearest to fulfilling the criteria for a modern sports stadium; namely of being fully utilized winter and summer. While the cricket ground uses one side of the main stand, the other faces out across the pitch of the leading Rugby League club in Yorkshire. Between the Old Pavilion and the Yorkshire County Club offices, which have housed the players' dressing-rooms since 1963, is a bowling-green. How this survives the pounding of the crowds during a wet Test match baffles the layman. Grass is a wondrous weed!

Since it became a Test ground in 1899, Headingley has had its share of misfortune. Fire destroyed one stand and so damaged the Pavilion that it had to be altered. Then, in 1975, vandals campaigning for the release of the convicted robber, George Davis, mutilated the pitch in the early hours of the last day of an England—Australia Test match then poised on a knife edge. One vandal was called Chappell; the same name as the Australian captain.

Headingley is not an easy ground for the players, especially when crowded. Many is the fielder who has run the wrong way, unable to see against a confused background. Behind the bowler on the open Kirkstall Lane end is the Chad stand, painted white, but with heads dotting the background. Peter May tells the story of how he pushed forward to his first ball in Test cricket as if he was playing in the dark. Fortunately the ball went off the edge for 4, and he survived to make a century.

Headingley is Bradman's ground in England. He played six innings there and scored 963 runs for an average of 192.6, a total which included one century made before lunch which grew into a treble hundred by the end of the day. Worse still, from England's point of view, when Bradman was captain in 1948 Australia became the first team to top 400 in the fourth innings—404 for 3, to be exact. That innings was Jim Laker's baptism of fire, never forgotten. Hedley Verity took 10 for 10 against Nottinghamshire at Headingley in 1932, the best bowling figures yet recorded. One game which particularly deserves a replay features the greatest in a batch of famous cricketing fightbacks, Somerset's victory over Yorkshire in 1901 when, having been bowled out for 87, they made 630 in their second innings, and then under the direction of that great and popular Australian games player, Sammy Woods, bowled out Yorkshire for 113 to win by 279 runs.

Some find Headingley somewhat featureless. How can that be when there are so many famous Yorkshire cricketers always in attendance? To me it is the richest ground of all in terms of the fellowship which it inspires.

Edgbaston

Edgbaston holds a special place in many affections, for it was here, during the Second World War, that top-class players like Walter Hammond and Learie Constantine kept cricket alive for schoolchildren in those troubled years.

Edgbaston became a Test ground in 1909. It then had a tiny pavilion behind the bowler's arm, an old and, it transpired, solidly built stand on one side, and a great bank of Midland cinders stretching round the other to a plesant scoreboard at the City end. Warwickshire adopted the ground in 1856. Facilities were no better than adequate in the early years, although the playing area was both large and well kept. Already the Birmingham populace were identifiably keener on soccer than on cricket—Edgbaston crowds have always been a disappointment.

Nonetheless, a huge expansion programme was undertaken after the Second World War, when money was raised by lotteries and pools systems pioneered by Warwickshire under the dynamic leadership of Leslie Deakins, the Secretary. 'If we gave him his head we'd have stands back in the Bull Ring,' his chairman once said. (The Bull Ring is fully two miles distant!) Thus the old double-decker stand was pulled down, the steel as good as new, and huge terraces constructed under which the

ground's superb banqueting and catering facilities provide Birmingham with an ideal focal point, winter and summer. However, the running-costs of the ground are such that it seems unlikely that Edgbaston will ever make a profit, however well it is managed. We live in an age when the cost of upkeep for such a magnificently appointed ground is too great for its revenue, actual or potential. It is an amenity, but it cannot survive without support.

Only the Pavilion remains of the old ground, and it is quite dwarfed by the stands on either side. Reorganization has required that the Long Room be on the first floor, but in reality the old building is a hotch potch retained only out of a sense of respect for tradition.

Edgbaston is famous as a Test ground on two counts: in 1924, on their first visit, the South Africans were bowled out by Maurice Tate and Arthur Gilligan for 30, and in 1957 an epic stand between Peter May and Colin Cowdrey prevented the West Indies from winning their series easily. On the county front a result similar to that mentioned under Headingley was recorded in 1922, when Hampshire were all out for 15 and then made 521 runs on the follow-on to defeat Warwickshire by 155 runs.

Edgbaston has one other attraction for the journalist: it is the one Test ground in this country that has a Press box looking down the wicket. Judging cricket is almost impossible unless you are perched on the umpire's shoulder. If anyone tells you that you can tell as much about a cricket match by standing square as from standing behind, then I will show you a man who knows little about cricket.

Australia
Sydney

Sydney Cricket Ground is owned and managed by Trustees, among whom sit some notable former cricketers and rugby players—for this is an all-the-year-round field—as well as politicians, lawyers and businessmen.

The first cricket played here was in 1877 against Lord Harris and his party, an occasion when an unpopular umpire from Victoria—most Victorians tend to be unpopular in Sydney, especially umpires who interfere with the batting—found himself in the middle of a riot.

The Pavilion, tiny and old-fashioned, is in the corner of the field at an angle of 45 degrees to the wicket. Behind the line, wicket to wicket, is the fine Noble Stand whence spectators look across the field to the green slope of the hill, at once biting, vulgar, witty, generous, crowded and smelly, especially if it is hot.

Years ago, when the famous Bulli soil was used on

Right: Derek Randall, caught Marsh, bowled Lillee, stands disconsolate in the Centenary Test at Melbourne

the pitch, the wickets at Sydney were kind to batsmen, except when there was heavy rain to transform them into a sticky bog. When England visit, either Sydney or Melbourne has two Tests. Sydney is the smaller ground with a capacity of just under 60,000—still huge by English or West Indian standards.

Melbourne

The Melbourne cricket ground is the largest in the world and on first visit is breathtaking. The first Test between England and Australia was played here in 1877, as all the cricketing world now knows after the huge success of the Centenary Test in Queen Elizabeth's Jubilee Year. The Australian MCC (Melbourne Cricket Club) was formed in the 1830s and took up residence in Yarra Park in 1953. Now the ground holds well over 100,000, and if large crowds appear for the Grand Final of the Australian Rules competition, attendances for the Test matches played during the Christmas holiday period break records year after year. For many years Melbourne was the only cricket ground with triple-decker stands, although in the mid-1970s a small triple-decker was built on the Queen's Park ground in Trinidad. With the entire ground encircled by high yet deep and spacious stands, the atmosphere of a big occasion at Melbourne transmits itself even on the walk down the hill through the gum trees. Like its counterpart at Lord's, the Melbourne pavilion is full of treasures from times past, a living museum of cricket.

Adelaide

The Adelaide Oval was named by a Surrey member who settled in South Australia, and the ground was first used for cricket in the 1880s. Of all the grounds in Australia, or indeed in the world, it deserves the title Oval, for the long boundaries are very long, much longer than those square to the wickets. Like the Melbourne Ground, the Oval is set in a glorious park, just across the river from the city; it is in this park that St Peter's Cathedral is sited, its spires visible from the Pavilion, and although this adds a certain picturesqueness to the appearance of the ground it has in all honesty to be mentioned that just as Worcester's cathedral is by no means an architectural masterpiece, no more is Adelaide's, being more an object of reverent interest than ecstatic admiration. Away from Sydney and Melbourne ground capacities decline, but Adelaide, with its Bradman tradition, can and has accommodated more than 40,000 spectators.

Brisbane

As the Queensland Cricket Association was not formed until the 1926-27 season, Test cricket is relatively recent in Brisbane. Its first Test—that of the Percy Chapman tour of 1928-29—was not played in the present stadium, but on the Exhibition Ground across the river. Now touring Test sides play in the suburb of Woolloongabba, in the arena known as the Gabba. From the city, the approach is either over a fine new bridge over the Queensland River or else by way of the old ferry, still one of the busiest passenger ferries in the world.

In the 1960-61 season, the greatest cricket match ever played, the exhilarating tie between Australia and the West Indies, was played on the Gabba. In the following decade much work was done on extending the covered accommodation, and more stands were opened for the visit of England in the 1974-75 season. The then Australian Prime Minister, Gough Whitlam, opened the new stand just before departing on a European tour, with the wry comment that he was leaving the Australian summer

for a European winter, whereas his predecessor, that enthusiastic supporter of cricket Sir Robert Menzies, always visited London in the summer when he spent half his time 'with Lords and the other half at Lord's'. Mr Whitlam was the leader of the Labour Party to which Clem Jones, the Mayor of Brisbane, belonged. You cannot discuss Brisbane's cricket without reference to Mayor Jones. John Gunther's book, *Inside Australia*, refers to him as a well-known 'fixer' in the new city of Brisbane, but one who, on the whole, fixed things pretty well. Just before the 1974 Test Clem Jones sacked the groundsman, or curator as the Australians call the job, and took over the work himself. After one of the thunderstorms typical of Test cricket in Brisbane, he moved the pitch nine yards from its intended site: remarkable though Australian grounds are for their speed of recovery from the lacerations of footballers, this move ensured a difficult wicket for the visiting English team.

Perth

The Western Australian Cricket Association's ground at Perth—the WACA as it is familiarly known—was not used for Test matches until the visit of England under Ray Illingworth in 1970-71. By then the seemingly endless flow of Western Australians into the Australian eleven (the two great fast bowlers Graham McKenzie and Dennis Lillee being outstanding examples) had dictated that Perth should become a Test ground and that Australian series should contain six rather than five Tests. With the addition of two new stands the capacity of the ground has been increased to almost 30,000, and with a park full of black swans on one side and the Gloucester Park racecourse (where Packer's World Series Cricket Super Test was staged) on the other, the ground has a pleasantly rural outlook, with the beautiful Swan River only a few hundred yards distant. Traditionally, Perth is the fastest wicket in Australia and arguably in the world, and the quality of the cricket played reflects the excellence of the pitches. The playing area used to be long enough for two games to be played simultaneously, but with new stands spreading from the Pavilion this is ceasing to be possible as the ground is developed to bring gate receipts in line with those from other Australian Test grounds.

South Africa
Capetown

As the gap between Test matches in South Africa

lengthens, so more and more cricketers are deprived of the pleasure of playing on Newlands, arguably the loveliest cricket ground in all the world. Trees, not concrete, circle the field, thus differentiating it from the huge rugby ground which is just visible. On the day I saw cricket there a black man, John Shepherd of Barbados and Kent, was playing. 'We have come a very long way,' said a Judge of impeccable Afrikaaner background, 'and I never thought I would see this.'

The first English team played there in 1888 under the captaincy of Charles (later Sir Charles) Aubrey Smith. Johnny Briggs, the Lancashire left-hander, took 15 wickets for 28 in the match, 14 of them bowled, the fifteenth leg-before, thus needing no help from his colleagues. Briggs died at the age of thirty-nine after a lifetime's battle against epilepsy, a condition he shared with a number of other cricketers including Tony Greig, but which was harder to treat then than now. Since that first game South Africa have fared only moderately on a ground which has a good record for producing results.

Johannesburg

Cricket began in Johannesburg on the old Wanderer's Ground at the beginning of the century. The new Wanderer's Ground has been little used for Test cricket, as it was only opened in time for the MCC series of 1956-57. It is the largest ground in South Africa, holding over 36,000, and in an annual five-match series two games are played here. Much of the accommodation is under the burning African sun, but there is an aluminium stand on the ground built on the cantilever principle which is a marvel of structural engineering and allows an uninterrupted view.

Port Elizabeth

This is the oldest ground in South Africa, dating from 1843; a Test match was played there in 1888-89. There is a vast stand on one side of the ground, and although I have only seen it myself under incessant rain it is clearly a glorious place for cricket with a tradition too strong to be allowed to die.

Durban

The principal cricket ground in Natal is called Kingsmead, and it was here that a never-to-be-repeated Test experiment resulted in the timeless Test of 1939, a match terminated on the tenth day because the boat taking the players back to England could wait for them no longer. England were set 696 to win in the fourth innings, and eventually finished with 656 for 6. The ground is close to the Indian Ocean; it has been steadily, if slowly, modernized. Indeed, in the 1960s there was a scheme to turn the site into a development project, but the Durban City Council vetoed the scheme, thus saving the many trees planted by famous players to commemorate great deeds, a charming custom on this ground.

The West Indies
Bridgetown, Barbados

The size of the Isle of Wight, but much more densely populated, Barbados is the cradle of more West Indian cricketers than any other of the islands. The three 'W's, Weekes, Walcott and Worrell, all learned the game here; another of the

Left: Newlands, headquarters of Western Province cricket, is majestically set at the foot of Table Mountain

island's citizens is Sir Garfield Sobers, perhaps the greatest cricketer of all time. The Pavilion here houses many memories, a host of them visible because, as in other, older cricket centres, the walls are covered in photographs. The ground now has a covered stand halfway around the boundary, a new ladies' stand to the left of the Pavilion named after George Challenor, and a scoreboard to rival the best in the world. How many people can be crammed into the available space I know not—perhaps 20,000—but they are capable of as much noise as Indian or Australian crowds four times as large. The first team from England played on what was the Pickwick Club's ground in 1895, but the first Test match was not staged there until 1930. Since 1947-48, when MCC resumed visits after the Second World War, hardly a season has passed without a Test on the Kensington as opposed to the Kennington Oval. Furthermore, although there have been moments of friskinesss and some danger due to overcrowding, there has never been the sort of riotous behaviour which has occurred on other grounds in the West Indies.

Kingston, Jamaica

The two principal grounds in the City are within a mile of each other—Melbourne Park and the Test ground at Sabina Park, where Test matches have been played for the past 49 years. It was on this ground that Sobers overtook the record individual Test aggregate by hitting 365 against the Pakistanis in 1957-58, taking full advantage of an ideal ground for big scores where the boundary is little more than 60 yards from the bat; a West Indian fast bowler like Wes Hall covered all but a few yards of the radius with every ball he bowled. It was here that the notorious riot occurred in 1978 when the Australians were deprived of victory by an invading mob and by the umpires refusing to allow play to continue on the seventh day to compensate for the loss of time on the sixth.

Georgetown, Guayna

The Bourda Ground boasts the best batting wicket in the West Indies. Seldom does it deteriorate in normal conditions, and this is strange in a city full of wide avenues and dykes whose presence indicates that the ground is close to if not below sea-level. The stands at the Bourda, which spread out from the old wooden pavilion, are not large but they virtually circle the ground. The West Indies' first win against England came in the first match ever played here. The crowd approaches 20,000 on a good day, and it was just such a large multitude were present when the first bottle-throwing incident of modern times occurred on England's tour under Len Hutton: Clifford McWatt, known from 1954 onwards as McCatt because he had so many lives, was finally run out for 99. Large bets had been placed on the local man to score a century, and once the first bottle appeared others followed in profusion. These days, a few bottles are normal: a quarter of a century ago this shower made world headlines.

Port of Spain, Trinidad

The home of the Queen's Park Club, the Queen's Park Oval is the best-appointed ground in the West Indies. It can hold about 30,000 most of them seated, and is a thoroughly modern ground. The building of new stands has deprived the members of one of the best views on any cricket field—that of the northern range of the island of Trinidad, wooded tropical hillsides on which the old pwi trees blaze into their flowers of yellow and red. Sadly the ground shares with Lord's large areas where spectators are unable to obtain a reasonable view: in this case it is because of a positive forest of stanchions, many of which could perhaps have been saved by spending more on reinforcement. For years after other centres had gone over to turf, Test and other cricket in Trinidad was played on the mat—first coconut fibre and then jute. On the latter surface not one Test was finished, but since the mid-1950s one groundsman, a Trinidad Indian called Kanhai—no relation to the batsman—has had charge of the ground and supervised the change to turf. Often there have been results in Trinidad because a well-equipped bowling side can either make a breakthrough with speed or, once the early sap has gone, with spin. Such bowlers are often helped by the dust from the wicket, and in recent years Trinidad has held an impressive record as the home of such spinners, whether orthodox or back-of-the-hand. Jumadeen and Inshan Ali are two such.

As with the Bourda, Queen's Park has known ugly crowd scenes. It was outside its splendid gates that the Trinidadians protested about the great divide caused in West Indian cricket by the Packer Circus, and by the West Indian Cricket Board of Control's

very reasonable insistence that anyone playing for West Indies in the second Test against Australia (the first was won with a full side) must indicate availability for the West Indies' tour of India. None of the star players did so, and all were dropped.

India
Bombay

Bombay is a city which contributes 75 per cent of all taxes paid by Indians to the central government in Delhi. Nevertheless, even for such a wealthy port and manufacturing centre, the existence in the heart of the city of two stadia, each capable of holding well over 50,000 people, does seem something of a waste. The story of cricket is riddled with politics, and there is no clearer evidence of this than the history of the Brabourne and Wankhede stadia. Originally, matches with touring teams were played on the Bombay Gymkhana, still a huge open space for cricket with a graceful pavilion and all the facilities of a Raj club-house: bars, billiard-rooms and deep, comfortable chairs. However, the Brabourne Stadium, named after the peer who was Governor in the 1930s, has a pavilion of true luxury, where a man may move, if he so chooses, from the breakfast table to the crease—not such a startling idea when play starts at 10.30 a.m. at the latest. Visiting teams have traditionally been accommodated here, and for the 1972-73 season, when MCC were the visitors, the ground was improved so that covered stands surrounded the playing area, and the capacity was increased to above 50,000. Yet the Cricket Club of India, the CCI, a private club, was not able to satisfy the needs of those mainly responsible for running provincial cricket on Bombay—the Parsees, a powerful community, strongly entrenched, and with the Gujeratis and Maharastrans also having their say resentment became bitter. Eventually the CCI defied its opponents to build a second stadium, feeling that the central government would never release the necessary steel

Left: Bridgetown, Barbados, during a drawn match between West Indies and Australia in 1973

and cement for the construction work. M. Wankhede, a member of the Lok Sabba, the Indian Parliament, presided over the creation and implementation of the design, and the stadium was built in record time. When England next visited Bombay in 1977 the new ground already had one Test under its belt, and the familiar figure of Polly Umrigar, then a selector, in charge. Wankhede too is a superbly appointed stadium, more comfortable for the vast crowds which are the rule in India than the older arena, a ghost ground now used for school sports. Whether the Wankhede wicket will produce more results than the Brabourne remains to be seen. Neither one was built on firm ground, and without a necessary level of bounce it is hard to finish matches in India.

Calcutta Eden Gardens

Calcutta and Bombay were for a long period regarded as equally important cities, the natural richness of Calcutta's Bengal hinterland perhaps giving the eastern city the edge because it was also a key manufacturing centre. But now Calcutta has lost its former glory, its corporate energy and will sucked out by the humid climate, the city itself showing unmistakeable signs of decay. Against this background, and pleasantly situated between the Maidan and the Hooghly river, Eden Gardens is the outstanding exception to this general rule. Second only to Melbourne in its size, it boasts three-decker stands—an uninterrupted circle of stalls in this open-air theatre. The noise when the ground if full—and in the days of more bizarre administration, all seats were sold twice over for one series—is awe-inspiring from a distance of a mile and more. There have been some unruly series in Calcutta; one of the most dangerous of all incidents was the stoning of the bus containing Bill Lawry's Australians as they left for the airport.

The original invitations that Calcutta extended to the MCC came in fact from Englishmen—like R. B. Lagden, who invited Arthur Gilligan's team in 1926-27, and Tom Longfield, Ted Dexter's father-in-law, who was President in 1954-55. But soon there will be no Englishmen or Scots remaining in the great Bengal merchant houses.

Traditionally Calcutta has provided a fair wicket. England won a Test there for the first time in 1977, Tony Greig playing a superb innings as he recovered from a fever, proving that there is nothing like batting for sweating it out!

Delhi

The leading light of the Delhi stadium is R. P. Mehra, whose family were important merchants in Lahore in the days before Partition; Mehra re-established the family fortune in Delhi. The ground, just outside the city walls, is the least developed of all the main Indian grounds, holding fewer than 30,000 people. Because cricket is, in effect, played in the winter in Delhi, a city almost in sight of the Himalayas, the hours of play tend to be contracted, and there is often a mist or heavy dew in the morning. Seam bowlers often have field days in these conditions, which makes it all the more strange that India has produced so few fast bowlers.

Since 1948, when the first Test match was played in Delhi, a total of twenty Tests have been played at the Feroz Shah Kotla ground. In the very first Test here West Indies scored 631. India replied with 454 and went on to save the match dramatically.

Right: Chandrasekhar is bowled by Lever in the Madras Test in 1977. The ground can comfortably hold 80,000 spectators

Kanpur

Both communities remember the tragedies that befell them. Thus while the Martyrs' Gate is close by the Delhi Ground where, it is alleged, those who started the Mutiny were executed, so in Kanpur, then known as Cawnpore, the cricket ground is close to the site of the wall from which more than 1,000 victims of the Mutiny were unceremoniously thrown. Kanpur is a textile city, and big crowds are attracted to the cricket; they have more than once burned down the awnings designed to keep the hot sun from the Indian plains off their heads. The wickets at Kanpur are, in the modern idiom, flat: there is seldom a result.

Bangalore

Bangalore, headquarters of the Karnataka State side, which has supplied Viswanath and Chandrasekhar to the best Indian elevens in history, staged its most recent Test match against West Indies in 1978-79: abandoned because of riots. It has been expanded in no small measure, and the concrete stands will soon encircle this ground as they do the others. Bangalore, the city after which the land-torpedo was named, is a garrison-town in which the wide open spaces of the suburbs with their detached new villas contrast sharply with the old city.

Hyderabad

The ground at Hyderabad is a most attractive setting for cricket. An old Moslem city in a predominantly Hindu area, the entire region reeks of old times. Only occasionally are Tests played there now, but the ground is well appointed and the wicket a beauty, far too good for mere three-day fixtures.

Madras

The ground at Madras, the most southerly of all, is currently, of all the Indian grounds, undergoing the greatest change. Originally, a wooden pavilion with a coconut floor in front of it led on to the field, and on either side temporary stands made of bamboo scaffolding poles, covered with dry palm-fronds, were built for the great matches. Now the new pavilion of concrete has taken over, the old is reduced to the status of club-house, and vast concrete stands will within the next decade completely encircle the ground, enabling Madras, the earliest centre in India for cricket, to hold a crowd of 80,000 without undue discomfort. Traditionally the Madras wicket has favoured spin, but it has produced results, of which India have won their share. Undoubtedly the game has a secure base in Tamil Nadu, the Madras province.

New Zealand
Wellington

Wellington's ground is called Basin Reserve, a God-given arena if ever there was one. Until the earthquake of 1853 this area was a lake; it subsequently became a swamp and the land was reclaimed. The first match played there was between HMS *Falcon* and a Wellington team; the first inter-provincial match was also played on the ground. Close to the centre of the city, the ground presents a walk almost as long for the batsman making a duck as does St Helen's at Swansea. In the winter the ground is used for soccer, but because the two games are not as popular as rugby the facilities at Wellington are less comprehensive than in other cities. Nevertheless, it was here that New Zealand registered its first victory, and a splendid one at that, against England in 1978.

Christchurch

Lancaster Park in Christchurch is a rugby ground, but it was opened for cricket in 1882. On this ground the England side of 1906-07 was beaten by the locals at New Year: they had suffered a rough sea-voyage from Wellington in order to arrive at the fixture, and they twice collapsed. The headquarters of New Zealand cricket are in this city, in the province of Canterbury, and the surroundings are very akin to those of the other Canterbury ground—all trees and spires.

In this most English of New Zealand's cities, with its lovely colonial buildings and flat terraine, the summer climate is so dry and so blisteringly hot that fast bowlers can offer devastatingly effective, if exhausting, attack.

Auckland

Eden Park is New Zealand's chief rugby centre, and it was on this ground that New Zealand gained their first Test victory in their twenty-sixth Test match on the ground when West Indies were defeated there in the fourth match of the 1955-56 series.

Auckland, sea-girt on two sides, has a humid, sub-tropical, climate making Eden Park an ideal pitch for slow and spin bowlers.

Below: Basin Reserve, Wellington, New Zealand is a glorious place to play, or watch, cricket. Here Australia and New Zealand fight it out

7up
GET
REAL
ACTION
7up
SUNNY BISCUITS

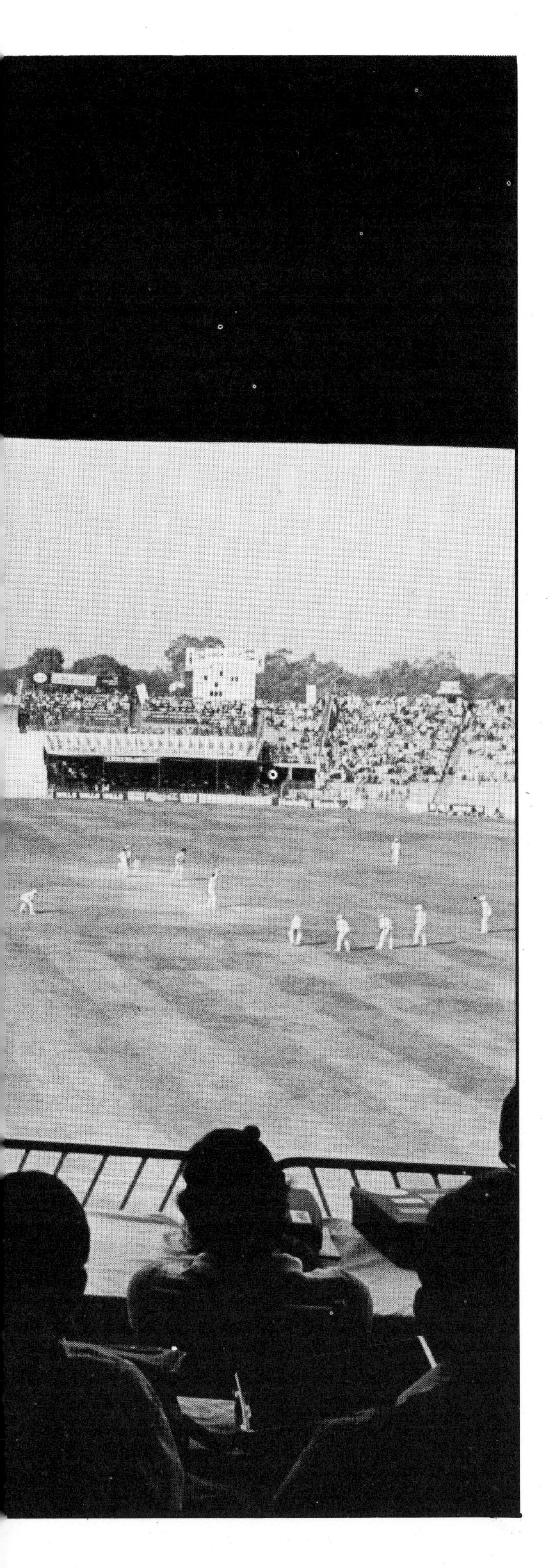

Left: a view of the ground at Lahore taken from the Press Box, where the noise of typewriters must sometimes be deafening

Pakistan
Lahore

The Gymkhana Club was a bastion of the Indian Army and Civil Service in the days of the British Empire and much cricket was played there. However, in 1959, twelve years after the foundation of the country, Pakistan had a new stadium ready for the Australians, complete with the type of turf wicket for which Lahore, with its cooler climate, had always been known.

Karachi

The headquarters of Pakistan cricket are in Karachi; here, the wicket is theoretically turf, but in practice it is simply rolled mud. The National Stadium was opened for cricket in 1955 when India visited the country; since then it has become more famous for crowd incidents than for results, which are almost impossible to achieve on such a pitch.

Hyderabad

Close by the River Indus, the ground at Hyderabad looks out across temple gardens into the vast expanse of the Sind desert. It is a country ground not yet built up, with a country wicket, where a result is more likely than in the big cities.

Bangladesh
Dacca

Pakistan's third huge concrete stadium was at Dacca in East Bengal, a ground built to hold 40,000, the whole concourse overlooked by the white minarets of the Central Mosque. The cricket ground is the very centre of life in Dacca, with its shops all round the ground, reminding the visitor of Hyderabad in India. Now the ground is the headquarters of Bangladesh cricket, this country being the only Associate Member of the International Cricket Conference with an authentic Test ground. When MCC took a scratch side containing only one current regular in county cricket, Barclay of Sussex, to the country in January 1977, a crowd of almost 30,000 turned out to watch Friday's play, on the Moslem rest day.

WORLD SERIES CRICKET
AUST V WEST INDIES
BOWLER
OVER 44
BATSMAN
DAVIS
08
E 0 26
H 0 19
O 0 0
C 0 0
D 2 20
R 0 22
CHAPPELLG
33
EXTRAS 3
8:34
2
090
NO YOU CAN USE
LAST WICKET 64
WESSELS 38
Dial S.T.D.
GOODYEAR GOODYEAR

THE FUTURE

It is easier to assess a cricket ball than a crystal ball, but perhaps it is as well for our peace of mind that we are not able to see clearly into the game's future.

Preceding page: a sprinkling of spectators at Melbourne's VFL Park in 1979 watch a World Series match between Australia and West Indies

Right: a man with much to smile about. Kerry Packer, the newspaper magnate who has affected the game of cricket for all time

Those of us who have seen cricket in dire distress in our lifetime must be more than content that it appears to be so healthy now; for all its occasional aberrations, enthusiasm for the game in such places as India and the West Indies means that cricket is unlikely to perish in this century or the next.

Nevertheless, there are many factors which should persuade those responsible for nurturing such a delicate plant that cricket needs careful handling if it is to survive. The greatest tragedy in the history of the game so far is that it has perished as a major sport in the United States of America. It now seems that the team games that the Americans have developed by themselves, American football and baseball, will go into a decline. It will be a slower decline than that which assailed cricket in the early part of this century, but the causes of the decline are plain for all to see: chief among them is the inability of the United States to compete internationally. As far as team games are concerned, her finest athletes are engaged in sports exclusively contained within the North American Continent. Furthermore, the emphasis within American football, basketball and other popular professional sports is on athletes of outsize dimensions. This has given a properly organized team game like soccer, in which height and weight are not all-important, the opportunity to grow like a tropical plant.

The popularity of baseball, tennis and soccer means that it will be impossible to re-establish cricket in the United States. The American experience suggests that, once it fades, cricket is more likely to die or survive in a diminished form than be revived as a major sport.

A second factor is the question of cost. Polo apart, cricket is by far the most complicated and expensive game of all to stage. Not only is there a full complement of twenty-eight engaged in each contest, but the preparation of the playing area and the upkeep of the accommodation, pavilions and seating required for matches lasting for the best part of a week, are such that the construction of new stadia for the game is almost out of the question, except in India where the revenues and population are huge. Furthermore, the cost factor means that educational establishments, whose season, especially in the northern hemisphere, is very short, can hardly justify capital expenditure on cricket fields. Already in England we have seen universities foregoing cricket grounds in favour of the installation of sporting facilities for more instant forms of exercise such as squash. As inflation is likely to remain with us, this high-cost factor presents a big threat to the future prosperity of the game.

Then there is the threat of schism, such as that posed by Kerry Packer. Optimists have to believe that in the long run order will triumph over chaos, and that the threat to cricket from the private promoter will fade away as it has done in other sports like tennis—the example of the eventual decline of privately promoted professional cricket in the nineteenth century is relevant here. There will of course be players who resist the present temptation to defection, and cricketing authorities who support that resistance. Furthermore, history suggests that private promotions have a way of fragmenting once the pirates begin to fall out over the booty; this too is an interesting possibility in the present circumstances. The use of private promotional money to establish top-class cricket outside the existing international framework is undesirable, and avoidable so long as one pre-condition is met—namely, that outstanding players be rewarded in proportion to their capacity as entertainers for attracting public money, whether this be from private individuals paying at the gate or companies paying in the form of sponsorship. If the rates of reward for cricketers get out of step with reality, as they did in Australia and threatened to do in England, then there is always scope for a private promoter to enter the arena. Again, one need only look back a short while into the history of cricket to see how successful Sir Julien Cahn was in raising teams to play in England and all over the world in the 1930s. Order in cricket is essential, because only by creating a pyramidal structure can the best talent approach the apex and so provide a real stimulus. Cricket needs to be organized from the most junior level up to the governing body of the game itself, and this formal organization must apply to every cricketing country, whether they have a framework of first-class cricket or not, whether they are Full or Associate Members of the International Cricket Conference.

For the strongest countries there seems no alternative to the Test match format as the true pinnacle of the international game. Certainly, the programme for tours to these countries may be in need of change from time to time but the five- or six-day match played against touring sides is the truest test of the real merit of cricket teams. And no country can expect to produce an adequately skilful Test team unless it has a first-class structure which brings forward sufficient numbers of talented cricketers to form a reservoir from which a Test squad can be selected. It would be inappropriate for any country which did not have such a first-class structure ever to acquire full Test status, although there are a number of countries like Sri Lanka and Bangladesh which could well justify short tours by first-class touring sides, like those which toured the

West Indies in the early days.

A successful future for cricket lies not only in maintaining a formal structure for the game at national level, but also in monitoring evolutionary changes in laws, equipment, technique and in the pattern of the first-class game. After the catastrophic committees of the 1960s it will be some time before it again becomes fashionable to meddle for the sake of it with the laws of cricket. During the lifetime of today's cricketers, their fathers and grandfathers, there have been only two areas of legislation which have been seen as a constant and recurring problem. Both concern the bowler. In the first place the bowler's action is likely to remain under intense scrutiny. When Tony Lock was showing just what could be accomplished with a bent arm, certain *avant garde* spirits thought it just possible that a bent-arm action akin to that used in baseball would represent the next development in bowling technique, extending the progression from under-arm to over-arm. Recognition of this heresy, for heresy it was, came when batsmen established the point that a ball thrown at speed represented a danger to life and limb. It was intolerable that the best batsmen in the world should become targets in a 22-yard coconut shy. The thrown ball was just too hard to pick up in line and length. The outcome of the acceptance of the batsman's viewpoint was a massive and successful attempt to straighten the action of bowlers all over the world. Lock himself, by far the most interesting and successful thrower of the cricket ball, was so horrified at the affront that his filmed 'bowling' represented to the traditional left-arm spin bowlers' high-wheeling arm, that he himself reverted to the action he had employed before going to work in the Croydon store where a low ceiling had obliged him to drop and bend his arm. Proof of Lock's ability to change his style was evident in his extraordinary success as a finger-spinner in Australian cricket, with Western Australia. Since then bowlers whose actions have been suspect have been reported, and then either straightened out or barred from first-class cricket. The most recent case has been that of Geoff Cope, who has twice had to accept the view of his peers that he was throwing the ball and enter a clinic to have his arm straightened. But obviously the rule as written lacks definition. The problem with the written word is that it is so often inexact and therefore leaves the verdict of legality open to interpretation. The price of fair bowling in the years ahead will be eternal vigilance.

We may safely pass over the other element in the bowler's action which has been subject to a change in the laws, namely the ball delivered from less than twenty-two yards, for this seems to be a problem which has been cured to most people's satisfaction. My own personal opinion is that dragging is an insignificant offence and that more damage has been caused by calling 'No-ball' for a front-foot offence (in terms of the danger to bowlers' ankles presented by an accumulation of foot-marks on the batting crease) than ever was done by allowing the occasional dragger to extend his rear foot over the bowling crease. It was only the coincidence in the late 1950s of both dragging *and* throwing which led to the outcry against both abuses: only throwing was truly dangerous.

The other serious problem for bowlers to face concerns what is or is not acceptable in terms of short-pitched bowling. It would hardly be desirable to revert to the customs of former days, when bowlers were expected to pitch the ball up on the off-stump so that a batsman could display his off-side driving capabilities. Nor would it be practical. No-one, whether batsman or bowler, seeks to eliminate completely the element of danger inherent in the short-pitched ball. The bouncer is a test for both the batsman's skill and his temperament, and as such is a valuable shock delivery in any bowler's armoury. It is the abuse of the short-pitched ball, the frequent 'firing one in' (to use contemporary jargon), that poses a real threat to cricket in the future. Not only has it become a persistent form of attack designed not to bowl a batsman out but to knock him out, totally antipathetic to the traditions of the game, but it also leads to a boring spectacle. No-one who saw it can ever forget the battering that Edrich and Close took at Manchester in 1976 against four West Indian fast bowlers, bowling persistently short yet receiving condemnation neither from the umpire nor from informed spectators around the ring. It has become clear to me that there is no common interpretation of what is meant by short-pitched bowling. Whether in future we shall see a line drawn in the middle of the wicket, short of which no bowler may deliver more than once or possibly twice in an over, remains to be seen. The idea of painting a line in front of the batsman would be a hard one to accept for any traditionalist; nor would it be easy to define where that line should be drawn, because the essence of cricket is that wickets are different all over the world. Because the bounce of the pitch varies as much as it does the drawing of a line can not be a matter for standardization.

I believe cricketers instinctively recognize what constitutes persistent short-pitched bowling. The only sensible solution to this problem is that umpires should judge what may be regarded as a proper form of attack by a bowler on a batsman, or if they cannot themselves judge it, then they should listen to the ground-swell of opinion among the cricketers themselves. This means that umpires and players should remain on close and friendly terms, although at the moment we are seeing quite the opposite trend. Umpires are locking themselves in their own changing-rooms like soccer referees, and are often manifestly out of touch with the thoughts and intentions of the players on the field. Umpiring and refereeing are perhaps the hardest tasks in sport, but it is in the excellence of the arbitrators rather than in the exactness of the legislators that I see the solutions to cricket's most difficult problems.

The great debates about the leg-before-wicket law belong to our grandfathers' rather than to our fathers' day. True, there have been minor amendments in the law during the last twenty years, but the major reform which allowed a batsman to be dismissed by a ball pitching outside the off-stump, but not by a ball pitching outside the leg-stump, has by and large succeeded in eliminating play with the pad. Nonetheless, the essential feature of the present leg-before law is based on what many people consider to be an historical irrelevance, namely that the pads should be in line wicket to wicket. Originally, of course, the ball had to pitch in line wicket to wicket, the reason for this being that were it not so the side winning the toss could choose where they would pitch the wickets in order to help their own bowlers to take advantage of local topographical undulations. The leg-before law is designed to protect the fielding side from the resistance of a batsman deliberately obstructing by padding off the ball so that it should not hit his wicket. One suggestion that I find very attractive is that any batsman hit three times on the leg when the ball would otherwise have hit the wicket should be out. The leg-before law is an area in which experiments can and possibly should be made in order to try and eliminate a deliberate padding-away of the ball. It is argued still, as it was most passionately in the past, that the leg-spin bowler has been unfairly punished by the leg-before law, introduced in the 1930s, which favoured the off-spin bowler. There is much truth in this. The answer may be to experiment with a law similar to the American system of batting and pitching—namely, that if any bowler hits a batsman on the pad when he would otherwise have hit the wicket, an appeal should be made and a mark scored against the batsman, no matter where the ball bounced. Any other bowler who achieved a similar hit on a batsman's pad could likewise appeal, and once a batsman had been convicted by the umpires of three such hits, he would automatically be adjudged to be out. This seems to me to be an experiment well worth conducting. Perhaps it would fail, doubtless there would be difficulties, but the leg-before-wicket law above all others is a law which should always be kept under review and subject to experimentation.

Not so the present law restricting the captain's right to place his field. This still seems an affront to one of the essential principles of the game, an unjustified restriction on the inalienable right of bowlers and their captain. This is a law which I find odious and which I would like to see repealed. Alas the chance of any further amendment seems slim. These days it is a law accepted through use and hardly ever contested by the players.

Other laws of the game may well be amended, but there seems to me to be no law equal in significance to the four I have mentioned. Questions as to whether the catch is fairly made inside or over the boundary, about the follow-on, the length of the tea interval and such other matters are trivial by comparison.

We move on now to the equipment of the game. From time to time, when either the bat or the ball has been in the ascendant, there have been suggestions that either the bat should be widened, or the stumps widened or made taller. At one time it was mooted that a smaller ball should be introduced, until Ray Lindwall, in a devastating rebuttal of the legislators' intentions, showed exactly what he could do with such a small ball, namely deliver six quite unplayable deliveries. In the nets at Lord's I was privileged to watch Ray Lindwall, to order, bowl three inswingers and three away-swingers which were of such devastating quality that it was clear that the small ball was designed to disappear into the realms of the curious rather than of the practical.

What we have since seen is an increase in the protective equipment which batsmen have developed to suit their needs, which also reflects changes in the assault on body and wicket mounted by bowlers. Whereas it was normal in the 1930s to field a team with two fast bowlers and three spinners, in the late 1970s it is becoming normal for the West Indies, the World Cup winners, to field four fast bowlers if they are available, with perhaps one spinner for Tests and not necessarily even one for one-day cricket. The idea of a balanced attack which was part of cricket's strategic thinking even ten years ago has become old hat. All-out sustained assault now seems the simplest way to victory. In recent years I have grown much out of sympathy, and sadly so, with West Indian cricket, as crowds, players and administrators seem to gain more and more pleasure from watching a succession of fast bowlers deliver their overs at barely ten or twelve to the hour, most deliveries pitched short—and not a spinner to be seen. This is of course a far cry from the days not thirty years ago when West Indian cricket came of age with those two extraordinary spinners, Ramadhin and Valentine. Against fast bowling, batsmen have developed their own methods of protection, the most notable of which has been the helmet. At first this was a guard worn under the cap by Mike Brearley, who set the fashion and whom I personally regarded as a brave innovator at a time when some form of head protection was necessary. The number of batsmen almost killed by fast bowlers has been mounting, and the near-death of Ewan Chatfield, the New Zealand bowler, when struck by a bouncer from that mildest man among pace bowlers, Peter Lever, seemed to indicate that the situation had got almost out of control. From the padded cap, we moved swiftly to the kind of helmet worn by motorcyclists and American footballers, an ugly piece of headgear. The days when batsmen went to the wicket without a box and wearing on their hands the gloves they had sported at the opera the previous night seemed far away. Attention to the design of the glove, which batsmen like Boycott supervised so that fingers should be effectively protected no matter what their angle on the bat, showed the way for protective clothing. Gloves were rapidly followed by pads worn under the clothes. At first it was the thigh pad, worn in most instances on the front leg above the conventional pad to save the fleshy part of the upper thigh from the kind of bruising which could keep a man out of cricket for a week or longer; then chest pads, a protection for the heart; protection for the arms, especially for those who had suffered breaks in their career; and finally the helmet itself. The future will see no diminution of this trend, nor can there be legislation to prevent batsmen protecting themselves. On the contrary, with the possibility spilling over from other games of a batsman taking a bowler who has inflicted injury upon him to Court, I see our batsmen being condemned to protecting themselves totally against the ball. The school of thought that believes that cricket crowds want to see blood and bouncers is in the ascendant. Protective armour is unavoidable while the danger inherent in short-pitched bowling continues to mount.

It is quite another matter for fielders to protect themselves. It would be a sad development if this trend were allowed to continue. No short-leg, no silly point, should be encouraged or allowed to stand closer than he feels is safe, without the false courage derived from the wearing of protective armour. There has been an increasing encroachment by close fielders on the batsman's swinging area, and the only occasion on which the umpires will uphold a batsman's appeal against this encroachment is when the fielders throw shadows across the path of the oncoming ball. There have been a number of serious accidents caused by batsmen swinging at a ball which has struck a fielder—usually at short-leg. One thinks of Sidney Barnes, the Australian batsman, in 1948, and of Roger Davis, the Glamorgan all-rounder who was almost killed by such a blow. It seems inevitable that the legislators will have to make a ruling as to whether or not helmets can be worn by members of the fielding side. My own view is that if the legislators do go into print on this subject it should be to ban their use.

As for the bats themselves, the process of experimentation continues, much to the advantage of batting skill. At the present time, the trend is towards heavier bats, a number of players using bats weighting 3 lbs or even more. Twenty-five years ago the fashion was for batsmen to prefer light bats, and bats of 2 lbs 2 oz were not uncommon. Subsequently we saw bats made with sloping shoulders, which at the time it was thought helped batsmen to hook, and since then we have seen bats with the middle gouged out in order to give additional weight to the sides; we have seen bats made with holes in order to distribute the weight evenly, and we know that manufacturers are capable of shaping bats so that the batsmen can have the driving weight of their striking implement wherever they choose. Bat-makers cannot, however, manufacture fashion-bats for general consumption. Some of the ideas which have been put into practice in the first-class game seem to have little relevance to the schoolboy cricketer who needs a basic implement which will survive unbroken against the harder balls which will inevitably be used as the skills of ball-making decline and machines take over from craftsmen. It has always been possible for bat-makers to press the face of their bats harder in order that they might cope with the treatment that they will receive; indeed, a combination of considerable pressing and close grain with adequate weight at the drive will continue to be the basic design for bats. The use of steel in the handle has also been tried to good effect, particularly in periods when the cane, most of which has come from the East Indies, has been of less than first-class quality.

As for the ball, obviously a key part of the game, few detailed studies of its development have been made, simply because too few balls of earlier generations survive to enable one to test the difference between present-day balls and those made years ago, whether of first-class quality or the kind used in club cricket. Time was when the trade union of cricket-ball-makers, one of Britain's smallest, declined to bring in apprentices with the result that the average age of men in the industry, who mostly worked in small factories along the Kent and Sussex borders, rose almost to that of the old-age pension. It was at this time that Australian balls, factory-made, came into use all over the world, in preference to those made in India, which tended to be hard and lose their shape. Since then the quality of machine-made balls has risen, and now it is normal for hand-stitching to be reserved for only a few of the best balls. However, the number of balls used in Test cricket which lose their shape and need replacement, often with devastating effect on a game since one ball may swing more than another, reflects a serious decline in the quality of cricket balls as the old techniques are phased out by reason of expense. On the subject of equipment costs in general, these have risen very sharply in recent years because even now the game's implements are labour-intensive. This is one of the trends which the cricketing authorities should watch carefully. Compared with the cost of equipment for soccer—even at artificially inflated prices—cricket gear is expensive for a young man who has to kit himself out.

Rising costs are also affecting the grounds themselves. Without a doubt the labour costs of preparing wickets are going to become a luxury which only the large grounds will be able to afford in the future: unless, that is, we ever attain the promised increase in leisure-time, in which case there may be no shortage of volunteers for the weeding, forking, sifting, sowing, dressing, patching and cutting which are necessary if a club or village cricket-square is to be kept in good repair. Even now conditions in schools are causing anxiety, with pitches only being mowed under contract and at scheduled intervals, regardless of whether a cricket match is being played at the time. All this explains the intensity of research work which is currently being put into the development of artificial wickets. There is no doubt that the standard of artificial pitches has improved following research into new materials undertaken not only by the National Cricket Association in England, but also in other countries. It could well be that future generations will play all their cricket on non-grass pitches. This will not be a new development. It is rare in Australia for young players to come forward who have not played on concrete or matting wickets.

Below: probably set to be one of the outstanding fast bowlers on the Test circuit for some years, Richard Hadlee of New Zealand

There seems to be no shortage of talent because of that. Sir Don Bradman has always said that it is better to learn to play on a surface with a regular bounce than to have the youngsters of ten, twelve and fourteen trying to play the game on bad grass pitches where the ball may shoot along the ground or hit them between the eyes.

As to technique, we have seen considerable changes in recent years as a result of the increase in one-day cricket. Many of these stem from the increased fitness of the players, not only their fitness in terms of demands made by the game itself, but also their general fitness as athletes. It would have been unthinkable twenty-five years ago for Test players to be given the daily training routine which is now normal for England teams, whether in this country or abroad. Men like Bernard Thomas have insured a high degree of fitness for our teams overseas, and the demands made by one-day cricket, especially the need for speed over the ground on the part of both batsmen and fielders, have been satisfactorily met, and this has helped to check the growing trend of recent years for a slowing-down of the action. Sometimes sloth is deliberate for tactical reasons, to save fast bowlers from fatigue during the course of a series, or to deprive opposing batsmen of the strike in key periods of the game. Whatever the reasons, the slowing-down of the action in cricket is a deplorable trend and one which many legislators are determined to counter. Certainly the system of fines which applies now to all first-class cricket in England, and indeed to most Test cricket throughout the world, has been the best method yet found of reversing this trend. I raise this matter under the heading of technique because that is how it began. It is not an easy subject on which to legislate. Fundamentally the resolution of this question, like so many others in cricket, remains in the hands of captains and umpires. However, in the coming years I predict a measurable increase in the average number of overs bowled per hour during a Test match. If this indeed turns out to be the case, it will also mean that spin bowlers will have more of a chance than they have had in recent years because fast bowlers will not be able to cope with the increased pace of the action, and this must add to the game's essential and precious variety.

As far as batsmen are concerned, we have already noted their increasing ability to take, as opposed to make, their runs faster. This also implies a greater eagerness for the short run and a method of play designed to achieve it. This has been a feature of many great players in the past—Hobbs and Sutcliffe, for instance—but now it is becoming almost a universal attribute in batsmen.

Over the years batsmen have had to adopt more of a leg-side leaning, because far fewer of the balls they receive are on the off-side than was the case say fifty years ago. The ability to work the ball off the legs, whether the stroke is made on the front or the back foot, is one of the most difficult skills to acquire in batting, and it is one which has become more and more necessary for young players to master. There is some evidence that in future batsmen who swing the bat at the ball are going to be better received by coaches than those with minimal back-lift whose approach is to let the ball hit the bat. If this is indeed a trend then it will also mean that young players will be encouraged to work on their individual shots, and this is the ultimate glory in the game for those who come to watch. Three players who made certain new strokes their trademark come immediately to mind: Denis Compton, with his sweep; Rohan Kanhai, whose ability to get down on one knee either before or during a stroke has meant that he has despatched many a ball considered to be unhittable in that direction far over the square-leg boundary; and Ted Dexter with his drive off the back foot which, if it was ever played so well before his arrival in Test cricket, has certainly not been equalled since for its power and timing. There is now every indication that coaching policies are concentrating more on the encouragement of these personal styles of batting.

The great development in bowling has been the use of the seam to make the ball move off the wicket, and there is no sign of any diminution in the regard for this skill as the most significant which the bowler can possess. Speed too remains a fearsome weapon, and those countries which are developing a succession of fast bowlers are fortunate indeed; compare, for instance, the character of West Indian cricket with that of India. The balance of their two attacks is totally different. But this particular comparison serves to underline the significance of wickets in the development of the bowlers that are produced on them; whereas there seems to be an endless procession of fast bowlers in the West Indies, in India there are even more spin bowlers being developed. Other countries would be pleased to have them among their ranks.

Spin bowling in England will not survive while so much grass is left on wickets up and down the country, and it is idle to pretend that either finger-spin or wrist-spin can be developed on pitches from which the ball does not deviate even at the end of a three-day match. The trend over the years has been to overlook the spinner, and only in my most optimistic moments do I see the slide to sameness in bowling being reversed. Not only pitches, but the increase in one-day cricket has restricted the spin bowler; there are few spinners who are capable of developing a flat-arc style for one-day cricket and a flighty one for the two-innings game. For the leg-spinner, whether his delivery be flat or flighty, the future looks particularly grim. It is not part of today's cricketing tactics to admit that a bowler may bowl one bad ball an over and so risk four runs; but make no mistake, if a bad ball is bowled by a spinner it will be struck for four runs. So skilful have the modern batsmen become in their resistance to fast bowling that whatever loose balls are delivered to them at a slower speed are despatched with ease.

As for the pattern of the first-class game, the tendency will be for shorter Test tours. The players believe that the four-month tour is on the way out—these tours become tedious and unprofitable when a five-Test match tour can be completed in eight or nine weeks and a three-Test tour in six weeks with sufficient time for practice and acclimatization. I believe there is sufficient built-in conservatism for the first-class structure in the various cricketing countries to survive, that the three- and four-day matches between first-class teams will be saved, at least for the next decade. In every case it is recognized that this is good preparation for Test cricket, whether or not club cricket is of a high standard. The longer two-innings match is seen as an essential feature of the cricket of every country. It will be maintained as long as it can be sustained on financial grounds—the English counties will only abandon the County Championship and the Australian states the Sheffield Shield under the direst financial pressure. Although there are moves to bring in a two- or four-day County Championship, the weight of opinion among players and administrators is in favour of the three-day match. Perhaps such an experiment would be no bad thing, but cricket has never been good at taking a chance with its structure.

Overall hangs the threat, either incipient or actual, of rampant commercialism. Cricket is always vulnerable to private promoters or pirate captains motivated only by the need for more money from it. Kerry Packer, his eye on the exclusive T.V. contract put his head down and stormed the game's citadel, Test cricket, burgling it for talent. By throwing a match to secure added revenue for his team Brian Rose's Somerset were convicted by their peers of being too clever by half and flung out of a valuable cup competition. In the end the game heals its own wounds. At the end of the 1970s an inherent sense of fair play seems to have pulled cricket through both the major crisis of Packer's assault and the minor one of Rose's misjudgement. It will survive: and at an appropriate level of prosperity.

GREAT PLAYERS

W. G. Grace, the *eminence gris* of English cricket. A match was halted at the announcement of his mother's death

We all love to choose our best elevens, whether they are a school, club, county, or international eleven, or indeed, even an eleven where each member has the same peculiar attribute in common—a love of fishing, perhaps. I have selected here what I consider to be the best possible squad of players in each particular country from the beginning of cricket to the present day—if we could assemble them all, what a World Cup event could be staged! In some countries a squad comprises fourteen, in some only twelve. Who to leave out on the day is a familiar enough problem for selectors in cricket. If it is hard enough to sift the talent available in a single generation, it is impossible to justify a selection through the years; and especially hard for anyone who believes that comparisons in cricket are a dangerous irrelevance and that the contribution each talented player gives in his own time is in itself of unique value. It is equally difficult to avoid the conclusion that standards of play—and players—are rising; this in itself bodes well for the game, though it is a judgment that is bound to be challenged.

England

Alfred Mynn
1807-1852

Of all the great cricketers in the game's developing years, Alfred Mynn stands out as the most powerful player and personality. Over six feet in height and almost eighteen stone in weight, he had the strength of the countryman and limbs to match. In a period of small scores, he was a successful batsman and his bowling was of such speed that he was alleged to have struck a long stop in the chest so hard that the poor fellow spat blood. He won his two great single-wicket matches with his rival and friend, Felix. With Fuller Pilch, these two were the leading cricketers in the country—it is not surprising that Kent were such a powerful combination at this time. However, the most interesting feature of Alfred Mynn's career is that he was a precursor of W. G. Grace himself—in skill and in personality the two men stand comparison, as they do in their impact on their contemporaries. Mynn's epitaph is the most famous in all cricket:

With his tall and stately presence, with his nobly moulded form,
His broad hand was ever open, his brave heart was ever warm.
All were proud of him, all loved him. As the changing seasons pass,
As our champion lies a-sleeping 'neath the Kentish grass,
Proudly, sadly, we will name him—to forget him were a sin.
Lightly lie the turf upon thee,
kind and manly Alfred Mynn.

Teams: Kent
Test Series: Nil
Career runs: 8,853 Average: 12.42
Career wickets: 342 Average: 9.18

W. G. Grace
1848-1915

William Gilbert Grace was almost fifteen years old when he made his first score in an important match—32 against an All-England eleven—and he was fifty-eight when he made his last—74 for the Gentlemen against the Players.

A career of forty-three years in cricket at a time when the game was becoming a significant feature of the English summer is the reason why he and Mr Gladstone were the best-known Englishmen of their age. Others have scored more runs, taken more wickets, caught more catches than W.G., but no-one has ever achieved his status. He knew everybody in cricket and everybody knew him. In his fifty-first year he retired from Test cricket because, as he said, 'the ground was getting a bit too far away.'

W.G.'s batting was forthright and uncomplicated, and his bowling followed the round-arm action of old, with variations of pace and the ball moving a little from leg. Considering the wickets on which he played, and the variety of bowlers that he met, his run-making feats are truly astonishing. He and his two brothers played together in a Test for England against Australia at The Oval in 1880; a month after this match, in which he sadly got a pair, G.F. Grace died of a chill.

Teams: Gloucestershire, London County, and England

Test series		Tests	Runs	100s	Aver-age	Wkts	Aver-age
1880	v Australia	1	161	1	161.00	3	22.66
1882	v Australia	1	36	—	18.00	—	—
1884	v Australia	3	72	—	18.00	3	12.66
1886	v Australia	3	200	1	50.00	1	22.00
1888	v Australia	3*	73	—	18.25	—	—
1890	v Australia	2*	91	—	30.33	2	6.00
1891-92	in Australia	3	164	—	32.80	0	—
1893	v Australia	2†	153	—	51.00	—	—
1896	v Australia	3†	119	—	19.83	0	—
1899	v Australia	1†	29	—	14.50	0	—
Total		22	1,098	2	32.29	9	26.22

Career runs: 54,904 Average: 39.52
Highest Test score: 170 v Australia, Oval, 1886
Highest career score: 344, MCC v Kent, Canterbury, 1876
Career wickets: 2,876 Average: 17.92
Best Test bowling: 2-12 v Australia, Lord's, 1890
Best career bowling: 10-49, MCC v Oxford University, 1886

* Captain (in two Tests in 1888) † Captain

Sydney Barnes
1873-1967

Sydney Barnes is the best argument in history in favour of a cricketer saving himself for Test matches. He played only a few first-class county games for Warwickshire in the mid-nineties and for Lancashire between 1899 and 1903, although his record for Staffordshire is astonishing; in 1934 he was still capable, at the age of fifty-eight of taking 61 wickets for 11 runs each. His Test bag was 189 wickets. When he was in his late thirties, in 1911-12, his bowling alone won a series for England in Australia. In South Africa he took 49 wickets in four Test matches.

His high arm action gave him the ability to move the ball in either direction on any wicket—his greatest asset. His deadliest ball was one delivered from the outside of the crease which swung in and then came back from leg, a constant threat to the off-stump.

Not the easiest of men, he had one other remarkable attribute—his beautiful handwriting. He was still inscribing in perfect copper-plate in his eighties.

Teams: Warwickshire, Lancashire and England

Test series		Tests	Runs	100s	Aver-age	Wkts	Aver-age
1901-02	in Australia	3				19	17.00
1902	in England	1				7	14.14
1907-08	in Australia	5				24	26.08
1909	in England	3				17	20.00
1911-12	in Australia	5				34	22.88
1912	in England	6				39	10.35
1913-14	in S. Africa	4				49	10.93
Total		27			8.06	189	16.43

Career wickets: 719 Average: 16.92
Best Test and Career bowling: 9-103 v South Africa (Johannesburg) 1913-14

Gilbert Jessop
1874-1955

Jessop was the man who consistently scored his runs at a rate of almost 100 an hour. His greatest innings was in the Oval Test match against Australia in 1902, when he made 104 in seventy-five minutes on a difficult pitch; after this, Hirst and Rhodes were able to see England home.

Compared to many of the earlier giants, who were huge in both stature and achievement, Jessop was a small man whose exceptional strength was concentrated in his hands and long arms.

He was known as 'The Croucher' because he seemed to fling himself at the ball, taking it very early and attacking it always. In the field, too, he was always a joy to watch—as a stopper and thrower he was unequalled among his generation.

Teams: Cambridge University, Gloucestershire and England

Test series		Tests	Runs	100s	Average
1899	in England	1	55	—	27.50
1901-02	in Australia	5	166	—	18.44
1902	in England	4	190	1	38.00
1905	in England	1	0	—	0
1907	in England	3	116	—	23.20
1909	in England	2	22	—	22.00
1912	in England	2	20	—	6.66
Total		18	569	1	21.88

Career runs: 26,698 Average: 32.63
Highest Test score: 104 v Australia, Oval, 1902
Highest career score: 286 Gloucestershire v Sussex, Hove, 1903

Wilfred Rhodes
1877-1973

Wilfred Rhodes was statistically the greatest all-round cricketer that England has ever seen. He heads the list of those who have achieved the double of 1,000 runs and 100 wickets, having managed this feat in no fewer than sixteen seasons. He played for Yorkshire as a twenty-year-old and was still playing at the age of fifty-two. In the course of his career with England he moved himself from number eleven in the batting order to number one, and was called back to play for England at the age of forty-eight, when he took 4 for 44 in The Oval test of 1926, having been first capped in 1899. In 1930, at Scarborough, he took a wicket with the last ball he bowled in first-class cricket. His bowling was

beautiful in its simplicity, his batting somewhat pedestrian by comparison; as a coach he taught boys at Harrow to be safe rather than adventurous. Sadly, in his last years he lost his sight, but even so was a frequent visitor to cricket matches where he was able to follow the game with his ears alone, and surprised all who came to know and respect him with his continuing knowledge of the game and his admiration for each succeeding generation.

Teams: Yorkshire and England

Test series		Tests	Runs	100s	Aver-age	Wkts	Aver-age
1899	in England	3	18	—	6.00	13	26.23
1902	in England	5	67	—	67.00	22	15.27
1903-04	in Australia	5	126	—	18.00	31	15.74
1905	in England	4	146	—	48.66	10	31.40
1907-08	in Australia	5	205	—	20.50	7	60.14
1909	in England	4	168	—	33.60	11	22.00
1909-10	in S Africa	5	226	—	25.11	2	73.50
1911-12	in Australia	5	463	1	57.87	—	—
1912	in England	6	257	—	32.12	3	24.66
1913-14	in S Africa	5	289	1	41.28	6	32.50
1920-21	in Australia	5	238	—	23.80	4	61.25
1921	in England	1	29		14.50	2	16.50
1926	in England	1	42	—	21.00	6	13.16
1929-30	in W Indies	4	51	—	25.50	10	45.30
Total		58	2,325	2	30.19	127	26.96

Career runs: 39,802 Average: 30.83
Highest Test score: 179 v Australia, Melbourne, 1911-12
Highest career score: 267* Yorkshire v Leicestershire, Leeds, 1921
Career wickets: 4187 Average: 16.71
Best Test bowling: 8-68 v Australia, Melbourne, 1903-04
Best career bowling: 9-24, C. I. Thornton's XI v Australians, Scarborough, 1899
* Not out

Jack Hobbs
1882-1963

In the course of his career John Berry Hobbs, the boy who went from Cambridge to The Oval, made 61,237 runs. He hit 197 first-class 100s, ninety-eight of them after the age of forty.

Statistics are too dry to convey his magic—Jack Hobbs was a lovely man, a perfect gentleman, who inspired such love and affection in others that the most famous of all cricket dining clubs—the Masters—was founded to celebrate his very existence.

Apart from his batting he was a great fielder, luring batsmen (no fewer than fifteen Australians on one tour) to destruction as they attempted to take singles to him in the covers. He was also a great practical joker and liked nothing better than to liven up the dressing-room. It was not unknown for him to set fire to the newspapers some of his team-mates were reading in The Oval dressing-room, as Herbert Strudwick, the great wicketkeeper, was fond of reminding him. Together these two liked nothing better than to scrap on the golf-course at West Hove when both were well into pensionable age.

Teams: Surrey and England

Test series		Tests	Runs	100s	Average
1907-08	in Australia	4	302	—	43.14
1909	v Australia	3	132	—	26.40
1909-10	in South Africa	5	539	1	67.37
1911-12	in Australia	5	662	3	82.75
1912	v Australia	3	224	1	56.00
1912	v South Africa	3	163	—	40.75
1913-14	in South Africa	5	443	—	63.28
1920-21	in Australia	5	505	2	50.50
1921	v Australia	1	—	—	—
1924	v South Africa	4	355	1	71.00
1924-25	in Australia	5	573	3	63.66
1926	v Australia	5	486	2	81.00
1928	v West Indies	2	212	1	106.00
1928-29	in Australia	5	451	1	50.11
1929	v South Africa	1	62	—	31.00
1930	v Australia	5	301	—	33.44
Total		61	5,410	15	56.94

Career runs: 61,237 Average: 50.65
Highest Test score: 211 v South Africa, Lord's, 1924
Highest career score: 316*, Surrey v Middlesex, Lord's, 1926
* Not out

Walter Hammond
1903-1965

Walter Reginald Hammond is so associated with Gloucestershire that it is easy to forget that he was born in Dover. His batting was simple but powerful and his ability to drive the ball unparalleled. In his early days he was capable of striking such form that it was impossible to bowl at him. He was a fine bowler, at above-medium pace, especially with the new ball, and England has never had a better slip catcher.

Teams: Gloucestershire and England

Test series	Tests	Runs	100s	Average	Wkts	Average
1927-28 in S Africa	5	321	—	40.12	15	26.60
1928 v W Indies	3	111	—	37.00	3	34.33
1928-29 in Australia	5	905	4	113.12	5	57.40
1929 v S Africa	4	352	2	58.66	1	95.00
1930 v Australia	5	306	1	34.00	5	60.40
1930-31 in S Africa	5	517	1	64.62	9	26.66
1931 v N Zealand	3	169	1	56.33	2	34.00
1932 v India	1	47	—	23.50	3	8.00
1932-33 in Australia	5	440	2	55.00	9	32.33
1932-33 in N Zealand	2	563	2	563.00	0	—
1933 v W Indies	3	74	—	24.66	0	—
1934 v Australia	5	162	—	20.25	5	72.80
1934-35 in W Indies	4	175	—	25.00	0	—
1935 v S Africa	5	389	—	64.83	6	24.33
1936 v India	2	389	2	194.50	1	94.00
1936-37 in Australia	5	468	1	58.50	12	25.08
1937 v N Zealand	3	204	1	51.00	4	25.25
1938 v Australia	4†	403	1	67.16	0	—
1938-39 in S Africa	5†	609	3	87.00	3	53.66
1939 v W Indies	3†	279	1	55.80	—	—
1946 v India	3†	119	—	39.66	0	—
1946-47 in Australia	4†	168	—	21.00	—	—
1946-47 in N Zealand	1†	79	—	79.00	—	—
Total	85	7,249	22	58.45	83	37.83

Career runs: 50,551 Average: 56.10
Highest Test and career score:
336* v New Zealand, Auckland, 1932-33
Career wickets: 732 Average: 30.58
Best Test bowling: 5-36 v South Africa, Johannesburg, 1927-28
Best career bowling: 9-23, Gloucestershire v Warwickshire, Cheltenham, 1928

* Not out † Captain

Harold Larwood
1904-

Harold Larwood first appeared for Nottinghamshire as a nineteen-year-old. He had long arms, although he was not a tall man, about 5 ft 8 in. He ran about eighteen yards to the wicket, accelerating with every stride, his knuckles almost touching the ground at the end of his follow-through. He was without doubt the fastest bowler of his generation. It is his speed which is always emphasized by those to whom he bowled, but it was speed and accuracy which made him such a fearsome opponent for cricketers throughout the world, particularly on the county cricket circuit. It was this accuracy too which made him an ideal person to implement Douglas Jardine's plan to contain Bradman: namely, to bowl short at the batsman with a ring of fielders close in on the leg-side. These were the tactics which were employed very successfully from an English point of view in the 1932-3 series and Larwood, as Jardine's foil, naturally received much criticism for the role he played. However, the Australians held Larwood in great esteem, and he has been living in their country since 1950.

Teams: Nottinghamshire and England

Test series	Tests	Wkts	Average
1926 v Australia	2	9	28.00
1928 v West Indies	2	6	19.00
1928-29 in Australia	5	18	40.44
1929 v South Africa	3	8	23.25
1930 v Australia	3	4	73.00
1931 v New Zealand	1	—	—
1932-33 in Australia	5	33	19.51
Total	21	78	28.41

Career wickets: 1,427 Average: 17.51
Best Test bowling: 6-32 v Australia, Brisbane, 1928-29
Best career bowling: 9-41, Nottinghamshire v Kent, Trent Bridge, 1931
Highest Test score: 98 v Australia, Sydney, 1932-33
Highest career score: 102*, Nottinghamshire v Sussex, Trent Bridge, 1931

* Not out

Leonard Hutton
1916-

Leonard Hutton, knighted in 1956, will always be remembered for his record score of 364 at The Oval in 1938, and for becoming the first professional in modern times to captain England; successfully too.

A batsman in the classic mould, Len Hutton's cover-drive was unforgettable to those who saw it, cricketing perfection. Like many other cricketers who suffer physical damage, he had to make a difficult adjustment following an injury to his left and guiding forearm during the Second World War, but he remained a fine player to the day he retired.

Captaincy tried him, as it has tried many who have led teams in Test matches and on tour, but Hutton's victory in Australia and his shared series in the West Indies, admittedly with superb teams to back him, still represent the greatest achievement by an England captain in recent times.

A shrewd man, his humour has a waspish quality which is a delight to his friends and colleagues.

Teams: Yorkshire and England

Test series		**Tests**	**Runs**	**100s**	**Average**
1937	v New Zealand	3	127	1	25.40
1938	v Australia	3	473	2	118.25
1938-39	in South Africa	4	265	—	44.16
1939	v West Indies	3	480	2	96.00
1946	v India	3	123	—	30.75
1946-47	in Australia	5	417	1	52.12
1947	v South Africa	5	344	1	43.00
1947-48	in West Indies	2	171	—	42.75
1948	v Australia	4	342	—	42.75
1948-49	in South Africa	5	577	2	64.11
1949	v New Zealand	4	469	2	78.16
1950	v West Indies	3	333	1	66.60
1950-51	in Australia	5	533	1	88.83
1950-51	in New Zealand	2	114	—	38.00
1951	v South Africa	5	378	1	54.00
1952	v India	4†	399	2	79.80
1953	v Australia	5†	443	1	55.37
1953-54	in West Indies	5†	677	2	96.71
1954	v Pakistan	2†	19	—	6.33
1954-55	in Australia	5†	220	—	24.44
1954-55	in New Zealand	2†	67	—	22.33
Total		79	6,971	19	56.67

Career runs: 40,140 Average: 55.51
Highest Test and career score: 364, England v Australia, Oval, 1938

* Captain

Denis Compton
1918-

Denis Charles Scott Compton is arguably the finest natural batsman that England has ever produced. A superb natural athlete with a delightful free-ranging personality that could not be restrained, Compton played cricket as if he enjoyed every moment of it. It showed, and it was this quality which made him so popular wherever he travelled.

He was a marvellous batsman to bowl at because despite his genius and unpredictability he gave the bowler a chance to attack him. The sweep was his great stroke and the one which he patented. His driving square on the off-side was also unique. One of the few men to play both cricket and football at the highest level, his greatest season was in 1947 when he scored eighteen 100s and a total of 3,816 runs. He was also a fine left-arm googly bowler and a splendidly instinctive catcher, although arguably the worst runner between the wickets the game has ever seen, his most disastrous call running out his brother Leslie in his benefit match.

Teams: Middlesex and England

Test series		**Tests**	**Runs**	**100s**	**Average**
1937	in England	1	65	—	65.00
1938	in England	4	214	1	42.50
1939	in England	3	189	1	63.00
1946	in England	3	146	—	73.00
1946-47	in Australia	5	459	2	51.00
1946-47	in New Zealand	1	38	—	38.00
1947	in England	5	753	4	94.12
1948	in England	5	562	2	62.44
1948-49	in S Africa	5	406	1	50.75
1949	in England	4	300	2	50.00
1950	in England	1	55	1	27.50
1950-51	in Australia	4	53	—	7.57
1950-51	in New Zealand	2	107	—	35.66
1951	in England	4	312	1	52.00
1952	in England	2	59	—	29.50
1953	in England	5	234	—	33.42
1953-54	in West Indies	5	348	1	49.71
1954	in England	4	453	1	90.60
1954-55	in Australia	4	191	—	38.20
1955	in England	5	492	1	54.66
1956	in England	1	129	—	129.00
1956-57	in South Africa	5	242	—	24.20
Total		78	5,807	17	50.06

Career runs: 38,942 Average: 51.85
Highest Test score: 278 v Pakistan, Nottingham, 1954
Highest career score: 300 MCC v N.E. Transvaal. Benoni, 1948-49

Jim Laker
1922-

Jim Laker was a Yorkshireman who began work in a Bradford bank and became the best off-spinner the game has ever seen. He was twenty-five when he started to play regularly for Surrey, but it was not until he was thirty-four that he won a regular place in the England side in 1956, having previously taken much punishment at the hands of the 1948 Australian side. In that summer he not only took all 10 wickets for Surrey against the Australians for 88, but in the Test match at Old Trafford just a month later took 10 wickets for 53, following first-innings figures of 9 for 37. He is the only bowler in the game's history to have taken 19 wickets in a first-class match. It is a performance which could hardly be bettered and may never be equalled. He retired in 1959 at the age of thirty-seven, an early age for spin bowlers, having been troubled with an arthritic finger. He wrote a book called *Over to Me* which created some controversy, left Surrey, and subsequently played just a few games for Essex. He has been able to maintain his connection with cricket as a television commentator of high renown. Succeeding generations of cricketers know him to be not only one of the best analysts in the game but also one of the leading coaches.

Teams: Surrey, Essex and England

Test series		Tests	Wickets	Average
1947-48	in West Indies	4	18	30.33
1948	v Australia	3	9	52.44
1949	v New Zealand	1	4	22.25
1950	v West Indies	1	1	86.00
1951	v South Africa	2	14	14.85
1952	v India	4	8	23.62
1953	v Australia	3	9	23.55
1953-54	in West Indies	4	14	33.50
1954	v Pakistan	1	2	19.50
1955	v South Africa	1	7	12.00
1956	v Australia	5	46	9.60
1956-57	in South Africa	5	11	29.45
1957	v West Indies	4	18	24.88
1958	v New Zealand	4	17	10.17
1958-59	in Australia	4	15	21.20
Total		46	193	21.23

Career wickets: 1,944 Average: 18.40
Best Test and career bowling: 10-53 v Australia, Old Trafford, 1956
Highest Test score: 63 v Australia, Trent Bridge, 1948
Highest career score: 113, Surrey v Gloucestershire, Oval, 1954

Fred Trueman
1931-

Frederick Sewards Trueman, born in 1931, follows Alfred Mynn, W. G. Grace and Jack Hobbs as a legend in his own lifetime. A Yorkshireman every inch of the way, a miner's son with coal-black hair, Fred Trueman became a magnificently hostile yet totally graceful fast bowler with as fine an action as the game has ever seen. In his early days 'Fiery Fred' had more brushes with authority than with batsmen; but for this he would have established an unassailable Test record. With 307 wickets at 21.57 apiece he heads the England bowlers. 'Will anybody else get more than 300?' he was once asked. 'If he does he'll be bloody tired,' was Fred's answer.

Teams: Yorkshire and England

Test series		Tests	Wkts	Average
1952	v India	4	29	13.31
1953	v Australia	1	4	22.50
1953-54	in West Indies	3	9	46.66
1955	v South Africa	1	2	56.00
1956	v Australia	2	9	20.44
1957	v West Indies	5	22	20.68
1958	v New Zealand	5	15	17.06
1958-59	in Australia	3	9	30.66
1958-59	in New Zealand	2	5	21.00
1959	v India	5	24	16.70
1959-60	in West Indies	5	21	26.14
1960	v South Africa	5	25	20.32
1961	v Australia	4	20	26.45
1962	v Pakistan	4	22	19.95
1962-63	in Australia	5	20	26.05
1962-63	in New Zealand	2	14	11.71
1963	v West Indies	5	34	17.47
1964	v Australia	4	17	23.47
1965	v New Zealand	2	6	39.50
Total		67	307	21.57

Career wickets: 2,304 Average: 18.29
Best Test bowling: 8-31 v India, Old Trafford, 1952
Best career bowling: 8-28, Yorkshire v Kent, Dover, 1954
Highest Test score: 39* v New Zealand, Oval, 1958
Highest career score: 104, Yorkshire v Northamptonshire, Northampton, 1963
* Not out

Alan Knott
1946-

A. P. E. Knott is one of a long line of wicketkeeper-batsmen to originate in Kent: Leslie Ames and Godfrey Evans are two others of the highest class. Les Ames hit 100 centuries, kept wicket to men like Tich Freeman, and was a key member of the great batting side England fielded between the wars; subsequently, Godfrey Evans, an agile and stimulating wicketkeeper, stamped his exuberant personality on the England side. However, for consistency of performance both behind the stumps and with the bat, together with his ability to come in and play a great innings just when it is needed, Alan Knott takes the palm. Certainly his career is ample justification for the theory that any batsman-wicketkeeper is a more useful member of a team than a wicketkeeper who cannot bat, however brilliant he may be.

Teams: Kent, Tasmania and England

Test series		Tests	Runs	100s	Average
1967	in England	2	28	—	14.00
1967-68	in West Indies	2	149	—	149.00
1968	in England	5	116	—	16.57
1968-69	in Pakistan	3	180	—	60.00
1969	in England	6	193	—	21.44
1970-71	in Australia	6	222	—	31.71
1970-71	in New Zealand	1	197	1	98.50
1971	in England	6	360	1	45.00
1972	in England	5	229	—	28.62
1972-73	in India	5	168	—	21.00
1972-73	in Pakistan	3	199	—	49.75
1973	in England	6	107	—	11.89
1973-74	in West Indies	5	365	—	45.62
1974	in England	6	158	—	26.33
1974-75	in Australia	6	364	1	36.40
1974-75	in New Zealand	2	29	—	—
1975	in England	4	261	—	37.28
1976	in England	5	270	1	30.00
1976-77	in India	5	268	—	38.28
1976-77	in Australia	1	57	—	28.50
1977	in England	5	255	1	36.42
Total		89	4,175	5	33.66

Career runs: 14,000 Average: 30.56
Highest Test score: 135 v Australia, Nottingham, 1977
Highest career score: 156, MCC v South Zone, Bangalore, 1972-73
Career dismissals: 928 catches + 104 stumpings = 1032
Test dismissals: 233 catches + 19 stumpings = 252

Australia

F. R. Spofforth
1853-1926

Frederick Robert Spofforth missed the first Test match ever but played in the second at Melbourne at the age of twenty-three. He was twenty-nine when his bowling won the Ashes Test match of 1882. Changing ends, he began a spell of three overs in which he took 4 wickets for 2 runs and brought his figures in the match to 14 wickets for 90.

He was 6 ft 2 in tall. Originally he was very fast off a run of less than ten yards, with a great leap in his action before a full follow-through, but as he grew older, 'the Demon', as he was well named, acquired all the known subtleties, and by the end of his Test career used his speed just as an occasional variation.

Teams: New South Wales, Victoria, Derbyshire and Australia

Test series		Tests	Wkts	Average
1876-77	in Australia	1	4	27.75
1878-79	in Australia	1	3	8.12
1881-82	in Australia	1	1	128.00
1882	in England	1	14	6.57
1882-83	in Australia	4	18	22.66
1884	in England	3	10	30.10
1884-85	in Australia	3	19	16.10
1886	in England	3	14	18.57
1886-87	in Australia	1	1	17.00
Total		18	94	18.41

Career wickets: 840 Average: 15.05
Best Test bowling: 7-44 v England, Oval, 1882 and Sydney, 1882-83
Best career bowling: 9-18, Australians v Oxford University, Oxford, 1886

Hugh Trumble
1867-1938

There were many splendid bowlers in the early days of Australian Test cricket—Ferris, Cotter and many others—but the most successful of all was Hugh Trumble, who bowled at medium pace with a break from the off. He had an outstanding cricket brain and was adept in adapting his field and his line against different batsmen. Like many other Australian bowlers he was also adept with the bat, and a good slip fielder.

After his retirement he was for many years secretary of the Melbourne Cricket Club, then Australia's most prestigious position in cricket administration.

Test series		Tests	Wkts	Average
1890	in England	2	2	22.50
1893	in England	3	6	39.00
1894-95	in Australia	1	3	29.00
1896	in England	3	18	18.83
1897-98	in Australia	5	19	28.15
1899	in England	5	15	25.00
1901-02	in Australia	5	28	20.03
1902	in England	3	26	14.26
1902-03	in South Africa	1	—	—
1903-04	in Australia	4	24	16.58
Total		32	141	21.78

Career wickets: 929 Average: 18.44
Best Test bowling: 8-65 v England, Oval, 1902
Best career bowling: 9-39, Australia v South of England, Bournemouth, 1902

Victor Trumper
1877-1915

Victor Thomas Trumper was born in 1877, the same year as Clem Hill. In his first innings as a twenty-one-year-old he scored 292 for New South Wales against Tasmania; in 1902, at the age of twenty-four, he established himself as one of the all-time greats by making 2,570 runs, a total which included eleven centuries—and this in one of the wettest of English summers. He was a superb player on bad wickets, and his drive is the subject of the most famous of all photographs from the golden age of the game.

Teams: New South Wales and Australia

Test series		Tests	Runs	100s	Average
1899	in England	5	280	1	35.00
1901-02	in Australia	5	219	—	21.90
1902	in England	5	247	1	30.87
1902-03	in South Africa	3	239	—	47.80
1903-04	in Australia	5	574	2	63.77
1905	in England	5	125	—	17.85
1907-08	in Australia	5	338	1	33.80
1909	in England	5	211	—	26.37
1910-11	in Australia	5	661	2	94.42
1911-12	in Australia	5	209	1	29.88
Total		48	3,164	8	39.06

Career runs: 16,939 Average: 44.57
Highest Test score: 214* v South Africa, Adelaide, 1910-11
Highest career score: 300*, Australians v Sussex, Hove, 1899

Clem Hill
1877-1945

Clem Hill first played for Australia at the age of nineteen, and remained a member of the Test team for fifteen years. He was one of the greatest left-handed batsmen of all time, despite the fact that his stance was far from classic, for he stood with his feet apart and the bat held low on the handle. He was nevertheless a very attacking batsman, merciless with anything short of a length. He also enjoyed coming in third, not normally the favourite position in a Test batting order. Hill sustained the Australian left-handed tradition whose earlier exponents included Warren Bardsley, Arthur Morris, Neil Harvey and Bill Lawry.

Teams: South Australia and Australia

Test series		Tests	Runs	100s	Average
1896	in England	3	30	—	5.00
1897-98	in Australia	5	452	1	56.50
1899	in England	3	301	1	60.20
1901-02	in Australia	5	521	—	52.10
1902	in England	5	258	1	36.85
1902-03	in South Africa	3	327	1	81.75
1903-04	in Australia	5	276	—	27.60
1905	in England	5	188	—	20.88
1907-08	in Australia	5	360	1	36.00
1910-11	in Australia	5	425	2	53.12
1911-12	in Australia	5	274	—	27.40
Total		49	3,412	7	39.21

Career runs: 17,216 Average: 43.47
Highest Test score: 191 v South Africa, Sydney, 1910-11
Highest career score: 365*, South Australia v New South Wales, Adelaide, 1900-01

Warwick Armstrong
1879-1947

Warwick Armstrong was a huge man, twenty-two stone when he retired, who captained Australia ten times without defeat. In all he played fifty Test matches, enjoying frequent success with both bat and ball. However, it was as a captain that he made his mark, for he was a tough disciplinarian and a man who liked to dominate his opponents. Armstrong gave his country its tradition of cricketing one-upmanship in the early 1920s, a tradition which has helped Australian sides to play above their potential ever since.

Teams: Victoria and Australia

Test series		Tests	Runs	100s	Average	Wkts	Average
1901-02	in Australia	4	159	—	53.00	—	—
1902	in England	5	97	—	13.85	2	61.50
1902-03	in S Africa	3	281	1	20.25	2	64.00
1903-04	in Australia	3	125	—	20.83	2	79.00
1905	in England	5	252	—	31.50	16	33.62
1907-08	in Australia	5	410	1	45.55	14	25.78
1909	in England	5	189	—	23.62	14	20.92
1910-11	in Australia	5	410	1	51.25	11	46.09
1911-12	in Australia	5	324	—	32.40	9	37.11
1920-21	in Australia	5†	464	3	77.33	9	22.66
1921	in England	5†	152	—	30.40	8	26.50
Total		50	2,863	6	38.68	87	33.59

Career runs: 16,177 Average: 46.75
Highest Test score: 159* v South Africa, Johannesburg, 1902-03
Highest career score: 303* Australians v Somerset Bath, 1905
Career wickets: 828 Average: 19.76
Best Test bowling: 6-35 v England, Lord's, 1909

Best career bowling: 8-47, Australians v Notts, Nottingham, 1902

† Captain

Ted McDonald
1892-1937

Edgar Arthur McDonald was a Tasmanian who, like Max Walker half a century later, played his cricket in Australia for Victoria. He appeared in only a few Test matches for his country because he came to England to play for Lancashire. He had a perfect bowling action, a sharp contrast with his famous partner Jack Gregory. However, together these two spearheaded the bowling of the Australian eleven that beat England just after the first World War, when England's batting was exceptionally strong. At the age of forty-five MacDonald died in a car accident.

Teams: Tasmania, Victoria, Lancashire and Australia

Test series		Tests	Wkts	Average
1920-21	in Australia	3	6	65.33
1921	in England	5	27	26.50
1921-22	in South Africa	3	10	37.10
Total		11	43	33.27

Career wickets: 1395 Average: 20.76
Best Test bowling: 5-32 v England, Oval, 1921
Best career bowling: 8-41, Australians v Leicestershire, Leicester, 1921

Bert Oldfield
1894-1976

Bert Oldfield was keeping wicket for New South Wales immediately after the First World War at the age of twenty-six. He played in fifty-four Test matches for Australia and was a key member of some of the greatest teams ever to leave his country. He was by no means a poor batsman, averaging over 22 in Test matches. He was a great and popular Test match cricketer, and subsequently did much work in encouraging young cricketers in Australia, at one point taking a side to East Africa. His career gave him a close view of the then great Australian left-handed spinners Arthur Mailey, Clarrie Grimmett and Bill O'Reilly.

Teams: New South Wales and Australia

Test series		Tests	Runs	100s	Average
1920-21	in Australia	3	107	—	21.40
1921	in England	1	28	—	—
1921-22	in South Africa	1	2	—	2.00
1924-25	in Australia	5	291	—	41.57
1926	in England	5	112	—	28.00
1928-29	in Australia	5	159	—	19.87
1930	in England	5	96	—	19.20
1930-31	in Australia	5	90	—	22.50
1931-32	in Australia	5	98	—	19.60
1932-33	in Australia	4	136	—	27.20
1934	in England	5	108	—	18.00
1935-36	in South Africa	5	121	—	24.20
1936-37	in Australia	5	79	—	9.87
Total		54	1,427	—	22.65

Career runs: 6135 Average 23.77
Highest Test score: 65* v England, Sydney, 1924-25
Highest career score: 137, Australians v Canterbury, Christchurch, 1927-28
Career dismissals: 78 catches, 52 stumpings = 130

Bill Woodfull
1897-1965

Bill Woodfull was captain of Australia in twenty-five of the thirty-five Test matches in which he played. He and Ponsford made a splendid opening pair for both Victoria and Australia. Despite a restricted back-lift he was a hard man to move; not quick on his feet, he took the worst of the bodyline bowling. A schoolmaster by career he was very different from Armstrong, his predecessor, yet no less respected.

Teams: Victoria and Australia

Test series		Tests	Runs	100s	Average
1926	in England	5	306	2	51.00
1928-29	in Australia	5	491	3	54.55
1930	in England	5†	345	1	57.50
1930-31	in Australia	5†	195	—	32.50
1931-32	in Australia	5†	430	1	71.67
1932-33	in Australia	5†	305	—	33.88
1934	in England	5†	228	—	28.50
Total		35	2,300	7	46.00

Career runs: 13,392 Average: 65.00
Highest Test score: 161 v South Africa, Melbourne, 1931-32
Highest career score: 284 Australia v New Zealand XI, Auckland, 1927-28

† Captain

Bill O'Reilly
1905-

Bill O'Reilly first played for Australia in 1931-32, when the South Africans visited the country, and he continued in the Test side until after the Second World War. His nickname was 'Tiger' and he well deserved it, for no bowler, certainly no spin bowler, ever attacked a batsman with greater gusto. He was a leg-spinner and googly bowler; his googly turned less than the heavily spun deliveries of Clarrie Grimmett or the flighted ones of Arthur Mailey, his two great predecessors, but O'Reilly's particular gift was an ability to make the ball bounce on Australian pitches, and any batsman instructed to attack him or to knock him off his length was almost bound to fail. He has continued to follow the game from the Press box, where he is recognized as one of the shrewdest Australian judges, critical but fair.

Teams: New South Wales and Australia

Test series	Tests	Wkts	Average
1931-32 in Australia	2	7	24.85
1932-33 in Australia	5	27	26.81
1934 in England	5	28	24.92
1935-36 in S. Africa	5	27	17.03
1936-37 in Australia	5	25	22.20
1938 in England	4	22	27.72
1945-46 in New Zealand	1	8	4.13
Total	27	144	22.59

Career wickets: 774 Average: 16.60
Best Test bowling: 7-54 v England, Nottingham, 1934
Best career bowling: 9-38, Australians v Somerset, Taunton, 1934

Don Bradman
1908-

Donald George Bradman was the greatest batsman of all time. He was such an outstanding player that bodyline bowling had to be invented in order to contain him. Once this was judged unacceptable he began to score runs again, though never with such profusion as in his salad days.

As a captain, he lost not one rubber. When he retired at the end of the 1948 season his tally in Test cricket was four runs short of 7,000, and his average a staggering 99.94. He made twenty-nine 100s, three more than Sobers and seven more than Cowdrey, his nearest rivals. Subsequently he became an outstanding selector and a major influence in cricketing administration, a man whose opinion was sought not only in Australia, but all over the world.

Teams: New South Wales, South Australia and Australia

Test series	Tests	Runs	100s	Average
1928-29 v England	4	468	2	66.85
1930 in England	5	974	4	139.14
1930-31 v West Indies	5	447	2	74.50
1931-32 v South Africa	5	806	4	201.50
1932-33 v England	4	396	1	56.57
1934 in England	5	756	2	94.75
1936-37 v England†	5	810	3	90.00
1938 in England†	4	434	3	108.50
1946-47 v England†	5	680	2	97.14
1947-48 v India†	5	715	4	178.75
1948 in England†	5	508	2	72.57
Total	52	6,996	29	99.94

Career runs: 28,067 Average: 95.14
Highest Test score: 334 v England, Leeds, 1930
Highest career score: 452* New South Wales v Queensland, Sydney, 1929-30
* Not out † Captain

Keith Miller
1919-

Keith Ross Miller was the most glamorous cricketer of his generation, and his cricket was as exciting as his personality. He was not the best batsman on bad wickets, although he could be devastating on good ones, but it was as a bowler that he was so memorable. Almost casual, he nonetheless generated considerable pace and bounce from his short run and glorious body action; he and Lindwall made a formidable opening pair. Miller was an emotional cricketer, unusual in his moods and his apparent carelessness. He is gifted with an astonishing ear for classical music.

Teams: Victoria, New South Wales, and Australia

Test series	Tests	Runs	100s	Average	Wkts	Average
1945-46 in N Zealand	1	30	—	30.00	2	3.00
1946-47 v England	5	384	1	76.80	16	20.87
1947-48 v India	5	185	—	37.00	9	24.77
1948 in England	5	184	—	28.26	13	23.15
1949-50 in S Africa	5	246	—	41.00	17	22.94
1950-51 v England	5	350	1	43.75	17	17.70
1951-52 v W Indies	5	362	1	40.22	20	19.90
1952-53 v S Africa	4	153	—	25.50	13	18.53
1953 in England	5	223	1	24.77	10	30.30
1954-55 v England	4	167	—	23.85	10	24.30
1954-55 in W Indies	5	439	3	73.16	20	32.00
1956 in England	5	203	—	22.55	21	22.23
1956-57 in Pakistan	1	32	—	16.00	2	29.00
Total	55	2,958	7	36.97	170	22.97

Career runs: 14,183 Average: 48.90
Highest Test score: 147 v West Indies, Kingston, 1954-55
Highest career score: 281*, Australians v Leicestershire, Leicester, 1956
Career wickets: 497 Average: 22.29
Best Test bowling: 7-60 v England, Brisbane, 1946-47
Best career bowling: 7-12, New South Wales v South Australia, 1955-56
* Not out

Ray Lindwall
1921-

Raymond Russell Lindwall was the most complete fast bowler of all time. Throughout a long smooth run to the wicket his action was perfectly balanced, even if his arm was carried lower than the purists would have liked. At first, like many others, he relied principally upon speed, but later his control became such that a suggestion that the cricket ball should be made smaller was dropped after Lindwall had demonstrated how he could perform with it. He was able to specify how and how much he would swing the ball, and did so with devastating control. He tried never to waste a delivery and was an example of the 'If you miss I'll hit' school, consistently directing the ball at the stumps. He was a more than useful batsman and a key figure in the 1948 Australian team.

Teams: New South Wales, Queensland, and Australia

Test series	Tests	Wkts	Average
1945-46 in New Zealand	1	2	14.50
1946-47 v England	4	18	20.38
1947-48 v India	5	18	16.88
1948 in England	5	27	19.62
1949-50 in South Africa	4	12	20.66
1950-51 v England	5	15	22.93
1951-52 v West Indies	5	21	23.04
1952-53 v South Africa	4	19	20.15
1953 in England	5	26	18.84
1954-55 v England	4	14	27.21
1954-55 in West Indies	5	20	32.15
1956 in England	4	7	34.00
1956-57 in Pakistan	1	1	64.00
1956-57 in India	3†	12	16.58
1958-59 v England	2	7	29.85
1959-60 in Pakistan	2	3	40.66
1959-60 in India	2	6	37.00
Total	61	228	23.05

Career wickets: 794 Average: 21.36
Best Test bowling: 7-38 v India, Adelaide, 1947-48
Best career bowling: 7-20, Australians v Minor Counties, Stoke-on-Trent, 1953
Highest Test score: 118 v West Indies, Bridgetown, 1954-55
Highest career score: 134*, New South Wales v Queensland, Sydney, 1945-46

* Not out †Captain in one Test

Bill Johnston
1922-

William Johnston was the third member, with Lindwall and Miller, of the most skilful trio of fast bowlers of any generation. Unusually, he started his career as a left-arm spinner, but then gradually developed into the most devastating of all the Australian left-arm over-the-wicket bowlers, having a better record even than Alan Davidson, who in the next generation had to carry so much of his country's burden. Bill Johnston ran some ten yards to the wicket and had a beautiful delivery, alway sideways-on to the batsman, just like Gary Sobers, a later exponent in the same mould. He was the leading Australian wicket-taker in four consecutive series. Sadly, his knee let him down on his second tour of England and he retired from the game at an age when many of the previous generation would still have been bowling. Due to his ability to avoid getting out as a number eleven batsman, he invariably finished a tour as high in the batting averages as he was in the bowling.

Teams: Victoria and Australia

Test series	Tests	Wkts	Average
1947-48 in Australia	4	16	12.33
1948 in England	5	27	23.33
1949-50 in South Africa	5	23	17.04
1950-51 in Australia	5	22	19.18
1951-52 in Australia	5	23	22.08
1952-53 in Australia	5	21	35.09
1953 in England	3	7	49.00
1954-55 in Australia	4	19	22.26
1954-55 in West Indies	4	2	94.00
Total	40	160	23.90

Career wickets: 554 Average: 23.34
Best Test bowling: 6-44 v South Africa, Johannesburg, 1949-50
Best career bowling: 8-52 Victoria v Queensland, Melbourne, 1952-53

Richie Benaud
1930-

Richie Benaud was the finest illustration of the adage that in bowling 'practice makes perfect'. Unlike good wine, bowlers do not mature without hard work and plenty of travel. By his third tour of England, Benaud had become a master of the art of leg-spin bowling, one of the last in the history of the game. He was also a splendidly robust batsman and a magnificent gully fielder. However, it was as Australia's captain, a position in which he was universally successful, that he made his mark. Benaud was one of the few cricketers to choose journalism as a profession and he subsequently became a television commentator. As such he was crucially involved in the original plotting which led to the formation of World Series Cricket as a counter-attraction to Test cricket, an ignominious role for one who owed so much to the Test game.

Teams: New South Wales and Australia

Test series	Tests	Runs	100s	Average	Wkts	Average
1951-52 in Australia	1	22	—	11.00	1	14.00
1952-53 in Australia	4	124	—	20.66	10	30.60
1953 in England	3	15	—	3.00	2	87.00
1954-55 in Australia	5	148	—	16.44	10	37.70
1954-55 in W Indies	5	246	1	41.00	18	27.00
1956 in England	5	200	—	25.00	8	41.25
1956-57 in Pakistan	1	60	—	30.00	1	36.00
1956-57 in India	3	53	—	13.25	23	16.86

1957-58 in S Africa	5	329	2	54.83	30	21.93
1958-59 in Australia	5†	132	—	26.40	31	18.83
1959-60 in Pakistan	3†	84	—	28.00	18	21.17
1959-60 in India	5†	91	—	15.17	29	19.59
1960-61 in Australia	5*	194	—	21.55	23	33.86
1961 in England	4†	45	—	9.00	15	32.53
1962-63 in Australia	5†	227	—	32.42	17	40.47
1963-64 in Australia	4*	231	—	33.00	12	37.41
Total	63	2,201	3	24.45	248	27.03

Career runs: 11,432 Average: 36.29
Highest Test score: 122 v South Africa, Johannesburg, 1957-58
Highest career score: 187, Australians v Natal, Pietermaritzburg, 1957-58
Career wickets: 9-35 Average: 24.80
Best Test bowling: 7-72 v India, Madras, 1956-57
Best career bowling: 7-32, New South Wales v Victoria, Melbourne, 1958-59
† Captain * Captain in 1 Test

Bill Lawry
1937-

Bill Lawry bent over his bat, hardly lifting it off the ground, and played his shots with extremely ungainly movements; he looked a far cry from such classic left-handed batsmen as Frank Woolley. However, he was a most practical operator, his judgment and eye probably unequalled at the time; many Australian left-handers have had the capacity to judge line and length to the last centimetre (Ken Mackay was another such) but Lawry was a hungry batsman who used this gift to make runs in such quantity that he virtually carried Australian batting in what was far from a vintage period for Australian cricket. As a captain he was practical, sensible and fair.

Teams: Victoria and Australia

Test series	Tests	Runs	100s	Average
1961 in England	5	420	2	52.50
1962-63 in Australia	5	310	—	34.44
1963-64 in Australia	5	496	1	55.11
1964 in England	5	317	1	39.62
1964-65 in India	3	284	—	56.80
1964-65 in Pakistan	1	29	—	14.50
1964-65 in Australia	1	60	—	30.00
1964-65 in West Indies	5	368	1	52.57
1965-66 in Australia	5	592	3	84.57
1966-67 in South Africa	5	296	—	29.60
1967-68 in Australia	4	369	1	52.71
1968 in England	4†	270	1	45.00
1968-69 in Australia	5†	667	3	83.37
1969-70 in India	5†	239	—	34.14
1969-70 in South Africa	4†	193	—	24.12
1970-71 in Australia	5*	324	—	40.50
Total	67	5,234	13	47.15

Career runs: 18,725 Average: 50.88
Highest Test score: 210 v West Indies, Bridgetown, 1964-65
Highest career score: 266, Victoria v New South Wales, Sydney, 1960-61
† Captain

Greg Chappell
1948-

Greg Chappell and his elder brother Ian, for several seasons his captain, were the mainstay of one of the best-ever Australian sides. Grandsons of Victor Richardson, both men seemed to have batting in their blood, Ian, who continued to develop in later years, being only marginally less successful than Greg. However, it was the younger brother's style which marked him out as one of the greatest batsmen of all time: he stood upright at the wicket showing more of his left shoulder to the bowler than many Australian right-handers; there was no stroke that he could not play, and his ability to master any bowling attack gave him a measure of consistency not enjoyed by equally prolific but less skilled colleagues.

Teams: South Australia, Somerset and Australia

Test series	Tests	Runs	100s	Average
1970-71 in Australia	5	243	1	34.71
1972 in England	5	437	2	48.55
1972-73 in Australia	3	242	1	60.50
1972-73 in West Indies	5	342	1	48.85
1973-74 in Australia	3	110	—	36.67
1973-74 in New Zealand	3	449	2	89.80
1974-75 in Australia	6	608	2	55.27
1975 in England	4	106	—	21.20
1975-76 in Australia	6*	702	3	117.00
1976-77 in Australia	4*	385	1	48.13
1976-77 in New Zealand	2*	102	—	34.00
1977 in England	5*	371	1	41.22
Total	51	4,097	12	53.20

Career runs: 18,685 Average: 50.91
Highest Test and career score: 247* Australia v New Zealand, Wellington, 1973-74
* Captain

Pakistan

A. H. Kardar
1925-

Abdul Hafeez Kardar is the father of Pakistan Test cricket. He came to England as a member of the Indian team in 1946, stayed on to win a Blue at Oxford, and then played for Warwickshire before returning to become his country's first Test captain. Having demonstrated considerable intelligence and skill as a slow left-arm bowler and capable batsman, as well as a successful captain, Kardar subsequently became a chief administrator of cricket in Pakistan—this at a time when the country's Test teams were building up their reputation by showing that they could take on the world's best on equal terms.

Teams: Northern India, Oxford University, Warwickshire, India (1946) and Pakistan 1952-53 onwards

Test series	Tests	Runs	100s	Average
1946 in England	3	80	—	16.00
1952-53 in India	5†	173	—	24.71
1954 in England	4†	96	—	16.00
1954-55 in Pakistan	5†	207	—	25.87
1955-56 in Pakistan	3†	49	—	12.25
1956-57 in Pakistan	1†	69	—	69.00
1957-58 in West Indies	5†	253	—	31.62
Total	26	927	—	23.76

Career runs: 6,814 Average: 29.76
Highest Test score: 93 Pakistan v India, Karachi, 1954-55
Highest career score: 173, North Zone v Australian Services, Lahore, 1945-46
† Captain

Fazal Mahmood
1927-

Fazal Mahmood was the founding father of Pakistan's bowling. He just failed to win selection for the Indian side that came in 1946; nevertheless, after Partition he developed into one of the finest medium-pace bowlers the game has ever seen, capable of bowling hour after hour to a fine length and with movement from leg. He once returned figures of 7 for 42 in a Test at Lucknow, remarkable figures for a pace bowler in India.

Teams: Punjab and Pakistan

Test series	Tests	Wkts	Average
1952-53 in India	5	20	25.60
1954 in England	4	20	20.40
1954-55 in Pakistan	5	15	22.06
1955-56 in Pakistan	2	5	18.60
1956-57 in Pakistan	1	13	8.77
1957-58 in West Indies	5	20	38.20
1958-59 in Pakistan	3†	21	15.85
1959-60 in Pakistan	2†	11	19.26
1960-61 in India	5†	9	26.55
1961-62 in Pakistan	1	—	—
1962 in England	2	5	66.40
Total	34	139	24.72

Career wickets: 459 Average: 18.96
Best Test bowling: 7-42 v India, Lucknow, 1952-53
Best career bowling: 9-43, Punjab v Services, Lahore, 1956-57
† Captain

Imtiaz Ahmed
1928-

Imtiaz Ahmed was Pakistan's first and, as yet, finest wicketkeeper-batsman who, after a distinguished career as a Test match player and Air Force officer, became both a coach and a selector. A quiet man, he was universally popular among both his own team and his opponents, with a reputation as a staunch and reliable cricketer.

Teams: Northern India, Karachi Blues and Pakistan

Test series	Tests	Runs	100s	Average
1952-53 in India	5	145	—	18.12
1954 in England	4	104	—	17.33
1954-55 in Pakistan	5	233	—	25.88
1955-56 in Pakistan	3	284	1	71.00
1956-57 in Australia	1	15	—	15.00
1957-58 in West Indies	5	344	1	38.22
1958-59 in Pakistan	3	79	—	15.80
1959-60 in Pakistan	3	116	—	19.33
1960-61 in India	5	375	1	41.66
1961-62 in Pakistan	3	102	—	17.00
1962 in England	4	282	—	35.25
Total	41	2,079	3	29.28

Career runs: 10,005 Average: 37.75
Highest Test score: 209 v New Zealand, Lahore, 1955-56
Highest career score: 300*, P.M.'s XI v Commonwealth XI, Bombay, 1950-51
Test dismissals: 77 catches and 16 stumpings = 93

Hanif Mohammad
1934-

Hanif Mohammad started his Test career at the age of seventeen, and quickly established records for a Pakistani batsman which have not yet been surpassed. His 337 not out for Pakistan against the West Indies at Bridgetown ranks third behind Sobers' 365 and Hutton's 364, and he is still both the most prolific Test scorer for his country as well as the batsman with the best average.

Teams: Karachi and Pakistan

Test series	Tests	Runs	100s	Average
1952-53 in India	5	287	1	35.87
1954 in England	4	181	—	22.62
1954-55 in Pakistan	5	273	1	34.12
1955-56 in Pakistan	3	151	1	37.75
1956-57 in Pakistan	1	5	—	2.50
1957-58 in West Indies	5	628	1	69.77
1958-59 in Pakistan	1	108	1	54.00
1959-60 in Pakistan	3	304	1	60.80
1960-61 in India	5	410	1	51.25
1961-62 in Pakistan	3	407	2	67.83
1962 in England	5	177	—	17.70
1964-65 in Pakistan	4†	262	—	33.71
1964-65 in Australia	1†	197	1	98.50
1964-65 in New Zealand	3†	194	1	38.80
1967 in England	3†	228	1	57.00
1968-69 in Pakistan	3	46	—	15.33
1969-70 in Pakistan	1	57	—	22.00
Total	55	3,915	12	43.98

Career runs: 15,179 Average: 53.79
Highest Test score: 337 v West Indies, Bridgetown, 1957-58
Highest career score: 499, Karachi v Bahawalpur, Karachi, 1958-59
† Captain

Saeed Ahmed
1937-

Saeed Ahmed is the elder brother of Younis Ahmed, the Surrey left-hander. A fine attacking batsman and useful off-spin bowler, he was his country's leading all-rounder in the 1960s when he also captained the team in one series. He averages over 40 in Test cricket. A controversial character, he has tangled from time to time with the Pakistan Board and its managers.

Teams: Punjab University, Lahore and Pakistan

Test series	Tests	Runs	100s	Average
1957-58 in West Indies	5	508	1	56.44
1958-59 in Pakistan	3	199	—	39.80
1959-60 in Pakistan	3	334	1	55.66
1960-61 in India	5	460	2	51.11
1962-62 in Pakistan	3	191	—	31.83
1962 in England	5	302	—	30.20
1964-65 in Pakistan	4	328	1	25.43
1964-65 in Australia	1	104	—	52.00
1964-65 in New Zealand	3	136	—	22.66
1967 in England	3	162	—	32.40
1968-69 in Pakistan	3	109	—	27.25
1971 in England	1	27	—	13.50
1972-73 in Australia	2	131	—	32.75
Total	41	2,991	5	40.41

Career runs: 12,866 Average 38.93
Highest Test score: 172 v New Zealand, Karachi, 1964-65
Highest career score: 203* Karachi Blues v P.W.D (Karachi) 1970-71

Intikhab Alam

Intikhab Alam is a genuine leg-spinner of the old school, capable of bowling out entire sides on good wickets. He is also a cheerful and often successful middle-order batsman, capable of hitting the ball as hard as any man. He has occasionally been favoured with the captaincy of his country, but his career as a Test player has been somewhat intermittent, perhaps because he is not one of the world's greatest fielders.

Teams Karachi, Pakistan International Airways, Surrey and Pakistan.

Test Series	Tests	Runs	100s		Wkts	Ave
1959-60 in Pakistan	1	6	–	3.00	3	20.66
1960-61 in India	3	90	–	22.50	5	36.80
1961-62 in Pakistan	2	64	–	16.00	3	71.33
1962 in England	3	45	–	11.25	3	91.66
1964-65 in Pakistan	1	74	–	74.00	2	65.50
1964-65 in Australia	1	74	–	37.00	–	–
1964-65 in New Zealand	3	135	–	27.00	2	94.00
1964-65 in Pakistan	3	19	–	9.50	9	21.23
1967 in England	3	104	–	20.80	4	67.00
1968-69 in Pakistan	3	56	–	28.00	8	44.87
1969-70 in Pakistan	3*	87	–	17.40	10	28.20
1971 in England	3*	48	–	12.00	8	45.75
1972-73 in Australia	3*	227	–	37.83	4	77.00
1972-73 in New Zealand	3*	108	–	27.00	18	17.94
1972-73 in Pakistan	3	202	1	50.50	15	28.53
1974 in England	3*	50	–	12.50	8	29.37
1974-75 in Pakistan	2*	88	–	22.00	6	33.33
1976-77 in Pakistan	3	4	–	1.33	15	22.06
1976-77 in West Indies	1	12	–	12.00	2	48.00
Total	47	1493	1	22.28	125	35.93

*Captain

Career runs 13,301, Average 22.43.
Highest Test Score 138 v England (Hyderabad) 1972-73.
Highest Career Score 182 Karachi Blues v Pakistan International Airways "B" (Karachi) 1970-71
Career Wickets 1451, Average 27-64
Best Test Bowling 7.52 v New Zealand (Dunedin) 1972-73.
Best Career Bowling 8.54 Pakistanis v Tasmania (Hobart) 1972-73.

Asif Iqbal
1943-

Asif Iqbal is a Pakistan all-rounder of rare grace and touch who at his best can turn a match if not win it outright. He has also been the leading recruiting agent for Packer cricket in Pakistan and, as such, a principal agent of the schism which has affected his own country's cricket as much as it has the game in the West Indies. His reputation in Kent, to whom he has contributed so much, is high.

Teams: Hyderabad, Karachi, Kent and Pakistan

Test series	Tests	Runs	100s	Average
1964-65 in Australia	1	16	—	8.00
1964-65 in New Zealand	3	108	—	21.60
1964-65 in Pakistan	4	179	—	29.83
1967 in England	3	267	1	53.40
1968-69 in Pakistan	3	130	—	32.50
1969-70 in Pakistan	3	172	—	28.66
1971 in England	3	160	1	53.33
1972-73 in Pakistan	3	212	1	53.00
1972-73 in Australia	3	130	—	21.67
1972-73 in New Zealand	3	310	1	62.00
1974 in England	3	53	—	10.60
1974-75 in Pakistan	2	157	—	39.25
1976-77 in Pakistan	3	282	1	70.50
1976-77 in Australia	3	313	2	78.25
1976-77 in West Indies	5	259	1	25.90
Total	45	2,748	8	37.64

Career runs: 12,197 Average: 41.38
Highest Test score: 175 v New Zealand, Dunedin, 1972-73
Highest career score: 196 National Bank v Pakistan International Airways, Lahore, 1976-77

Mushtaq Mohammad
1943-

Mushtaq Mohammad, like his elder brother Hanif, captained his country successfully. (Two other brothers, Wazir and Sadiq, have also played for Pakistan.) Mushtaq was one of the best leg-spin bowlers of his time, and a more dashing batsman in the middle order than his brother—an all-rounder capable of turning and winning a Test match.

Teams: Karachi Whites, Northamptonshire and Pakistan

Test series	Tests	Runs	100s	Average
1958-59 in Pakistan	1	18	—	9.00
1960-61 in India	5	263	1	43.83
1961-62 in Pakistan	3	186	—	31.00
1962 in England	5	401	1	44.55
1967 in England	3	146	—	29.20
1968-69 in Pakistan	3	121	—	40.33
1969-70 in Pakistan	2	59	—	14.75
1971 in England	3	164	1	41.00
1972-73 in Pakistan	3	327	1	81.75
1972-73 in Australia	3	244	1	40.66
1972-73 in New Zealand	2	314	1	104.66
1974 in England	3	209	—	34.83
1974-75 in Pakistan	2	156	1	39.00
1976-77 in Pakistan	3†	284	2	71.00
1976-77 in Australia	3†	77	—	15.40
1976-77 in West Indies	5†	314	1	31.40
Total	49	3,283	10	40.53

Career runs: 29,896 Average 42.40
Highest Test score: 201 v New Zealand, Dunedin, 1972-73
Highest career score: 303*, Karachi Blues v Karachi University, Karachi, 1967-68
† Captain

Majid Khan
1946-

Majid Khan, son of another Test player for India, Jehangir Khan, is one of Pakistan's finest all-rounders. A more than useful bowler, he is a batsman of such skill that he is capable of totally destroying an attack when in the mood to do so. Some of his batting in England has been erratic, but when on form, whether for Pakistan or Glamorgan he is one of the best players in the world to watch on account of his fine judgment of the ball.

Teams: Lahore, Punjab, Cambridge University, Glamorgan, Queensland and Pakistan

Test series	Tests	Runs	100s	Average
1964-65 in Pakistan	4	147	—	29.40
1967 in England	3	38	—	6.33
1968-69 in Pakistan	3	162	—	54.00
1971 in England	2	44	—	22.00
1972-73 in Pakistan	3†	214	—	42.80
1972-73 in Australia	3	239	1	39.83
1972-73 in New Zealand	3	327	1	65.40
1974 in England	3	262	—	43.67
1974-75 in Pakistan	2	137	1	34.25
1976-77 in Pakistan	3	304	1	60.80
1976-77 in Australia	3	247	—	49.40
1976-77 in West Indies	5	530	1	53.00
Total	37	2,651	5	42.75

Career runs: 23,252 Average 43.46
Highest Test score: 167 v West Indies, Georgetown, 1976-77
Highest career score: 241, Lahore Greens v Bahawalpur, Lahore, 1965-66
† Captain

Zaheer Abbas
1947-

Zaheer Abbas plays cricket in spectacles, although from his play no-one could detect any shortcomings in his eyesight. He is Pakistan's finest stroke-player, one of the few Test batsmen of his generation to play with the full swing of the bat and to be identifiably a double-century man. Zaheer has been not only a prolific scorer but also a rapid one, not only for his country but also for his adopted county, Gloucestershire, where he is seen at his happiest.

Teams: Karachi Whites, Pakistan International Airways, Gloucestershire and Pakistan

Test series	Tests	Runs	100s	Average
1969-70 in Pakistan	1	39	—	19.50
1971 in England	3	386	1	96.50
1972-73 in Pakistan	2	50	—	25.00
1972-73 in Australia	3	144	—	24.00
1972-73 in New Zealand	3	35	—	7.00
1974 in England	3	324	1	54.00
1974-75 in Pakistan	2	71	—	17.75
1976-77 in Pakistan	3	60	—	12.00
1976-77 in Australia	3	343	1	57.16
1976-77 in West Indies	3	131	—	21.83
Total	26	1,583	3	34.41

Career runs: 19,804 Average: 49.75
Highest Test and career score: 274 v England Birmingham, 1971

Sarfraz Narwaz
1948-

Sarfraz Narwaz, known to the Pakistan team as 'Horse', can be a capable bowler at above fast-medium pace. He has on many occasions sustained Pakistan's quick bowling effort sufficiently to enable their prolific batsmen to keep the side in the game. Sarfraz has had many brushes with the Pakistan Test Authorities during the course of his career, and his temperament has occasionally taken the edge off his consistency. Northamptonshire, like Pakistan, have known not only his potential but also the problems involved in harnessing the 'Horse'.

Teams: Lahore, Northamptonshire and Pakistan

Test series	Tests	Wkts	Average
1968-69 in Pakistan	1	0	—
1972-73 in Pakistan	2	1	156.00
1972-73 in Australia	2	12	25.87
1972-73 in New Zealand	3	5	55.00
1974 in England	3	9	28.77
1974-75 in Pakistan	2	8	33.67
1976-77 in Pakistan	3	13	21.76
1976-77 in Australia	2	8	27.25
1976-77 in West Indies	4	16	36.18
1977-78 in Pakistan	2	5	30.40
1978 in England	2	5	10.20
Total	26	82	32.01

Career wickets: 700 Average: 23.37
Best Test bowling: 6-89 v West Indies, Lahore, 1974-75
Best career bowling: 8-27, Pakistanis v Nottinghamshire, Nottingham, 1974

Imran Khan
1952-

Imran Khan has developed into one of the world's

leading all-rounders. Not only is he a batsman of great skill, capable of scoring quickly, he has also become a most dangerous fast bowler, well able to ensure that the Pakistan attack has adequate pace to be able to cope with the demands of modern top-class cricket.

Teams: Lahore, Worcestershire, Sussex and Pakistan

Test series	Tests	Wkts	Average
1971 in England	1	0	—
1974 in England	3	5	51.60
1976-77 in Pakistan	3	14	30.21
1976-77 in Pakistan	3	18	28.83
1976-77 in West Indies	5	25	31.60
Total	15	62	32.98

Career wickets: 496 Average: 26.51
Best Test bowling: 6-63 v Australia, Sydney, 1976-77
Best career bowling: 7-53 Worcestershire v Lancashire (Worcester) 1976

India

K. S. Ranjitsinhji
1872-1933

Ranji, who became Maharajah the Jam Sahib of Nawanagar in 1907, played cricket in England for twenty-seven years, from 1893, when he first played in the Cambridge side, until he last played for Sussex in 1920, having captained the county from 1899 to 1903. He did not get a Blue until his last year at Cambridge, when he had played the game but little. Like other truly great cricketers Ranji made a considerable contribution to the technique of batting: he founded the system of back-foot defence and yet was a fearsome driver off the front foot, but it was the leg glance which became his own special stroke and enabled him to score hundreds of the thousands of runs he made in first-class cricket.

Teams: Cambridge University, Sussex and England

Test series		Tests	Runs	100s	Average
1896	in England	2	235	1	78.33
1897-98	in Australia	5	457	1	50.77
1899	in England	5	278	—	46.33
1902	in England	3	15	—	3.75
Total		15	985	2	44.77

Career runs: 24,692 Average: 56.37
Highest Test score: 175 v Australia, Sydney, 1897-98
Highest career score: 285* Sussex v Somerset, Taunton, 1901

K. S. Duleepsinhji
1905-1959

Duleep was a nephew of Ranji, who cared very much for the young man and made Charles Fry his guardian. When he first came to England, Duleep was sent to Aubrey Faulkner, the South African googly bowler, for coaching; he began his first-class career at Cambridge as a nineteen-year-old and played for Sussex until he was twenty-seven. Unlike Ranji he was not a man of robust health, and he died at the relatively early age of fifty-four. Nevertheless, he was a marvellous batsman whom people loved to watch —his strokes were played with a grace and timing that enabled him to play the ball earlier than most of his contemporaries. Like many other batsmen, he was also a superb slip fielder. Duleep was the first victim of the colour bar in cricket, and was excluded from an MCC team to South Africa. Although little was spoken of this incident at the time, many of those who cared for and admired him had become decision-makers when the time came to break off relations with South Africa in the 1960s. The best story told about Duleep concerns a Sussex–Kent match played at Tunbridge Wells, where the wicket had been unfairly watered to help the bowling of Tich Freeman. When Duleep became aware of what had happened he said, 'They are cheats; when they come to Hastings I will show them.' At Hastings he scored a superb double century.

Teams: Cambridge University, Sussex, England

Test series		Tests	Runs	100s	Average
1929	in England	1	13	—	6.50
1929-30	in New Zealand	4	358	1	89.50
1930	in England	4	416	1	59.42
1931	in England	3	208	1	52.00
Total		12	995	3	58.52

Career runs: 15-485 Average 49.95
Highest Test score: 173 v Australia (Coros) 1930
Highest career score: 333 Sussex v Northants (Home) 1930

Mahomed Nissar
1910-1963

Nissar was the only genuine fast bowler India has produced. He came from the Punjab, and he and Amar Singh, a bowler of fast-medium pace, made a formidable pair in the 1930s, though never in a class to justify a mention ahead of dozens of opening bowlers in England and elsewhere during that period.

Teams: South Punjab, United Provinces, Pakistan Railways, Northern India and India

Test series		Tests	Wkts	Average
1932	in England	1	6	19.16
1933-34	in India	2	7	32.71
1936	in England	3	12	28.58
Total		6	25	28.58

Career wickets: 379 Average: 17.85
Best Test bowling: 5-90 v England, Bombay, 1933-34
Best career bowling: 6-17 South Punjab v Sind, Patalia, 1938-39

V. M. Merchant
1911-

India's most effective batsman, Merchant hit forty-three centuries in a career which spanned over twenty years, including the Second World War. An ambitious cricketer, he would very much like to have brought India to England as captain in 1946. When he retired after the 1951-52 season, he continued to be involved with Indian cricket as a selector and as a stalwart member of the Cricket Club of India. Subsequently he became involved in discussions which ultimately led to the sad and wasteful move from the Brabourne Stadium to the new Wankhede Stadium in Bombay. This must have been an even more bitter pill to swallow than his failure to captain India on a tour of England despite the fact that he was twice, in 1936 and 1946, unquestionably the team's leading batsman.

Teams: Bombay and India

Test series		Tests	Runs	100s	Average
1933-34	in India	3	178	—	29.66
1936	in England	3	282	1	47.00

1946 in England	3	245	1	49.00
1951-52 in India	1	154	1	154.00
Total	10	859	3	47.72

Career runs: 12,876 Average: 72.74
Highest Test score: 154 v England, Delhi, 1951-52
Highest career score: 359*, Bombay v Maharashtra, Bombay, 1943-44

Lala Amarnath
1911-

Amarnath was India's leading all-rounder for many seasons on either side of the Second World War, and indeed during it. An opening bowler and lively batsman, he captained India in Australia. He has remained close to cricket as both commentator and parent—his two sons are both with the Indian team.

Teams: Punjab and India

Test series	Test	Runs	100s	Average	Wkts	Average
1933-34 in India	3	203	1	40.60	4	28.25
1946 in England	3	69	—	13.80	13	25.38
1947-48 in Australia	5†	140	—	14.00	13	28.15
1948-49 in India	5†	294	—	36.75	3	87.66
1951-52 in India	3	67	—	16.75	3	69.00
1952-53 in India	5	105	—	26.25	9	22.44
Total	24	878	1	24.38	45	32.91

Career runs: 10,269 Average: 42.08
Highest Test score: 118 v England, Bombay, 1933-34
Highest career score: 262, India in England v Rest of India, Calcutta, 1946-47
Career wickets: 451 Average: 22.59
Best Test bowling: 5-96 v England, Manchester, 1946
Best career bowling: 6-29 Indians v Middlesex Lord's 1936

V. Mankad
1917-

Vinoo Mankad was the finest all-round cricketer India has produced, a most steady batsman and an outstanding left-arm bowler. He is the only Indian to have done the double on a tour of England. His ability to maintain length and spin for hour after hour was largely instrumental in keeping India in contention during many games in which they would otherwise have been routed.

Teams: Nawanagar, Hindus, Gujerat, Rajasthan and India

Test series	Tests	Runs	100s	Average	Wkts	Average
1946 in England	3	124	—	24.80	11	26.54
1947-48 in Australia	5	306	2	30.60	12	52.50
1948-49 in India	5	143	—	15.88	17	43.76
1951-52 in India	5	223	—	31.85	34	16.79
1952 in England	3	271	1	54-20	9	42.85
1952-53 in India	5	129	—	32.25	25	20.56
1952-53 in W Indies	5	229	—	28.62	15	53.06
1954-55 in Pakistan	5	51	—	10.20	12	33.25
1955-56 in India	4	526	2	105.20	12	27.33
1956-57 in India	3	82	—	13.67	11	28.45
1958-59 in India	2	25	—	8.33	4	65.50
Total	44	2.109	5	31.47	162	32.31

Career runs: 11,554 Average: 34.69
Highest Test and career score: 231 v New Zealand, Madras, 1955-56
Best Test bowling: 8-52 v Pakistan, New Delhi, 1952-53
Best career bowling: 8-35, Indians v Ceylon, Colombo, 1944-45
Career wickets: 776 Average: 24.60

V. Manjrekar
1931-

Vijay Manjrekar was the best of a poor generation of Indian cricketers in the 1950s. He wins a place in this company ahead of, say, Umrigar, who scored more runs, because he was a batsman .who steeled himself to face pace bowling to a greater extent than most of his colleagues, although he did display one rather disturbing tendency, namely, an excessively forceful swing and follow-through which, on one occasion, felled Billy Griffith, then MCC Secretary. 'Has this happened often?' he was asked, to which he replied, 'Yes, you are my third victim.' Manjrekar was also a useful wicketkeeper.

Teams: Bombay, Bengal, Andaha, Uttar Pradesh and India

Test series	Tests	Runs	100s	Average
1951-52 in India	2	74	—	24.66
1952 in England	4	162	1	23.14
1952-53 in India	3	58	—	14.50
1952-53 in West Indies	4	254	1	36.28
1954-55 in Pakistan	5	270	—	45.00
1955-56 in India	5	386	2	77.20
1956-57 in India	3	197	—	32.83
1958-59 in India	4	148	—	24.66
1959 in England	2	134	—	33.50
1960-61 in India	5	247	—	49.40
1961-62 in India	5	586	1	83.71
1961-62 in West Indies	5	167	—	16.70
1963-64 in India	4	225	1	37.50
1964-65 in India	4	301	1	121.00
Total	55	3,209	8	39.13

Career runs: 12,717 Average: 50.86

Highest Test score: 189* v England, Delhi, 1961-62
Highest career score: 283, Vizianagram XI v Tata Sports Club XI, Hyderabad, 1963-64

E. A. S. Prasanna
1940-
Prasanna is arguably the best off-spinner that India has ever produced. His rivals for this title have been Ghulam Ahmed and Venkat, but year in and year out this tiny, somewhat roly-poly figure has kept India's Test flag flying higher than it has ever flown. In company with Bedi and Chandra, his ability to maintain length and spin over a long period has made him more successful in wicket-taking than other Indian off-spinners. With his power of spin he too can turn a match in a short time, another vital attribute in any attacking, match-winning bowler.

Teams: Mysore and India

Test series	Tests	Wkts	Average
1961-62 in India	1	1	39.00
1961-62 in West Indies	1	3	40.66
1966-67 in India	1	5	44.80
1967 in England	3	9	47.77
1967-68 in Australia	4	25	27.44
1967-68 in New Zealand	4	24	18.79
1969-70 in India	8	46	24.02
1970-71 in West Indies	3	11	37.00
1972-73 in India	3	10	20.20
1974 in England	2	3	89.00
1974-75 in India	5	15	40.40
1975-76 in New Zealand	3	11	20.27
1975-76 in West Indies	1	—	—
1976-77 in India	4	18	21.61
1977-78 in Australia	4	6	46.50
Total	47	187	29.36

Career wickets: 930 Average: 23.12
Best Test bowling: 8-76 v New Zealand, Auckland, 1975-76
Best career bowling: 8-50 Mysore v Andhra Belgaum 1970-71

Pataudi Mansur Ali Khan
1941-
The two Nawabs of Pataudi, father and son, both captained India. Pataudi senior died at the age of forty-two while playing polo, at which time his son was eleven. But the young Pataudi went on to score over 2,000 runs at Winchester College, a record aggregate, and he played his first first-class match at the age of sixteen. At twenty, with one century in a university match behind him, he had an accident in a motor-car on the sea-front at Hove, and this affected his sight. Nonetheless, within a few months of the accident he was playing in Test matches for

India, and he captained his country against Australia, England, New Zealand and the West Indies. His strokemaking and the power and timing of his batting were such that but for his accident he could well have become the greatest Indian batsman of all time.

Teams: Delhi, Oxford University, Sussex and India

Test series	Tests	Runs	100s	Average
1961-62 in India	3	222	1	44.40
1961-62 in West Indies	3	114	—	19.00
1963-64 in India	5†	308	1	38.50
1964-65 in India	7†	586	3	58.60
1966-67 in India	3†	144	—	24.00
1967 in England	3†	269	1	44.83
1967-68 in Australia	3†	339	—	56.50
1967-68 in New Zealand	4†	221	—	31.57
1969-70 in India	8†	349	—	23.27
1972-73 in India	3†	147	—	36.75
1974-75 in India	4†	94	—	11.75
Total	46	2,793	6	34.95

Career runs: 15,425 Average 33.60
Highest Test and career score: 203*, v England Delhi, 1963-64
† Captain

B. S. Chandrasekhar
1945-
Chandra is the finest wrist-spinning bowler of his generation in the world; sadly, he does not have many rivals, but even if he did his ability to make the ball spin and bounce even on the deadest wickets and at a pace approaching medium would make him a formidable bowler. What is especially remarkable about him is that he bowls with a right arm which was affected by polio when he was a child. He is the kind of bowler who can turn a match in two or three overs, and yet he has always been accurate enough to justify a number of fielders standing close to the bat—a rare attribute in a bowler of his type.

Teams: Mysore and India

Test series	Tests	Wkts	Average
1963-64 in India	4	10	33.90
1964-65 in India	2	9	21.00
1965-66 in India	2	8	36.50
1966-67 in India	3	18	28.50
1967 in England	3	16	27.18
1967-68 in Australia	2	1	174.00
1971 in England	3	13	29.15
1972-73 in India	5	35	18.91
1974 in England	2	2	63.00
1974-75 in India	4	14	41.35
1975-76 in West Indies	4†	21	31.23
1975-76 in New Zealand	3†	11	26.72
1976-77 in India	8†	36	25.78
1977-78 in Australia	5	28	25.14
Total	50	222	28.24

Career wickets: 971 Average: 22.85
Best Test bowling: 8-79 v England, Delhi, 1972-73
Best career bowling: 9-72 v Mysore v Kerala, Bijapur, 1969-70

† Captain

B. S. Bedi
1946-

Bishan Singh Bedi is a colourful Indian cricketer and was, in his time, the finest slow left-arm bowler in the world. His variations and subtlety in the air, as well as his ability to spin the ball, made him the perfect bowler on all wickets, and his duels with great batsmen such as Barry Richards were a fascinating spectacle, particularly at a time when cricket was characterized by medium-pace containment, with few batsmen able to break the stranglehold. In Bedi's case the batsmen, whether they were playing in the Tropics or in more temperate climates, were set problems by an artist who also had the merit of being a proud competitor. For this reason he was made captain of India, but bowlers are not often suited to this work and Bedi's term of office compares unfavourably in its results with that of A. L. Wadekar, his predecessor.

Teams: Northern Punjab, Delhi, Northamptonshire and India

Test series	Tests	Wkts	Average
1966-67 in India	2	7	32.57
1967 in England	2	7	33.71
1967-68 in Australia	2	4	55.75
1967-68 in New Zealand	4	16	23.18
1969-70 in India	8	36	20.56
1970-71 in West Indies	5	15	43.73
1971 in England	3	11	29.54
1972-73 in India	5	25	25.28
1974 in England	3	10	52.30
1974-75 in India	4	15	33.27
1975-76 in New Zealand	2	4	30.50
1975-76 in West Indies	4	18	25.33
1976-77 in India	8	47	18.38
1977-78 in Australia	5	31	23.87
Total	58	246	26.89

Career wickets: 1438 Average: 21.26
Best Test bowling: 7-98 v Australia, Calcutta, 1969-70
Best career bowling: 7-5, Delhi v Jammu and Kashmir, New Delhi, 1974-75

S. M. Gavaskar
1949-

Sunil Gavaskar first came to the fore in the Caribbean, where he helped India to win their first series —his off-driving was particularly fine. Subsequently his Test career has been somewhat less consistent. He developed a penchant for outrageous strokes, but nonetheless, throughout his career in Test cricket he has been India's most reliable batsman. He has been particularly valuable as an opener, and having been the only real Indian success on the tour to Pakistan, he took over the captaincy from Bedi for the visit of Kallicharran's West Indians.

Teams: Bombay and India

Test series	Tests	Runs	100s	Average
1970-71 in West Indies	4	774	4	154.80
1971 in England	3	144	—	24.00
1972-73 in India	5	224	—	24.88
1974 in England	3	217	1	36.16
1974-75 in India	2	108	—	27.00
1975-76 in New Zealand	3	266	1	66.60
1975-76 in West Indies	4	390	2	55.71
1976-77 in India	8	653	2	65.30
1977-78 in Australia	5	450	2	50.00
Total	37	3,226	13	48.87

Career runs: 11,512 Average: 48.36
Highest Test score: 220 v West Indies,

Port-of-Spain, 1970-71
Highest career score: 282, Bombay v Bihar, Bombay, 1971-72

S. M. H. Kirmani
1949-

Syed Kirmani is India's longest-serving and most reliable wicketkeeper. India has had a series of keepers who have been sound rather than spectacular, but Kirmani has played more Tests with India's trio of great spin bowlers than any other, and his experience of standing up to the wicket against these men has meant that he has been tested under all conditions, more frequently than any of his predecessors—keeping wicket to slow bowlers is recognized as being the hardest task of all. Batting at number seven or eight in a relatively weak batting side is not an easy role either, and Kirmani has often had to prove himself a durable if never truly prolific batsman.

Teams: Mysore, Karnataka and India

Test series	Tests	Runs	100s	Average
1975-76 in New Zealand	3	92	—	33.00
1975-76 in West Indies	4	35	—	11.66
1976-77 in India	8	363	—	30.25
1977-78 in Australia	5	305	—	33.88
Total	20	795	—	28.39

Career runs: 3,515 Average: 28.12
Highest Test score: 88 v New Zealand, Bombay, 1976-77
Highest career score: 101* Karataka v Hyderabad, Bangalore, 1976-77
Test dismissals: 35 caught = 15 stumped + 50

Amar Singh
1910-1940

Amar Singh, a magnificent right-arm fast medium bowler and a brilliant fielder, first came to England in 1932 and took over 100 wickets on the tour. In 1936, already playing for Colne Cricket Club in the Lancashire League, he was released for the three Test matches, taking six wickets for thirty-five runs in one innings at Lord's. His early death at the age of twenty-nine from pneumonia was a sad blow to Indian cricket.

Teams: Western India States, Nawangar and India

Test series	Tests	Wkts	Average
1932 in England	1	4	39.75
1933-34 in India	3	14	27.28
1936 in England	3	10	31.70
Total	7	28	30.64

Career wickets: 484 Average: 20.49
Best Test bowling: 7-86 v England, Madras, 1933-34
Best career bowling: 8-23 All India v Rest of India, New Delhi, 1931-32

West Indies

George Challenor
1888-1947

George Challenor was the father of West Indian batsmanship. A member of a plantation-owning family in Barbados, he was one West Indian batsman with the style and run-scoring capabilities to take his place among the greats of the golden age. He was an off-side player who was merciless with short deliveries, but when the in-swing attack was developed to contain his style of batting, Challenor's patience and play suffered.

Teams: Barbados and West Indies

Test series	Tests	Runs	100s	Average
1928 in England	3	101	—	14.83

Career runs: 5,822 Average: 38.55
Highest Test score: 46 v England, Oval, 1928
Highest career score: 237*, Barbados v Jamaica, Bridgetown, 1924-25

Learie Constantine
1902-1971

Learie Nicholas Constantine was a man of only medium height, and yet he was as lively on the cricket field as a rubber ball. There has never been a better fielder—his party trick was to hit the stumps from the outfield. His Test figures were not as good as many others', but it is as a character able to communicate with his public the world over that Learie Constantine will be remembered as one of the greatest of all cricketers. He was also one of the few who went on to play a full part in public life as a lawyer and politician, and finally as Trinidad's High Commissioner in London.

Teams: Trinidad and West Indies

Test series	Tests	Runs	100s	Average	Wkts	Average
1928 in England	3	89	—	14.83	5	52.40
1929-30 in W Indies	3	106	—	17.66	18	27.61
1930-31 in Australia	5	72	—	7.20	8	50.87
1933 in England	1	95	—	47.50	1	55.00
1934-35 in W Indies	3	169	—	33.80	15	13.13
1939 in England	3	110	—	27.50	11	29.81
Total	18	641	—	19.42	58	30.10

Career runs: 8,738 Average: 20.60
Highest Test score: 90 v England, Trindad, 1934-35

Highest career score: 133, Trinidad v Barbados, Port-of-Spain, 1928-29
Career wickets: 424 Average: 20.60
Best Test bowling: 5-75 v England, Oval, 1939
Best career bowling: 8-38, Trinidad v Barbados, Bridgetown, 1923-24

George Headley
1909-

George Alphonso Headley carried West Indian batting single-handedly in the years between their admission to the Test match circle and the outbreak of the Second World War, earning him the nickname 'the black Bradman'. Born in Panama, the only game he played as a child was rounders. Originally he was weak on the on-side, but under pressure from the Australians, who concentrated on this stump, he became a master all round the wicket, his technique based on an initial movement on to the back foot which made him, like Bradman, a fierce hooker and cutter of the ball.

Teams: Jamaica and West Indies

Test series	Tests	Runs	100s	Average
1929-30 in West Indies	4	703	4	87.87
1930-31 in Australia	5	336	2	37.33
1933 in England	3	277	1	55.40
1934-35 in West Indies	4	485	1	97.00
1939 in England	3	334	2	66.80
1947-48 in West Indies	1	36	—	36.00
1948-49 in India	1	2	—	2.00
1953-54 in West Indies	1	17	—	8.50
Total	22	2,190	10	60.83

Career runs: 9,921 Average: 69.86
Highest Test score: 270* v England, Kingston, 1934-35
Highest career score: 344* Jamaica v Lord Tennyson's XI, Kingston, 1931-32

G. E. Gomez
1919-

Gerry Gomez was the first West Indian all-rounder to dominate a Test series. This he did in Australia in 1951-52. Like the other West Indian all-rounders of his generation, Dennis Atkinson and John Goddard, Gomez bowled at above medium pace and batted in the middle of the order. An enthusiastic fielder, he developed a reputation for taking impossible catches close to the wicket. He and Jeff Stollmeyer, both from Trinidad, held their places in the West Indian side throughout the Second World War, coming to England on both the 1939 and 1950 tours.

Teams: Trinidad and West Indies

Test series	Tests	Runs	100s	Average	Wkts	Average
1939 in England	2	22	—	7.33	—	—
1947-48 in W Indies	4	232	—	46.40	1	31.00
1948-49 in India	5	256	1	36.57	16	28.37
1950 in England	4	207	—	41.40	2	81.50
1951-52 in Australia	5	324	—	36.00	18	14.22
1951-52 in N Zealand	1	14	—	14.00	3	26.00
1952-53 in W Indies	4	62	—	12.40	11	31.90
1953-54 in W Indies	4	126	—	21.00	7	37.57
Total	29	1,243	1	30.31	55	27.41

Career runs: 6,764 Average: 43.63
Highest Test score: 101 v India, New Delhi, 1948-49
Highest career score: 216*, Trinidad v Barbados, Port-of-Spain, 1942-43
Career wickets: 200 Average: 25.26
Best Test bowling: 7-55 v Australia, Sydney, 1951
Best career bowling: 9-24, West Indians v South Zone, Madras, 1948-49

Frank Worrell
1924-1967

Frank Mortimer Maglinne Worrell was the first West Indian cricketer to be knighted. A glorious batsman, one of the famous three 'W's, he played stylist to the pugnacity of Everton Weekes and the sheer power of Clyde Walcott. A beautifully balanced quick left-arm bowler or spinner, he was the precursor of Gary Sobers, the super-cricketer. However, it is as a man and as a captain that Frank Worrell stands out from the pack. At one stage in danger of losing his ability through an addiction to drink, he recovered and established himself as the greatest captain the West Indies are ever likely to see, the first black man to do the job in a manner which excited the admiration of the entire world. No cricketer ever more deserved Chaucer's description 'a very parfait gentle knight'. Had fatal illness not removed him before his time, Worrell would have been a priceless, statesman-like influence on West Indian cricket now that it is in danger of losing its outstanding reputation.

Teams: Barbados, Jamaica and West Indies

Test series	Tests	Runs	100s	Average
1947-48 in West Indies	3	294	1	147.00
1950 in England	4	539	2	89.83
1951-52 in Australia	5	337	1	33.70
1951-52 in New Zealand	2	233	1	116.50
1952-53 in West Indies	5	398	1	49.75
1953-54 in West Indies	4	334	1	47.71
1954-55 in West Indies	4	206	—	25.75
1957 in England	5	350	1	38.88
1959-60 in West Indies	4	320	1	64.00

1960-61 in Australia	5*	375	—	37.50
1961-62 in West Indies	5*	332	—	88.00
1963 in England	5*	142	—	70.28
Total	51	3,860	9	49.48

Career runs: 15,025 Average: 54.24
Highest Test score: 261 v England, Nottingham, 1950
Highest career score: 308*, Barbados v Trinidad, Bridgetown, 1943-44
* Captain

Sonny Ramadhin
1930-

No spin bowler made a greater impact on cricket than Sonny Ramadhin. A tiny figure, he always bowled with his sleeve buttoned at the wrist and usually wore a cap. He had the ability on English wickets to make the ball turn from both leg and off with the use of wrist- and finger-spin, without needing to roll his wrist to bowl the leg-spinner. Not since the advent of the South African googly bowlers in 1907 had a young spinner created such havoc among his opponents as did the twenty-year-old Ramadhin on his first tour of England in 1950. Apart from any of his other virtues he was exceptionally accurate. In the end batsmen learned how to deal with him through psychological means, by establishing a pattern of controlled, frequent and vigorous hitting which would affect his rhythm and length. However, in that first season he mesmerized the best batsmen in England. Subsequently people sought to challenge his action and suggested that his sleeves were always kept buttoned because his arm was bent at the elbow, but nothing, neither subsequent failures nor envious accusations, could take away the glory which he shared with Alf Valentine as the West Indies won their first victory over England in a Test match rubber.

Teams: Trinidad, Lancashire and West Indies

Test series	**Tests**	**Wkts**	**Average**
1950 in England	4	26	23.33
1951-52 in Australia	5	14	49.64
1951-52 in New Zealand	2	13	12.76
1952-53 in West Indies	4	12	13.83
1953-54 in West Indies	5	23	24.30
1954-55 in West Indies	4	5	75.80
1955-56 in New Zealand	4	20	15.80
1957 in England	5	14	39.07
1958-59 in India	2	2	45.40
1958-59 in Pakistan	2	9	13.44
1959-60 in West Indies	4	17	28.88
1960-61 in Australia	2	3	44.50
Total	43	158	28.96

Career wickets: 758 Average: 20.24
Best Test bowling: 7-49 v England, Birmingham, 1957
Best career bowling: 8-15 West Indies v Gloucestershire, Cheltenham, 1950

Lance Gibbs
1934-

Lance Gibbs is the most prolific Test wicket-taker yet. An off-spinner with a high, wheeling action, he set the pattern for whole generations of West Indian spin bowlers. An essential member of a West Indian attack that was growing to depend more and more on fast bowling, Gibbs could be relied upon to bowl entire sides out when the wicket suited him. His only fault was that he never really mastered the art of bowling round the wicket, and that is why he left Warwickshire and England after a few seasons to return to his home in Guyana, where he is now established as a leading coach to a never-ending stream of new talent.

Teams: Guyana, Warwickshire, South Australia and West Indies

Test series	**Tests**	**Wkts**	**Average**
1957-58 in West Indies	4	17	23.05
1958-59 in India	1	—	—
1958-59 in Pakistan	3	8	22.25
1960-61 in Australia	3	19	20.78
1961-62 in West Indies	5	24	20.41
1963 in England	5	26	21.30
1964-65 in West Indies	5	18	30.83
1966 in England	5	21	24.76
1966-67 in India	3	18	22.05
1967-68 in West Indies	5	20	30.50
1968-69 in Australia	5	24	38.45
1968-69 in New Zealand	3	8	45.25
1969 in England	3	6	52.83
1970-71 in West Indies	1	—	—
1971-72 in West Indies	2	3	89.00
1972-73 in West Indies	5	26	26.76
1973 in England	3	9	25.22
1973-74 in West Indies	5	18	36.72
1974-75 in India	5	21	21.61
1974-75 in Pakistan	2	7	30.00
1975-76 in Australia	6	16	40.75
Total	79	309	29.09

Career wickets: 1,024 Average: 27.16
Best Test bowling: 8-38 v India, Bridgetown, 1961-62
Best career bowling: 8-37 Warwickshire v Glamorgan, Birmingham, 1970

Gary Sobers
1936-

Garfield St Aubrun Sobers was the greatest all-round cricketer the world has ever seen. As a batsman few have possessed either the power or the variety of his stroke-making; he was capable of playing an innings which would captivate the stoniest observers of the cricketing world. Bradman thought him a superb player. For all his skill with the bat, it is as a bowler that he has unique claims to fame: a left-hander, he could bowl fast, at medium pace, and with both orthodox and back-of-the-hand spin at a level which would have made him a Test cricketer as a specialist in any of these skills. A generous and easy opponent, Gary Sobers is one of the few Test players to have had at one stage a more brilliant Test than career record.

Teams: Barbados, South Australia, Nottinghamshire and West Indies

Test series	Tests	Runs	100s	Aver-age	Wkts	Aver-age
1953-54 v England	1	40	—	40.00	4	20.25
1954-55 v Australia	4	231	—	38.50	6	35.50
1955-56 in N Zealand	4	81	—	16.20	2	24.50
1957 in England	5	320	—	32.00	5	71.00
1957-58 v Pakistan	5	824	3	137.33	4	94.25
1958-59 in India	5	557	3	92.83	10	29.20
1958-59 in Pakistan	3	160	—	32.00	—	—
1959-60 v England	5	709	3	101.28	9	39.55
1960-61 in Australia	5	430	2	43.00	15	39.20
1961-62 v India	5	424	2	70.66	23	20.56
1963 in England	5	322	1	40.25	20	28.55
1964-65 v Australia	5†	352	—	39.11	12	41.00
1966 in England	5†	722	3	103.14	20	27.25
1966-67 in India	3†	342	0	114.00	14	25.00
1967-68 v England	5†	545	2	90.83	13	39.07
1968-69 in Australia	5†	497	2	49.70	18	40.72
1968-69 in N Zealand	3†	70	—	14.00	7	43.00
1969 in England	3†	150	—	30.00	11	28.90
1971 v India	5	597	3	74.62	12	33.50
1971-72 v N Zealand	5	253	1	36.14	10	33.20
1973 in England	3	306	1	76.50	6	28.17
1973-74 in W Indies	4	100	—	20.00	14	30.07
Total	93	8.032	26	57.78	235	34.03

Career runs: 28,315 Average: 54.87
Highest Test and career score: 365* v Pakistan, Kingston, 1957-58
Career wickets: 1,043 Average: 27.74
Best Test bowling: 6-73 v Australia, Brisbane, 1968-69
Best career bowling: 9-49, West Indians v Kent, Canterbury, 1966
* Not out † Captain

Wes Hall
1937-

Wesley Winfield Hall bowled at only medium pace when he first played for Barbados; he was an away-swinger, and the ability to swing the ball is always highly valued in the West Indies. Only later did he develop into the fastest bowler of his time. His stamina was as remarkable as his speed, and overall Hall won much praise for being one of the fairest opponents in the game. But it is for the sheer beauty of his action that he will be remembered by all who saw him: full of energy and yet controlled, his approach and delivery were graceful and powerful enough to earn the ultimate adjective for a bowler's action—perfect. He was also strong enough to hit a cricket ball as far as any man before or since.

Teams: Barbados, Queensland and West Indies

Test series	Tests	Wkts	Average
1958-59 in India	5	30	17.66
1958-59 in Pakistan	3	16	17.93
1959-60 v England	5	22	30.66
1960-61 in Australia	5	21	29.33
1961-52 v India	5	27	15.74
1963 in England	5	16	33.37
1964-65 v Australia	5	16	28.37
1966 in England	5	18	30.83
1966-67 in India	3	8	33.25
1967-68 v England	4	9	39.22
1968-69 in Australia	2	8	40.62
1968-69 in New Zealand	1	1	42.00
Total	48	192	26.38

Career wickets: 546 Average: 26.14
Best Test bowling: 7-69 v England, Kingston, 1959-60
Best career bowling: 7-51, West Indians v Glamorgan, Swansea, 1963
Highest Test score: 50* v India, Port-of-Spain, 1961-62; 50 v Australia, Brisbane, 1960-61
Highest career score: 102*, West Indians v Cambridge University, Cambridge, 1963
* Not out

Gordon Greenidge
1951-

Gordon Greenidge is a strange cricketer in that he is playing for the wrong country. Born in the West Indies yet educated in England, all his cricketing knowledge was acquired in Hampshire long before he began to play Test cricket for the West Indies. With Vivian Richards he has been an essential force in perhaps the greatest West Indian Test team in all history. As an opening batsman there is no-one better in his generation; he and Barry Richards comprised an opening pair of enormous skill and run-making capability, largely responsible for Hampshire's success in both Championship and one-day cricket. Unlike so many other West Indian Test cricketers who have shone and then faded, Greenidge has matured season by season and is now among the top half-dozen batsmen in the world.

Teams: Hampshire, Barbados and West Indies

Test series	Tests	Runs	100s	Average
1974-75 in India	5	371	1	41.22
1975-76 in Australia	2	11	—	2.75
1976 in England	5	592	3	65.77
1976-77 in West Indies	5	536	1	53.60
1977-78 in West Indies	2	131	—	65.50
Total	19	1,641	5	48.26

Career runs: 15,159 Average: 42.58
Highest Test score: 134 v England, Manchester, 1976
Highest career score: 273*, D. H. Robins' XI v Pakistanis, Eastbourne, 1974

Vivian Richards
1952-

It is a curiosity of cricket that one man called Richards should succeed another as the greatest batsman of his generation, one white, the other black, and it is one of the sadder aspects of the game that they could never play Test cricket against each other because one was a South African and the other a West Indian. Viv Richards as a batsman is capable of the most varied stroke-making and the most powerful hitting of any man. In his early Tests he was not a success, but once he gained control and learned through experience to adapt his game to any wicket, he began to put bowlers all around the world to the sword in a blaze of century-making. His place in the record books is uncertain because of his involvement with the Packer series.

Teams: Leeward Islands, Combined Islands, Somerset and West Indies

Test series	Tests	Runs	100s	Average
1974-75 in India	5	353	1	50.42
1974-75 in Pakistan	2	17	—	5.67
1975-76 in Australia	6	426	1	38.72
1975-76 in West Indies	4	556	3	92.66
1976 in England	4	829	3	118.42
1976-77 in West Indies	5	257	—	28.55
1977-78 in West Indies	2	62	—	31.00
Total	28	2,500	8	55.55

Career runs: 13,065 Average: 48.03
Hightest Test and career score: 291 v England Oval, 1976

Michael Holding
1954-

Together with Andy Roberts, Wayne Daniel, Colin Croft and Joel Garner, Michael Holding is one of a battery of West Indian fast bowlers to achieve remarkable results in cricket all over the world. Some of them have proved more durable than Holding, but the latter's feat for the West Indies at The Oval, when he took 14 England wickets, 11 of them clean-bowled or lbw, entitles him to be chosen ahead of all the others. His action, consisting of the approach of a sprinter and the delivery of a classic fast bowler, also entitle him to recognition as the senior member of a great squad, despite the challenge of the bustling, aggressive yet silent Roberts.

Teams: Jamaica and West Indies

Test series	Tests	Wkts	Average
1975-76 in Australia	5	10	61.40
1975-76 in West Indies	4	19	19.89
1976 in England	4	28	12.71
Total	13	57	23.64

Career wickets: 117 Average: 25.61
Best Test and career bowling: 8-92 v England, Oval, 1976

New Zealand

C. S. Dempster
1903-1974

Scotty Dempster began to play for Wellington at the age of eighteen, and was still playing first-class cricket at the age of forty-three. He captained Leicestershire for three years in the 1930s, and in 1936 made three centuries in succession. Like all great batsmen he averaged over 40 throughout his first-class career, and played a key role in putting New Zealand cricket on the world map.

Teams: Wellington, Scotland, Leicestershire, Warwickshire and New Zealand

Test series	Tests	Runs	100s	Average
1929-30 in New Zealand	4	341	1	34.75
1931 in England	2	173	1	86.50
1931-32 in New Zealand	2	104	—	26.00
1932-33 in New Zealand	2	105	—	105.00
Total	10	723	2	65.72

Career runs: 12,098 Average: 44.97
Highest Test score: 136 v England, Wellington, 1929-30
Highest career score: 212, New Zealanders v Essex, Leyton, 1927

Bill Merritt
1908-1977

Bill Merritt came to England in 1927 as a nineteen-year-old member of the first major tour by a New Zealand side captained by Tom Lowry. Merritt took 107 wickets with his leg-spinners at an average of 23.64. He returned to play Test matches in 1931, when he was the chief bowler of the side and took 99 wickets at an average of 26.48. The greatest moment of his career was when he was asked by his captain to open the bowling against MCC at Lord's and took 7 wickets for 28. Subsequently he came to England to play, and for years he was the leading member of the Northamptonshire team, then the Cinderella of the Championship.

Teams: Canterbury, Northants and New Zealand

Test series	Tests	Wkts	Average
1929-30 in New Zealand	4	8	54.40
1931 in England	2	4	45.25
Total	6	12	51.41

Career wickets: 536 Average: 25.50
Best Test bowling: 4-104 v England, Lord's, 1931
Best career bowling: 8-41, New Zealand v Essex, Leyton, 1931

Jack Cowie
1912-

Jack Cowie was New Zealand's opening bowler in the years before and after the Second World War. A solid figure, he bowled at a lively fast-medium pace, and had the frame to sustain this attack hour after hour. He was mainly an in-swing bowler and, like Martin Donnelly, lost the best years of his career to the War.

Teams: Auckland and New Zealand

Test series	Tests	Wkts	Average
1937 in England	3	19	20.78
1945-46 in New Zealand	1	6	6.67
1946-47 in New Zealand	1	6	13.83
1949 in England	4	14	33.41
Total	9	45	21.53

Career wickets: 359 Average: 22.29
Best Test bowling: 6-36 v Australia, Wellington, 1945-46
Best career bowling: 6-3, New Zealand v Ireland, Dublin, 1937

Tom Burtt
1915-

Tom Burtt was New Zealand's best-ever spin-bowler, capable of wheeling away with his left-arm tweakers for hour after hour after the classic manner of the 1930s. Every English county had a bowler such as Burtt, and many of them have the same roly-poly shape and personality.

Teams: Canterbury and New Zealand

Test series	Tests	Wkts	Average
1946-47 in New Zealand	1	—	—
1949 in England	4	17	33.41
1950-51 in New Zealand	2	6	30.17
1951-52 in New Zealand	2	8	28.25
1952-53 in New Zealand	1	2	70.00
Total	10	33	35.45

Career wickets: 408 Average: 22.19
Best Test bowling: 6-162 v England, Manchester, 1949
Best career bowling: 8-35 Canterbury v Otago, 1953-54

Walter Hadlee
1915-

Captain of New Zealand on the 1949 tour of England, the dignified Walter Hadlee set out to ensure that his country was never second-graded in Test cricket. Only thus, he reasoned, could cricket thrive or even survive in a country where rugby was and is the ruling passion of a small population. As batsman, captain and administrator, Hadlee has served New Zealand well, not least by siring two more Test cricketers, Dayle and Richard.

Teams: Canterbury, Otago and New Zealand

Test series	Tests	Runs	100s	Average
1937 in England	3	151	1	25.16
1945-46 in New Zealand	1†	9	—	4.50
1946-47 in New Zealand	1†	116	1	116.00
1949 in England	4†	193	—	32.16
1950-51 in New Zealand	2†	74	—	24.67
Total	11	543	2	30.16

Career runs: 7,421 Average: 40.11
Highest Test score: 116 v England, Christchurch, 1946-47
Highest career score: 198, Otago v Australians, Dunedin, 1945-46
† Captain

Martin Donnelly
1917-

Martin Patterson Donnelly lost his best cricketing years to the Second World War. He was a left-handed batsman of rare ability, rated by no less a judge than C. B. Fry as the best left-hander that he had ever seen. His cricket career was a short one, but he brought to it the gifts of a great athlete, for he had played rugby for England. He was also a superb fielder, the man responsible for filling the Parks at Oxford in the summers following the War.

Teams: Wellington, Canterbury, Oxford University, Middlesex, Warwickshire and New Zealand

Test series	Tests	Runs	100s	Average
1937 in England	3	120	—	24.00
1949 in England	4	462	1	77.00
Total	7	582	1	52.90

Career runs: 9,212 Average: 47.74
Highest Test score: 206, New Zealand v England, Lord's, 1949
Highest career score: 208* MCC v Yorkshire, Scarborough, 1948

Bert Sutcliffe
1923-

Bert Sutcliffe was another New Zealand left-hander, and holds the record for the highest score by a left-hander, 385 for Otago versus Canterbury in the 1952-53 season. A most graceful player, he was tried only by the fastest bowling. After being struck on the head he never quite recaptured his original fluency, but his contribution to New Zealand cricket both as player and coach has been valuable and sustained.

Teams: Auckland, Otago and New Zealand

Test series	Tests	Runs	100s	Average
1946-47 in New Zealand	1	58	—	58.00
1949 in England	4	423	1	60.42
1950-51 in New Zealand	2	147	1	49.00
1951-52 in New Zealand	2	103	—	25.75
1952-53 in New Zealand	2	150	—	37.50
1953-54 in South Africa	5	305	—	38.12
1954-55 in New Zealand	2	169	—	42.25
1955-56 in New Zealand	2	93	—	23.25
1955-56 in Pakistan	3	81	—	13.50
1955-56 in India	5	611	2	87.28
1958 in England	4	112	—	17.42
1958-59 in New Zealand	2	73	—	24.33
1964-65 in India	4	274	1	45.66
1964-65 in Pakistan	3	61	—	15.25
1965 in England	1	57	—	57.00
Total	42	2,727	5	40.10

Career runs: 17,196 Average: 47.50
Highest Test score: 230* v India, Delhi, 1955-56
Highest career score: 385, Otago v Canterbury, Christchurch, 1952-53

John Reid
1928-

John Reid first played cricket for Wellington as a nineteen-year-old, and became one of the most versatile players in the history of the game. He opened the bowling and batting and kept wicket for his country. On tour in South Africa he became the first player to make 1,000 runs and take 50 wickets in a South African season. A powerful, athletic man, very strong in the drive, he is memorable for having one of the hairiest chests in cricket. He was also a splendid captain, and one of the best of the many fine ambassadors for New Zealand who have come with cricket teams from that country.

Teams: Wellington, Otago, and New Zealand

Test series	Tests	Runs	100s	Average	Wkts	Average
1949 in England	2	173	—	43.25	—	—
1950-51 v England	2	72	—	24.00	—	—
1952-52 v W Indies	2	9	—	3.00	—	—
1952-53 v S Africa	2	17	—	5.66	2	56.00
1953-54 in S Africa	5	263	1	29.22	12	32.00
1954-55 v England	2	106	—	26.50	4	19.00
1955-56 in Pakistan	3	136	—	22.68	7	31.57
1955-56 in India	5	493	2	70.42	6	45.16
1955-56 v W Indies	4*	203	—	25.37	7	36.85
1958 in England	5†	147	—	16.33	6	31.16
1958-59 v England	2†	44	—	14.66	3	17.66
1961-62 in S Africa	5†	546	1	60.66	11	19.72
1962-63 v England	3†	263	1	52.60	2	85.50

1963-64 v S Africa	3†	88	—	14.66	12	23.16
1964-65 v Pakistan	3†	229	—	38.16	4	35.50
1964-65 in India	4†	198	—	28.28	3	59.33
1964-65 in Pakistan	3†	296	1	59.20	5	27.00
1965 in England	3†	148	—	24.66	1	54.00
Total	58	3.431	6	33.31	85	33.41

Career runs: 16,067 Average: 41.62
Highest Test score: 142 v South Africa, Johannesburg, 1961-62
Highest career score: 296, Wellington v Northern Districts, Wellington, 1962-63
Career wickets: 458 Average: 22.51
Best Test bowling: 6-60 v South Africa, Dunedin, 1963-64
Best career bowling: 7-20, Otago v Central Districts, Dunedin, 1956-57

† Captain * Captain in 3 Tests

Bevan Congdon
1938-

Bev Congdon is New Zealand's most frequently capped player. An all-rounder of great skill, whether batting in the middle order or bowling his medium-pace away-swingers, he was always one of New Zealand's shrewdest cricketers. He has also been one of the most popular, and was given a great ovation at Lord's on his last appearance there by a crowd who recalled his innings of 175 in 1973, one of his three centuries against England.

Teams: Central Districts, Wellington, Otago, Canterbury and New Zealand

Test series	Tests	Runs	100s	Average
1964-65 in India	3	81	—	13.50
1964-65 in Pakistan	1	74	—	37.00
1964-65 in New Zealand	3	152	—	30.75
1965 in England	3	111	—	18.33
1965-66 in New Zealand	3	214	1	35.67
1967-68 in New Zealand	4	240	—	34.28
1968-69 in New Zealand	3	233	—	38.80
1969 in England	3	179	—	35.80
1969-70 in India	3	174	—	29.00
1969-70 in Pakistan	3	55	—	9.20
1970-71 in New Zealand	2	56	—	18.67
1971-72 in West Indies	5	531	2	88.50
1972-73 in New Zealand	3	91	—	18.20
1973 in England	3	362	2	72.40
1973-74 in Australia	3	150	—	30.00
1973-74 in New Zealand	3	150	1	30.00
1974-75 in New Zealand	2	58	—	19.33
1975-76 in New Zealand	3	218	—	54.50
1976-77 in New Zealand	2	156	1	52.00
1977-78 in New Zealand	3	89	—	14.83
1978 in England	3	74	—	12.33
Total	61	3,448	7	32.22

Career runs: 13,101 Average 34.84
Highest Test score: 176 v England, Nottingham, 1973
Highest career score: 202*, Central Districts v Otago, Nelson, 1968-69

Bruce Taylor
1943-

Bruce Taylor was one of New Zealand's finest all-rounders, winning thirty caps. He was capable of bowling an entire side out, and also of hitting Test centuries. A fine figure of a man, he bowled at medium pace and occasionally faster, but he was able to make the ball move and won a reputation as a bowler who could attack without sacrificing accuracy.

Teams: Canterbury, Wellington and New Zealand

Test series	Tests	Runs	100s	Average	Wkts	Average
1964-65 in Pakistan	3	117	—	39.00	6	35.15
1964-65 in India	3	158	1	31.60	15	18.40
1965 in England	2	60	—	15.00	4	64.25
1965-66 in N Zealand	1	24	—	12.00	5	13.20
1967-68 in N Zealand	3	73	—	12.16	8	29.37
1968-69 in N Zealand	3	209	1	69.70	5	53.60
1969 in England	2	7	—	1.70	10	15.50
1969-70 in India	2	64	—	16.00	6	17.50

1969-70 in Pakistan	1	0	—	0.00	3	12.70
1971-72 in W Indies	4	114	—	38.00	27	17.70
1972-73 in N Zealand	3	10	—	2.50	13	32.00
1973 in England	3	62	—	12.40	9	43.88
Total	30	898	2	20.40	111	26.60

Career runs: 4,183 Average: 25.50
Highest Test score: 124 v West Indies, Auckland, 1968-69
Career wickets: 384 Average 25.26
Highest career score: 173, Wellington v Otago, Dunedin, 1972-73
Best Test and career bowling: 7-74 v West Indies, Bridgetown, 1971-72

Glenn Turner
1947-

One of the many products of coaching by English county players, Glenn Turner was spotted in Otago by Billy Ibadulla, Warwickshire's Pakistani batsman. Warwickshire could not offer him a place but Worcestershire did, and Turner, who had a reputation for slow scoring in his early days, developed into New Zealand's finest right-handed batsman. He broke an old Worcestershire record by scoring 10 centuries in a season, and then by the end of May 1973, for New Zealand, he scored 1,000 runs. A combative character, he has stood his ground in fierce action against both the Australians and Indians.

Teams: Otago, Worcestershire and New Zealand

Test series	Tests	Runs	100s	Average
1968-69 in New Zealand	3	183	—	30.50
1969 in England	2	126	—	42.00
1969-70 in India	3	105	—	21.00
1969-70 in Pakistan	1	136	1	68.00
1970-71 in New Zealand	2	160	—	53.33
1971-72 in West Indies	5	672	2	96.00
1972-73 in New Zealand	3	235	—	47.00
1973 in England	3	116	—	23.20
1973-74 in Australia	2	60	—	20.00
1973-74 in New Zealand	3	403	2	100.75
1974-75 in New Zealand	2	108	—	36.00
1975-76 in New Zealand	3	217	1	54.25
1976-77 in India	3	261	1	43.50
1976-77 in Pakistan	2	60	—	15.00
1976-77 in New Zealand	2	78	—	19.50
Total	39	2,920	7	45.62

Career runs: 27,128 Average: 48.27
Highest Test and career score: 259 v West Indies, Georgetown, 1971-72 and 259, New Zealanders v Guyana, Georgetown, 1971-72

Richard Hadlee
1951-

Richard Hadlee and his brother Dayle were New Zealand's opening bowlers in some of their country's best years in Test cricket. As Hadlee's action matured and gave him increasing pace, he became one of the most feared of all the fast-medium bowlers of his generation. No mean batsman, he joined Nottinghamshire in a time of crisis and at once made his mark on English county cricket.

Teams: Canterbury, Nottinghamshire and New Zealand

Test series	Tests	Wkts	Average
1972-73 in New Zealand	1	2	56.00
1973 in England	1	1	143.00
1973-74 in Australia	3	7	36.43
1973-74 in New Zealand	2	10	22.90
1975-76 in New Zealand	2	12	16.41
1976-77 in India	3	13	33.61
1976-77 in Pakistan	3	10	44.70
1976-77 in New Zealand	2	6	59.00
1977-78 in New Zealand	3	15	24.73
1978 in England	3	13	20.76
Total	23	89	31.58

Career wickets: 323 Average: 23.77
Best Test and career bowling: 7-23 v India, Wellington, 1975-76

South Africa

Aubrey Faulkner
1881-1930

George Aubrey Faulkner, together with Vogler, Pegler and Schwarz, was one of four South African googly bowlers who spread alarm and uncertainty in batsmen all over the world in the 1900s, shortly after B. J. T. Bosanquet (an Englishman and a fine batsman, incidentally) had invented his version of the off-break bowled with a leg break-action. Faulkner was a successful all-round cricketer, and later opened a school of cricket in England which built a deserved reputation for training young players in orthodox methods. Sadly, he was one of several cricketers to die by his own hand.

Teams: Transvaal, MCC and South Africa

Test series	Tests	Runs	100s	Average	Wkts	Average
1905-06 in S Africa	5	129	—	18.42	14	19.42
1907 in England	3	117	—	23.40	12	18.16
1909-10 in S Africa	5	545	1	60.55	29	21.89
1910-11 in Australia	5	732	2	73.20	10	51.40
1912 in England	6	194	1	19.40	17	26.70
1924 in England	1	37	—	18.50	—	—
Total	25	1,754	4	40.79	82	26.58

Career runs: 6,392 Average: 36.31
Highest Test and career score: 204 v Australia,

Melbourne, 1910-11
Career wickets: 449 Average: 17.42
Best Test bowling: 7-84 v England, Oval, 1912
Best career bowling: 7-26, South Africans v Victoria, Melbourne, 1910-11

Herbie Taylor
1889-1973
Herbert Wilfred Taylor was a magnificent player in the early days of South African cricket, at his best on the matting wickets on which he was brought up. He demonstrated to those who wished to study his method how batting should be based on a full stride, whether backward or forward. He was not such a good player on turf, but nonetheless helped the South African team through the period of transition from matting wickets. He was captain from 1913-24.

Teams: Natal, Transvaal and South Africa

Test series	Tests	Runs	100s	Average
1912 in England	6	194	—	19.40
1913-14 in South Africa	5	508	1	50.80
1921-22 in South Africa	3	200	—	33.33
1922-23 in South Africa	5	582	3	64.66
1924 in England	5	197	—	32.83
1927-28 in South Africa	5	412	1	41.20
1929 in England	3	221	1	55.25
1930-31 in South Africa	4	299	1	49.83
1931-32 in Australia	5	314	—	31.40
1931-32 in New Zealand	1	9	—	9.00
Total	42	2,936	7	40.77

Career runs: 13,105 Average: 41.87
Highest Test score: 176 v England, Johannesburg, 1922-23
Highest career score: 250*, Natal v Transvaal, Johannesburg, 1912-13

Bruce Mitchell
1909-
Bruce Mitchell played for Transvaal for twenty-five years. He came to England on his first tour at the age of twenty, and scored more runs than any other member of the 1929 side. He was peerless among his generation as a defensive batsman. In 1935 he made 164 not out in five and a half hours when South Africa won her first Test match at Lord's. Quite apart from his batting, he was as good a specialist first slip as South Africa, renowned for her fielding and catching talent, ever produced.

Teams: Transvaal and South Africa

Test series	Tests	Runs	100s	Average
1929 in England	5	251	—	31.37
1930-31 v England	5	455	1	50.55
1931-32 in Australia	5	322	—	32.20
1931-32 in New Zealand	2	166	1	55.33
1935 in England	5	488	2	69.71
1935-36 v Australia	5	251	—	31.37
1938-39 v England	5	466	1	58.25
1947 in England	5	597	2	66.33
1948-49 v England	5	475	1	52.77
Total	42	3,471	8	48.88

Career runs: 11,395 Average: 45.39
Highest Test score: 189* v England, Oval, 1947
Highest career score: 195, South Africans v Surrey, Oval, 1935
* Not out

Arthur Dudley Nourse
1910-
Like the Pataudis, Dave Nourse and his son Dudley became the two best-known South African batsmen of their generations. Dave Nourse played for Natal for twenty-nine years, for Transvaal for two years, and for Western Province for nine seasons, his career spanning an astonishing forty years. He was a left-hander of great persistence at the wicket, and the batsman on whom so much of South Africa's early cricket depended. Arthur Dudley Nourse had a relatively short career by comparison, playing for Natal for a mere twenty-two years! As a run-maker he was more successful than his father. His most famous innings was as captain in 1951 when he made 208 in the first Test match at Trent Bridge, batting with a broken thumb, and was largely responsible for South Africa's victory.

Teams: Natal and South Africa

Test series	Tests	Runs	100s	Average
1935 in England	4	157	—	26.16
1935-36 in South Africa	5	518	1	57.55
1938-39 in South Africa	5	422	2	60.28
1947 in England	5	621	2	69.00
1948-49 in South Africa	5	536	2	76.57
1949-50 in South Africa	5	405	1	45.00
1951 in England	5	301	1	37.62
Total	34	2,960	9	53.81

Career runs: 12,472
Highest Test score: 231 v Australia, Johannesburg, 1935-36
Highest career score: 260*, Natal v Transvaal, Johannesburg, 1935-36

Athol Rowan
1921-
Athol Rowan was a splendid figure—tall, fair and good-looking, with a glorious action for an off-spinner. Sadly, a bad knee terminated his Test career. He and his brother Eric Rowan, a tough

opening batsman and one of the last to take the field in Test cricket without a box or even gloves, were stalwarts of a strong Transvaal team. Athol's particular merit was that he combined both spin and flight, and thus was able to establish his mastery on hard South African wickets.

Teams: Transvaal and South Africa

Test series	Tests	Wkts	Average
1947 in England	5	12	55.91
1948-49 in S Africa	5	24	33.08
1951 in England	5	18	34.38
Total	15	54	38.59

Career wickets: 273 Average: 23.47
Best Test bowling: 5-68 v England, Nottingham, 1951
Best career bowling: 9-19 Transvaal v Australians, Johannesburg, 1949-50

Hugh Tayfield
1928-

Hugh Joseph Tayfield succeeded Athol Rowan as South Africa's leading off-spinner. He was the first spin bowler to achieve single-handed domination of batsmen on good wickets by depriving them of runs, thanks to his own accuracy and the extraordinary fielding of the South African elevens in which he played. He had a habit of stubbing his toe on the ground before beginning to bowl which gave him his nickname 'Toey'. He also developed a catching position which could either be described as a short mid-on or a deep forward-short-leg, almost on the crease, where Jack Cheetham, his captain, took many catches when batsmen drove early at the ball having failed to 'read' its flight through the air.

Teams: Natal, Rhodesia and South Africa

Test series	Tests	Wkts	Average
1949-50 in South Africa	5	17	42.70
1952-53 in Australia	5	30	28.10
1952-53 in New Zealand	2	10	16.20
1953-54 in South Africa	5	21	17.95
1955 in England	5	26	21.84
1956-57 in South Africa	5	37	17.18
1957-58 in Australia	5	17	37.58
1960 in England	5	12	37.83
Total	37	170	25.91

Career wickets: 851 Average: 21.96
Best Test and career bowling: 9-113 v England, Johannesburg, 1956-57

John Waite
1930-

John Waite was perhaps the best of the many outstanding wicketkeeper-batsmen in South Africa's history, capable of opening the batting or going in lower down the order. He was a fine player on his own wickets, very correct. As a wicketkeeper he was outstanding, both up to the wicket and back, establishing for himself a reputation for spectacular and athletic competence. He was also one of the most popular members of the South African teams to tour abroad, an open, warm and happy man.

Teams: Eastern Province and South Africa

Test series	Tests	Runs	100s	Average
1951 in England	4	152	—	21.71
1952-43 in Australia	5	293	—	29.30
1952-53 in New Zealand	2	133	—	44.33
1953-54 in South Africa	5	144	—	24.00
1955 in England	5	265	1	29.44
1956-57 in South Africa	5	169	—	21.12
1957-58 in South Africa	5	362	2	40.22
1960 in England	5	267	—	38.14
1961-62 in South Africa	5	263	1	29.22
1963-64 in Australia	4	184	1	36.86
1963-64 in New Zealand	3	103	—	25.75
1964-65 in South Africa	2	70	—	35.00
Total	50	2,405	4	30.44

Career runs: 9,698 Average: 34.76
Highest Test score: 134 v Australia, Durban, 1957-58
Highest career score: 219 Eastern Province v Griqualand West, Kimberley, 1950-51
Test Dismissals: 124 catches 17 stumpings = 141

Neil Adcock
1931-

Neil Adcock was a tall fast bowler, with a long approach to the wicket. In partnership with Peter Heine he gave South Africa a marvellously penetrative opening attack in the 1950s. These two were feared all over the world, Adcock for his natural ability and the movement he obtained even on hard wickets, and Heine for his hostility. With this pair as its spearhead in the field, the South Africans recaptured third place in the world ranking which they had not held since the early days of their googly bowlers.

Teams: Transvaal and South Africa

Test series	Tests	Wkts	Average
1953-54 in South Africa	5	24	20.20
1955 in England	4	10	25.20
1956-57 in South Africa	5	21	14.90
1957-58 in South Africa	5	14	29.28
1960 in England	5	26	22.57

1961-62 in South Africa	2	9	16.44
Total	26	104	21.10

Career wickets: 405 Average: 17.23
Best Test bowling: 6-43 v Australia, Durban, 1957-58
Best career bowling: 8-39 Transvaal v Orange Free State, Johannesburg, 1953-54

Eddie Barlow
1940-

Eddie Barlow was perhaps the most competitive of all South Africa's cricketers. An immensely strong figure of a man, he was a powerful batsman, at times overshadowed by great stroke-makers like Richards or Pollock, but none the less a key member of the South African side which was coming to the fore in the early 1960s. He was also a rumbustious bowler capable of astonishing feats, his whole technique based on body-power rather than any fluency of action. Add to these qualities his athletic and safe slip fielding, and it is easy to see why he has won a reputation as an all-round cricketer of the highest renown. For many seasons a splendid captain of Western Province, he proved his qualities of leadership during his season with one of the 'Cinderella' counties of England, Derbyshire, whose players he endowed with a new self-respect.

Teams: Transvaal, Eastern Province, Western Province, Derbyshire and South Africa

Test series	Tests	Runs	100s	Average	Wkts	Average
1961-62 in S Africa	5	330	—	36.51	—	—
1963-64 in Australia	5	603	3	32.85	7	32.85
1963-64 in N Zealand	2	295	—	49.16	2	50.50
1964-65 in S Africa	5	558	1	55.80	5	39.00
1965 in England	3	184	—	30.66	—	—
1966-67 in S Africa	5	186	—	20.66	15	21.60
1969-70 in S Africa	4	360	2	51.42	11	23.36
Total	30	2.516	6	45.74	40	34.05

Career runs: 16,330 Average: 39.34
Highest Test score: 201 v Australia, Adelaide, 1963-64
Highest career score: 217, Derbyshire v Surrey, Ilkeston, 1976
Career wickets: 512 Average: 24.90
Best Test bowling: 5-85 v Australia, Cape Town, 1966-67
Best career bowling: 7-24 Western Province v Natal, Durban, 1972-73

Graeme Pollock
1944-

Graeme Pollock was the finest left-handed batsman that South Africa ever produced. A glorious stroke-maker, he could annihilate bowling attacks and frequently did so. He and his brother Peter, an outstanding fast bowler, formed the nucleus of a strong Eastern Province side. Sadly, Pollock's opportunities in Test cricket were limited, but in all his twenty-three tests he was a great stylist: he never made runs badly.

Teams: Eastern Province and South Africa

Test series	Tests	Runs	100s	Average
1963-64 in Australia	5	399	2	57.00
1963-64 in New Zealand	1	53	—	26.50
1964-65 v England	5	459	1	57.37
1965 in England	3	291	1	48.50
1966-67 v Australia	5	537	2	76.71
1969-70 v Australia	4	517	1	73.85
Total	23	2,256	7	60.97

Career runs: 14,760 Average: 53.67
Highest Test and career score: 274 v Australia, Durban, 1969-70

Barry Richards
1945-
Barry Richards was the greatest batsman of his generation in the ten years from 1965 to 1975. Sadly, he was never able to prove this in a full programme of Test cricket. In his only series, against Australia in 1970, he scored 508 runs in seven innings. He was a century-maker rather than a double-century man, but the frequency with which he made runs and the ease and fluency with which they sped from his bat suggested that he had the ability to charm the ball. His ability to adapt to both three- and one-day cricket was proof of the theory that great players can create opportunities in either form. Essentially, the reason for Richards success was his adherence, conscious or unconscious, to the principles of classic batting, and because of this he was a joy to watch. Like Roy Marshall, whose place he took in the Hampshire side, he was occasionally a clever bowler and always a splendid slip fielder.

Teams: Natal, Hampshire and South Africa

Test series	Tests	Runs	100s	Average
1969-70 v Australia	4	508	2	72.57

Career runs: 27,293 Average: 55.70
Highest Test score: 140 v Australia, Durban, 1969-70
Highest career score: 356, South Australia v Western Australia, Perth, 1970-71

Mike Procter
1946-
It would be hard to imagine a better all-round cricketer than Gloucestershire's captain. A batsman capable, on his day, of taking an attack to pieces by sustained yet soundly based hitting, Procter's bowling skills brought him even more obvious successes. His whirling action, with delivery at least half a stride away from the norm, is astonishing enough in itself, but like Sobers Procter can also turn his hand to off-spin. Most significant of all, he recovered from the type of knee operation that would have crippled others and in his maturity led his adopted county to success in Cup cricket, winning the Benson and Hedges in 1977.

Teams: Gloucestershire, Natal, Western Province, Rhodesia and South Africa

Test series	Tests	Runs	100s	Average	Wkts	Average
1966-67 in S Africa	3	17	—	5.66	15	17.53
1969-70 in S Africa	4	209	—	34.83	26	13.57
Total	7	226	—	25.11	41	15.02

Career runs: 17,997 Average: 37.41
Highest Test score: 48 v Australia, Cape Town, 1969-70
Highest career score: 254, Rhodesia v Western Province, Salisbury, 1970-71
Career wickets: 1132 Average: 19.22
Best Test bowling: 6-73 v Australia, Port Elizabeth, 1969-70
Best career bowling: 9-71, Rhodesia v Transvaal, Bulawayo, 1972-73

Right: Cape Coloured cricketers play on a mat wicket in South Africa

TABLES & STATISTICS

CRICKET Test Matches
In England

1880 v Australia
England won the only Test
Oval
England won by 5 wickets
England 420 (W. G. Grace 152) and 57-5 Australia 149 and 327 (W. L. Murdoch 153*)
1882 v Australia
Australia won the only Test
Oval
Australia won by 7 runs
Australia 63 and 122 England 101 (F. Spofforth 7-46) and 77 (F. Spofforth 7-44)
1884 v Australia
Series won by England
Manchester
Match drawn
England 95 and 180-9
Australia 182
Lord's
England won by an innings and 5 runs
Australia 229 and 145 (G. Ulyett 7-36) England 379
Oval
Match drawn
Australia 551 (W. L. Murdoch 211) England 346 and 85-2
1886 v Australia
Series won by England
Manchester
England won by 4 wickets
Australia 205 and 123 (R. Barlow 7-44) England 223 and 107-6
Lord's
England won by an innings and 106 runs
England 353 (A. Shrewsbury 164) Australia 121 and 126
Oval
England won by an innings and 217 runs
England 434 (W. G. Grace 170) Australia 68 (G. Lohmann 7-36) and 149
1888 v Australia
Series won by England
Lord's
Australia won by 61 runs
Australia 116 and 60
England 53 and 62
Oval
England won by an innings and 137 runs
Australia 80 and 100
England 317
Manchester
England won by an innings and 21 runs
England 172
Australia 81 (R. Peel 7-31) and 70
1890 v Australia
Series won by England
Lord's
England won by 7 wickets
Australia 132 and 176
England 173 and 137-3
Oval
England won by 2 wickets
Australia 92 and 102
England 100 and 95-8
Manchester
Match abandoned
1893 v Australia
Series won by England
Lord's
Match drawn
England 334 and 234-8d
Australia 269
Oval
England won by an innings and 43 runs
England 483 (G. Giffen 7-128)
Australia 91 and 349
Manchester
Match drawn
Australia 204 and 236
England 243 and 118-4
1896 v Australia
Lord's
England won by 6 wickets
Australia 53 and 347
England 292 and 111-4
Manchester
Australia won by 3 wickets
Australia 412 (T. Richardson 7-168) and 125-7 England 231 and 305 (K. Ranjitsinhji 154*)
Oval
England won by 66 runs
England 145 and 84
Australia 119 and 44
1899 v Australia
Series won by Australia
Nottingham
Match drawn
Australia 252 and 230-8d
England 193 and 155-7
Lord's
Australia won by 10 wickets
England 206 (E. Jones 7-88) and 240 Australia 421 and 28-0
Leeds
Match drawn
Australia 172 and 224
England 220 and 19-0
Manchester
Match drawn
England 372 and 94-3
Australia 196 and 346-7d
Oval
Match drawn
England 576 Australia 352 (W. Lockwood 7-71) and 254-5
1902 v Australia
Series won by Australia
Birmingham
Match drawn
England 376-9d Australia 36 (W. Rhodes 7-17) and 46-2
Lord's
Match drawn
England 102-2
Sheffield
Australia won by 143 runs
Australia 194 and 289
England 145 and 195
Manchester
Australia won by 3 runs
Australia 299 and 86 England 262 and 120
Oval
England won by 1 wicket
Australia 324 and 121 England 183 (H. Trumble 8-65) and 263-9
1905 v Australia
Series won by England
Nottingham
England won by 213 runs
England 196 (F. Laver 7-64) and 426-5d Australia 221 and 188 (B. Bosanquet 8-107)
Lord's
Match drawn
England 282 and 151-5
Australia 181
Leeds
Match drawn
England 301 and 295-5d
Australia 195 and 224-7
Manchester
England won by an innings and 80 runs
England 446 Australia 197 and 169
Oval
Match drawn
England 430 (A. Cotter 7-148) and 261-6d Australia 363 and 124-4
1907 v South Africa
Series won by England
Lord's
Match drawn
England 428 (A. Vogler 7-128)
South Africa 140 and 185-3
Leeds
England won by 53 runs
England 76 and 162 South Africa 110 (C. Blythe 8-59) and 75 (C. Blythe 7-40)
Oval
Match drawn
England 295 and 138 South Africa 178 and 159-5
1909 v Australia
Series won by Australia
Birmingham
England won by 10 wickets

Australia 74 and 151
England 121 and 105-0
Lord's
Australia won by 9 wickets
England 269 and 121
Australia 350 and 41-1
Leeds
Australia won by 126 runs
Australia 188 and 207 England 182 (C. Macartney 7-58) and 87
Manchester
Match drawn
Australia 147 and 279-9d
England 119 (F. Laver 8-31) and 108-3
Oval
Match drawn
Australia 325 and 339-5d
England 352 and 104-3

1912 Triangular Tournament

England v Australia
Lord's
Match drawn
England 310-7d
Australia 282-7
Manchester
Match drawn
England 203 Australia 14-0
Oval
England won by 244 runs
England 245 and 175 (G. Hazlitt 7-25)
Australia 111 and 65
England v South Africa
Lord's
England won by an innings and 62 runs
South Africa 58 and 217
England 337 (S. Pegler 7-65)
Leeds
England won by 174 runs
England 242 and 238
South Africa 147 and 159
Oval
England won by 10 wickets
South Africa 95 and 93 (S. Barnes 8-29) England 176 (G. Faulkner 7-84) and 14-0
Australia v South Africa
Manchester
Australia won by an innings and 88 runs
Australia 448 South Africa 265 and 95
Lord's
Australia won by 10 wickets
South Africa 263 and 173
Australia 390 (W. Bardsley 164) and 48-0
Nottingham
Match drawn
South Africa 329 Australia 219

1921 v Australia
Series won by Australia
Nottingham
Australia won by 10 wickets
England 112 and 147
Australia 232 and 30-0
Lord's
Australia won by 8 wickets
England 187 and 283
Australia 342 and 131-2
Leeds
Australia won by 219 runs
Australia 407 and 273-7d
England 259 and 202
Manchester
Match drawn
England 362-4d and 44-1
Australia 175
Oval
Match drawn
England 403-8d (C. Mead 182*) and 244-2 Australia 389
1924 v South Africa
Series won by England
Birmingham
England won by an innings and 18 runs
England 438
South Africa 30 (A. E. R. Gilligan 6-7) and 390
Lord's
England won by an innings and 18 runs
South Africa 273 and 240
England 531-2d (J. B. Hobbs 211)
Leeds
England won by 9 wickets
England 396 and 60-1
South Africa 132 and 323
Manchester
Match drawn
South Africa 116-4
Oval
Match drawn
South Africa 342 England 421-8
1926 v Australia
Series won by England
Nottingham
Match drawn
England 32-0
Lord's
Match drawn
Australia 383 (W. Bardsley 193*) and 194-5 England 475-3d
Leeds
Match drawn
Australia 494 (C. Macartney 151)
England 294 and 254-3
Manchester
Match drawn
Australia 335 England 305-5
Oval
England won by 289 runs
England 280 and 436
(H. Sutcliffe 161) Australia 302 and 125
1928 v West Indies
Series won by England
Lord's
England won by an innings and 58 runs
England 401 West Indies 177 and 166
Manchester
England won by an innings and 30 runs
West Indies 206 and 115
England 351
Oval
England won by an innings and 71 runs
West Indies 238 and 129
England 438 (J. B. Hobbs 159)
1929 v South Africa
Series won by England
Birmingham
Match drawn
England 245 and 308-4d
South Africa 250 and 171-1
Lord's
Match drawn
England 302 and 312-8d
South Africa 322 and 90-5
Leeds
England won by 5 wickets
South Africa 236 (A. Freeman 7-115) and 275 England 328 and 186-5
Manchester
England won by an innings and 32 runs
England 427-7d (F. Woolley 154)
South Africa 130 (A. Freeman 7-71) and 265
Oval
Match drawn
England 258 and 264-1
South Africa 492-8d
1930 v Australia
Series won by Australia
Nottingham
England won by 93 runs
England 270 and 302
Australia 144 and 335
Lord's
Australia won by 7 wickets
England 425 (K. Duleepsinhji 173) and 375
Australia 729-6d (D. Bradman 254, W. M. Woodfull 155) and 72-3
Leeds
Match drawn
Australia (D. Bradman 334)
England 391 and 95-3
Manchester
Match drawn
Australia 345 England 251-8

Oval
Australia won by an innings and 39 runs
England 405 (H. Sutcliffe 161) and 251 (P. Hornibrook 7-92) Australia 695 (D. Bradman 232)
1931 v New Zealand
Series won by England
Lord's
New Zealand 224 and 469-9d
England 454 and 146-5
Oval
England won by an innings and 26 runs
England 416-4d
New Zealand 193 and 197
Manchester
Match drawn
England 224-3
1932 v India
England won the only Test
Lord's
England won by 158 runs
England 259 and 275-8d
India 189 and 187
1933 v West Indies
Series won by England
Lord's
England won by an innings and 27 runs
England 296 West Indies 97 and 172
Manchester
Match drawn
West Indies 375 (G. Headley 169*) and 225 (J. Langridge 7-56)
England 374
Oval
England won by an innings and 17 runs
England 312 West Indies 100 and 195
1934 v Australia
Series won by Australia
Nottingham
Australia won by 238 runs
Australia 374 and 273-8d
England 268 and 141
(W. O'Reilly 7-54)
Lord's
England won by an innings and 38 runs
England 440 Australia 284
(H. Verity 7-61) and 118 (H. Verity 8-43)
Manchester
Match drawn
England 627-9d (M. Leyland 153, W. O'Reilly 7-189) and 123-0d
Australia 491 and 66-1
Leeds
Match drawn
England 200 and 229-6
Australia 584 (D. Bradman 304, W. Ponsford 181)
Oval
Australia won by 562 runs
Australia 701 (W. Ponsford 266, D. Bradman 244) and 327 England 321 and 145
1935 v South Africa
Series won by South Africa
Nottingham
Match drawn
England 384-7d South Africa 220 and 17-1
Lord's
South Africa won by 157 runs
South Africa 228 and 278-7d (B. Mitchell 164*) England 198 and 151
Leeds
Match drawn
England 216 and 294-7d
South Africa 171 and 194-5
Manchester
Match drawn
England 357 and 231-6d
South Africa 318 and 169-2
Oval
Match drawn
South Africa 476 and 287-6
England 534-6d (M. Leyland 161)
1936 v India
Series won by England
Lord's
England won by 9 wickets
India 147 and 93
England 134 and 108-1
Manchester
Match drawn
India 203 and 390-5 England 571-8d (W. Hammond 167)
Oval
England won by 9 wickets
England 471-8d (W. Hammond 217) and 64-1 India 222 and 312 (G. O. Allen 7-80)
1937 v New Zealand
Series won by England
Lord's
Match drawn
England 424 and 226-4d
New Zealand 295 and 175-8
Manchester
England won by 130 runs
England 358-9d and 187
New Zealand 281 and 134
Oval
Match drawn
New Zealand 249 and 187
England 254-7d and 31-1
1938 v Australia
Series drawn
Nottingham
Match drawn
England 658-8d (E. Paynter 216*)
Australia 411 (S. McCabe 232) and 427-6
Lord's
Match drawn
England 494 (W. Hammond 240) and 242-8d Australia 422 (W. A. Brown 206*) and 204-6
Leeds
Australia won by 5 wickets
England 223 and 123
Australia 242 and 107-5
Manchester
Match abandoned
Oval
England won by an innings and 579 runs
England 903-7d (L. Hutton 364, M. Leyland 187, J. Hardstaff 169*)
Australia 201 and 123
1939 v West Indies
Series won by England
Lord's
England won by 8 wickets
West Indies 277 and 225 England 404-5d (L. Hutton 196) and 100-2
Manchester
Match drawn
England 164-7d and 128-6d
West Indies 133 and 43-4
Oval
Match drawn
England 352 and 366-3 (L. Hutton 165*) West Indies 498
1946 v India
Series won by England
Lord's
England won by 10 wickets
India 200 (A. Bedser 7-49) and 275
England 428 (J. Hardstaff 205*) and 48-0
Manchester
Match drawn
England 294 and 153-5d
India 170 and 152-9 (A. Bedser 7-52)
Oval
Match drawn
India 331 England 95-3
1947 v South Africa
Series won by England
Nottingham
Match drawn
South Africa 533 (A. Melville 189) and 166-1 England 208 and 551 (D. Compton 163)
Lord's
England won by 10 wickets
England 554-8d (D. Compton 208, W. Edrich 189) and 26-0 South Africa 327 and 252
Manchester
England won by 7 wickets
South Africa 339 and 267
England 478 (W. Edrich 191) and 130-3

Leeds
England won by 10 wickets
South Africa 175 and 184
England 317-7d and 47-0
Oval
Match drawn
England 427 and 325-6d
South Africa 302 and 423-7 (B. Mitchell 189*)
1948 v Australia
Series won by Australia
Nottingham
Australia won by 8 wickets
England 165 and 441 (D. Compton 184) Australia 509 and 89-2
Lord's
Australia won by 409 runs
Australia 350 and 460-7d
England 215 and 186
Manchester
Match drawn
England 363 and 174-3d
Australia 221 and 92-1
Leeds
Australia won by 7 wickets
England 496 and 365-8d Australia 458 and 404-3 (A. Morris 182, D. Bradman 173*)
Oval
Australia won by an innings and 149 runs
England 52 and 188
Australia 389 (A. Morris 196)
1949 v New Zealand
Series drawn
Leeds
Match drawn
England 372 and 267-4d
New Zealand 341 and 195-2
Lord's
Match drawn
England 313-9d and 306-5
New Zealand 484 (M. Donnelly 206)
Manchester
Match drawn
New Zealand 293 and 348-7
England 440-9d
Oval
Match drawn
New Zealand 345 and 308-9d
England 482 (L. Hutton 206)
1950 v West Indies
Series won by West Indies
Manchester
England won by 202 runs
England 312 (A. Valentine 8-104) and 288 West Indies 215 and 183
Lord's
West Indies won by 326 runs
West Indies 326 and 425-6d (C. Walcott 168*) England 151 and 274
Nottingham
West Indies won by 10 wickets
England 223 and 436
West Indies 558 (F. Worrell 261) and 103-0
Oval
West Indies won by an innings and 56 runs
West Indies 503 England 344 (L. Hutton 202*) and 103
1951 v South Africa
Series won by England
Nottingham
South Africa won by 71 runs
South Africa 483-9d (A. D. Nourse 208) and 121 England 419-9d and 114
Lord's
England won by 10 wickets
England 311 and 16-0 South Africa 115 (R. Tattersall 7-52) and 211
Manchester
England won by 9 wickets
South Africa 158 (A. Bedser 7-58) and 191 England 211 and 142-1
Leeds
Match drawn
South Africa 538 (E. A. Rowan 236) and 87-0 England 505
Oval
England won by 4 wickets
South Africa 202 and 154
England 194 and 164-6
1952 v India
Series won by England
Leeds
England won by 7 wickets
India 293 and 165
England 334 and 128-3
Lord's
England won by 8 wickets
India 235 and 378 (V. Mankad 184) England 537 (L. Hutton 150) and 79-2
Manchester
England won by an innings and 207 runs
England 347-9d India 58 (F. Trueman 8-31) and 82
Oval
Match drawn
England 326-6d India 98
1953 v Australia
Series won by England
Nottingham
Match drawn
Australia 249 (A. Bedser 7-55) and 123 (A. Bedser 7-44) England 144 and 120-1
Lord's
Match drawn
Australia 346 and 368
England 372 and 282-7
Manchester
Match drawn
Australia 318 and 35-8
England 276
Leeds
Match drawn
England 167 and 275
Australia 266 and 147-4
Oval
England won by 8 wickets
Australia 275 and 162
England 306 and 132-2
1954 v Pakistan
Series drawn
Lord's
Match drawn
Pakistan 87 and 121-3
England 117-9d
Nottingham
England won by an innings and 129 runs
Pakistan 157 and 272 England 558-6d (D. Compton 278)
Manchester
Match drawn
England 359-8d
Pakistan 90 and 25-4
Oval
Pakistan won by 24 runs
Pakistan 133 and 164
England 130 and 143
1955 v South Africa
Series won by England
Nottingham
England won by an innings and 5 runs
England 334 South Africa 181 and 148
Lord's
England won by 71 runs
England 133 and 353 South Africa 304 and 111 (J. B. Statham 7-39)
Manchester
South Africa won by 3 wickets
England 284 (D. Compton 158) and 381 South Africa 521-8d and 145-7
Leeds
South Africa won by 224 runs
South Africa 171 and 500
England 191 and 256
Oval
England won by 92 runs
England 151 and 204
South Africa 112 and 151
1956 v Australia
Series won by England
Nottingham
Match drawn
England 217-8d and 188-3d
Australia 148 and 120-3
Lord's
Australia won by 185 runs

Australia 285 and 257
England 171 and 186
Leeds
England won by an innings and 42 runs
England 325 Australia 143 and 140
Manchester
England won by an innings and 170 runs
England 459 Australia 84 (J. C. Laker 9-37) and 205 (J. C. Laker 10-53)
Oval
Match drawn
England 247 and 182-3d
Australia 202 and 27-5
1957 v West Indies
Series won by England
Birmingham
Match drawn
England 186 (S. Ramadhin 7-49) and 583-4d (P. May 285*, M. C. Cowdrey 154) West Indies 474 (O. G. Smith 161) and 72-7
Lord's
England won by an innings and 36 runs
West Indies 127 (T. Bailey 7-44) and 261 England 424 (M. C. Cowdrey 152)
Nottingham
Match drawn
England 619-6d (T. Graveney 258) and 64-1 West Indies 372 (F. Worrell 191*) and 367 (O. G. Smith 168)
Leeds
England won by an innings and 5 runs
West Indies 142 and 132
England 279 (F. Worrell 7-70)
Oval
England won by an innings and 237 runs
England 412 (T. Graveney 164)
West Indies 89 and 86
1958 v New Zealand
Series won by England
Birmingham
England won by 205 runs
England 221 and 215-6d
New Zealand 94 and 137
Lord's
England won by an innings and 148 runs
England 269 New Zealand 47 and 74
Leeds
England won by an innings and 71 runs
New Zealand 67 and 129 (A. Lock 7-51) England 267-2d
Manchester
England won by an innings and 13 runs
New Zealand 267 and 85 (A. Lock 7-35) England 365-9d
Oval
Match drawn
New Zealand 161 and 91-3
England 219-9d
1959 v India
Series won by England
Nottingham
England won by an innings and 59 runs
England 422
India 206 and 157
Lord's
England won by 8 wickets
India 168 and 165
England 226 and 108-2
Leeds
England won by an innings and 173 runs
India 161 and 149 England 483-8d (M. C. Cowdrey 160)
Manchester
England won by 171 runs
England 490 and 265-8d
India 208 and 376
Oval
England won by an innings and 27 runs
India 140 and 194 England 361
1960 v South Africa
Series won by England
Birmingham
England won by 100 runs
England 292 and 203
South Africa 186 and 209
Lord's
England won by an innings and 73 runs
England 362-8d South Africa 152 and 137
Nottingham
England won by 8 wickets
England 287 and 49-2
South Africa 88 and 247
Manchester
Match drawn
England 260 and 153-7d
South Africa 229 and 46-0
Oval
Match drawn
England 155 and 479-9d (G. Pullar 175, M. C. Cowdrey 155) South Africa 419 and 97-4
1961 v Australia
Series won by Australia
Birmingham
Match drawn
England 195 and 401-4 (E. Dexter 180) Australia 516-9d
Lord's
Australia won by 5 wickets
England 206 and 202
Australia 340 and 71-5
Leeds
England won by 8 wickets
Australia 237 and 120
England 299 and 62-2
Manchester
Australia won by 54 runs
Australia 190 and 432
England 367 and 201
Oval
Match drawn
England 256 and 370-8
Australia 494 (P. Burge 181)
1962 v Pakistan
Series won by England
Birmingham
England won by an innings and 24 runs
England 544-5d (M. C. Cowdrey 159) Pakistan 246 and 274
Lord's
England won by 9 wickets
Pakistan 100 and 355
England 370 (T. Graveney 153) and 86-1
Leeds
England won by an innings and 117 runs
England 428 Pakistan 131 and 180
Nottingham
Match drawn
England 428-5d Pakistan 219 and 216-6
Oval
England won by 10 wickets
England 480-5d (M. C. Cowdrey 182, E. Dexter 172) and 27-0
Pakistan 183 and 323
1963 v West Indies
Series won by West Indies
Manchester
West Indies won by 10 wickets
West Indies 501-6d (C. Hunte 182) and 1-0 England 205 and 296
Lord's
Match drawn
West Indies 301 and 229
England 297 and 228-9
Birmingham
England won by 217 runs
England 216 and 278-9d
West Indies 186 and 91 (F. Trueman 7-44)
Leeds
West Indies won by 221 runs
West Indies 397 and 229
England 174 and 231
Oval
West Indies won by 8 wickets
England 275 and 223
West Indies 246 and 255-2

1964 v Australia
Series won by Australia

Nottingham
Match drawn
England 216-8d and 193-9d
Australia 168 and 40-2
Lord's
Match drawn
Australia 176 and 168-4
England 246
Leeds
Australia won by 7 wickets
England 268 and 229
Australia 389 (P. Burge 160) and 111-3
Manchester
Match drawn
Australia 656-8d (R. B. Simpson 311) and 4-0 England 611 (K. Barrington 256, E. Dexter 174, G. McKenzie 7-153)
Oval
Match drawn
England 182 and 381-4
Australia 379
1965 v New Zealand
Series won by England
Birmingham
England won by 9 wickets
England 435 and 96-1
New Zealand 116 and 413
Lord's
England won by 7 wickets
New Zealand 175 and 347
England 307 and 218-3
Leeds
England won by an innings and 187 runs
England 546-4d (J. Edrich 310*, K. Barrington 163)
New Zealand 193 and 166
1965 v South Africa
Series won by South Africa
Lord's
Match drawn
South Africa 280 and 248
England 338 and 145-7
Nottingham
South Africa won by 94 runs
South Africa 269 and 289
England 240 and 224
Oval
Match drawn
South Africa 208 and 392
England 202 and 308-4
1966 v West Indies
Series won by West Indies
Manchester
West Indies won by an innings and 40 runs
West Indies 484 (G. Sobers 161)
England 167 and 277
Lord's
Match drawn
West Indies 269 and 369-5d (G. Sobers 163*) England 355 and 197-4
Nottingham
West Indies won by 139 runs
West Indies 235 and 482-5d (B. Butcher 209*) England 325 and 253
Leeds
West Indies won by an innings and 55 runs
West Indies 500-9d (G. Sobers 174)
England 240 and 205
Oval
England won by an innings and 34 runs
West Indies 268 and 225
England 527 (T. Graveney 165)
1967 v India
Series won by England
Leeds
England won by 6 wickets
England 550-4d (G. Boycott 246*) and 126-4 India 164 and 510
Lord's
England won by an innings and 124 runs
India 152 and 110
England 386 (T. Graveney 151)
Birmingham
England won by 132 runs
England 298 and 203
India 92 and 277
1967 v Pakistan
Series won by England
Lord's
Match drawn
England 369 and 241-9d
Pakistan 354 (Hanif Mohammad 187*) and 88-3
Nottingham
England won by 10 wickets
Pakistan 140 and 114
England 252-8d and 3-0
Oval
England won by 8 wickets
Pakistan 216 and 255
England 440 and 34-2
1968 v Australia
Series drawn
Manchester
Australia won by 159 runs
Australia 357 and 220
England 165 and 253
Lord's
Match drawn
England 351-7d Australia 78 and 127-4
Birmingham
Match drawn
England 409 and 142-3d
Australia 222 and 68-1
Leeds
Match drawn
Australia 315 and 312
England 302 and 230-4
Oval
England won by 226 runs
England 494 (J. Edrich 164, B. d'Oliveira 158) and 181 Australia 324 and 125 (D. Underwood 7-50)
1969 v West Indies
Series won by England
Manchester
England won by 10 wickets
England 413 and 12-0
West Indies 147 and 275
Lord's
Match drawn
West Indies 380 and 295-9d
England 344 and 295-7
Leeds
England won by 30 runs
England 223 and 240
West Indies 161 and 272
1969 v New Zealand
Series won by England
Lord's
England won by 230 runs
England 190 and 340 New Zealand 169 and 131 (D. Underwood 7-32)
Nottingham
Match drawn
New Zealand 294 and 66-1
England 451-8d (J. Edrich 155)
Oval
England won by 8 wickets
New Zealand 150 and 229
England 242 and 138-2
1971 v Pakistan
Series won by England
Birmingham
Match drawn
Pakistan 608-7d (Zaheer Abbas 274)
England 353 and 229-5
Lord's
Match drawn
England 241-2d and 117-0
Pakistan 148
Leeds
England won by 25 runs
England 316 and 264
Pakistan 350 and 205
1971 v India
Series won by India
Lord's
Match drawn
England 304 and 191
India 313 and 145
Manchester
Match drawn
England 386 and 245-3d
India 212 and 65-3
Oval
India won by 4 wickets
England 355 and 101
India 284 and 174-6
1972 v Australia
Series drawn

Manchester
England won by 89 runs
England 249 and 234
Australia 142 and 252
Lord's
Australia won by 8 wickets
England 272 (R. Massie 8-84) and 116 (R. Massie 8-53) Australia 308 and 81-2
Nottingham
Match drawn
Australia 315 and 423-4d (R. Edwards 170)
England 189 and 290-4
Leeds
England won by 9 wickets
Australia 146 and 136
England 263 and 21-1
Oval
Australia won by 5 wickets
England 284 and 356
Australia 399 and 242-5
1973 v New Zealand
Series won by England
Nottingham
England won by 38 runs
England 250 and 325-8d
New Zealand 97 and 440 (B. Congdon 176)
Lord's
Match drawn
England 253 and 463-9 (K. Fletcher 178)
New Zealand 551-9 (B. Congdon 175)
Leeds
England won by an innings and 1 run
New Zealand 276 and 142
England 419
1973 v West Indies
Series won by West Indies
Oval
West Indies won by 158 runs
West Indies 415 and 255
England 257 and 255
Birmingham
Match drawn
West Indies 327 (G. Sobers 150) and 302 England 305 and 182-2
Lord's
West Indies won by an innings and 226 runs
West Indies 652-8d (R. Kanhai 157; G. Sobers 150*)
England 233 and 193
1974 v India
Series won by England
Manchester
England won by 113 runs
England 328-9d and 213-3d
India 246 and 182
Lord's
England won by an innings and 285 runs
England 629 (D. Amiss 188)
India 302 and 42
Birmingham
England won by an innings and 78 runs
India 165 and 216
England 459-2d (D. Lloyd 214*)
1974 v Pakistan
Series drawn
Leeds
Match drawn
Pakistan 285 and 179
England 183 and 238-6
Lord's
Match drawn
Pakistan 130-9d. and 216 (D. Underwood 8-51)
England 270 and 27-0
Oval
Match drawn
Pakistan 600-7d (Zaheer Abbas 240) and 94-4
England 545 (D. Amiss 183)
1975 v Australia
Series won by Australia
Birmingham
Australia won by an innings and 85 runs
Australia 359
England 101 and 173
Lord's
Match drawn
England 315 and 436-7d (J. Edrich 175) Australia 268 and 329-3
Leeds
Match drawn
England 288 and 291
Australia 135 and 220-3
Oval
Match drawn
Australia 532-9d (I. Chappell 192) and 40-2
England 191 and 538
1976 v West Indies
Series won by West Indies
Nottingham
Match drawn
West Indies 494 (I. Richards 232) and 176-5d
England 332 and 156-2
Lord's
Match drawn
England 250 and 254
West Indies 182 and 241-6
Manchester
West Indies won by 425 runs
West Indies 211 and 411-5d
England 71 and 126
Leeds
West Indies won by 55 runs
West Indies 450 and 196
England 387 and 204
Oval
West Indies won by 231 runs
West Indies 687-5d (I. Richards 291) and 182-0d
England 435 (D. Amiss 203, A. M. Holding 8-92) and 203
1977 v Australia
Series won by England
Lord's
Match drawn
England 216 and 305
Australia 296 (R. Willis 7-78) and 114-6
Manchester
England won by 9 wickets
Australia 297 and 218
England 437 and 82-1
Nottingham
England won by 7 wickets
Australia 243 and 309
England 364 and 189-3
Leeds
England won by an innings and 85 runs
England 436 (G. Boycott 191)
Australia 103 and 248
Oval
Match drawn
England 214 and 57-2
Australia 385
1978 v Pakistan
Series won by England
Birmingham
England won by an innings and 57 runs
Pakistan 164 (C. Old 7-50) and 231
England 452-8d
Lord's
England won by an innings and 120 runs
England 364
Pakistan 105 and 139 (I. Botham 8-34)
Leeds
Match drawn
Pakistan 201
England 119
1978 v New Zealand
Series won by England
Oval
England won by 7 wickets
New Zealand 234 and 182
England 279 and 138
Nottingham
England won by an innings and 119 runs
England 429
New Zealand 120 and 190
Lord's
England won by 7 wickets
New Zealand 339 and 67
England 289 and 118-3

In Australia

1876-77 v England
Series drawn
Melbourne
Australia won by 45 runs
Australia 245 (C. Bannerman 165*) and 104 England 196 and 108 (T. Kendall 7-55)
Melbourne
England won by 4 wickets
Australia 122 and 259
England 261 and 122-6
1878-79 v England
Australia won only Test
Melbourne
Australia won by 10 wickets
England 113 and 160 (F. Spofforth 7-62) Australia 256 (T. Emmett 7-68) and 19-0
1881-82 v England
Series won by Australia
Melbourne
Match drawn
England 294 and 308
Australia 320 and 127-3
Sydney
Australia won by 5 wickets
England 133 (G. Palmer 7-68) and 232 Australia 197 and 169-5
Sydney
Australia won by 6 wickets
England 188 and 134
Australia 260 and 66-4
Melbourne
Match drawn
England 309 and 234-2
Australia 300
1882-83 v England
Series drawn
Melbourne
Australia won by 9 wickets
Australia 291 and 58-1
England 177 (G. Palmer 7-65) and 169
Melbourne
England won by an innings and 27 runs
England 294 Australia 114 (W. Bates 7-28) and 153
Sydney
England won by 69 runs
England 247 and 123 (F. Spofforth 7-44) Australia 218 and 83 (R. Barlow 7-40)
Sydney
Australia won by 4 wickets
England 263 and 197
Australia 262 and 199-6
1884-85 v England
Series won by England
Adelaide
England won by 8 wickets
Australia 243 and 191
England 369 and 67-2
Melbourne
England won by 10 wickets
England 401 and 7-0
Australia 279 and 126
Sydney
Australia won by 6 runs
Australia 181 and 165
England 133 and 207
Sydney
Australia won by 8 wickets
England 269 (G. Giffen 7-117) and 77 Australia 309 and 38-2
Melbourne
England won by an innings and 98 runs
Australia 163 and 125 England 386
1886-87 v England
Series won by England
Sydney
England won by 13 runs
England 45 and 184
Australia 119 and 97
Sydney
England won by 71 runs
England 151 and 154
Australia 84 (G. Lohmann 8-35) and 150
1887-88 v England
England won the only Test
Sydney
England won by 126 runs
England 113 and 137 (C. Turner 7-43) Australia 42 and 82
1891-92 v England
Series won by Australia
Melbourne
Australia won by 54 runs
Australia 240 and 236
England 264 and 158
Sydney
Australia won by 72 runs
Australia 144 (G. Lohmann 8-58) and 391 England 307 and 156
Adelaide
England won by an innings and 230 runs
England 499 Australia 100 and 169
1894-95 v England
Series won by England
Sydney
England won by 10 runs
Australia 586 (S. Gregory 201, G. Giffen 161) and 166
England 325 and 437
Melbourne
England won by 94 runs
England 75 and 475 (A. Stoddart 173)
Australia 123 and 333
Adelaide
Australia won by 382 runs
Australia 238 and 411
England 124 and 143 (A. Trott 8-43)
Sydney
Australia won by an innings and 147 runs
Australia 284 England 65 and 72
Melbourne
England won by 6 wickets
Australia 414 and 267
England 385 and 298-4
1897-98 v England
Series won by Australia
Sydney
England won by 9 wickets
England 551 (K. Rantjisinhji 175) and 96-1 Australia 237 and 408
Melbourne
Australia won by an innings and 55 runs
Australia 520 England 315 and 150
Adelaide
Australia won by an innings and 13 runs
Australia 573 (J. Darling 178)
England 278 and 282
Melbourne
Australia won by 8 wickets
Australia 323 (C. Hill 188) and 115-2 England 174 and 263
Sydney
Australia won by 6 wickets
England 335 and 178
Australia 239 (T. Richardson 8-94) and 276-4 (J. Darling 160)
1901-02 v England
Series won by Australia
Sydney
England won by an innings and 124 runs
England 464 Australia 168 and 172
Melbourne
Australia won by 229 runs
Australia 112 and 353 (S. F. Barnes 7-121)
England 61 (M. A. Noble 7-17) and 175
Adelaide
Australia won by 4 wickets
England 388 and 247
Australia 321 and 315-6
Sydney
Australia won by 7 wickets
England 317 and 99
Australia 299 and 121-3
Melbourne
Australia won by 32 runs
Australia 144 and 255
England 189 and 178
1903-04 v England
Series won by England
Sydney
England won by 5 wickets
Australia 285 and 485 (V. Trumper 185*) England 577 (R. E. Foster 287) 194-5

Melbourne
England won by 185 runs
England 315 and 103
Australia 122 (W. Rhodes 7-56) and 111 (W. Rhodes 8-68)
Adelaide
Australia won by 216 runs
Australia 388 and 351
England 245 and 278
Sydney
England won by 157 runs
England 249 (M. Noble 7-100) and 210 Australia 131 and 171
Melbourne
Australia won by 218 runs
Australia 247 (L. Braund 8-81) and 133 England 61 and 101 (H. Trumble 7-28)
1907-08 v England
Series won by Australia
Sydney
Australia won by 2 wickets
England 273 and 300
Australia 300 and 275-8
Melbourne
England won by 1 wicket
Australia 266 and 397
England 382 and 282-9
Adelaide
Australia won by 245 runs
Australia 285 and 506 (C. Hill 160) England 363 and 183
Melbourne
Australia won by 308 runs
Australia 214 and 385
England 105 and 186
Sydney
Australia won by 49 runs
Australia 137 (S. F. Barnes 7-60) and 422 (V. Trumper 166) England 281 and 229
1910-11 v South Africa
Series won by Australia
Sydney
Australia won by an innings and 114 runs
Australia 528 (C. Hill 191)
South Africa 174 and 240
Melbourne
Australia won by 89 runs
Australia 348 and 327 (V. Trumper 159) South Africa 506 (G. Faulkner 204) and 80
Adelaide
South Africa won by 38 runs
South Africa 482 and 360
Australia 465 (V. Trumper 214*) and 339
Melbourne
Australia won by 530 runs
Australia 328 and 578 South Africa 205 and 171
Sydney
Australia won by 7 wickets
Australia 364 and 198-3 South Africa 160 and 401 (J. Zulch 150)
1911-12 v England
Series won by England
Sydney
Australia won by 146 runs
Australia 447 and 308
England 318 and 291 (H. Hordern 7-90)
Melbourne
England won by 8 wickets
Australia 184 and 299
England 265 and 219-2
Adelaide
England won by 7 wickets
Australia 133 and 476
England 501 (J. B. Hobbs 187) and 112-3
Melbourne
England won by an innings and 225 runs
Australia 191 and 173
England 589 (W. Rhodes 179, J. B. Hobbs 178)
Sydney
England won by 70 runs
England 324 and 214
Australia 176 and 292
1920-21 v England
Series won by Australia
Sydney
Australia won by 377 runs
Australia 267 and 581 (W. Armstrong 158) England 190 and 281
Melbourne
Australia won by an innings and 91 runs
Australia 499 England 251 (J. M. Gregory 7-69) and 157
Adelaide
Australia won by 119 runs
Australia 354 (H. L. Collins 162) and 582 England 447 and 370
Melbourne
Australia won by 8 wickets
England 284 and 315 (A. Mailey 9-121) Australia 389 and 211-2
Sydney
Australia won by 9 wickets
England 204 and 280
Australia 392 (C. Macartney 170) and 93-1
1924-25 v England
Series won by Australia
Sydney
Australia won by 193 runs
Australia 450 and 452
England 298 and 411
Melbourne
Australia won by 81 runs
Australia 600 and 250
England 479 (H. Sutcliffe 176, J. Hobbs 154) and 290
Adelaide
Australia won by 11 runs
Australia 489 (J. Ryder 201*) and 250 England 365 and 363
Melbourne
England won by an innings and 29 runs
England 548 Australia 269 and 250
Sydney
Australia won by 307 runs
Australia 295 and 325
England 167 and 146
1928-29 v England
Series won by England
Brisbane
England won by 675 runs
England 521 (E. Hendren 169) and 342-8d Australia 122 and 66
Sydney
England won by 8 wickets
Australia 253 and 397
England 636 (W. Hammond 251) and 16-2
Melbourne
England won by 3 wickets
Australia 397 and 351
England 417 (W. Hammond 200) and 332-7
Adelaide
England won by 12 runs
England 334 and 383 (W. Hammond 177) Australia 369 (A. Jackson 164) and 336 (J. C. White 8-126)
Melbourne
Australia won by 5 wickets
England 519 and 257
Australia 491 and 287-5
1930-31 v West Indies
Series won by Australia
Adelaide
Australia won by 10 wickets
West Indies 296 (C. Grimmett 7-87) and 249 Australia 376 and 172-0
Sydney
Australia won by an innings and 172 runs
Australia 369 (W. Ponsford 183)
West Indies 107 and 90
Brisbane
Australia won by an innings and 217 runs
Australia 558 (D. Bradman 223)
West Indies 193 and 148
Melbourne
Australia won by an innings and 122 runs
West Indies 99 (H. Ironmonger 7-23) and 107 Australia 328-8d (D. Bradman 152)
Sydney
West Indies won by 30 runs

West Indies 350-6d and 124-5d
Australia 224 and 220

1931-32 v South Africa

Series won by Australia

Brisbane
Australia won by an innings and 163 runs
Australia 450 (D. Bradman 226)
South Africa 170 and 117

Sydney
Australia won by an innings and 155 runs
South Africa 153 and 161
Australia 469

Melbourne
Australia won by 169 runs
Australia 198 and 554 (D. Bradman 167, W. Woodfull 161) South Africa 358 and 225

Adelaide
Australia won by 10 wickets
South Africa 308 (C. Grimmett 7-116) and 274 (C. Grimmett 7-83)
Australia 513 (D. Bradman 299*) and 73-0

Melbourne
Australia won by an innings and 72 runs
South Africa 36 and 45 Australia 153

1932-33 v England

Series won by England

Sydney
England won by 10 wickets
Australia 360 (S. McCabe 187*) and 164 England 524 (H. Sutcliffe 194 and 1-0)

Melbourne
Australia won by 111 runs
Australia 228 and 191
England 169 and 139

Adelaide
England won by 338 runs
England 341 and 412
Australia 222 and 193

Brisbane
England won by 6 wickets
Australia 340 and 175
England 356 and 162-4

Sydney
England won by 8 wickets
Australia 435 and 182
England 454 and 168-2

1936-37 v England

Series won by Australia

Brisbane
England won by 322 runs
England 358 and 256
Australia 234 and 58

Sydney
England won by an innings and 22 runs
England 426-6d (W. Hammond 231*) Australia 80 and 324

Melbourne
Australia won by 365 runs
Australia 200-9d and 564 (D. Bradman 270) England 76-9d and 323

Adelaide
Australia won by 148 runs
Australia 288 and 433 (D. Bradman 212) England 330 and 243

Melbourne
Australia won by an innings and 200 runs
Australia 604 (D. Bradman 169)
England 239 and 165

1946-47 v England

Series won by Australia

Brisbane
Australia won by an innings and 332 runs
Australia 645 (D. Bradman 187)
England 141 (K. Miller 7-60) and 172

Sydney
Australia won by an innings and 33 runs
England 255 and 371
Australia 659-8d (S. G. Barnes 234, D. Bradman 234)

Melbourne
Match drawn
Australia 365 and 536 (A. Morris 155) England 351 and 310-7

Adelaide
Match drawn
England 460 and 340-8d
Australia 487 and 215-1

Sydney
Australia won by 5 wickets
England 280 (R. Lindwall 7-63) and 186 Australia 253 (D. Wright 7-105) and 214-5

1947-48 v India

Series won by Australia

Brisbane
Australia won by an innings and 226 runs
Australia 382-8d (D. Bradman 185)
India 58 and 98

Sydney
Match drawn
India 188 and 61-7 Australia 107

Melbourne
Australia won by 233 runs
Australia 394 and 255-4d
India 291-9d and 125

Adelaide
Australia won by an innings and 16 runs
Australia 674 (D. Bradman 201, A. Hassett 198) India 381 and 277 (R. Lindwall 7-38)

Melbourne
Australia won by an innings and 177 runs
Australia 575-8d (R. N. Harvey 153) India 331 and 67

1950-51 v England

Series won by Australia

Brisbane
Australia won by 70 runs
Australia 228 and 32-7d
England 68-7d and 122

Melbourne
Australia won by 28 runs
Australia 194 and 181
England 197 and 150

Sydney
Australia won by an innings and 13 runs
England 290 and 123
Australia 426

Adelaide
Australia won by 274 runs
Australia 371 (A. Morris 206) and 403-8d England 272 (L. Hutton 156*) and 228

Melbourne
England won by 8 wickets
Australia 217 and 197
England 320 (R. T. Simpson 156*) and 95-2

1951-52 v West Indies

Series won by Australia

Brisbane
Australia won by 3 wickets
West Indies 216 and 245
Australia 226 and 236-7

Sydney
Australia won by 7 wickets
West Indies 362 and 290
Australia 517 and 137-3

Adelaide
West Indies won by 6 wickets
Australia 82 and 255
West Indies 105 and 233-4

Melbourne
Australia won by 1 wicket
West Indies 272 and 203
Australia 216 and 260-9

Sydney
Australia won by 202 runs
Australia 116 (G. Gomez 7-55) and 377 West Indies 78 and 213

1952-53 v South Africa

Series drawn

Brisbane
Australia won by 96 runs
Australia 280 and 277 South Africa 221 and 240

Melbourne
South Africa won by 82 runs
South Africa 227 and 388 (W. Endean 162*) Australia 243 and 290 (H. Tayfield 7-81)

Sydney
Australia won by an innings and 38 runs

South Africa 173 and 232
Australia 443 (R. N. Harvey 190)
Adelaide
Match drawn
Australia 530 (A. Hassett 163, C. McDonald 154) and 233-3d
South Africa 387 and 177-6
Melbourne
South Africa won by 6 wickets
Australia 520 (R. N. Harvey 205) and 209 South Africa 435 and 297-4
1954-55 v England
Series won by England
Brisbane
Australia won by an innings and 154 runs
Australia 601-8d (R. N. Harvey 162, A. Morris 153) England 190 and 257
Sydney
England won by 38 runs
England 154 and 296
Australia 228 and 184
Melbourne
England won by 128 runs
England 191 and 279
Australia 231 and 111 (F. Tyson 7-27)
Adelaide
England won by 5 wickets
Australia 323 and 111
England 341 and 97-5
Sydney
Match drawn
England 371-7d
Australia 221 and 118-6
1958-59 v England
Series won by Australia
Brisbane
Australia won by 8 wickets
England 134 and 198
Australia 186 and 147-2
Melbourne
Australia won by 8 wickets
England 259 and 87
Australia 308 (R. N. Harvey 167, J. B. Statham 7-57) and 42-2
Sydney
Match drawn
England 219 and 287-7d
Australia 357 and 54-2
Adelaide
Australia won by 10 wickets
Australia 476 (C. McDonald 170) and 36-0 England 240 and 270
Melbourne
Australia won by 9 wickets
England 205 and 214
Australia 351 and 69-1
1960-61 v West Indies
Series won by Australia
Brisbane
A tie
West Indies 453 and 284
Australia 505 (N. O'Neill 181) and 232
Melbourne
Australia won by 7 wickets
Australia 348 and 70-3
West Indies 181 and 233
Sydney
West Indies won by 222 runs
West Indies 339 (G. Sobers 168) and 326 Australia 202 and 241
Adelaide
Match drawn
West Indies 393 and 432-6d
Australia 366 and 273-9
Melbourne
Australia won by 2 wickets
West Indies 292 and 321
Australia 356 and 258-8
1962-63 v England
Series drawn
Brisbane
Match drawn
Australia 404 and 362-4d
England 389 and 278-6
Melbourne
England won by 7 wickets
Australia 316 and 248
England 331 and 237-3
Sydney
Australia won by 8 wickets
England 279 and 104
Australia 319 (F. Titmus 7-79) and 67-2
Adelaide
Match drawn
Australia 393 (R. Harvey 154) and 293 England 331 and 223-4
Sydney
Match drawn
England 321 and 268-8d
Australia 349 and 152-4
1963-64 v South Africa
Series drawn
Brisbane
Match drawn
Australia 435 (B. Booth 169) and 144-1d South Africa 346 and 13-1
Melbourne
Australia won by 8 wickets
South Africa 274 and 306
Australia 447 (W. Lawry 157) and 136-2
Sydney
Match drawn
Australia 260 and 450-9d
South Africa 302 and 326-5
Adelaide
South Africa won by 10 wickets
Australia 345 and 331 South Africa 595 (E. Barlow 201, R. G. Pollock 175) and 82-0
Sydney
Match drawn
Australia 311 (J. Partridge 7-91) and 270 South Africa 411 and 76-0
1964-65 v Pakistan
Only Test drawn
Melbourne
Match drawn
Pakistan 287 and 326
Australia 448 and 88-2
1965-66 v England
Series drawn
Brisbane
Match drawn
Australia 443-6d (W. Lawry 166, K. Walters 155) England 280 and 186-3
Melbourne
Match drawn
Australia 358 and 426
England 558 and 5-0
Sydney
England won by an innings and 93 runs
England 488 (R. Barber 185, N. Hawke 7-105) Australia 221 and 174
Adelaide
Australia won by an innings and 9 runs
England 241 and 266
Australia 516 (R. Simpson 225)
Melbourne
Match drawn
England 485-9d and 69-3
Australia 543-8d (R. Cowper 307)
1967-68 v India
Series won by Australia
Adelaide
Australia won by 146 runs
Australia 335 and 369
India 307 and 251
Melbourne
Australia won by an innings and 4 runs
India 173 (G. McKenzie 7-66) and 352 Australia 529 (I. Chappell 151)
Brisbane
Australia won by 39 runs
Australia 379 and 294
India 279 and 355
Sydney
Australia won by 144 runs
Australia 317 and 292 (R. Cowper 165) India 268 and 197
1968-69 v West Indies
Series won by Australia
Brisbane
West Indies won by 125 runs
West Indies 296 and 353
Australia 284 and 240
Melbourne
Australia won by an innings and 30 runs
West Indies 200 (G. McKenzie 8-71) and 280 Australia 510 (W.

Lawry 205, I. Chappell 165)
Sydney
Australia won by 10 wickets
West Indies 264 and 324
Australia 547 and 42-0
Adelaide
Match drawn
West Indies 276 and 616
Australia 533 and 339-9
Sydney
Australia won by 382 runs
Australia 619 (K. Walters 242, W. Lawry 151) and 394-8d West Indies 279 and 352
1970-71 v England
Series won by England
Brisbane
Match drawn
Australia 433 (K. Stackpole 207) and 214 England 464 and 39-1
Perth
Match drawn
England 397 and 287-6d
Australia 440 (I. Redpath 171) and 100-3
Melbourne
Match abandoned
Sydney
England won by 299 runs
England 332 and 319-5d
Australia 236 and 116 (J. Snow 7-40)
Melbourne
Match drawn
Australia 493-9d and 169-4d
England 392 and 161-0
Adelaide
Match drawn
England 470 and 233-4d
Australia 235 and 328-3
Sydney
England won by 62 runs
England 184 and 302
Australia 264 and 160
1972-73 v Pakistan
Series won by Australia
Adelaide
Australia won by an innings and 114 runs
Pakistan 257 and 214
Australia 585 (I. Chappell 196)
Melbourne
Australia won by 92 runs
Australia 441-5d and 425
Pakistan 574-8d (Majid Khan 158) and 200
Sydney
Australia won by 52 runs
Australia 334 and 184
Pakistan 360 and 106
1973-74 v New Zealand
Series won by Australia
Melbourne
Australia won by an innings and 25 runs
Australia 462-8d
New Zealand 237 and 200
Sydney
Match drawn
New Zealand 312 and 305-9d
Australia 162 and 30-2
Adelaide
Australia won by an innings and 57 runs
Australia 477
New Zealand 218 and 202
1974-75 v England
Series won by Australia
Brisbane
Australia won by 166 runs
Australia 309 and 285-5d
England 265 and 166
Perth
Australia won by 9 wickets
England 208 and 293
Australia 481 and 23-1
Melbourne
Match drawn
England 242 and 244
Australia 241 and 238-8
Sydney
Australia won by 171 runs
Australia 405 and 289-4d
England 295 and 228
Adelaide
Australia won by 163 runs
Australia 304 (D. Underwood 7-113)
England 172 and 241
Melbourne
England won by an innings and 4 runs
Australia 152 and 373
England 529 (M. Denness 188, M. Walker 8-143)
1975-76 v West Indies
Series won by Australia
Brisbane
Australia won by 8 wickets
West Indies 214 and 370
Australia 366 and 219-2
Perth
West Indies won by an innings and 87 runs
Australia 329 (I. Chappell 156) and 169 (A. Roberts 7-54)
West Indies 585 (R. Fredericks 169)
Melbourne
Australia won by 8 wickets
West Indies 224 and 312
Australia 485 and 55-2
Sydney
Australia won by 7 wickets
West Indies 355 and 128
Australia 405 (G. Chappell 182) and 82-3
Adelaide
Australia won by 190 runs
Australia 418 and 345-7d
West Indies 274 and 299
Melbourne
Australia won by 165 runs
Australia 351 and 300-3d
West Indies 160 and 326
1976-77 v Pakistan
Series drawn
Adelaide
Match drawn
Pakistan 272 and 466 (Asif Iqbal 152*) Australia 454 and 261-6
Melbourne
Australia won by 348 runs
Australia 517-8d (G. Cosier 168) and 315-8d
Pakistan 333 and 151
Sydney
Pakistan won by 8 wickets
Australia 211 and 180
Pakistan 360 and 32-2
1976-77 v England
Centenary Test
Melbourne
Australia won by 45 runs
Australia 138 and 419-9d
England 95 and 417 (D. Randall 174)
1977-78 v India
Series won by Australia
Brisbane
Australia won by 16 runs
Australia 166 and 327
India 153 and 324
Perth
Australia won by 2 wickets
India 402 and 330-9d
Australia 394 (R. Simpson 176) and 342-8
Melbourne
India won by 222 runs
India 256 and 343
Australia 213 and 164
Sydney
India won by an innings and 2 runs
Australia 131 and 263
India 396-8d
Adelaide
Australia won by 47 runs
Australia 505 and 256
India 269 and 445
1978-79 v England
See end of statistics section

In South Africa

1888-89 v England
Series won by England
Port Elizabeth
England won by 8 wickets
South Africa 84 and 129

England 148 and 67-2
Cape Town
England won by an innings and 202 runs
England 292 (W. Ashley 7-95) South Africa 47 (J. Briggs 7-17) and 43 (J. Briggs 8-11)
1891-92 v England
England won the only Test
Cape Town
England won by an innings and 189 runs
South Africa 97 and 83 (J. Ferris 7-37) England 369
1895-96 v England
Series won by England
Port Elizabeth
England won by 288 runs
England 185 and 226 South Africa 93 (G. Lohmann 7-38) and 30 (G. Lohmann 8-7)
Johannesburg
England won by an innings and 197 runs
England 482 South Africa 151 (G. Lohmann 9-28) and 134
Cape Town
England won by an innings and 33 runs
South Africa 115 (G. Lohmann 7-42) and 117 England 265
1898-99 v England
Series won by England
Johannesburg
England won by 32 runs
England 145 and 237
South Africa 251 and 99
Cape Town
England won by 210 runs
England 92 and 330
South Africa 177 and 35
1902-03 v Australia
Series won by Australia
Johannesburg
Match drawn
South Africa 454 and 101-4
Australia 296 and 372-7d
Johannesburg
Australia won by 159 runs
Australia 175 and 309 (W. Armstrong 159*)
South Africa 240 and 85 (J. Saunders 7-34)
Cape Town
Australia won by 10 wickets
Australia 252 and 59-0
South Africa 85 and 225
1905-06 v England
Series won by South Africa
Johannesburg
South Africa won by 1 wicket
England 184 and 190 South Africa 91 and 287-9
Johannesburg
South Africa won by 9 wickets
England 148 and 160 South Africa 277 and 33-1
Johannesburg
South Africa won by 243 runs
South Africa 385 and 349-5d
England 295 and 196 (S. Snooke 8-70)
Cape Town
England won by 4 wickets
South Africa 218 and 138
England 198 and 160-6
Cape Town
South Africa won by an innings and 16 runs
England 187 and 130
South Africa 333
1909-10 v England
Series won by South Africa
Johannesburg
South Africa won by 19 runs
South Africa 208 and 345
England 310 and 224 (A. Vogler 7-94)
Durban
South Africa won by 95 runs
South Africa 199 and 347
England 199 and 252
Johannesburg
England won by 3 wickets
South Africa 305 and 237
England 322 and 221-7
Cape Town
South Africa won by 4 wickets
England 203 and 178
South Africa 207 and 175-6
Cape Town
England won by 9 wickets
England 417 (J. Hobbs 187) and 16-1 South Africa 103 (C. Blythe 7-46) and 327
1913-14 v England
Series won by England
Durban
England won by an innings and 157 runs
South Africa 182 and 111
England 450
Johannesburg
England won by an innings and 12 runs
South Africa 160 (S. F. Barnes 8-56) and 231 (S. F. Barnes 9-103)
England 403 (W. Rhodes 152)
Johannesburg
England won by 91 runs
England 238 and 308
South Africa 151 and 304
Durban
Match drawn
South Africa 170 (S. F. Barnes 7-56) and 305-9d (S. F. Barnes 7-88) England 163 and 154-5
Port Elizabeth
England won by 10 wickets
South Africa 193 and 228
England 411 and 11-0
1921-22 v Australia
Series won by Australia
Durban
Match drawn
Australia 299 and 324-7d
South Africa 232 and 184-7
Johannesburg
Match drawn
Australia 450 (H. L. Collins 203) and 7-0 South Africa 243 and 472-8d (C. Frank 152)
Cape Town
Australia won by 10 wickets
South Africa 180 and 216
Australia 396 and 1-0
1922-23 v England
Series won by England
Johannesburg
South Africa won by 168 runs
South Africa 148 and 420 (H. W. Taylor 176) England 182 and 218
Cape Town
England won by 1 wicket
South Africa 113 and 242
England 183 and 173-9 (A. Hall 7-63)
Durban
Match drawn
England 428 (C. Mead 181) and 11-1 South Africa 368
Johannesburg
Match drawn
England 244 and 376-6d
South Africa 295 and 247-4
Durban
England won by 109 runs
England 281 and 241
South Africa 179 and 234
1927-28 v England
Series drawn
Johannesburg
England won by 10 wickets
South Africa 196 (G. Geary 7-70) and 170 England 313 and 57-0
Cape Town
England won by 87 runs
England 133 and 428
South Africa 250 and 224
Durban
Match drawn
South Africa 246 and 464-8d
England 430 and 132-2
Johannesburg
South Africa won by 4 wickets
England 265 and 215
South Africa 328 and 156-6
Durban
South Africa won by 8 wickets
England 282 and 118

(G. Bissett 7-29) South Africa 332-7d and 69-2
1930-31 v England
Series won by South Africa
Johannesburg
South Africa won by 28 runs
South Africa 126 and 306
England 193 and 211
Cape Town
Match drawn
South Africa 513-8d
England 350 and 252
Durban
Match drawn
South Africa 177 and 145-8
England 223-1d
Johannesburg
Match drawn
England 442 and 169-9d
South Africa 295 and 280-7
Durban
Match drawn
South Africa 252 and 219-7d
England 230 and 72-4
1935-36 v Australia
Series won by Australia
Durban
Australia won by 9 wickets
South Africa 248 and 282
Australia 429 and 102-1
Johannesburg
Match drawn
South Africa 157 and 491
(A. D. Nourse 231)
Australia 250 and 274-2
(S. McCabe 189*)
Cape Town
Australia won by an innings and 78 runs
Australia 362-8d South Africa 102 and 182
Johannesburg
Australia won by an innings and 184 runs
South Africa 157 and 98 (C. Grimmett 7-40) Australia 439
Durban
Australia won by an innings and 6 runs
South Africa 222 (C. Grimmett 7-100)
and 227 Australia 455
1938-39 England
Series won by England
Johannesburg
Match drawn
England 422 and 291-4d
South Africa 390 and 108-1
Cape Town
Match drawn
England 559-9d
(W. Hammond 181)
South Africa 286 and 201-2
Durban
England won by an innings and 13 runs
England 469-4d (E. Paynter 243) South Africa 103 and 353
Johannesburg
Match drawn
England 215 and 203-4
South Africa 349-8d
Durban
Match drawn
South Africa 530 and 481
England 316 and 654-5 (W. J. Edrich 219)
1948-49 v England
Series won by England
Durban
England won by 2 wickets
South Africa 161 and 219
England 253 and 128-8
Johannesburg
Match drawn
England 608 (C. Washbrook 195, L. Hutton 158) South Africa 315 and 270-2 (E. Rowan 156*)
Cape Town
Match drawn
England 308 and 276-3d
South Africa 356 and 142-4
Johannesburg
Match drawn
England 379 and 253-7d
South Africa 257-9d and 194-4
Port Elizabeth
England won by 3 wickets
South Africa 379 and 187-3d
England 395 and 174-7
1949-50 v Australia
Series won by Australia
Johannesburg
Australia won by an innings and 85 runs
Australia 413 South Africa 137 and 191
Cape Town
Australia won by 8 wickets
Australia 526-7d (R. Harvey 178) and 87-2 South Africa 278 and 333
Durban
Australia won by 5 wickets
South Africa 311 and 99
Australia 75 (H. Tayfield 7-23) and 336-5 (R. Harvey 151*)
Johannesburg
Match drawn
Australia 465-8d and 259-2
South Africa 352
Port Elizabeth
Australia won by an innings and 259 runs
Australia 549-7d (A. Hassett 167, A. Morris 157) South Africa 158 and 132
1953-54 v New Zealand
Series won by South Africa
Durban
South Africa won by an innings and 58 runs
South Africa 437-9d New Zealand 230 and 149
Johannesburg
South Africa won by 132 runs
South Africa 271 and 148
New Zealand 187 and 100
Cape Town
Match drawn
New Zealand 505
South Africa 326 and 159-3
Johannesburg
South Africa won by 9 wickets
South Africa 243 and 25-1
New Zealand 79 and 188
Port Elizabeth
South Africa won by 5 wickets
New Zealand 226 and 222
South Africa 237 and 215-5
1956-57 v England
Series drawn
Johannesburg
England won by 131 runs
England 268 and 150
South Africa 215 and 72
Cape Town
England won by 312 runs
England 369 and 220-6d
South Africa 205 and 72 (J. Wardle 7-36)
Durban
Match drawn
England 218 and 254
(H. Tayfield 8-69) South Africa 283 and 142-6
Johannesburg
South Africa won by 17 runs
South Africa 340 and 142
England 251 and 214
(H. Tayfield 9-113)
Port Elizabeth
South Africa won by 58 runs
South Africa 164 and 134
England 110 and 130
1957-58 v Australia
Series won by Australia
Johannesburg
Match drawn
South Africa 470-9d and 201
Australia 368 and 162-3
Cape Town
Australia won by an innings and 141 runs
Australia 449 (J. Burke 189)
South Africa 209 and 99
Durban
Match drawn
Australia 163 and 292-7
South Africa 384

Johannesburg
Australia won by 10 wickets
Australia 401 and 1-0
South Africa 203 and 198
Port Elizabeth
Australia won by 8 wickets
South Africa 214 and 144
Australia 291 and 68-2
1961-62 v New Zealand
Series drawn
Durban
South Africa won by 30 runs
South Africa 292 and 149
New Zealand 245 and 166
Johannesburg
Match drawn
South Africa 322 and 178-6d
New Zealand 223
(G. Lawrence 8-53) and 165-4
Cape Town
New Zealand won by 72 runs
New Zealand 385 and 212-9d
South Africa 190 and 335
Johannesburg
South Africa won by an innings
and 51 runs
New Zealand 164 and 249
South Africa 464
Port Elizabeth
New Zealand won by 40 runs
New Zealand 275 and 228
South Africa 190 and 273
1964-65 v England
Series won by England
Durban
England won by an innings and
104 runs
England 485-5
South Africa 155 and 226
Johannesburg
Match drawn
England 531 (E. Dexter 172)
South Africa 317 and 336-6
Cape Town
Match drawn
South Africa 501-7d
(A. Pithey 154) and 346 England
442 and 15-0
Johannesburg
Match drawn
South Africa 390-6d and 307-3d
England 384 and 153-6
Port Elizabeth
Match drawn
South Africa 502 and 178-4d
England 435 and 29-1
1966-67 v Australia
Series won by South Africa
Johannesburg
South Africa won by 233 runs
South Africa 199 and 620
(J. Lindsay 182) Australia 325 and
261
Cape Town
Australia won by 6 wickets
Australia 542 (R. Simpson
153) and 180-4 South Africa 353
(R. G. Pollock 209) and 367
Durban
South Africa won by 8 wickets
South Africa 300 and 185-2
Australia 147 and 334
Johannesburg
Match drawn
Australia 143 and 148-8
South Africa 332-9d
Port Elizabeth
South Africa won by 7 wickets
Australia 173 and 278
South Africa 276 and 179-3
1969-70 v Australia
Series won by South Africa
Cape Town
South Africa won by 170 runs
South Africa 382 and 232
Australia 164 and 280
Durban
South Africa won by an innings
and 129 runs
South Africa 622-9d (R. Pollock
274) Australia 157 and 336
Johannesburg
South Africa won by 307 runs
South Africa 279 and 408
Australia 202 and 178
Port Elizabeth
South Africa won by 323 runs
South Africa 311 and 470-8d
Australia 212 and 246

In West Indies

1929-30 v England
Series drawn
Bridgetown
West Indies 369 and 384 (G.
Headley 176) England 467 (A.
Sandham 152) and 167-3
Port of Spain
England won by 167 runs
England 208 and 425-8d (E.
Hendren 205*) West Indies 254
and 212 (W. Voce 7-70)
Georgetown
West Indies won by 289 runs
West Indies 471 (C. Roach 209)
and 290 England 145 and 327
Kingston
Match drawn
England 849 (A. Sandham 325)
and 272-9d West Indies 286 and
408-5 (G. Headley 223)
1934-35 v England
Series won by West Indies
Bridgetown
England won by 4 wickets
West Indies 102 and 51-6d
England 81-7d and 75-6
Port of Spain
West Indies won by 217 runs
West Indies 302 and 280-6d
England 258 and 107
Georgetown
Match drawn
England 226 and 160-6d
West Indies 184 (E. Hollies 7-50)
and 104-5
Kingston
West Indies won by an innings and
161 runs
West Indies 535-7d (G. Headley
270*) England 271 and 103
1947-48 v England
Series won by West Indies
Bridgetown
Match drawn
West Indies 296 (J. Laker 7-103)
and 351-9d England 253 and 86-4
Port of Spain
Match drawn
England 362 and 275
West Indies 497 and 72-3
Georgetown
West Indies won by 7 wickets
West Indies 297-8d and 78-3
England 111 and 263
Kingston
West Indies won by 10 wickets
England 227 and 336
West Indies 490 and 76-0
1952-53 v India
Series won by West Indies
Port of Spain
Match drawn
India 417 and 294 West Indies 438
(E. Weekes 207, S. Gupte 7-162)
and 142-0
Bridgetown
West Indies won by 142 runs
West Indies 296 and 228
India 253 and 129
Port of Spain
Match drawn
India 279 and 362-7d
(M. Apte 163*) West Indies 315
(E. Weekes 161) and 192-2
Georgetown
Match drawn
India 262 and 190-5
West Indies 364
Kingston
Match drawn
India 312 and 444 (P. Roy 150)
West Indies 576 (F. Worrell 237)
and 92-4
1953-54 v England
Series drawn
Kingston
West Indies won by 140 runs
West Indies 417 and 290-6d

England 170 and 316
Bridgetown
West Indies won by 181 runs
West Indies 383 (C. Walcott 220) and 292-2d (J. Holt 166) England 181 and 313
Georgetown
England won by 9 wickets
England 435 (L. Hutton 169) and 75-1 West Indies 251 and 256
Port of Spain
Match drawn
West Indies 681-8d (E. Weekes 206, F. Worrell 167) and 212-4d England 537 and 98-3
Kingston
England won by 9 wickets
West Indies 139 (T. Bailey 7-34) and 346 England 414 (L. Hutton 205) and 72-1

1954-55 v Australia
Series won by Australia
Kingston
Australia won by 9 wickets
Australia 515-9d and 20-1
West Indies 259 and 275
Port of Spain
Match drawn
West Indies 382 and 273-4
Australia 600-9d
Georgetown
Australia won by 8 wickets
West Indies 182 and 207 (I. Johnson 7-44) Australia 257 and 133-2
Bridgetown
Match drawn
Australia 668 and 249
West Indies 510 (D. Atkinson 219) and 234-6
Kingston
Australia won by an innings and 82 runs
West Indies 357 (C. Walcott 155) and 319 Australia 758-8d (R. Harvey 204)

1957-58 v Pakistan
Series won by West Indies
Bridgetown
Match drawn
West Indies 579-9d (E. Weekes 197) and 28-0
Pakistan 106 and 657-8d (Hanif Mohammad 337)
Port of Spain
West Indies won by 120 runs
West Indies 325 and 312
Pakistan 282 and 235
Kingston
West Indies won by an innings and 174 runs
Pakistan 328 and 288 West Indies 790-3d (G. Sobers 365*, C. Hunte 260)
Georgetown
West Indies won by 8 wickets
Pakistan 408 (Saeed Ahmed 150) and 318 West Indies 410 and 317-2
Port of Spain
Pakistan won by an innings and 1 run
West Indies 268 and 227
Pakistan 496 (Wazir Mohammad 189)

1959-60 v England
Series won by England
Bridgetown
Match drawn
England 482 and 71-0
West Indies 563-8d (G. Sobers 226, F. Worrell 197*)
Port of Spain
England won by 256 runs
England 382 and 230-9d
West Indies 112 and 244
Kingston
Match drawn
England 277 (W. Hall 7-69) and 305 West Indies 353 and 175-6
Georgetown
Match drawn
England 295 and 334-8
West Indies 402-8d
Port of Spain
Match drawn
England 393 and 350-7d
West Indies 338-8d and 209-5

1961-62 v India
Series won by West Indies
Port of Spain
West Indies won by 10 wickets
India 203 and 98
West Indies 289 and 15-0
Kingston
West Indies won by an innings and 18 runs
India 395 and 218
West Indies 631-8d (G. Sobers 153)
Bridgetown
West Indies won by an innings and 30 runs
India 258 and 187 (L. Gibbs 8-38)
West Indies 475
Port of Spain
West Indies won by 7 wickets
West Indies 444-9d and 176-3
India 197 and 422 (P. Umrigar 172*)
Kingston
West Indies won by 123 runs
West Indies 253 and 283
India 178 and 235

1964-65 v Australia
Series won by West Indies
Kingston
West Indies won by 179 runs
West Indies 239 and 373
Australia 217 and 216
Port of Spain
Match drawn
West Indies 429 and 386
Australia 516
Georgetown
West Indies won by 212 runs
West Indies 355 and 180
Australia 179 and 144
Bridgetown
Match drawn
Australia 650-6d (W. Lawry 210, R. Simpson 201) and 175-4d West Indies 573 (S. Nurse 201) and 242-5
Port of Spain
Australia won by 10 wickets
West Indies 224 and 131
Australia 294 and 63-0

1967-68 v England
Series won by England
Port of Spain
Match drawn
England 568 West Indies 363 and 243-8
Kingston
Match drawn
England 376 and 68-8 West Indies 143 (J. Snow 7-49) and 391-9d
Bridgetown
Match drawn
West Indies 349 and 284-6
England 449
Port of Spain
England won by 7 wickets
West Indies 526-7d (R. Kanhai 153) and 92-2d
England 414 and 215-3
Georgetown
Match drawn
West Indies 414 (R. Kanhai 150, G. Sobers 152) and 264 England 371 and 206-9

1970-71 v India
Series won by India
Kingston
Match drawn
India 387 (D. Sardesai 212)
West Indies 217 and 385-5 (R. Kanhai 158*)
Port of Spain
India won by 7 wickets
West Indies 214 and 261
India 352 (J. Noreiga 9-95) and 125-3
Georgetown
Match drawn
West Indies 363 and 301-3d
India 376 and 123-0
Bridgetown
Match drawn
West Indies 501-5d (G. Sobers 178*) and 180-6d
India 347 (D. Sardesai 150) and 221-5

Port of Spain
Match drawn
India 360 and 427 (S. Gavaskar 220) West Indies 526 and 165-8
1971-72 v New Zealand
Series drawn
Kingston
Match drawn
West Indies 508-4d (L. Rowe 214, R. Fredericks 163) and 218-3d
New Zealand 386 (G. Turner 223*) and 236-6
Port of Spain
Match drawn
New Zealand 348 (B. Congdon 166*) and 288-3d
West Indies 341 and 121-5
Bridgetown
Match drawn
West Indies 133 (B. Taylor 7-74) and 564-8 (C. Davis 183)
New Zealand 422
Georgetown
Match drawn
West Indies 365-7d and 86-0
New Zealand 543-3d (G. Turner 259, T. Jarvis 182)
Port of Spain
Match drawn
West Indies 368 and 194
New Zealand 162 and 253-7
1972-73 v Australia
Series won by Australia
Kingston
Match drawn
Australia 428-7d and 260-2d
West Indies 428 and 67-3
Bridgetown
Match drawn
Australia 324 and 300-3d
West Indies 391 and 36-0
Port of Spain
Australia won by 46 runs
Australia 332 and 281
West Indies 280 and 289
Georgetøwn
Australia won by 10 wickets
West Indies 366 (C. Lloyd 178) and 109 Australia 341 and 135-0
Port of Spain
Match drawn 419-8d and 218-7d
West Indies 319 and 135-5
1973-74 v England
Series drawn
Port of Spain
West Indies won by 7 wickets
England 131 and 392 (D. Amiss 174) West Indies 392 (A. Kallicharran 158) and 132-3
Kingston
Match drawn
England 353 and 432-9 (D. Amiss 262*) West Indies 583-9d

Bridgetown
Match drawn
England 395 and 277-7
West Indies 596-8d (L. Rowe 302)
Georgetown
Match drawn
England 448
West Indies 198-4
Port of Spain
England won by 26 runs
England 267 and 263
West Indies 305 (A. Greig 8-86) and 199
1975-76 v India
Series won by West Indies
Bridgetown
West Indies won by an innings and 97 runs
India 177 and 214
West Indies 488-9d
Port of Spain
Match drawn
West Indies 241 and 215-8
India 402-5d (S. Gavaskar 156)
Port of Spain
India won by 6 wickets
West Indies 359 (I. Richards 177) and 271-6d
India 228 and 406-4
Kingston
West Indies won by 10 wickets
India 306-6d and 97
West Indies 391 and 13-0
1976-77 v Pakistan
Series won by West Indies
Bridgetown
Match drawn
Pakistan 435 and 291
West Indies 421 (C. Lloyd 157) and 251-9
Port of Spain
West Indies won by 6 wickets
Pakistan 180 (C. Croft 8-29) and 340
West Indies 316 and 206-4
Georgetown
Match drawn
Pakistan 194 and 540 (M. Khan 167) West Indies 448 and 154-1
Port of Spain
Pakistan won by 266 runs
Pakistan 341 and 301-9d
West Indies 154 and 222
Kingston
West Indies won by 140 runs
West Indies 280 and 359
Pakistan 198 and 301
1977-78 v Australia
Series won by West Indies
Port of Spain
West Indies won by an innings and 106 runs
Australia 90 and 209
West Indies 405

Bridgetown
West Indies won by 9 wickets
Australia 250 and 178
West Indies 288 and 141-1
Georgetown
Australia won by 3 wickets
West Indies 205 and 439
Australia 286 and 362
Port of Spain
West Indies won by 198 runs
West Indies 292 and 290
Australia 290 and 94
Kingston
Match drawn
Australia 343 and 305-3d
West Indies 280 and 258-9

In New Zealand

1929-30 v England
Series won by England
Christchurch
England won by 8 wickets
New Zealand 112 and 131
England 181 and 66-2
Wellington
Match drawn
New Zealand 440 (F. Woolley 7-76) and 164-4d England 320 and 107-4
Auckland
Match drawn
England 330-4d New Zealand 96-1
Auckland
Match drawn
England 540 (G. B. Legge 196) and 22-3 New Zealand 387
1931-32 v South Africa
Series won by South Africa
Christchurch
South Africa won by an innings and 12 runs
New Zealand 293 and 146
South Africa 451
Wellington
South Africa won by 8 wickets
New Zealand 364 and 193
South Africa 410 and 150-2
1932-33 v England
Series drawn
Christchurch
Match drawn
England 560-8d
(W. Hammond 227) New Zealand 223 and 35-0
Auckland
Match drawn
New Zealand 158 and 16-0
England 548-7d (W. Hammond 336*)
1945-46 v Australia
Australia won the only Test

Wellington
Australia won by an innings and 103 runs
New Zealand 42 and 54
Australia 199-8d
1946-47 v England
Only Test drawn
Christchurch
Match drawn
New Zealand 345-9d
England 265-7d
1950-51 v England
Series won by England
Christchurch
Match drawn
New Zealand 417-8d and 46-3
England 550
Wellington
England won by 6 wickets
New Zealand 125 and 189
England 227 and 91-4
1951-52 v West Indies
Series won by West Indies
Christchurch
West Indies won by 5 wickets
New Zealand 236 and 189
West Indies 287 and 142-5
Auckland
Match drawn
West Indies 546-6d (J. Stollmeyer 152) New Zealand 160 and 17-1
1952-53 v South Africa
Series won by South Africa
Wellington
South Africa won by an innings 180 runs
South Africa 524-8d (D. McGlew 255*) New Zealand 172 and 172
Auckland
Match drawn
South Africa 377 and 200-5d
New Zealand 245 and 31-2
1954-55 v England
Series won by England
Dunedin
England won by 8 wickets
New Zealand 125 and 132
England 209-8d and 49-2
Auckland
England won by an innings and 20 runs
New Zealand 200 and 26
England 246
1955-56 v West Indies
Series won by West Indies
Dunedin
West Indies won by an innings and 71 runs
New Zealand 74 and 208
West Indies 353
Christchurch
West Indies won by an innings and 64 runs
West Indies 386 New Zealand 158 and 164
Wellington
West Indies won by 9 wickets
West Indies 404 (E. Weekes 156) and 13-1 New Zealand 208 and 208
Auckland
New Zealand won by 190 runs
New Zealand 255 and 157-9d (D. Atkinson 7-53) West Indies 145 and 77
1958-59 v England
Series won by England
Christchurch
England won by an innings and 99 runs
England 374 New Zealand 142 and 133
Auckland
Match drawn
New Zealand 181
England 311-7d
1962-63 v England
Series won by England
Auckland
England won by an innings and 215 runs
England 562-7d New Zealand 258 and 89
Wellington
England won by an innings and 47 runs
New Zealand 194 and 187
England 428-8d
Christchurch
England won by 7 wickets
New Zealand 266 (F. Trueman 7-75) and 159
England 253 and 173-3
1963-64 v South Africa
Series drawn
Wellington
Match drawn
South Africa 302 and 218-2d
New Zealand 253 and 138-6
Dunedin
Match drawn
New Zealand 149 and 138
South Africa 223 and 42-3
Auckland
Match drawn
South Africa 371 and 200-5d
New Zealand 263 and 191-8
1964-65 v Pakistan
Series drawn
Wellington
Match drawn
New Zealand 266 and 179-7d
Pakistan 187 and 140-7
Auckland
Match drawn
Pakistan 226 and 207
New Zealand 214 and 166-7
Christchurch
Match drawn
Pakistan 206 and 309-8d
New Zealand 202 and 223-5
1965-66 v England
Series drawn
Christchurch
Match drawn
England 342 and 201-5d
New Zealand 347 and 48-8
Dunedin
Match drawn
New Zealand 192 and 147-9
England 254-8d
Auckland
Match drawn
New Zealand 296 and 129
England 222 and 159-4
1967-68 v India
Series won by India
Dunedin
India won by 5 wickets
New Zealand 350 and 208
India 359 and 200-5
Christchurch
New Zealand won by 6 wickets
New Zealand 502 (G. Dowling 239) and 88-4 India 288 and 301
Wellington
India won by 8 wickets
New Zealand 186 and 199
India 327 and 61-2
Auckland
India won by 272 runs
India 252 and 261-5d
New Zealand 140 and 101
1970-71 v England
Series won by England
Christchurch
England won by 8 wickets
New Zealand 65 and 254
England 231 and 89-2
Auckland
Match drawn
England 321 and 237
New Zealand 313-7d and 40-0
1972-73 v Pakistan
Series won by Pakistan
Wellington
Match drawn
Pakistan 357 (Sadiq Mahommad 166) and 290-6d
New Zealand 325 and 78-3
Dunedin
Pakistan won by an innings and 166 runs
Pakistan 507-6d (Mushtaq Mohammad 201, Asif Iqbal 175)
New Zealand 156 (Intikhab Alam 7-52) and 185
Auckland
Match drawn
Pakistan 402 and 271
New Zealand 402 and 92-3

1973-74 v Australia
Series drawn
Wellington
Match drawn
Australia 511-6d (G. Chappell 247) and 460-8 New Zealand 484
Christchurch
New Zealand won by 5 wickets
Australia 223 and 259
New Zealand 255 and 230-5
Auckland
Australia won by 297 runs
Australia 221 and 346
New Zealand 111 and 158
1974-75 v England
Series won by England
Auckland
England won by an innings and 83 runs
England 593-6d (K. Fletcher 216, M. Denness 181) New Zealand 326 and 184
Christchurch
Match drawn
New Zealand 342
England 272-2 (D. Amiss 164*)
1975-76 v India
Series drawn
Auckland
India won by 8 wickets
New Zealand 266 and 215
India 414 and 71-2
Christchurch
Match drawn
India 270 and 255-6
New Zealand 403
Wellington
New Zealand won by an innings and 33 runs
India 220 and 81 (R. Hadlee 7-23) New Zealand 334
1976-77 v Australia
Series won by Australia
Christchurch
Match drawn
Australia 552 (K. Walters 250) and 154-4d
New Zealand 357 and 293-8
Auckland
Australia won by 10 wickets
New Zealand 229 and 175
Australia 377 and 28-0
1977-78 v England
Series drawn
Wellington
New Zealand won by 72 runs
New Zealand 228 and 123
England 215 and 64
Christchurch
England won by 174 runs
England 418 and 96-4d
New Zealand 235 and 105
Auckland
Match drawn
New Zealand 315 and 382-8
England 429 (C. Radley 158)
1978-79 v Pakistan
See end of statistics section

In India

1933-34 v England
Series won by England
Bombay
England won by 9 wickets
India 219 and 258
England 438 and 40-1
Calcutta
Match drawn
England 403 and 7-2
India 247 and 237
Madras
England won by 202 runs
England 335 (Amar Singh 7-86) and 261-7d India 145 (H. Verity 7-49) and 249
1948-49 v West Indies
Series won by West Indies
New Delhi
Match drawn
West Indies 631 (C. Walcott 152)
India 454 and 220-6
Bombay
Match drawn
West Indies 629-6d (E. Weekes 194) India 273 and 333-3
Calcutta
Match drawn
West Indies 366 (E. Weekes 162) and 336-9d India 272 and 325-3
Madras
West Indies won by an innings and 193 runs
West Indies 582 (J. Stollmeyer 160, D. Phadkar 7-159) India 245 and 144
Bombay
Match drawn
West Indies 286 and 267
India 193 and 355-8
1951-52 v England
Series drawn
New Dehli
Match drawn
England 203 and 368-6
India 418-6d (V. Merchant 154, V. Hazare 164*)
Bombay
Match drawn
India 485-9d (V. Hazare 155) and 208 England 456 (T. Graveney 175) and 55-2
Calcutta
Match drawn
England 342 and 252-5d
India 344 and 103-0
Kanpur
England won by 8 wickets
India 121 and 157
England 203 and 76-2
Madras
India won by an innings and 8 runs
England 266 (V. Mankad 8-55) and 183 India 457-9d
1952-53 v Pakistan
Series won by India
New Dehli
India won by an innings and 70 runs
India 372 Pakistan 150 (V. Mankad 8-52) and 152
Lucknow
Pakistan won by an innings and 43 runs
India 106 and 182 (F. Mahmood 7-42) Pakistan 331
Bombay
India won by 10 wickets
Pakistan 186 and 242
India 387-4d and 45-0
Madras
Match drawn
Pakistan 344 India 175-6
Calcutta
Match drawn
Pakistan 257 and 236-7d
India 397 and 28-0
1955-56 v New Zealand
Series won by India
Hyderabad
Match drawn
India 498-4d (P. Umrigar 223)
New Zealand 326 (S. Gupte 7-128) and 212-2
Bombay
India won by an innings and 27 runs
India 421-8d (V. Mankad 223)
New Zealand 258 and 136
New Dehli
Match drawn
New Zealand 450-2d (B. Sutcliffe 230*) and 112-1
India 531-7d (V. Manjrekar 177)
Calcutta
Match drawn
India 132 and 438-7d
New Zealand 336 and 74-6
Madras
India won by an innings and 109 runs
India 537-3d (V. Mankad 231, P. Roy 173) New Zealand 209 and 219
1956-57 v Australia
Series won by Australia
Madras
Australia won by an innings and 5 runs
India 161 (R. Benaud 7-72) and 153 (R. Lindwall 7-43)

Australia 319
Bombay
Match drawn
India 251 and 250-5
Australia 523-7d (J. Burke 161)
Calcutta
Australia won by 94 runs
Australia 177 (G. Ahmed 7-49) and 189-9d India 136 and 136
1958-59 v West Indies
Series won by West Indies
Bombay
Match drawn
West Indies 227 and 323-4d
India 152 and 289-5
Kanpur
West Indies won by 203 runs
West Indies 222 (S. Gupte 9-102) and 443-7d (G. Sobers 198)
India 222 and 240
Calcutta
West Indies won by an innings and 336 runs
West Indies 614-5d (R. Kanhai 256) India 124 and 154
Madras
West Indies won by 295 runs
West Indies 500 and 168-5d
India 222 and 151
New Delhi
Match drawn
India 415 and 275
West Indies 644-8d
1959-60 v Australia
Series won by Australia
New Delhi
Australia won by an innings and 127 runs
India 135 and 206 Australia 468
Kanpur
India won by 119 runs
India 152 and 291 (A. Davidson 7-93) Australia 219 (J. Patel 9-69) and 105
Bombay
Match drawn
India 289 and 226-5d
Australia 387-8d (N. O'Neill 163) and 34-1
Madras
Australia won by an innings and 55 runs
Australia 342 India 149 and 138
Calcutta
Match drawn
India 194 and 339
Australia 331 and 121-2
1960-61 v Pakistan
Series drawn
Bombay
Match drawn
Pakistan 350 (Hanif Mohammad 160) and 166-4 India 449-9d
Kanpur
Match drawn
Pakistan 335 and 140-3
India 404
Calcutta
Match drawn
Pakistan 301 and 146-3d
India 180 and 127-4
Madras
Match drawn
Pakistan 448-8d and 59-0
India 539-9d (C. Borde 177*)
New Delhi
Match drawn
India 463 and 16-0
Pakistan 286 and 250
1961-62 v England
Series won by India
Bombay
Match drawn
England 500-8d (K. Barrington 151*) and 184-5d
India 390 and 180-5
Kanpur
Match drawn
India 467-8d England 244 and 497-5 (K. Barrington 172)
New Dehli
Match drawn
India 466 (V. Manjrekar 189*)
England 256-3
Calcutta
India won by 187 runs
India 380 and 252
England 212 and 233
Madras
India won by 128 runs
India 428 and 190 England 281 and 209
1963-64 v England
Series drawn
Madras
Match drawn
India 457-7d (B. Kunderam 192) and 152-9d England 317 and 241-5
Bombay
Match drawn
India 300 and 249-8d
England 233 and 206-3
Calcutta
Match drawn
India 241 and 300-7
England 267 and 145-2
New Dehli
Match drawn
India 344 and 463-4 (Nawab of Pataudi 203*) England 451 (M. C. Cowdrey 151)
Kanpur
Match drawn
England 559-8d India 266 and 347-3
1964-65 v Australia
Series drawn
Madras
Australia won by 139 runs
Australia 211 and 397
India 276 and 193
Bombay
India won by 2 wickets
Australia 320 and 274
India 341 and 256-8
Calcutta
Match drawn
Australia 174 and 143-1
India 235
1964-65 v New Zealand
Series won by India
Madras
Match drawn
India 397 and 199-2d
New Zealand 315 and 62-0
Calcutta
Match drawn
New Zealand 462-9d (B. Sutcliffe 151*) and 191-9d India 380 (Nawab of Pataudi 153) and 92-3
Bombay
Match drawn
New Zealand 297 and 80-8
India 88 and 463-5d (D. Sardesai 200*)
New Dehli
India won by 7 wickets
New Zealand 262 (S. Venkataraghavan 8-72) and 272
India 465-8d and 73-3
1966-67 v West Indies
Series won by West Indies
Bombay
West Indies won by 6 wickets
India 296 and 316 West Indies 421 (B. Chandrasekhar 7-157) and 192-4
Calcutta
West Indies won by an innings and 45 runs
West Indies 390 India 167 and 178
Madras
Match drawn
India 404 and 323 West Indies 406 and 270-7
1969-70 v New Zealand
Series drawn
Bombay
India won by 60 runs
India 156 and 260
New Zealand 229 and 127
Nagpur
New Zealand won by 167 runs
New Zealand 319 and 214
India 257 and 109
Hyderabad
Match abandoned as a draw following riots
New Zealand 181 and 175-8d
India 89 and 76-7

1969-70 v Australia
Series won by Australia
Bombay
Australia won by 8 wickets
India 271 and 137
Australia 345 and 67-2
Kanpur
Match drawn
India 320 and 312-7d
Australia 348 and 95-0
New Dehli
India won by 7 wickets
Australia 296 and 107
India 223 and 181-3
Calcutta
Australia won by 10 wickets
India 212 and 161
Australia 335 (S. Bedi 7-98) and 42-0
Madras
Australia won by 77 runs
Australia 258 and 153
India 163 and 171
1969-70 v New Zealand
Series drawn
Bombay
India won by 60 runs
India 156 and 260
New Zealand 229 and 127
Nagpur
New Zealand won by 167 runs
New Zealand 319 and 214
India 257 and 109
Hyderabad
Match drawn
New Zealand 181 and 175-8d
India 89 and 76-7
1969-70 v Australia
Series won by Australia
Bombay
Australia won by 8 wickets
India 271 and 137
Australia 345 and 67-2
Kanpur
Match drawn
India 320 and 312-7d
Australia 348 and 95-0
New Delhi
India won by 7 wickets
Australia 296 and 107
India 223 and 181-3
Calcutta
Australia won by 10 wickets
India 212 and 161
Australia 335 and 42-0
Madras
Australia won by 77 runs
Australia 258 and 153
India 163 and 171
1972-73 v England
Series won by India
New Delhi
England won by 6 wickets
India 173 and 233
England 200 (B. Chandrasekhar 8-79) and 208-4
Calcutta
India won by 28 runs
India 210 and 155
England 174 and 163
Madras
India won by 4 wickets
England 242 and 159
India 316 and 86-6
Kanpur
Match drawn
India 357 and 186-6
England 397
Bombay
Match drawn
India 448 and 244-5d
England 480 and 67-2
1974-75 v West Indies
Series won by West Indies
Bangalore
West Indies won by 267 runs
West Indies 289 and 356-6d (C. Lloyd 163) India 260 and 118
New Dehli
West Indies won by an innings and 17 runs
India 220 and 256
West Indies 493 (I. Richards 192*)
Calcutta
India won by 85 runs
India 233 and 316
West Indies 240 and 224
Madras
India won by 100 runs
India 190 (A. Roberts 7-64) and 256 West Indies 192 and 154
Bombay
West Indies won by 201 runs
West Indies 604-6d (C. Lloyd 242*) and 205-3d
India 406 (L. Gibbs 7-98) and 202
1976-77 v New Zealand
Series won by India
Bombay
India won by 162 runs
India 399 and 202-4d
New Zealand 298 and 141
Kanpur
Match drawn
India 524-9d and 208-2d
New Zealand 350 and 193-7
Madras
India won by 216 runs
India 298 and 201-5d
New Zealand 140 and 143
1976-77 v England
Series won by England
New Delhi
England won by an innings and 25 runs
England 381 (D. Amiss 179)
India 122 (J. Lever 7-46) and 234
Calcutta
England won by 10 wickets
India 155 and 181
England 321 and 16-0
Madras
England won by 200 runs
England 262 and 185-9d
India 164 and 83
Bangalore
India won by 140 runs
India 253 and 259-9d
England 195 and 177
Bombay
Match drawn
India 338 and 192
England 317 and 152-7
1978-79 v West Indies

In Pakistan

1954-55 v India
Series drawn
Dacca
Match drawn
Pakistan 257 and 158
India 148 and 147-2
Bahawalpur
Match drawn
India 235 and 209-5
Pakistan 312-9d
Lahore
Match drawn
Pakistan 328 and 136-5d
India 251 and 74-2
Peshawar
Match drawn
Pakistan 188 and 182
India 245 and 23-1
Karachi
Match drawn
Pakistan 162 and 241-5d
India 145 and 69-2
1955-56 v New Zealand
Series won by Pakistan
Karachi
Pakistan won by an innings and 1 run
New Zealand 164 and 124
Pakistan 289
Lahore
Pakistan won by 4 wickets
New Zealand 348 and 328
Pakistan 561 (Imitiaz Ahmed 209, W. Hassan 189) and 117-6
Dacca
Match drawn
New Zealand 70 and 69-6
Pakistan 195-6d
1956-57 v Australia
Pakistan won the only Test
Karachi
Pakistan won by 9 wickets
Australia 80 and 187 (Fazal Mahmood 7-80) Pakistan 199 and

69-1

1958-59 v West Indies

Series won by Pakistan

Karachi

Pakistan won by 10 wickets
West Indies 146 and 245
Pakistan 304 and 88-0

Dacca

Pakistan won by 41 runs
Pakistan 145 and 144
West Indies 76 and 172

Lahore

West Indies won by an innings and 156 runs
West Indies 469 (R. Kanhai 217)
Pakistan 209 and 104

1959-60 v Australia

Series won by Australia

Dacca

Australia won by 8 wickets
Pakistan 200 and 134
Australia 225 and 112-2

Lahore

Australia won by 7 wickets
Pakistan 146 and 366 (Saeed Ahmed 166, L. Kline 7-75)
Australia 391-9d and 122-3

Karachi

Match drawn
Pakistan 287 and 194-8d
Australia 257 and 83-2

1961-62 v England

Series won by England

Lahore

England won by 5 wickets
Pakistan 387-9d and 200
England 380 and 209-5

Dacca

Match drawn
Pakistan 393-7d and 216
England 439 (G. Pullar 165) and 38-0

Karachi

Match drawn
Pakistan 253 and 404-8
England 507 (E. Dexter 205)

1964-65 v Australia

Only Test drawn

Karachi

Match drawn
Pakistan 414 (K. Ibadulla 166) and 279-8d Australia 352 (R. Simpson 153) and 227-2

1964-65 v New Zealand

Series won by Pakistan

Rawalpindi

Pakistan won by an innings and 64 runs
New Zealand 175 and 79
Pakistan 318

Lahore

Match drawn
Pakistan 385-7d (Hanif Mohammad 203*) and 194-8d
New Zealand 482-6d

Karachi

Pakistan won by 8 wickets
New Zealand 285 and 223
Pakistan 307-8d (Saeed Ahmed 172) and 202-2

1968-69 v England

Series drawn

Lahore

Match drawn
England 306 and 225-9d
Pakistan 209 and 203-5

Dacca

Match drawn
Pakistan 246 and 195-6d
England 274 and 33-0

Karachi

Match abandoned as a draw owing to riots
England 502-7

1969-70 v New Zealand

Series won by New Zealand

Karachi

Match drawn
Pakistan 220 and 283-8d
New Zealand 274 (Nazir 7-99) and 112-5

Lahore

New Zealand won by 5 wickets
Pakistan 114 and 208
New Zealand 241 (S. Pervez 7-74) and 82-5

Dacca

Match drawn
New Zealand 273 and 200
Pakistan 290-7d and 51-4

1972-73 v England

Series drawn

Lahore

Match drawn
England 355 and 306-7d
Pakistan 422 and 124-3

Hyderabad

Match drawn
England 487 (D. Amiss 158) and 218-6 Pakistan 569-9d (Mushtaq Mohammad 157)

Karachi

Match drawn
Pakistan 445-6d and 199
England 386 and 30-1

1974-75 v West Indies

Series drawn

Lahore

Match drawn
Pakistan 199 and 373-7d
West Indies 214 and 258-4

Karachi

Match drawn
Pakistan 406-8d and 256
West Indies 493 and 1-0

1976-77 v New Zealand

Series won by Pakistan

Lahore

Pakistan won by 6 wickets
Pakistan 417 (Javed Miandad 163, Asif Iqbal 166) and 105-4
New Zealand 157 and 360

Hyderabad

Pakistan won by 10 wickets
Pakistan 473-8d and 4-0
New Zealand 219 and 254

Karachi

Match drawn
Pakistan 565-9d (Javed Miandad 206) and 290-5d
New Zealand 468 (W. Lees 152) and 262-7

1977-78 v England

Series drawn

Lahore

Match drawn
Pakistan 407 and 106-3
England 288

Hyderabad

Match drawn
Pakistan 275 and 259-4d
England 191 and 186-1

Karachi

Match drawn
England 266 and 222-5
Pakistan 281 (P. Edmonds 7-66)

1978-79 v India

Series won by Pakistan

Faisalabad

Match drawn
Pakistan 503-8d (Zaheer Abbas 176, Javed Miandad 154*) and 264-4d
India 462-9d and 43-0

Lahore

Pakistan won by 8 wickets
India 199 and 465
Pakistan 539-6d (Zaheer Abbas 235*)

Karachi

Pakistan won by 8 wickets
India 344 and 300
Pakistan 481 and 165-2

DOMESTIC CRICKET

County Championship Winners

1864	Surrey
1865	Nottinghamshire
1866	Middlesex
1867	Yorkshire
1868	Nottinghamshire
1869	Shared by Nottinghamshire Yorkshire
1870	Yorkshire
1871	Nottinghamshire
1872	Nottinghamshire
1873	Shared by Gloucestershire Nottinghamshire

1874 Gloucestershire
1875 Nottinghamshire
1876 Gloucestershire
1877 Gloucestershire
1878 Undecided
1879 Shared by Lancashire Nottinghamshire
1880 Nottinghamshire
1881 Lancashire
1882 Shared by Lancashire Nottinghamshire
1883 Nottinghamshire
1884 Nottinghamshire
1885 Nottinghamshire
1886 Nottinghamshire
1887 Surrey
1888 Surrey
1889 Shared by Lancashire Nottinghamshire, Surrey
1890 Surrey
1891 Surrey
1892 Surrey
1893 Yorkshire
1894 Surrey
1895 Surrey
1896 Yorkshire
1897 Lancashire
1898 Yorkshire
1899 Surrey
1900 Yorkshire
1901 Yorkshire
1902 Yorkshire
1903 Middlesex
1904 Lancashire
1905 Yorkshire
1906 Kent
1907 Nottinghamshire
1908 Yorkshire
1909 Kent
1910 Kent
1911 Warwickshire
1912 Yorkshire
1913 Kent
1914 Surrey
1919 Yorkshire
1920 Middlesex
1921 Middlesex
1922 Yorkshire
1923 Yorkshire
1924 Yorkshire
1925 Yorkshire
1926 Lancashire
1927 Lancashire
1928 Lancashire
1929 Nottinghamshire
1930 Lancashire
1931 Yorkshire
1932 Yorkshire
1933 Yorkshire
1934 Lancashire
1935 Yorkshire
1936 Derbyshire
1937 Yorkshire
1938 Yorkshire
1939 Yorkshire
1946 Yorkshire
1947 Middlesex
1948 Glamorgan
1949 Shared by Middlesex Yorkshire
1950 Shared by Lancashire Surrey
1951 Warwickshire
1952 Surrey
1953 Surrey
1954 Surrey
1955 Surrey
1956 Surrey
1957 Surrey
1958 Surrey
1959 Yorkshire
1960 Yorkshire
1961 Hampshire
1962 Yorkshire
1963 Yorkshire
1964 Worcestershire
1965 Worcestershire
1966 Yorkshire
1967 Yorkshire
1968 Yorkshire
1969 Glamorgan
1970 Kent
1971 Surrey
1972 Warwickshire
1973 Hampshire
1974 Worcestershire
1975 Leicestershire
1976 Middlesex
1977 Shared by Middlesex Kent
1978 Kent

Gillette Cup
1963

Preliminary Round
Lancashire beat Leicestershire

First Round
Glamorgan beat Somerset
Middlesex beat Gloucester
Derbyshire beat Hampshire
Sussex beat Kent
Lancashire beat Essex
Northants beat Warwicks
Worcestershire beat Surrey
Yorkshire beat Nottinghamshire

Second Round
Worcestershire beat Glamorgan
Lancashire beat Derbyshire
Northants beat Middlesex
Sussex beat Yorkshire

Semi-final
Sussex beat Northamptonshire
Worcestershire beat Lancashire

FINAL
Sussex 168 (J. Parks 57, N. Gifford 4-33) beat Worcestershire 154 by 14 runs.

1964

First Round
Essex beat Cambridgeshire
Surrey beat Cheshire
Durham beat Hertfordshire
Glamorgan beat Worcestershire
Northants beat Derbyshire
Hampshire beat Wiltshire

Second Round
Glamorgan beat Essex
Lancashire beat Kent
Northants beat Leics
Middlesex beat Yorkshire
Somerset beat Nottinghamshire
Surrey beat Gloucestershire
Sussex beat Durham
Warwickshire beat Hampshire

Third Round
Lancashire beat Glamorgan
Warwicks beat Northants
Sussex beat Somerset
Surrey beat Middlesex

Semi-final
Warwickshire beat Lancashire
Sussex beat Surrey

FINAL
Warwickshire 127 (N. Thomson 4-23) Sussex 131-2 (L. Lenham 47), Sussex won by 8 wickets.

1965

First Round
Middlesex beat Bucks
Somerset beat Berkshire
Derbyshire beat Essex
Warwicks beat Cambs
Hampshire beat Norfolk
Nottinghamshire beat Wiltshire

Second Round
Northants beat Glos
Hampshire beat Kent
Yorkshire beat Leicestershire
Middlesex beat Derbyshire
Somerset beat Nottinghamshire
Surrey beat Glamorgan
Warwickshire beat Lancashire
Sussex beat Worcestershire

Third Round
Middlesex beat Sussex
Yorkshire beat Somerset

Surrey beat Northamptonshire
Warwickshire beat Hampshire

Semi-final
Surrey beat Middlesex
Yorkshire beat Warwickshire

FINAL
Yorkshire 317-4 (G. Boycott 146) beat Surrey 142 (R. Tindall 57, R. Illingworth 5-29) by 175 runs.

1966

First Round
Lancashire beat Cheshire
Hampshire beat Lincolnshire
Berkshire beat Hertfordshire
Glamorgan beat Northants
Somerset beat Sussex
Kent beat Suffolk

Second Round
Gloucestershire beat Berkshire
Essex beat Derbyshire
Warwickshire beat Glamorgan
Hampshire beat Kent
Surrey beat Leicestershire
Lancashire beat Middlesex
Somerset beat Yorkshire
Worcester beat Notts

Third Round
Hampshire beat Surrey
Somerset beat Lancashire
Warwicks beat Gloucestershire
Worcestershire beat Essex

Semi-final
Warwickshire beat Somerset
Worcestershire beat Hampshire

FINAL
Worcestershire 155-8, Warwickshire 159-5 (R. Barber 66)
Warwickshire won by 5 wickets.

1967

First Round
Nottinghamshire beat Durham
Northants beat Bedfordshire
Somerset beat Leicestershire
Hampshire beat Lincolnshire
Sussex beat Worcestershire
Cambridge beat Oxfordshire

Second Round
Kent beat Essex
Hampshire beat Glamorgan
Northants beat Notts
Surrey beat Derbyshire
Sussex beat Middlesex
Lancashire beat Gloucestershire
Somerset beat Warwickshire
Yorkshire beat Cambridgeshire

Third Round
Lancashire beat Yorkshire
Somerset beat Northants
Kent beat Surrey
Sussex beat Hampshire

Semi-final
Kent beat Sussex
Somerset beat Lancashire

FINAL
Kent 193 (B. Luckhurst 54) beat Somerset 161 by 32 runs.

1968

First Round
Notts beat Lancashire
Worcestershire beat Durham
Middlesex beat Essex
Bedfordshire beat Dorset
Cheshire beat Norfolk
Northants beat Glamorgan

Second Round
Sussex beat Derbyshire
Hampshire beat Bedfordshire
Northants beat Ches
Gloucestershire beat Kent
Leicestershire beat Somerset
Middlesex beat Surrey
Warwickshire beat Yorkshire
Notts beat Worcestershire

Third Round
Warwickshire beat Hampshire
Middlesex beat Leicestershire
Gloucs beat Nottinghamshire
Sussex beat Northamptonshire

Semi-final
Warwickshire beat Middlesex
Sussex beat Gloucestershire

FINAL
Sussex 214-7 (J. Parks 57) Warwickshire 215-6 (W. Stewart 49) Warwickshire won by 4 wickets.

1969

First Round
Essex beat Wiltshire
Yorkshire beat Norfolk
Middlesex beat Bucks
Glamorgan beat Northants
Hertfordshire beat Devon
Derbyshire beat Somerset

Second Round
Derbyshire beat Worcestershire
Essex beat Warwickshire
Sussex beat Gloucestershire
Leicestershire beat Kent
Yorkshire beat Lancashire
Surrey beat Hampshire
Glamorgan beat Hertfordshire
Notts beat Middlesex

Third Round
Derbyshire beat Glamorgan
Sussex beat Leicestershire
Yorkshire beat Surrey
Nottinghamshire beat Essex

Semi-final
Derbyshire beat Sussex
Yorkshire beat Nottinghamshire

FINAL
Yorkshire 219-8 (B. Leadbeater 76) beat Derbyshire 150 by 69 runs.

1970

First Round
Nottinghamshire beat Warwickshire
Worcestershire beat Oxfordshire
Surrey beat Yorkshire
Glamorgan beat Cornwall
Middlesex beat Norfolk
Buckinghamshire beat Bedfordshire

Second Round
Lancashire beat Gloucestershire
Hampshire beat Buckinghamshire
Somerset beat Northamptonshire
Nottinghamshire beat Leicestershire
Sussex beat Essex
Kent beat Worcestershire
Surrey beat Glamorgan
Middlesex beat Derbyshire

Third Round
Lancashire beat Hampshire
Somerset beat Nottinghamshire
Sussex beat Kent
Surrey beat Middlesex

Semi-final
Lancashire beat Somerset
Sussex beat Surrey

FINAL
Sussex 184-9, Lancashire 185-4 (H. Pilling 70*) Lancashire won by 6 wickets.

1971

First Round
Lancashire beat Somerset
Glamorgan beat Staffordshire
Surrey beat Hertfordshire
Essex beat Bedfordshire
Lincolnshire beat Northumberland
Kent beat Northamptonshire

Second Round
Lancashire beat Worcestershire
Essex beat Glamorgan
Gloucestershire beat Sussex
Surrey beat Middlesex
Kent beat Yorkshire
Leicestershire beat Derbyshire
Warwickshire beat Lincolnshire
Hampshire beat Nottinghamshire

Third Round
Lancashire beat Essex
Gloucestershire beat Surrey
Kent beat Leicestershire
Warwickshire beat Hampshire

Semi-final
Lancashire beat Gloucestershire
Kent beat Warwickshire

FINAL
Lancashire 224-7 (C. Lloyd 66) beat Kent 200 (Asif Iqbal 89) by 24 runs.

1972

First Round
Hampshire beat Wiltshire
Worcestershire beat Sussex
Durham beat Oxfordshire
Glamorgan beat Northamptonshire
Warwickshire beat Yorkshire
Buckinghamshire beat Cambridgeshire

Second Round
Lancashire beat Somerset
Hampshire beat Nottinghamshire
Kent beat Gloucestershire
Essex beat Middlesex
Worcestershire beat Derbyshire
Surrey beat Durham
Glamorgan beat Buckinghamshire
Warwickshire beat Leicestershire

Third Round
Lancashire beat Hampshire
Kent beat Essex
Worcestershire beat Glamorgan
Warwickshire beat Glamorgan

Semi-final
Lancashire beat Kent
Warwickshire beat Worcestershire

FINAL
Warwickshire 234-9 (P. Whitehouse 68), Lancashire 235-6 (C. Lloyd 126) Lancashire won by 4 wickets.

1973

First Round
Gloucestershire beat Glamorgan
Durham beat Yorkshire
Sussex beat Northamptonshire
Hampshire beat Wiltshire
Lancashire beat Bedfordshire
Staffordshire beat Dorset

Second Round
Gloucestershire beat Surrey
Essex beat Durham
Worcestershire beat Warwickshire
Leicestershire beat Somerset
Sussex beat Derbyshire
Kent beat Hampshire
Middlesex beat Nottinghamshire
Lancashire beat Staffordshire

Third Round
Gloucestershire beat Sussex
Worcestershire beat Leicestershire
Sussex beat Kent
Middlesex beat Lancashire

Semi-final
Gloucestershire beat Worcestershire
Sussex beat Middlesex

FINAL
Gloucestershire 248-8 (M. Procter 94, A. Brown 77*) beat Sussex 208 (G. Greenidge 76, R. Knight 4-47) by 40 runs.

1974

First Round
Lancashire beat Gloucestershire
Hampshire beat Derbyshire
Lincolnshire beat Glamorgan
Essex beat Shropshire
Kent beat Buckinghamshire
Durham beat Hertfordshire

Second Round
Lancashire beat Middlesex
Yorkshire beat Hampshire
Nottinghamshire beat Warwickshire
Worcestershire beat Sussex
Surrey beat Lincolnshire
Somerset beat Essex
Leicestershire beat Northants
Kent beat Durham

Third Round
Lancashire beat Yorkshire
Worcestershire beat Nottinghamshire
Somerset beat Surrey
Kent beat Leicestershire

Semi-final
Lancashire beat Worcestershire
Kent beat Somerset

FINAL
Lancashire 118 (C. Lloyd 25)
Kent 122-6
Kent won by 4 wickets.

1975

First Round
Middlesex beat Buckinghamshire
Leicestershire beat Staffordshire
Northamptonshire beat Cambs.
Somerset beat Surrey
Nottinghamshire beat Sussex
Oxfordshire beat Cornwall

Second Round
Middlesex beat Warwickshire
Worcestershire beat Essex
Nottinghamshire beat Kent
Derbyshire beat Somerset
Gloucestershire beat Oxfordshire
Leicestershire beat Yorkshire
Lancashire beat Northamptonshire
Hampshire beat Glamorgan

Third Round
Middlesex beat Worcestershire
Derbyshire beat Nottinghamshire
Gloucestershire beat Leicestershire
Lancashire beat Hampshire

Semi-final
Middlesex beat Derbyshire
Lancashire beat Gloucestershire

FINAL
Middlesex 180 (H. Gomes 44), Lancashire 182-3 (C. Lloyd 73*, A. Kennedy 51). Lancashire won by 7 wickets.

1976

First Round
Staffordshire beat Essex
Derbyshire beat Lincolnshire
Gloucestershire beat Worcestershire
Warwickshire beat Glamorgan
Yorkshire beat Shropshire
Hertfordshire beat Berkshire

Second Round
Northamptonshire beat Nottinghamshire
Hertfordshire beat Essex
Leicestershire beat Hampshire
Derbyshire beat Surrey
Gloucestershire beat Yorkshire
Warwickshire beat Somerset
Sussex beat Kent
Lancashire beat Middlesex

Third Round
Northamptonshire beat Hertfordshire
Hampshire beat Derbyshire
Lancashire beat Gloucestershire
Warwickshire beat Sussex

Semi-final
Northamptonshire beat Hampshire
Lancashire beat Warwickshire

FINAL
Lancashire 195 (D. Lloyd 48), Northamptonshire 199-6 (P. Willey 65). Northamptonshire won by 4 wickets.

1977

First Round
Middlesex beat Kent
Nottinghamshire beat Hampshire
Northumberland beat Bedfordshire
Northamptonshire beat Durham
Leicestershire beat Hertfordshire
Lancashire beat Cornwall

Second Round
Middlesex beat Warwickshire
Hampshire beat Yorkshire
Somerset beat Northumberland
Derbyshire beat Sussex
Surrey beat Lancashire
Northamptonshire beat Gloucestershire
Leicestershire beat Essex
Glamorgan beat Worcestershire

Third Round
Leicestershire beat Northants
Glamorgan beat Surrey
Somerset beat Derbyshire
Middlesex beat Hampshire

Semi-final
Glamorgan beat Leicestershire
Middlesex beat Somerset

FINAL
Glamorgan 177 (M. Llewellyn 62)
Middlesex 178-5 (C. Radley 85*)
Middlesex won by 5 wickets.

1978

First Round
Derbyshire beat Worcestershire
Somerset beat Warwickshire
Staffordshire beat Devon
Surrey beat Shropshire
Sussex beat Suffolk
Yorkshire beat Durham

Second Round
Essex beat Surrey
Glamorgan beat Somerset
Kent beat Northamptonshire
Lancashire beat Gloucestershire
Leicestershire beat Hampshire
Middlesex beat Derbyshire
Sussex beat Staffordshire
Yorkshire beat Nottinghamshire

Third Round
Essex beat Leicestershire
Lancashire beat Middlesex
Somerset beat Kent
Sussex beat Yorkshire

Semi-final
Somerset beat Essex
Sussex beat Lancashire

FINAL
Somerset 207-7 (I. Botham 80)
Sussex 211-5 (P. Parker 62*)
Sussex won by 5 wickets.

Benson & Hedges Cup
1972

Quarter-final
Leicestershire beat Lancashire
Gloucestershire beat Middlesex
Warwickshire beat Glamorgan
Yorkshire beat Sussex

Semi-final
Leicestershire beat Warwickshire
Yorkshire beat Gloucestershire

FINAL
Yorkshire 136-9 (B. Leadbeater 32)
Leicestershire 140-5 (J. Balderstone 41*). Leicestershire won by 5 wickets.

1973

Quarter-final
Kent beat Hampshire
Essex beat Leicestershire
Lancashire beat Glamorgan
Worcestershire beat Nottinghamshire

Semi-final
Kent beat Essex
Worcestershire beat Lancashire

FINAL
Kent 225-7 (B. Luckhurst 79)
beat Worcestershire 186
(B. d'Oliveira 47, Asif Iqbal 4-43)
by 39 runs.

1974

Quarter-final
Leicestershire beat Kent
Lancashire beat Worcestershire
Surrey beat Yorkshire
Somerset beat Hampshire

Semi-final
Surrey beat Lancashire
Leicestershire beat Somerset

FINAL
Surrey 170 (Younis Ahmed 43, K. Higgs 4-10) beat Leicestershire 143 (J. Balderstone 32) by 27 runs.

1975

Quarter-final
Hampshire beat Somerset
Leicestershire beat Lancashire
Middlesex beat Yorkshire
Warwickshire beat Essex

Semi-final
Leicestershire beat Hampshire
Middlesex beat Warwickshire

FINAL
Middlesex 146 (M. Smith 83, N. McVicker 4-20), Leicestershire 150-5 (J. Steele 49). Leicestershire won by 5 wickets.

1976

Quarter-final
Kent beat Nottinghamshire
Surrey beat Essex
Warwickshire beat Lancashire
Worcestershire beat Leicestershire

Semi-final
Kent beat Surrey
Worcestershire beat Warwickshire

FINAL
Kent 236-7 (G. Johnson 78) beat

Worcestershire 193 (B. d'Oliveira 50, K. Jarvis 4-34) by 43 runs.

1977

Quarter-final
Gloucestershire beat Middlesex
Hampshire beat Glamorgan
Kent beat Sussex
Northamptonshire beat Warwickshire

Semi-final
Gloucestershire beat Hampshire
Kent beat Northamptonshire

FINAL
Gloucestershire 237-6 (A. Stovold 71, Zaheer Abbas 70) beat Kent 173 (R. Woolmer 64, J. Shepherd 55) by 64 runs.

1978

Quarter-final
Derbyshire beat Middlesex
Somerset beat Sussex
Kent beat Nottinghamshire
Warwickshire beat Glamorgan

Semi-final
Kent beat Somerset
Derbyshire beat Warwickshire

FINAL
Derbyshire 147 (P. Kirsten 41, J. Shepherd 4-25), Kent 151-4 (R. Woolmer 79). Kent won by 6 wickets.

John Player League Winners

1969 Lancashire
1970 Lancashire
1971 Worcestershire
1972 Kent
1973 Kent
1974 Leicestershire
1975 Hampshire
1976 Kent
1977 Leicestershire
1978 Hampshire

Cricket in Australia

Sheffield Shield Winners

1892-93 Victoria
1893-94 South Australia
1894-95 Victoria
1895-96 New South Wales
1896-97 New South Wales
1897-98 Victoria
1898-99 Victoria
1899-1900 New South Wales
1900-01 Victoria
1901-02 New South Wales
1902-03 New South Wales
1903-04 New South Wales
1904-05 New South Wales
1905-06 New South Wales
1906-07 New South Wales
1907-08 Victoria
1908-09 New South Wales
1909-10 South Australia
1910-11 New South Wales
1911-12 New South Wales
1912-13 South Australia
1913-14 New South Wales
1914-15 Victoria
1919-20 New South Wales
1920-21 New South Wales
1921-22 Victoria
1922-23 New South Wales
1923-24 Victoria
1924-25 Victoria
1925-26 New South Wales
1926-27 South Australia
1927-28 Victoria
1928-29 New South Wales
1929-30 Victoria
1930-31 Victoria
1931-32 New South Wales
1932-33 New South Wales
1933-34 Victoria
1934-35 Victoria
1935-36 South Australia
1936-37 Victoria
1937-38 New South Wales
1938-39 South Australia
1939-40 New South Wales
1946-47 Victoria
1947-48 Western Australia
1948-49 New South Wales
1949-50 New South Wales
1950-51 Victoria
1951-52 New South Wales
1952-53 South Australia
1953-54 New South Wales
1954-55 New South Wales
1955-56 New South Wales
1956-57 New South Wales
1957-58 New South Wales
1958-59 New South Wales
1959-60 New South Wales
1960-61 New South Wales
1961-62 New South Wales
1962-63 Victoria
1963-64 South Australia
1964-65 New South Wales
1965-66 New South Wales
1966-67 Victoria
1967-68 Western Australia
1968-69 South Australia
1969-70 Victoria
1970-71 South Australia
1971-72 Western Australia
1972-73 Western Australia
1973-74 Victoria
1974-75 Western Australia
1975-76 South Australia
1976-77 Western Australia
1977-78 Western Australia

Cricket in India

Ranji Trophy Winners

1934-35 Bombay
1935-36 Bombay
1936-37 Nawanagar
1937-38 Hyderabad
1938-39 Bengal
1939-40 Maharashtra
1940-41 Maharashtra
1941-42 Bombay
1942-43 Baroda
1943-44 Western India States
1944-45 Bombay
1945-46 Holkar
1946-47 Baroda
1947-48 Holkar
1948-49 Bombay
1949-50 Baroda
1950-51 Holkar
1951-52 Bombay
1952-53 Holkar
1953-54 Bombay
1954-55 Madras
1955-56 Bombay
1956-57 Bombay
1957-58 Baroda
1958-59 Bombay
1959-60 Bombay
1960-61 Bombay
1961-62 Bombay
1962-63 Bombay
1963-64 Bombay
1964-65 Bombay
1965-66 Bombay
1966-67 Bombay
1967-68 Bombay
1968-69 Bombay
1969-70 Bombay
1970-71 Bombay
1971-72 Bombay
1972-73 Bombay
1973-74 Karnataka
1974-75 Bombay
1975-76 Bombay
1976-77 Bombay
1977-78 Karnataka

Cricket in New Zealand

Plunket Shield Winners

From 1906 to 1921 the Shield was competed for on a challenge basis (in the manner of sailing's America's Cup). From that time onwards it has maintained a league format.

1906-07 Canterbury won the first contest but were defeated in the first challenge.
1907-1911 Auckland defeated 7 challengers.
1911-1912 Canterbury defeated 2 challengers.
1912-1913 Auckland defeated only one challenger.
1913-1918 Canterbury defeated 9 challengers.
1918-1919 Wellington were defeated at their first defence.
1919-1920 Canterbury defeated 2 challengers.
1920-1921 Auckland defeated 3 challengers.
1921 Wellington won the Cup from Auckland but the system was changed before they faced their first challenge.

1921-22	Auckland
1922-23	Canterbury
1923-24	Wellington
1924-25	Otago
1925-26	Wellington
1926-27	Auckland
1927-28	Wellington
1928-29	Auckland
1929-30	Wellington
1930-31	Canterbury
1931-32	Wellington
1932-33	Otago
1933-34	Auckland
1934-35	Canterbury
1935-36	Wellington
1936-37	Auckland
1937-38	Auckland
1938-39	Auckland
1939-40	Auckland
1945-46	Canterbury
1946-47	Auckland
1947-48	Otago
1948-49	Canterbury
1949-50	Wellington
1950-51	Otago
1951-52	Canterbury
1952-53	Otago
1953-54	Central Districts
1954-55	Wellington
1955-56	Canterbury
1956-57	Wellington
1957-58	Otago
1958-59	Auckland
1959-60	Canterbury
1960-61	Wellington
1961-62	Wellington
1962-63	Northern Districts
1963-64	Auckland
1964-65	Canterbury
1965-66	Wellington
1966-67	Central Districts
1967-68	Central Districts
1968-69	Auckland
1969-70	Otago
1970-71	Central Districts
1971-72	Otago
1972-73	Wellington
1973-74	Wellington
1974-75	Otago

Cricket in South Africa

Currie Cup Winners

1889-90	Transvaal
1890-91	Griqualand West
1892-93	Western Province
1893-94	Western Province
1894-95	Transvaal
1896-97	Western Province
1897-98	Western Province
1902-03	Transvaal
1903-04	Transvaal
1904-05	Transvaal
1906-07	Transvaal
1908-09	Western Province
1910-11	Natal
1912-13	Natal
1920-21	Western Province
1921-22	Shared by Transvaal, Natal & Western Province
1923-24	Transvaal
1925-26	Transvaal
1926-27	Transvaal
1929-30	Transvaal
1931-32	Western Province
1933-34	Natal
1934-35	Transvaal
1936-37	Natal
1937-38	Shared by Transvaal and Natal
1946-47	Natal
1947-48	Natal
1950-51	Transvaal
1951-52	Natal
1952-53	Western Province
1954-55	Natal
1955-56	Western Province
1958-59	Transvaal
1959-60	Natal
1960-61	Natal
1962-63	Natal
1963-64	Natal
1965-66	Shared by Transvaal and Natal
1966-67	Natal
1967-68	Natal
1968-69	Transvaal
1969-70	Shared by Transvaal and Western Province
1970-71	Transvaal
1971-72	Transvaal
1972-73	Transvaal
1973-74	Natal
1974-75	Western Province
1975-76	Natal
1976-77	Natal
1977-78	Western Province

Shell Trophy Winners

1975-76	Canterbury
1976-77	Otago
1977-78	Auckland

Cricket In West Indies

Shell Shield Winners

1965-66	Barbados
1966-67	Barbados
1967-68	Barbados
1968-69	Jamaica
1969-70	Trinidad
1970-71	Trinidad
1971-72	Barbados
1972-73	Guyana
1973-74	Barbados
1974-75	Guyana
1975-76	Shared by Trinidad and Barbados
1976-77	Barbados
1977-78	Barbados

Cricket in Pakistan

Qaid-B-Azam Trophy

1953-54	Bahawalpur
1954-55	Karachi
1956-57	Punjab
1957-58	Bahawalpur
1958-59	Karachi
1959-60	Karachi
1961-62	Karachi Blues
1962-63	Karachi "A"
1963-64	Karachi Blues
1964-65 / **1965-66**	Karachi Blues
1966-67 / **1967-68**	Karachi

1968-69	Lahore
1969-70	Pakistan Int. Airways
1970-71	Karachi Blues
1971-72 / **1972-73**	Railways
1973-74	Railways
1974-75 / **1975-76**	National Bank
1976-77	Shared by National Bank and United Bank
1977-78	Habib Bank

Cricketing Records

(correct to the end of the 1978 English season)

Test Cricket

Highest individual innings

365* G. S. Sobers
WI v Pak Kingston 1957-58
364 L. Hutton
Eng v Aus Oval 1938
337 Hanif Mohammad
Pak v WI Bridgetown 1957-58
336* W. R. Hammond
Eng v NZ Auckland 1932-33
334 D. G. Bradman
Aus v Eng Headingley 1930
325 A. Sandham
Eng v WI Kingston 1929-30
311 R. B. Simpson
Aus v Eng Old Trafford 1964
310* J. H. Edrich
Eng v NZ Headingley 1965
307 R. M. Cowper
Aus v Eng Melbourne 1965-66
304 D. G. Bradman
Aus v Eng Headingley 1934
302 L. G. Rowe
WI v Eng Bridgetown 1973-74

Most runs in a career

8032 G. S. Sobers (WI)
93 Tests
7624 M. C. Cowdrey (Eng)
114 Tests
7249 W. R. Hammond (Eng)
85 Tests
6996 D. G. Bradman (Aus)
52 Tests
6971 L. Hutton (Eng)
79 Tests
6806 K. F. Barrington (Eng)
82 Tests
6149 R. N. Harvey (Aus)
79 Tests

Highest Totals

903-7d Eng v Aus Oval 1938
849 Eng v WI Kingston 1929-30
790-3d WI v Pak Kingston 1957-58
758-8d Aus v WI Kingston 1954-55
729-6d Aus v Eng Lord's 1930
701 Aus v Eng Oval 1934

Lowest Totals

26 NZ v Eng Auckland 1954-55
30 SA v Eng Port Elizabeth 1895-96
30 SA v Eng Edgbaston 1924
35 SA v Eng Cape Town 1898-99
36 Aus v Eng Edgbaston 1902
36 SA v Aus Melbourne 1931-32

Highest Match Run Aggregates

1981 SA v Eng Durban 1938-39
1815 WI v Eng Kingston 1929-30
1753 Eng v Aus Adelaide 1920-21
1723 Eng v Aus Headingley 1948

Lowest Match Run Aggregate

234 Aus v SA Melbourne 1931-32
291 Eng v Aus Lord's 1888
295 NZ v Aus Wellington 1945-46

Biggest Wins

Inns & 579 Eng v Aus Oval 1938
Inns & 336 WI v Ind Calcutta 1958-59
Inns & 332 Aus v Eng Brisbane 1946-47
675 runs Eng v Aus Brisbane 1928-29
562 runs Aus v Eng Oval 1934
530 runs Aus v SA Melbourne 1910-11

Closest Result

Tied match Aus v WI Brisbane 1960-61

Longest Matches

10 days SA v Eng Durban 1938-39
9 days WI v Eng Kingston 1929-30
8 days Aus v Eng Melbourne 1928-29

Most Consecutive Wins

8 Aus 1920-21 to 1921
7 Eng 1884-85 to 1887-88
7 Eng 1928 to 1928-29

Most Consecutive Losses

8 SA 1888-89 to 1898-99
8 Eng 1920-21 to 1921

Most Test appearances

114 M. C. Cowdrey (Eng)
93 G. S. Sobers (WI)
91 T. G. Evans (Eng)
89 A. P. E. Knott (Eng)
85 W. R. Hammond (Eng)
82 K. F. Barrington (Eng)
79 L. R. Gibbs (WI)
79 T. W. Graveney (Eng)
79 R. N. Harvey (Aus)
79 L. Hutton (Eng)
79 R. B. Kanhai (WI)
78 D. C. S. Compton (Eng)
77 J. H. Edrich (Eng)

Most Runs in Series

974 D. G. Bradman (Aus) v Eng 1930
905 W. R. Hammond (Eng) v Aus 1928-29
834 R. N. Harvey (Aus) v SA 1952-53
829 I. V. A. Richards (WI) v Eng 1976
827 C. L. Walcott (WI) v Aus 1954-55
824 G. S. Sobers (WI) v Pak 1957-58
810 D. G. Bradman (Aus) v Eng 1936-37
806 D. G. Bradman (Aus) v SA 1931-32

Most Centuries in Career

29 D. G. Bradman (Aus)
26 G. S. Sobers (WI)
22 M. C. Cowdrey (Eng)
22 W. R. Hammond (Eng)
21 R. N. Harvey (Aus)
20 K. F. Barrington (Eng)

Most Centuries in Series

5 C. L. Walcott (WI) v Aus 1954-55
(D. G. Bradman scored four centuries in a series three times.)

Most Centuries in Consecutive Innings

5 E. D. Weekes (WI) 1947-48 to 1948-49
4 J. H. Fingleton (Aus) 1935-36 to 1936-37
4 A. Melville (SA) 1938-39 to 1947

Most Runs in a Day

309 D. G. Bradman (Aus) v Eng Headingley 1930
295 W. R. Hammond (Eng) v NZ Auckland 1932-33
273 D. C. S. Compton (Eng) v Pak Trent Bridge 1954
271 D. G. Bradman (Aus) v Eng Headingley 1939

Fastest Centuries

70 mins J. M. Gregory (Aus) v SA Johannesburg 1921-22
75 mins G. L. Jessop (Eng) v Aus Oval 1902
78 mins R. Benaud (Aus) v WI Kingston 1954-55
80 mins J. H. Sinclair (SA) v Aus Cape Town 1902-03
86 mins B. R. Taylor (NZ) v WI Auckland 1968-69

Most Wickets in Innings

10-53 J. C. Laker (Eng) v Aus Old Trafford 1956
(9 wickets in an innings have been taken on eight occasions.)

Most Wickets in Match

19-90 J. C. Laker (Eng) v Aus Old Trafford 1956
17-159 S. F. Barnes (Eng) v SA Johannesburg 1913-14

Most Wickets in Series

49 S. F. Barnes (Eng) v SA 1913-14
46 J. C. Laker (Eng) v Aus 1956
44 C. V. Grimmett (Aus) v SA 1935-36
41 R. M. Hogg (Aus) v Eng 1978-79
39 A. V. Bedser (Eng) v Aus 1953
38 M. W. Tate (Eng) v Aus 1924-25

Most Wickets in a Day

15 J. Briggs (Eng) v SA Cape Town 1888-89
14 H. Verity (Eng) v Aus Lord's 1934

Most Catches in Series

15 J. M. Gregory (Aus) v Eng 1920-21

Most Wickets in Car eer

309 L. R. Gibbs (WI) in 79 Tests
307 F. S. Trueman (Eng) in 67 Tests
265 D. L. Underwood (Eng) in 74 Tests
252 J. B. Statham (Eng) in 70 Tests
248 R. Benaud (Aus) in 63 Tests
246 B. S. Bedi (Ind) in 58 Tests
246 G. D. McKenzie (Aus) in 60 Tests
236 A. V. Bedser (Eng) in 51 Tests
235 G. S. Sobers (WI) in 93 Tests
228 R. R. Lindwall (Aus) in 61 Tests
226 B. S. Chandrasekhar in 50 Tests
216 C. V. Grimmett (Aus) in 37 Tests
202 J. A. Snow (Eng) in 49 Tests

Most Catches in Career

120 M. C. Cowdrey in 114 Tests
110 W. R. Hammond in 85 Tests
110 R. B. Simpson in 62 Tests
110 G. S. Sobers in 93 Tests

Most Dismissals in Series

26 R. W. Marsh (Aus) v WI 1975-76
26 J. H. B. Waite (SA) v NZ 1961-62
24 A. P. E. Knott (Eng) v Aus 1970-71
24 D. Lindsay (SA) v Aus 1966-67
24 D. L. Murray (WI) v Eng 1963

Most Dismissals in Career

252 A. P. E. Knott (Eng) in 89 Tests
219 T. G. Evans (Eng) in 91 Tests
187 A. T. W. Grout (Aus) in 51 Tests
158 D. L. Murray (WI) in 51 Tests
141 J. H. B. Waite (SA) in 50 Tests
130 W. A. Oldfield (Aus) in 130 Tests

First Class Cricket

Highest Totals

1107 Victoria v NSW Melbourne 1926-27
1059 Victoria v Tasmania Melbourne 1922-23
951-7d Sind v Baluchistan Karachi 1973-74
918 NSW v S. Australia Sydney 1900-01
912-8d Holkar v Mysore Indore 1945-46
910-6d Railways v DIK Lahore 1964-65
903-7d Eng v Aus Oval 1938

Highest Individual Innings

499 Hanif Mohammad
Karachi v Bahawalpur Karachi 1958-59
452* D. G. Bradman
NSW v Queensland Sydney 1929-30
443* B. B. Nimbalkar
Maharashtra v WI States Poona 1948-49
437 W. H. Ponsford
Victoria v Queensland Melbourne 1927-28
429 W. H. Ponsford
Victoria v Tasmania Melbourne 1922-23
428 Aftab Baloch
Sind v Baluchistan Karachi 1973-74
424 A. C. MacLaren
Lancashire v Somerset Taunton 1895

Fastest Centuries

35 mins P. G. H. Fender
Surrey v Northamptonshire Northampton 1920
37 mins C. M. Old
Yorkshire v Warwickshire Birmingham 1977
40 mins G. L. Jessop
Gloucester v Yorkshire Harrogate 1897
42 mins G. L. Jessop
Gents of South v Players of South Hastings 1907

Wicket keepers
Most dismissals in career

1527 J. T. Murray (Middlesex) 1952-75
1493 H. Strudwick (Surrey)1902-27
1328 F. H. Hush (Kent) 1895-1914
1327 D. Hunter (Yorkshire) 1888-1909

Lowest Totals

12 Oxford University v MCC Oxford 1877
12 Northants v Gloucester 1907
13 Auckland v Canterbury Auckland 1877-78
13 Notts v Yorkshire Trent Bridge 1901

Highest Match Aggregates

2376 runs Maharashtra v Bombay Poona 1948-49
2078 runs Bombay v Holkar Bombay 1944-45
1981 runs SA v Eng Durban 1938-39
1929 runs NSW v S. Australia Sydney 1925-26

Lowest Match Aggregates

105 runs MCC v Australians Lord's 1878
134 runs England v The Bs Lord's 1831
147 runs Kent v Sussex Sevenoaks 1828
149 runs England v Kent Lord's 1858

Longest Match

10 days SA v Eng Durban 1938-39

Shortest Match

3 hrs 5 mins Middlesex v Somerset Lord's 1899

Biggest Wins

Inns & 851 Railways v DIK Lahore 1965-65
Inns & 666 Victoria v Tasmania Melbourne 1922-23
Inns & 656 Victoria v NSW Melbourne 1926-27
Inns & 605 NSW v S Australia Sydney 1900-01
685 runs NSW v Queensland Sydney 1929-30
675 runs England v Australia Brisbane 1928-29
638 runs NSW v S Australia Adelaide 1920-21

Most Runs in Season

3816 D. C. S. Compton (Mx) 1947
3539 W. J. Edrich (Mx) 1947
3518 T. W. Hayward (Sy) 1906
3429 L. Hutton (Yorks) 1949

Most Runs in Career

61237 J. B. Hobbs (Sy) 1905-34
58969 F. E. Woolley (Kent) 1906-38
57611 E. H. Hendren (Mx) 1907-38
55060 C. P. Mead (Hants) 1905-36

Most Centuries in Season

18 D. C. S. Compton (Mx) 1947
16 J. B. Hobbs (Sy) 1925
15 W. R. Hammond (Glos) 1938
14 H. Sutcliffe (Yorks) 1932

Most Centuries in Career

197 J. B. Hobbs (Sy)
170 E. H. Hendren (Mx)
167 W. R. Hammond (Glos)
153 C. P. Mead (Hants)

Most Centuries in Consecutive Innings

6 C. B. Fry (Sx) 1901
6 D. G. Bradman (S. Australia) 1938-39

Most Sixes in Innings

15 J. R. Reid (296) Wellington v N. Districts Wellington 1962-63
13 Majid Jehangir (147*) Pakistanis v Glamorgan Swansea 1967
13 C. G. Greenidge D. H. Robins' XI v Pakistanis Eastbourne 1974
13 C. G. Greenidge Hampshire v Sussex Southampton 1975

1,000 Runs in Season

28 times W. G. Grace (Glos)
28 times F. E. Woolley (Kent)
27 times M. C. Cowdrey
27 times C. P. Mead (Hants)
26 times J. B. Hobbs (Sy)
25 times E. H. Hendren (Mx)
24 times W. G. Quaife (Warks)
24 times H. Sutcliffe (Yorks)
23 times M. C. Cowdrey (Kent)
22 times W. R. Hammond (Glos)
22 times T. W. Graveney (Glos and Worcs)

Two Double-Centuries in Same Match

A. E. Fagg for Kent v Essex at Colchester in 1938. He scored 244 and 202 not out.

Two Centuries in Same Match

7 times W. R. Hammond (Glos)
6 times J. B. Hobbs (Sy)
5 times C. B. Fry (Sx)

Most Runs in a Day

345 C. G. Macartney Australians v Nottinghamshire Trent Bridge 1921
334 W. H. Ponsford Victoria v NSW Melbourne 1926-27
333 K. S. Duleepsinhji Sussex v Northamptonshire Hove 1930

Most Boundaries in Innings

68 fours P. A. Perrin Essex v Derbyshire Chesterfield 1904
64 fours Hanif Mohammad Karachi v Bahawalpur Karachi 1958-59

Longest Innings

999 mins Hanif Mohammad (337) Pak v WI Bridgetown 1957-58
797 mins L. Hutton (364) Eng v Aus Oval 1938
762 mins R. Simpson (311) Aus v Eng Manchester 1964
727 mins R. Cowper (307) Aus v Eng Melbourne 1955-56
708 mins L. Wight (262*) BG v Barbados Georgetown 1951-52

Ten Wickets in Innings

3 times A. P. Freeman (1929, 1930, 1931)
2 times V. W. Walker (1859, 1865)
2 times W. G. Grace (1873, 1886)
2 times H. Verity (1931, 1932)
2 times J. C. Laker (1956 twice)

Best Innings Analyses

10-10 H. Verity
Yorkshire v Nottinghamshire Headingley 1932
10-18 G. Geary
Leicestershire v Glamorgan Pontypridd 1929
9-2 G. Elliott
Victoria v Tasmania Launceston 1857-58
9-7 Ahad Khan
Railways v DIK Lahore 1964-65
8-2 J. C. Laker
England v Rest Bradford 1950

Most Wickets in Match

19 J. C. Laker Eng v Aus Old Trafford 1956

Most Wickets in a Day

17 C. Blythe Kent v Northants Northampton 1907
17 H. Verity Yorks v Essex Leyton 1933
17 T. W. Goddard Glos v Kent Bristol 1939

Most Wickets in Season

304 A. P. Freeman (Kent) 1928
298 A. P. Freeman (Kent) 1933
290 T. Richardson (Sy) 1895
283 C. T. B. Turner (Aus) 1888
276 A. P. Freeman (Kent) 1931
275 A. P. Freeman (Kent) 1930

Most Wickets in Career

4187 W. Rhodes (Yorks) 1898-1930
3776 A. P. Freeman (Kent) 1914-36
3278 C. W. L. Parker (Glos) 1903-35
3061 J. T. Hearne (Mx) 1888-1923

100 Wickets in Season

23 times W. Rhodes (Yorks)
20 times D. Shackleton (Hants)
17 times A. P. Freeman (Kent)
16 times T. W. Goddard (Glos)
16 times C. W. L. Parker (Glos)
16 times R. T. D. Perks (Worcs)
15 times J. T. Hearne (Mx)
15 times G. H. Hirst (Yorks)
15 times A. S. Kennedy (Hants)

Most Hat-Tricks

7 D. V. P. Wright (Kent)
6 T. W. Goddard (Glos)
6 C. W. L. Parker (Glos)
5 S. Haigh (Yorks)
5 V. W. C. Jupp (Sx & Northants)
5 A. E. G. Rhodes (Derby)
5 F. A. Tarrant (Mx)

Largest attendances Test Matches

350,534 Australia v England (Melbourne) 3rd Test 1936-37
325,000 India v England (Calcutta) 2nd Test 1972-73

In England
158,000 England v Australia (Leeds) 4th Test 1948

137,915 England v Australia (Lord's) 2nd Test 1953

Single Test Match Day
90,800 Australia v West Indies (Melbourne) 5th Test, 2nd day 1960-61

Test Series
943,000 Australia v England 5 Tests 1936-37

In England
549,650 England v Australia 5 Tests 1953

Other First Class Matches in England
80,000 Surrey v Yorkshire (Oval) 3 days 1906
78,792 Yorkshire v Lancashire (Leeds) 3 days 1904
78,617 Lancashire v Yorkshire (Manchester) 3 days 1926

Benefits and Testimonials

Pre 1915
£3,703 **G. H. Hirst** 1904
£3,111 **J. T. Tyldesley** 1906
£2,282 **J. T. Brown** 1901
£2,202 **W. Rhodes** 1911
£2,120 **W. S. Lees** 1906
£2,071 **S. Haigh** 1909
£2,000 **R. Peel** 1894

1919-1939
£4,016 **R. Kilner** 1925
£3,648 **M. Leyland** 1934
£3,059 **H. Sutcliffe** 1929
£2,906 **C. Hallows** 1928
£2,620 **P. Holmes** 1928
£2,620 **W. R. Hammond** 1934
£2,563 **A. Wood** 1939

1946-70
£14,000 **C. Washbrook** 1948
£13,047 **J. B. Statham** 1961
£12,866 **A. V. Bedser** 1953
£12,258 **D. C. S. Compton** 1949
£11,143 **A. L. Dixon** 1969
£11,086 **J. C. Laker** 1956

1971-78
£40,171 **D. Lloyd** 1978
£38,214 **J. N. Graham** 1977
£38,134 **R. Illingworth** 1977
£35,000 **D. B. Close** 1977
£35,000 **P. J. Graves** 1978
£34,747 **D. L. Amiss** 1975
£29,109 **D. J. Brown** 1973
£27,199 **C. H. Lloyd** 1977
£27,000 **B. L. d'Oliveira** 1975

All Round Cricket

1,000 Runs and 100 Wickets Most Times in Season
16 times W. Rhodes (Yorks)
14 times G. H. Hirst (Yorks)
10 times V. W. C. Jupp (Sx and Northants)
9 times W. E. Astill (Leics)

2,000 Runs and 200 Wickets in Season
G. H. Hirst (Yorks) 1906

3,000 Runs and 100 Wickets in Season
J. H. Parks (Sx) 1937

Fielders (excluding wicketkeepers)

Most Catches in Innings
7 M. J. Stewart (Sy) v Northants 1957
7 A. S. Brown (Glos) v Notts 1966

Most Catches in Match
10 W. R. Hammond (Glos) v Surrey 1928

Most Catches in Season
78 W. R. Hammond (Glos) 1928
77 M. J. Stewart (Sy) 1967

Wicketkeepers

Most Catches in Career
913 F. E. Woolley (Kent) 1906-38
871 W. G. Grace (Glos) 1865-1908

Most Dismissals in Innings
8 A. T. W. Grout (Queensland) v W. Australia 1959-60

Most Dismissals in Match
12 E. Pooley (Sy) v Sussex 1868
12 D. Tallon (Qu) v NSW 1938-39
12 H. B. Taber (NSW) v S. Australia 1968-69

Most Dismissals in Season
127 L. E. G. Ames (Kent) 1929
121 L. E. G. Ames (Kent) 1928
110 H. Yarnold (Worcs) 1949

Most Dismissals in Career
1493 H. Strudwick (Sy) 1902-27
1328 F. H. Huish (Kent) 1895-1914
1327 D. Hunter (Yorks) 1888-1909

Throwing the Cricket Ball
140 yds 2 ft R. Percival at Durham 1884
140 yds 9 in R. Mackenzie at Toronto 1872

1979

In New Zealand

1978-79 v Pakistan
Series
Christchurch
Pakistan won by 128 runs
Pakistan 271 and 176
New Zealand 290 and 176

Napier
Match drawn
Pakistan 360 and 234-3d
New Zealand 403

Auckland
New Zealand 254 and
Pakistan 359

In India

1978-1979 v West Indies
Series won by India

Bowlers taking 1,000 Wickets in First Class Cricket at an Average of less than 18 runs per wicket

NAME	TEAMS	CAREER DATES	WICKETS	AVERAGE
A. Shaw	Nottinghamshire	1864-97	**2001**	12.08
J. Grundy	Nottinghamshire	1850-69	**1045**	13.05
E. Wilsher	Kent	1850-74	**1188**	13.07
T. Emmett	Yorkshire	1866-88	**1582**	13.36
F. Morley	Nottinghamshire	1872-83	**1231**	13.38
A. Watson	Lancashire	1872-93	**1351**	13.41
E. Peate	Yorkshire	1879/90	**1076**	13.48
G. Lohmann	Surrey	1884-97/98	**1805**	13.91
J. Southerton	Surrey	1854-79	**1626**	14.30
H. Verity	Yorkshire	1930-39	**1956**	14.87
J. Lillywhite	Sussex	1862-81	**1140**	15.38
W. Attewell	Nottinghamshire	1881-1900	**1932**	15.39
A. Mold	Lancashire	1889-1901	**1673**	15.54
S. Haigh	Yorkshire	1895-1913	**2012**	15.94
J. Briggs	Lancashire	1879-1900	**2212**	15.95
W. Flowers	Nottinghamshire	1877-96	**1169**	15.98
R. Peel	Yorkshire	1882-99	**1754**	16.21
J. B. Statham	Lancashire	1950-68	**2260**	16.36
W. Rhodes	Yorkshire	1898-1930	**4187**	16.71
W. E. Bowes	Yorkshire	1928-47	**1638**	16.75
C. Blythe	Kent	1899-1914	**2506**	16.81
R. Tyldesley	Lancashire	1919-35	**1509**	17.21
H. L. Jackson	Derbyshire	1947/63	**1733**	17.36
F. Martin	Kent	1885-1900	**1317**	17.38
H. Larwood	Nottinghamshire	1924-38	**1427**	17.51
W. C. Smith	Surrey	1900-14	**1077**	17.55
C. H. Parkin	Lancashire	1906-26	**1048**	17.58
J. T. Hearne	Middlesex	1888-1923	**3061**	17.75
F. A. Tarrant	Victoria, Middlesex	1898/99-1936/37	**2876**	17.99
W. G. Grace	Gloucestershire	1865-1908	**2876**	17.99

Batsmen scoring 10,000 runs in First Class Cricket with an Average of 45 runs

NAME	TEAMS	CAREER DATES	RUNS	AVERAGE
D. G. Bradman	N.S.W.,S. Australia	1927/28—48/49	**28,067**	95.14
V. M. Merchant	Bombay	1929/30—51/52	**12,876**	72.74
W. H. Ponsford	Victoria	1920/21—34/35	**13,819**	65.18
W. M. Woodfull	Victoria	1921/22—34/35	**13,392**	65.00
A. L. Hassett	Victoria	1932/33—53/54	**16,890**	58.24
A. F. Kippax	N.S.W.	1918/19—35/36	**12,747**	57.69
V. S. Hazare	Baroda	1934/35—66/67	**17,972**	57.23
G. Boycott	Yorkshire	1962-78	**33,690**	56.81
C. L. Walcott	Barbados	1941/42—63/64	**11,820**	56.55
K. S. Ranjitsinhji	Sussex	1893 —1920	**24,692**	56.37
R. B. Simpson	N.S.W., Western Australia	1952/53—77/78	**21,029**	56.22
W. R. Hammond	Gloucestershire	1920 —1951	**50,493**	56.10
B. A. Richards	Natal, Glos, Hants, Western Australia	1964/65—1978	**27,293**	55.70
L. Hutton	Yorkshire	1934 —1960	**40,140**	55.51
A. R. Morris	N.S.W.	1940/41—54/55	**12,489**	55.01
G. S. Sobers	Barbados, S. Australia, Nottinghamshire	1952/53—1974	**28,315**	54.87
F. M. M. Worrell	Barbados, Jamaica	1941/42—1964	**15,025**	54.24
Hanif Mohammad	Karachi	1951/52—68/69	**15,171**	53.79
R. M. Cowper	Victoria, W. Australia	1959/60—69/70	**10,595**	53.78
R. G. Pollock	Eastern Prov.	1960/61—77/78	**14,760**	53.67
E. D. Weekes	Barbados	1944/45—1964	**12,010**	52.90
P. R. Umrigar	Bombay	1944/45—65/66	**16,023**	52.28
H. Sutcliffe	Yorkshire	1919 —1945	**50,135**	52.00
D. C. S. Compton	Middlesex	1936 —1964	**38,942**	51.85
A. D. Nourse	Natal	1931/32—52/53	**12,472**	51.53
W. A. Brown	N.S.W., Queensland	1932/33—49/50	**13,840**	51.44
P. B. H. May	Surrey	1948 —1963	**27,592**	51.00
N. C. O'Neill	N.S.W.	1955/56—67/68	**13,805**	50.95
R. N. Harvey	Victoria, N.S.W.	1946/47—62/63	**21,699**	50.92
G. S. Chappell	S. Australia, Somerset, Queensland	1966/67—1977	**18,685**	50.91
W. M. Lawry	Victoria	1955/56—71/72	**18,725**	50.88
V. L. Manjrekar	Bombay, Bengal, Andrha	1949/50—68/69	**12,717**	50.86
E. H. Hendren	Middlesex	1907 —1938	**57,611**	50.80
J. B. Hobbs	Surrey	1905 —1934	**61,237**	50.65
C. B. Fry	Sussex, Hants., Sussex	1892 —21/22	**30,886**	50.22
W. Bardsley	N.S.W.	1903/04—27/28	**17,028**	49.94
K. S. Duleepsinhji	Sussex	1924 —1932	**15,485**	49.95
C. H. Lloyd	Guyana, Lancashire	1963/64—1978	**21,521**	49.93
Zaheer Abbas	Karachi Whites, Gloucestershire	1965/55—1978	**19,804**	49.75
S. J. McCabe	N.S.W.	1928/29—41/42	**11,951**	49.35
R. B. Kanhai	Warwicks, W. Australia, Tasmania	1954/55—1977	**28,639**	49.29
K. R. Miller	Victoria, N.S.W., Notts	1937/38—1959	**14,183**	48.90
E. A. B. Rowan	Transvaal	1929/30—53/54	**11,710**	48.58
S. M. Gavaskar	Bombay	1966/67—76/77	**11,512**	48.36
G. M. Turner	Otago, Worcestershire	1964/65—1978	**27,128**	48.27
I. V. A. Richards	Leewards Islands, Combined Islands, Somerset	1971/72—1978	**13,065**	48.03
P. J. P. Burge	Queensland	1952/53—67/68	**14,640**	47.68
C. P. Mead	Hampshire	1905 —1936	**55,061**	47.67

Bowlers taking 1,000 Wickets in First Class Cricket at an Average of less than 18 runs per wicket

NAME	TEAMS	CAREER DATES	RUNS	AVERAGE
B. Sutcliffe	Auckland, Otago	1941/42—65/66	**17,196**	47.50
D. R. Jardine	Surrey	1920 —1948	**14,823**	46.90
W. W. Armstrong	Victoria	1898/99—1921/22	**16,177**	46,75
C. G. Macartney	N.S.W., Otago	1905/06—35/36	**15,050**	45.79
K. F. Barrington	Surray	1953 —1968	**31,714**	45.63
D. J. McGlew	Natal	1947/48—66/67	**12,070**	45.54
J. H. Edrich	Surrey	1956 —1978	**39,790**	45.47
E. Tyldesley	Lancashire	1909 —1936	**38,874**	45.46
B. C. Booth	N.S.W.	1954/55—68/69	**11,265**	45.42
B. Mitchell	Transvaal	1925/26—49/50	**11,395**	45.39
T. L. Livingston	N.S.W., Northants	1941/42—1964	**15,260**	45.01

Bombay
Match drawn
India 424 (S. Gavaskar 205) and 224-2
West Indies 493 (A. Kallicharran 187)
Bangalore
Match drawn
West Indies 437 and 200-8
India 371
Calcutta
Match drawn
India 300 and 361-1d
(S. M. Gavaskar 182* D. Vengsarkar 157*)
West Indies 327 and 197-9
Madras
India won by 3 wickets
West Indies 228 and 151
India 255 and 125
Delhi
Match drawn
India 556-8d
West Indies 172 and 179-3
Kanpur
Match drawn
India 644-7d (G. R. Vishwanath 79)
West Indies 451-8
(S. F. A. Bacchus 250)

In Australia

1978-79 v England
Series won by England
Brisbane
England won by 7 wickets
Australia 116 and 339
England 286 and 170-3
Perth
England won by 166 runs
England 309 and 208
Australia 190 and 161
Melbourne
Australia won by 103 runs
Australi 258 and 167
England 143 and 179
Sydney
England won by 93 runs
England 152 and 346
(D. W. Randall 150)
Adelaide
England won by 205 runs
England 169 and 360
Australia 164 and 160
Sydney
England won by 9 wickets
Australia 198 and 143
England 308 and 35-1

Bibliography

Altham & Swanton	*History of Cricket*	George Allen & Unwin, 1947
Arlott, John (Ed.)	*Cricket*	Burke, 1953
Bowen, Rowland	*Cricket: A History*	Eyre & Spottiswoode, 1970
Brookes, Christopher	*English Cricket*	Weidenfeld and Nicolson, 1978
Cardus, Neville	*Autobiography*	Collins, 1947
Cozier, Tony	*The West Indies: 50 Years of Cricket*	Angus & Robertson, 1978
Robinson, Ray	*The Wildest Tests*	Panther, 1972
Ross, Gordon	*A History of Cricket*	Arthur Barker, 1972
Swanton, E.W. (Ed.)	*World of Cricket*	
Thomson, A.A.	*The Great Cricketer*	Hale, 1957
Warner, Pelham	*Lord's*	Harrap, 1946
Wisden Cricketers Almanack		Michael Joseph, 1966
Whitington, R.S.	*Illustrated History of Cricket in Australia*	Pelham, 1974

INDEX

PICTURE ACKNOWLEDGEMENTS
Africamera: 99, 175, 176L&R
Central Press: 76T&B, 151
Colorsport: 54/5, 58/9, 61, 62/3, 82L&R, 103L, 109, 159
Copper-Bridgeman Library: 6/7, 12/13, 20/1, 30, 33, 37, 143
Patrick Eagar: 51, 52, 57, 70, 70/1, 77, 79, 84, 87, 88, 96 97, 111, 114, 115, 121, 123, 124/5, 128/9, 130, 132/3, 134/5, 137, 141, 162, 163, 167
Mary Evans: 16, 38/9, 62/3, 64/5
Indian High Commission: 94, 94/5
Ken Kelly: 36, 116/7, 149
Mansell Collection: 8, 9, 18/19, 24/7, 34/5, 44L&R, 146
M.C.C.: 72L, 74L
Robin Marlar: 22
New Zealand Airlines: 70T
New Zealand High Commission: 92/3, 131
Press Association: 48T&B, 73L, 81, 171
Radio Times Hulton Picture Library: 43, 47, 70C, 73R, 144
Anne Ronan Picture Library: 10, 15, 49
Sport and General: 74R, 91L&R, 100, 103R, 126
Topix: 107